WARRIORS OF DISINFORMATION

WARRIORS OF DISINFORMATION

American Propaganda, Soviet Lies, and
the Winning of the Cold War

< AN INSIDER'S ACCOUNT >

ALVIN A. SNYDER

ARCADE PUBLISHING · NEW YORK

FIRST EDITION

Library of Congress Cataloging-in-Publication Data

Snyder, Alvin A.
    Warriors of disinformation : American propaganda, Soviet lies, and the winning of the Cold War, an insider's account / Alvin A. Snyder. —1st ed.
        p.   cm.
    Includes index.
    ISBN 1-55970-321-0
    1. United States Information Agency. 2. Propaganda, American.
3. Cold War. I. Title.
    E744.5.S69   1995
    327.12730171'7'09045—dc20   95-12703

Published in the United States of America by Arcade Publishing, Inc., New York
Distributed by Little, Brown and Company

10   9   8   7   6   5   4   3   2   1

Designed by David Szanto

BP

PRINTED IN THE UNITED STATES OF AMERICA

To

Anne Snyder,

a warrior of boundless inspiration and patience,

to Carole and James Snyder,

and to the memory of my parents,

Jean and Gus Snyder

Contents

More than forty years ago, I was a pioneer in radio, a sports announcer. And I found myself broadcasting major league baseball games from telegraphed reports. I was not at the stadium . . .

Now, if the game was rather dull, you could say, "It's a hard-hit ball down toward second base. The shortstop is going over after the ball and makes a wild stab, picks it up, turns and gets him out just in time."

Now, I submit to you that I told the truth, if he was out from shortstop to first, and I don't know whether he really ran over toward second base and made a one-handed stab, or whether he just squatted down and took the ball when it came to him. But the truth got there, and in other words, it can be attractively packaged.

— Ronald Reagan,
speaking at the Voice of America's
fortieth anniversary ceremonies,
Washington, D.C.,
February 24, 1982

Preface

DURING THE COLD WAR, THE INTERNATIONAL PROPAGANDA MA-
chine of the U.S. government sported its own 120-piece symphony orchestra and ballroom dance band. The orchestra was said to be one
of the finest in Europe, and Horst Jankowski's dance band, headquartered in Berlin, swung with the best of them. All this was part of
cold war spin. Far from concert and dance halls, in the mountains of
Afghanistan, U.S. government media gurus were training sheepherders to be skilled TV cameramen so that they could chronicle the
nightmare of Soviet military occupation; in the Arctic, films extolling
the American way of life were carried on reindeer sleds to Lapland-
ers; TV programs designed to incite unrest were beamed from a helium balloon over Florida toward Castro's Cuba; the American
government's worldwide television network carried programs proclaiming the success of a high-tech Star Wars missile test that had
been secretly rigged so it could not fail.

Whatever worked was fair game. The U.S. government
ran a full-service public relations organization, the largest in the
world, about the size of the twenty biggest U.S. commercial PR firms
combined. Its full-time professional staff of more than 10,000,
spread out among some 150 countries, burnished America's image
and trashed the Soviet Union 2,500 hours a week with a tower of
babble comprised of more than 70 languages, to the tune of over
$2 billion per year. The biggest branch of this propaganda machine is
called the United States Information Agency.

With the cold war now over, America's prodigious international propaganda machine has been, in television lingo, fading to black, its practitioners dwindling in numbers and many of its programs going off the air as the result of Congress-imposed budget cutbacks. Gone is the familiar Communist enemy on which propaganda programs were focused and against whose threat congressional funding committees were rallied. The world is now awash in a sea of information from TV satellites, videocassettes, fax machines, cellular phones, computer networks, fiber-optic cable, and much more—all competing for people's attention. Government broadcast outlets are squeezed into receiving a smaller share of the available audience, and its purveyors are subjected to greater accountability by a better-informed public. There are still more than 4,500 state-run global radio stations touting their own national interests and competing against one another for listeners, but around the world people are tuning in to rapidly expanding commercial media. For the first time since it was established, the British Broadcasting Corporation's share of the domestic radio audience has fallen below 50 percent. People abroad now tune in local FM stereo stations, listen to compact discs, and watch TV programs like "Baywatch," with its young hard bodies, beamed in by satellite from Hollywood. The American TV quiz show "Jeopardy" is played worldwide in 65 languages. Computer hackers in Hanoi chat with counterparts around the world on their screens faster than they can telephone someone across town. Ted Turner's Cable News Network was even scooped by some residents of Kobe, Japan, who provided the world with live eyewitness updates on the devastating earthquake that killed more than 4,000 persons in January 1995 via the worldwide computer service Internet.

But just before it began its fade to black, the American propaganda machine enjoyed a Golden Age, as dramatic advances in information technology made propaganda more readily transmittable via satellite television. In this book, I have concentrated on the period 1982–1988, when I was director of the U.S. Information Agency's Television and Film Service, and the two most powerful countries on earth ratcheted up the intensity of their free-for-all to psych out and smash the other by any communicative means necessary. Leading the charge was USIA director Charles Z. Wick, a Hollywood entrepreneur who propelled his agency into the forefront of U.S. foreign policy efforts by the sheer force of his personality and by his close personal friendship with President Ronald Reagan. Wick—former bandleader from Cleveland, Hollywood agent, and movie producer—seemed a curious choice for the diplomatic position, but Ronald Reagan knew better.

"Now, people have asked me how I discovered this very effective public servant," Reagan said affectionately at a dinner honoring Wick in 1988 (who by then had served longer than any other USIA director). "I just looked for someone with the balance of two qualities: a greatness of vision, yet still able to understand Washington. And when I found the man who would produce the classic film that combined Snow White and the Three Stooges, I said, I have found that man."[1] Reagan had seen to it that Wick was given all the resources he needed. During Wick's eight years as director, USIA's expenditures increased from $486 million to $820 million annually. Wick knew that he would make his greatest impact with television, and so my annual budget soared from just over $6 million when I joined the Agency in 1982, to almost $37 million when I left in 1988 (I also had served longer than anyone in that job up to that point or since).

Recently declassified Russian documents illustrate the importance that Yuri Andropov and Mikhail Gorbachev and their aides placed on the manipulation of the international media to promote Soviet policies, and how much Reagan's public posturing—on such issues as targeting Russia with Euro-missiles and Soviet human rights abuses—confounded, outraged, and distracted Kremlin leaders. The USIA's exploitation of the international media on these and other issues clearly made it more difficult for Gorbachev to marshal public support throughout the fragile Communist bloc of nations for his reform programs and eroded his support at home. Internal secret documents detailing meetings of Soviet leaders, many of which relate to propaganda issues, have been released by Russian President Boris Yeltsin and made available through the Library of Congress and the Cold War International History Project of the Woodrow Wilson International Center for Scholars. I will refer to these records, to recently declassified documents from the State Department and the USIA, and to my own notes of the many sessions I personally attended with Soviet leaders.

Propagandizing means advocating a point of view favorable to one's own position, and that's precisely what we at the USIA did. The British government, too, admitted the venerable BBC's overseas service was a weapon of propaganda, consisting of British views concerning the news.[2] I had no problem with practicing advocacy journalism, because I felt we were transmitting "good" propaganda; an exaggerated version of the truth, perhaps, but still fundamentally the truth. I would later learn that many of us at the USIA were often duped by government officials from the intelligence community, the White House, the State Department, and the Pentagon into transmitting lies—disinformation—without realizing it at the time. We became unknowing warriors of disinformation, and then we became knowing ones.

This book highlights some of the crucial battles of the propaganda war, a war to influence public attitudes abroad and erode support for the Soviet system. Under Reagan, public diplomacy—dealing directly with foreign publics instead of with their governments—became a linchpin in American foreign policy. The president's National Security Council and the State Department drafted public diplomacy impact statements for most major foreign policy decisions; a senior USIA officer was assigned to the office of the White House press secretary to keep international public diplomacy in the forefront.

The propaganda war was fought on many fronts and included its share of heroes and goats. Ronald Reagan and Charles Z. Wick were respectively the commander in chief and the supreme commander in the war of propaganda, but I have attempted to focus equally on some of its foot soldiers. The strategies both sides used were effectively shielded from public scrutiny. The U.S. government erected an iron curtain of its own around the American public, which had virtually no idea what its agencies were broadcasting abroad. When Congress established America's foreign information service shortly after World War II, it wanted to ensure government propagandists couldn't brainwash domestic audiences the way Nazi propagandists had. Congress was also successfully lobbied by American broadcasters who didn't want competition from government-funded communicators. And so, for nearly fifty years, there has been a ban on the domestic dissemination of broadcasts and publications produced by the USIA, which was established in 1953. Given today's sophisticated technology, however, the law cannot be enforced, and it ought to have been repealed long before this was the case. Americans should have known how America was conducting its public diplomacy abroad during the cold war. This book will give them—belatedly—some perspective on it.

Some readers may never have heard of the USIA, though most will recognize the Voice of America, Radio Free Europe/Radio Liberty, and Radio Moscow, and believe them to be effective means of spreading information abroad. In fact, Radio Moscow, for example, had virtually no credibility. During the height of the cold war it averaged less than one percent of the listenership in those areas outside Russia where the signal could be heard. Conversely, listeners behind the Iron Curtain felt that programs from Radio Free Europe and Radio Liberty were suspect because they were written and produced by dissident exiles.

Propaganda is always most productive when it is least traceable. The image of America abroad was greatly damaged when Soviet-inspired stories about how the U.S. government had created the AIDS virus to kill off its African-American population surfaced in the Western media. When U.S.-provided footage of Soviet atrocities in Afghanistan showed up on TV in Communist-bloc countries, its effects were far more devastating than a decade's worth of shortwave radio broadcasts. Disinformation stories about America's Star Wars missile technology, the invasion of Grenada, and Soviet military activities in Afghanistan, as broadcast on the USIA's Worldnet television programs, were excerpted by foreign TV and by foreign newspapers, and had far greater impact than had those stories appeared solely in U.S. government media.

America's warriors of disinformation strove to stay on the offensive, to keep their Soviet counterparts off-balance. The astute Russian journalist Alexander Shalnev admitted to me recently that Soviet propagandists were ineffective because they were usually on the defensive. By using technology to get our stories out quickly, we rarely gave Soviet propagandists the chance to take the initiative. Social psychologists argue that propaganda is most productive when the messages containing it are timely and repeated often. "Air" Wick, as the USIA director was unaffectionately called by those who disapproved of his methods, never to my knowledge cracked a psychology book or a how-to bureaucratic manual during the entire time we were putting together a worldwide satellite TV network. He just did it. The one-time bandleader from Cleveland played a lot of hunches. But they were usually the right ones.

Political scientists tell me it is difficult to measure precisely what impact Western propaganda had in hastening the demise of communism, although Zbigniew Brzezinski has argued that "the loss of Communist monopoly over mass communications is the key to the breakdown of Communist totalitarianism."[3] During the cold war, those who were exposed to Western media behind the Iron Curtain could not, of course, be readily interviewed, and polling could only be conducted among émigrés to the west. Polling people about that period today is also imperfect, because conditions have changed so radically. And so anecdotal accounts of that period will help reconstruct it.

I make no claim to being a scholar of the cold war. Wick used to boast that he didn't know much about foreign affairs, but he could still make things happen. I was among those who were there to help him, and so I saw what he did to make it happen. I will leave it to cold war historians to determine to what extent the USIA helped to topple communism. What I relate in this book may be useful to them. I hope it contributes to our understanding of the period.

Today, Radio Moscow still opens with the first few bars of the familiar theme song, "Moscow Nights." But the most popular programs across Russia these days are a Mexican TV soap opera, "Rescue 911," and "Santa Barbara." They are not only escapist but satisfy Russian curiosity about life in the West. Radio Free Europe and Radio Liberty are pulling up stakes and setting out to find new audiences in Asia. The Voice of America is experimenting with talking computers. The cold war broadcast instruments are adrift; shortwave radio has become outdated. Even if communism were alive and well, government propagandists could no longer get away with what the USIA did in the 1980s. Rupert Murdoch's satellite TV service to Europe and Asia, and Ted Turner's CNN, seen in some 200 nations, did as much to kill off the VOA and other government-sponsored broadcast services as the fall of the Berlin Wall.

The multiplying forms of information may well spawn disinformation more insidious than any we have yet known. Studies show that when people become inundated with data they will seek simple, clear-cut messages. Confusion provides fertile ground for future warriors of disinformation with a clearly defined mission. What replaces 1980s-style disinformation may make it seem wholesome by comparison.

Acknowledgments

THERE WERE THOUSANDS OF WARRIORS ON BOTH SIDES OF THE IRON Curtain who fought the battle for the skies, and for what they considered to be a just cause. By recounting their own personal experiences, many of these individuals helped me to reconstruct some of the more significant propaganda battles of the 1980s, the decade in which the war of disinformation drew to a close. A list of those kind enough to be interviewed is included in the Appendix. I am deeply grateful to them, and to the Annenberg Washington Program in Communications Policy Studies of Northwestern University, Newton N. Minow, director, for providing me with a fellowship to complete the book.

My wife, Anne, was unwavering in her support, without which *Warriors* would have never happened.

Timothy Bent, senior editor at Arcade Publishing, made excellent suggestions to this television writer who is used to letting pictures tell the story. *Warriors* is ever better as a result.

My thanks to Maria Downs, my agent, who believed in the book, and provided valuable guidance.

Finally, to Yuri Solton, the Radio Moscow commentator, who thankfully gave us all a wrap when he announced on December 30, 1991, "The Soviet Union, or rather the totalitarian Communist system that once kept 300 million people in harness and toyed with the maniacal idea of a world revolution, has ceased to exist."

WARRIORS OF DISINFORMATION

↔ 1 ↔

Letting Wick Be Wick

IT SEEMED SOMEHOW FITTING THAT THE MAN WHO PRODUCED A movie entitled *Snow White and the Three Stooges* would be put in charge of waging psychological warfare against the Communist Evil Empire during the entire Reagan Administration. The man who claimed that British Prime Minister Maggie Thatcher had opposed the American invasion of Grenada because she was a woman, and who frequently sent anti-Communist jokes in the diplomatic pouch to the U.S. Embassy in Moscow, was no cerebral State Department diplomat. In fact, he was no diplomat at all, as became clear to everyone shortly after he arrived in Washington in 1981 to take over as America's chief overseas propagandist—director of the United States Information Agency—as the cold war was about to head into the home stretch. Charles Z. Wick admitted he was short on diplomatic skills but promised that he would make things happen. He did. For his Soviet counterparts, Wick was their worst nightmare come true. "Charles is a man who brought our international communications agency into the twentieth century," said Reagan. "And you know, this happens to be one of my favorite centuries."[1]

Charlie Wick was a Hollywood huckster who for eight

years stood U.S. foreign relations on its ear—and set the Kremlin's teeth on edge. He grew to admire his great adversary, Soviet leader Mikhail Gorbachev. "He's a guy with a great sense of humor," said Wick, who had acted as a press agent for such diverse clients as Rudy Vallee, Benny Goodman, and Francis Langford.

A self-made millionaire and member of Ronald Reagan's inner circle of Hollywood cronies, Wick was a Washington neophyte and soon became fair game for Reagan bashers. "Kiddiegate" was one of his first imbroglios. The USIA, a sprawling colossus of almost 10,000 employees, was on the A-list of the hottest employment agency in town—the White House personnel office—when positions had to be found for those who had helped elect Reagan in 1980, as well as their spouses, children, and relatives. Charlie Wick was a team player, and he wanted to do his duty for his buddy the president.

Job "referrals" arrived on Wick's desk for: the son of the secretary of defense, three daughters and a niece of two national security advisers, the nephew of the White House communications director, daughters of the secretary of state and the assistant secretary of the interior, the daughter of a former Voice of America director, and daughters of two prominent journalists. Jobs were found at the USIA for all of them. Also hired was a cashier from a Washington delicatessen down the block from USIA headquarters. The cashier was slated to become cultural affairs officer at the U.S. Embassy in Haiti.[2] When the story hit the *Washington Post,* the nomination was subsequently withdrawn, and Kiddiegate became an issue with the Senate Foreign Relations Committee. Most of the young relatives of administration officials were also let go. "It was a process of learning and growing for Charlie Wick," said Senate aide Peter Galbraith.[3]

Wick, a younger Richard Nixon lookalike[4] (which was where the similarity ended), was manic about security. He had reason to be. His friend the president had barely survived an assassination attempt in 1981, and he himself had received telephone threats against him and his family. For protection around his Washington office Wick was sworn in as a special deputy U.S. marshal so that he could pack a handgun. He had a $30,000 security system installed at his rented home in DuPont Circle (he reimbursed the government for $22,000 after a series of negative press reports). When he traveled abroad he did so with several armed State Department bodyguards. Wick also always wore a custom-made, lead-lined raincoat, under the weight of which he once fell on the sidewalk as he got out of a car.[5] Wick thought the hot dog stand on the sidewalk outside the entrance to the USIA's Washington headquarters posed a security threat to Agency employees and visiting foreign dignitaries, who had to pass by the stand on their way into the building from their limousines. The hot dog stand was real Americana, fitting in neatly with the USIA's mission to present our way of life to others, but Wick apparently thought it was carrying things too far. He asked Woody Kingman, his director of management, to complain to Marion Barry, District of Columbia mayor, in an attempt to bar the hot dog vendor from the sidewalk. "We remain convinced that vendor operations in front of the USIA are inappropriate and harmful to the national interest," Kingman wrote to D.C. officials in May 1987, in a feeble attempt to link the hot dog stand to potential terrorism. "Vendor tables and other equipment could be used to hide explosive devices."[6] D.C. officials were unimpressed, and Kingman's request was denied.

The hard-charging Wick demanded attention to the smallest detail, and became irritated on his first trip to Europe as the USIA's director, when he was stopped by a military security guard as he tried to breeze through the door at the U.S. Embassy in Belgrade without first showing any identification. The marine, who was female, had not been informed in advance of Wick's visit by his staff and bolted out from behind a thick glass door, shouting, "Stop! Don't go any farther. Identify yourself!"

"If you don't know who I am, that's your problem," Wick shouted back, irritated at his staff for not clearing his entry into the embassy in advance. The marine grabbed him by the arm and did her best to restrain the director, who became enraged, threatening to lodge a complaint of harassment with the commandant of the Marine Corps. Wick meant what he said. The guard was transferred, and word spread that she had been caught in Wick's "potato masher."[7] During his eight years as director, Wick was never stopped again by an embassy security guard. A nervous bureaucracy marked it down as another item for payback time. Not too long after the Belgrade incident, Wick was accused in press reports leaked by his detractors of not stopping his subordinates from compiling a so-called "enemies list"—to them, reminiscent of Joe McCarthy's—which reportedly included many prominent names.

Wick's legend and reputation grew. One disgruntled USIA

employee claimed that when Wick got mad at the slow-moving bureaucracy, he underwent "a physiological transformation: his eyes bulge, his mouth starts to quiver, and his flesh just seems to disintegrate."[8] His in-house critics drew up a list of twenty-five behavioral traits that one had to know to get along with him. It was summarized in a handout entitled *What to Do and What Not to Do to Behave Properly in the Presence of the Director,* the contents of which were promptly leaked to the press. "Never put Wick in the position of having to explain to anybody who he is," warned the publication. "He expects that everything is prepared so that he can pass along freely with the conviction that the proper people know who he is."

For his part, Wick beat up on Agency department heads for being too slow. Some lasted only a matter of weeks. "One of the problems with your department is by the time we get things done, the disease has either caused the patient to die or he is hopelessly gone," he wrote to one hapless executive he had asked to clean out his desk. "By that time the preventive inoculation is too late."[9]

The chairman of the House Foreign Affairs Subcommittee, Daniel Mica (D-FL), noted to Wick that "there is a fear of the director within the Agency." "So what!" Wick boomed in reply to Mica. "Everyone has his own management style."[10]

A lawyer by training, Wick unwisely began to tape telephone conversations without telling the other parties. He wanted records of his conversations so that follow-up actions could be taken to keep things moving quickly through the bureaucracy. They were often turned into what Wick's staff called "zingers," or "Z Grams," some thirty of which per day he would fire off to individuals for action and which were then tracked by Wick's staff to be certain items were followed up. It is not illegal to tape a telephone conversation in Washington without telling the other party, but the matter was pursued by appropriate law enforcement authorities in seven states where such tapings could be considered an invasion of privacy. Wick's lawyer was Leonard Garment, who during the Watergate years was counsel to President Richard Nixon, someone else who taped people without informing them in advance. Garment claimed Wick's invasion of privacy was small potatoes, and compared to Nixon's tapings it probably was.[11]

"There were hundreds of tapes about things like Frank

Sinatra's singing engagements," said Garment. But Wick was forced to back down, and with hat in hand, he traveled with Garment to several states to apologize personally to district attorneys. Letters of apology were written to persons who had been taped. Wick telephoned former president Jimmy Carter, with whom he held a repentant prayer session long-distance. Despite calls for his dismissal, a remorseful Wick kept his job.[12]

Wick was born Charles Zwick in Cleveland, Ohio, on October 12, 1917, the son of a successful Jewish businessman. He began to play the piano as a child, and by the time he was in high school he was arranging scores for the popular Fred Waring orchestra. He formed the Charles Zwick Orchestra to pay his way through Case Western Reserve University law school. When legendary band leader Tommy Dorsey came to Cleveland to play at the Palace Theater, he stayed at the Carter Hotel, where the Charles Zwick Orchestra was playing the Rainbow Room. Dorsey was impressed with young Charlie and hired him as his business manager and music arranger.[13]

Wick eventually settled in Los Angeles, where he went to work at the William Morris Agency as an agent for Hollywood stars. At a friend's house he met model Mary Jane Woods, whom he would marry. He later dropped the "Z" from his name, founded his own agency, and in addition to Reagan and Goodman, managed Eleanor Roosevelt and Sir Winston Churchill. Wick negotiated American film rights for the former British prime minister's series "History of the English-Speaking Peoples." And, of course, he also produced that classic Twentieth-Century Fox comedy, *Snow White and the Three Stooges,* which starred skater Carol Heiss and was based on a story Wick had written for his children. It was the only film featuring the Three Stooges that ever lost money.[14]

In the mid-1950s Wick and boat engine millionaire Ralph Evinrude founded United Convalescent Hospitals, a nursing home company, that grew into one of the country's largest. Wick later formed his own investment business and retired as a millionaire at age forty.

The Wicks lived in a fashionable neighborhood, next door to motion picture star Judy Garland and her daughter, Liza Minnelli. Eleven-year-old Liza would knock on the door and ask,

"Mr. Wick, can I use your pool?"[15] Charles Wick, Jr., went to the same private elementary school as Reagan's daughter, Patti. Nancy Reagan and Mary Jane Wick met and worked together on projects at the school's Mothers' Club. Mary Jane said she and Nancy would console each other when "Patti was a teenager and my boys went through a period of having long hair."[16]

The Wicks and the Reagans became fast friends, and Wick worked as a principal fund-raiser in Ronald Reagan's 1980 presidential campaign. After Reagan's victory, Wick was named co-chairman of the $8 million presidential inaugural balls and had to handle the arrival of Reagan supporters in Washington, which he described as the "Normandy invasion without water."[17] Reagan then appointed him as the director of the U.S. Information Agency.

We have already seen that Wick was no diplomat, and yet in 1981 he found himself in one of the most visible and diplomatic jobs in the U.S. government. Reagan and Wick had often discussed how the media could be used to further foreign policy objectives. When Wick arrived in Washington, Reagan gave him a *New York Times* article about how television might be used to undermine the Polish Communist government's crackdown on striking labor unions. Said the article: "Imagine the reaction if the average laborer knew of the latest happenings inside Poland. Picture what an effect TV images of the Polish strikers would have!"[18] Charlie Wick could imagine it. His first USIA-TV satellite show to slam the Communists would be a Polish-language musical starring Frank Sinatra and Pope Paul II, entitled "Let Poland Be Poland."

Charlie Wick wanted "Let Poland Be Poland" to be the biggest TV spectacular in the history of the world. To direct it he brought in Marty "Chains" Pasetta from Hollywood. Pasetta's credits included among others the annual motion picture Academy Award shows and "Paul Anka in Monte Carlo." USIA bureaucrats winked at each other at the sight of man they soon nicknamed "Chains," because he wore open sports shirts with heavy gold links dangling around his neck. Wick's idea was to beam the program by TV satellite to audiences around the world in order to draw attention to the Polish government's crackdown on striking labor unions led by Lech Walesa.

The new USIA director believed in a "big bang" theory of

public relations. The size of a TV spectacular and the hoopla surrounding it were as important as the program itself. Involving Reagan and other world leaders would give it the scale he wanted. To sell the idea, Wick invited to his office White House communications director David Gergen for a late-night meeting, along with a group of neo-conservative intellectuals including Ben Wattenberg, Michael Novak, and Norman Podhoretz. On December 21, 1981, for two and a half hours, they discussed how to deal with the Soviet-backed Polish military suppression of Solidarity. Gergen characterized it as a meeting "among friends" who shared Reagan's views on foreign policy. Wick presented his idea to the group: the program would be beamed around the world by satellite to encourage pro-democracy elements in Poland and to embarrass Communist leaders there, in the Soviet Union, and elsewhere in Eastern Europe.

Everyone concurred it would be a solid public relations opportunity, a golden opportunity for Reagan to establish his credentials as the leading spokesman against totalitarian threats. Gergen was convinced that Reagan could rally the forces of freedom and contribute to the breakup of the Soviet bloc. "The administration," he said, "has been walking on eggshells, saying little, and this has added to a general sense of gloom." Reagan's handling of the situation in Poland could be a "make-or-break" event for his young presidency. The group agreed that Gergen should write a memorandum to the public relations troika at the White House—Ed Meese, Mike Deaver, and James Baker—strongly endorsing Wick's idea. The TV spectacular, wrote Gergen in his White House memo, would "rouse the public, increase the sense of moral outrage, convince people both here and in Europe of the nature of the Soviets, and—hopefully—aid the cause of freedom in Eastern Europe."[19] Mike Deaver and the others loved the idea. Wick promptly called Frank Sinatra in Hollywood, who agreed to star in the production and even to sing in Polish. Wick, the former Hollywood agent, started thumbing through his dog-eared Rolodex for other celebrities.

Not everyone was so wild about the idea. "We've got to stop him," said a career foreign service officer in a panic.[20] And a staff member of the National Security Council, Richard Pipes, became alarmed over the number of Hollywood stars signing up to appear on Wick's show. Pipes, a noted historian on leave from Harvard, thought the project was becoming too show biz: "I think you're moving too fast, Charlie," said Pipes at a White House meeting. "This looks like the Academy Awards. We're supposed to make a political statement."[21]

Most of Wick's predecessors at USIA would have yielded to a senior member of the foreign policy staff, but not Wick. His face reddened and his voice rose in anger as he pointed his finger at Pipes. "You set the policy, and I'll produce the television show," Wick thundered. "The U.S. is against martial law in Poland, and this is how I want television to make the statement. Butt out!"[22] Pipes, aware that Wick would appeal directly to Reagan, backed off. "The only way to stop Charlie Wick is to shoot him," said a frustrated White House aide.[23]

To publicize the event and to help raise money to produce the program, Wick put together a group of high-powered public relations experts from Procter & Gamble, Philip Morris, General Motors, Walt Disney, and Exxon, among others. He called the meeting to order in New York City on the afternoon of January 6, 1982. Richard Holwill of the conservative Heritage Foundation reported that a tax-exempt organization called the National Center for Public Diplomacy had already been set up within his organization and could be used to funnel funds for the satellite program. Holwill said the Heritage Foundation had thought of using the center to organize protests against Soviet nuclear tests, which the United States claimed were causing acid yellow rain to fall in Afghanistan and Southeast Asia. "The Poland TV spectacular to help the Solidarity movement is a similar type mission," said Holwill. Stephen Stamus of the Exxon Corporation suggested that sponsoring organizations be expanded to include international labor union groups. The public relations gurus agreed to alert their overseas subsidiaries about the event.[24]

Meanwhile, "Chains" Pasetta was busy putting together the ninety-minute extravaganza, which would cost more than $500,000 (all but about $38,000 would eventually be covered by private donations; the Carthage Foundation, Mobil Oil, and Rockwell International each pledged $100,000). The program was taking shape. Ronald Reagan would speak from the White House, and Frank Sinatra would sing a Polish-language ballad. "Let Poland Be Poland" narrators would include Charlton Heston, Glenda Jackson,

Max Von Sydow, Kirk Douglas, Henry Fonda, Orson Welles, Bob Hope, and others. World political and religious leaders, including Pope John Paul II, would denounce Polish repression. Cellist Mstislav Rostropovich, a Russian émigré, would conduct a symphony orchestra. During the program—a mixture of music, poetry, and rhetoric—Reagan would indicate possible U.S. military action in Poland if the situation there continued to deteriorate. Pro-union rallies around the world were videotaped. Sixteen heads of state agreed to make special appearances. Congress provided a special dispensation permitting the program to be shown in the United States, so in addition to being broadcast overseas by stations in some 30 countries and in 39 languages, it was carried by 142 public television stations. According to audience estimates, more than 184 million persons in 46 countries saw 30 minutes or more of the program.[25] The Voice of America also transmitted the program to radio listeners worldwide.

Career foreign service diplomats within the Agency and State Department were aghast at the idea that Glenda Jackson and Frank Sinatra were hired to carry diplomatic water for the United States. At the very least it was a waste of time. According to USIA career minister Hans N. Tuch, Wick "was convinced beyond any doubt that such a show was the most dramatic method of condemning the rape of Poland. . . . There was no one who could persuade him that Frank Sinatra and his show business friends might effectively combat Soviet subversion in Peoria, but not in Bonn, Brussels, Bologna, or Bordeaux."[26]

"Let Poland Be Poland" got mixed review from the critics. After Central Intelligence Agency director William J. Casey saw the program, he flung his arms around Wick and exclaimed, "Hooray for you!" Casey said the CIA felt the program had a "positive impact" abroad, and that Polish dissenters were given a boost in morale. Viewers who watched the Hollywood spectacular expecting to see Pope Paul II and Frank Sinatra dancing a soft shoe were no doubt disappointed. "Let Poland be Poland" was tediously long and wordy.

"Only in the United States would quite such a vulgar spectacle be mounted," said the *London Daily Mail*. "Cold war rhetoric can be overdone," editorialized the *Washington Post*.

"But . . . what is the proper tone of voice in which to speak of the crushing of the Polish renewal?" the *Post* then pondered. The point was that *people all over were talking about it.* Who cared if it wasn't Shakespeare in the Park? It achieved its purpose by focusing attention worldwide on the plight of Poland's free labor movement and, according to follow-up USIA research, had generated some support for it. The Russians had put up such a fuss over the program in advance that people tuned in from curiosity. "The Soviet Union's commissars must have watched the satellite television broadcast with much concern," said the *Toronto Star.* Reported Vienna's *Daily Kurier,* "The broadcast . . . dominated world affairs on Sunday" (January 31).

Moscow pronounced the program a dud. But just to be certain, on the night Wick's special was being broadcast, Soviet TV aired a film about American espionage in Poland. The Polish government, for its part, denounced the American broadcast as constituting interference in its internal affairs and claimed the program was filled with lies. Jailed Solidarity union leaders were actually in a "good mood," said a Polish government official.

During the week that followed, the Soviets mounted a campaign to discredit Wick. "He is a millionaire who made his money from real estate, show business, and brothels," said one Soviet weekly. "Veterans of psychological warfare are concerned only that the super expert in presidential publicity has now been instructed to work in a market which, in their opinion, he does not understand." Soviet propagandists were receiving anti-Wick material from magazines and newspapers in this country, to which Wick's enemies within the USIA were leaking stories with increasingly regularity. "The . . . Agency has been in turmoil ever since its boss, Charles Wick, a Reagan chum, took over and began trying to transform it from an independent news and information operation into a propaganda arm of the administration," wrote the King Features syndicate, a charge soon echoed by Soviet critics.

"Charlie Wick slammed into the USIA with a body punch," recalled Terrence A. Catherman, a senior foreign service officer and former deputy director of the Voice of America. "You did what he said immediately and picked up the pieces later on. He was demanding things at the time that no one was prepared to deliver. He scared the hell out of people. We hadn't seen another director like this, ever."[27]

That's because in the past stoic State Department bureaucrats had called the shots and not a Hollywood huckster by the name of Charles Z. Wick.

↔ 2 ↔

Toward a Public Diplomacy

SHORTLY AFTER THE END OF WORLD WAR II, WILLIAM BENTON, AN AS-
sistant secretary of state, concluded that Hollywood movies were tar-
nishing America's image abroad, so he journeyed west to the film
capital to meet with studio moguls and straighten things out. Many
in Congress shared his view. Some even suggested that the government should censor films such as *Tobacco Road* and *The Lost Weekend,* which they thought gave America a bad rap overseas.[1] They
even claimed the Bing Crosby–Barry Fitzgerald movie *Going My
Way,* in which a priest named Father O'Malley uses unconventional
methods to tame unruly street kids, was considered insulting by Europe's Protestant countries because it "played up" the Catholic religion too much. One Congressman argued that the American film
classic *Life With Father,* the William Powell–Irene Dunne comedy,
was harmful to America's relations with Italy because audiences
there considered the movie too juvenile.[2] The State Department was
also unhappy with Hollywood film purchases by the Soviet Union.
The State Department was pushing the Charlie Chaplin film *The Dictator,* but the Kremlin instead bought *The Grapes of Wrath,* based on

John Steinbeck's realistic but unflattering novel about America during the Depression.

Benton opposed government censorship, but nonetheless felt Hollywood would not comply unless a little "vinegar" was thrown in. He held four days of nonstop meetings with studio executives. "I met constantly with the key groups of the motion picture industry—morning, afternoon, and night," he wrote in his report upon returning to Washington. "The motion picture industry is potentially the most valuable ally in the conduct of our foreign relations and conversely it is a first-class headache."[3] Despite his exhaustive and exhausting (he never went to bed before two A.M.) schedule of meetings, Benton admitted having failed to convince Hollywood "to eliminate many of the petty annoyances and distorted representations of American life."[4] President Harry Truman also met with a group of Hollywood motion picture leaders, which included legendary filmmaker Cecil B. DeMille, to discuss ways of achieving greater cooperation between the government and the motion picture industry, but nothing much came out of the session.[5] There is no record that Truman lost any sleep as the result of the encounter, as Secretary Benton had under similar conditions. A government study would later reveal that the impact Hollywood movies made abroad was more favorable than unfavorable.[6]

Unable to exert influence in Hollywood, the State Department decided to establish its own film unit, even though government officials openly admitted it would never achieve Hollywood's level of professionalism. But it could offer safe alternatives, such as a cowboy documentary showing that American ranchers worked most of the time just like Siamese sheepherders, instead of gunslinging and killing each other in high-noon showdowns.[7] One State Department documentary film was shot at the New York School for Home Economics and featured average American women rather than Hollywood starlets, preparing for a career in marriage by learning to care for home and family. The women were pictured in a laboratory testing different types of foods, or studying the quality of bedding so that they could make the proper consumer choices as wives and mothers.[8] It was all propaganda, or, as the USIA later preferred to call it, public diplomacy.

Until Ronald Reagan was elected president in 1980, U.S.

diplomacy hadn't changed very much. American politicians had always tried to devise ways to influence foreign public opinion overseas as a way of helping foreign policy initiatives, a concept advanced by Benjamin Franklin beginning in 1757, when as envoy to England he tried to rally support for the Colonies, and later by Thomas Jefferson, as America's representative to France and after he left the presidency. Jefferson had time to ponder things from his retirement at Monticello. The War of 1812 had just ended, and American interests were getting bad press in Europe. "I hope," Jefferson wrote, "that to preserve this weather gauge of public opinion, and to counteract the slanders and falsehoods disseminated by the British papers, the government will make it a standing instruction to their ministers at foreign courts to keep Europe truly informed of occurrences here, by publishing in their papers the naked truth always, whether favorable or unfavorable. For they will believe the good, if we tell them the bad also."[9]

Jefferson believed the United States would be able to wield more influence abroad by showcasing its democratic values and institutions. As minister to France after the Revolutionary War, Jefferson established the first American information center with public affairs officers to promote America, laying the groundwork for the future USIA. Information offices quickly spread elsewhere in Europe and beyond. Traditional diplomacy was changed even more radically when the first transatlantic cable was laid in 1866, and again when radio hobbyists discovered in 1924 that shortwave signals could travel huge distances, bounding up and down like a ball for thousands of miles between the ground and an upper layer of atmosphere. Suddenly, everyone wanted to get into the act. The Netherlands was the first European country to use short-wave radio to maintain contact with its Dutch colonies abroad. Britain, France, Portugal, and Belgium followed soon after: they also wanted to strengthen ties with their overseas possessions. Telegraph messages were sent first but were soon replaced by voice transmissions, when it was determined that the spoken word enhanced the effectiveness of the message.[10] As veteran Radio Netherlands reporter Jonathan Marks recalls, many nations already had their own airlines and decided that they should have their own international radio voice as well, "to tell the world what a great place their country was, providing you were only visiting on a tourist visa."[11]

In 1942, President Roosevelt set up the Office of War Information (OWI), predecessor of the U.S. Information Agency, to combat German and Italian propaganda. The first Voice of America radio broadcast was transmitted on February 24, 1942. It consisted of a program, in German, carried across the Atlantic via shortwave and relayed by the British Broadcasting Corporation. "The news may be good. The news may be bad," said German Service staff announcer Robert Bauer. "But we shall tell you the truth." The VOA's life was imperiled by controversy in 1943, when one of its commentaries referred to Italy's king Victor Emmanuel as "the moronic little king"[12] while the State Department was in the middle of secret negotiations with Fascist Italy. Roosevelt himself admonished the VOA, and its broadcast studios were later moved from New York to Washington, where staff could be watched more closely. Despite the move, the marriage between journalism and diplomacy became no less strained.

The OWI was disbanded following World War II because it was thought that "psychological warfare" was no longer necessary. President Harry S Truman, however, noting the strength of such programs transmitted by other nations, such as the BBC, argued, "The nature of present-day foreign relations makes it essential for the United States to maintain information activities abroad as an integral part of the conduct of our foreign affairs." Still, in 1948, one State Department official remarked that the objectives of diplomacy were best served by releasing as little information as possible.[13]

Truman met opposition from isolationists who maintained that it wasn't necessary for the United States to send propaganda during peacetime. They were joined by the major American wire services, the Associated Press and United Press, who withdrew their services from the State Department. An AP spokesman said, "Government cannot engage in newscasting without creating the fear of propaganda, which necessarily would reflect upon the objectivity of the news services from which such newscasts are prepared."[14] But a stubborn Truman ordered the State Department to take the lead in coordinating the effort, and the Office of International Information and Cultural Affairs was established. The Office of Educational Exchange was also set up, and American libraries and cultural centers were established in foreign countries.

All this effort was to counter Soviet propaganda and

what the United States perceived as the distorted versions of its foreign policies disseminated by the Communists. To pursue vigorously Truman's "Campaign of Truth," and to take over the job of selling America abroad, President Dwight D. Eisenhower established the United States Information Agency in 1953. He was particularly dismayed that so many Europeans were too young to realize how much the Marshall Plan had done to rebuild the war-devastated continent. "Western Europe," said Eisenhower, "was rapidly being rebuilt, modernized industrially, and restored to prosperity, but European governments did little to inform their own people about the steps we were taking to help them."[15] Eisenhower, who believed in what he called diplomacy's "P-factor"—people-to-people communication—met personally at least once a month with the USIA's first director, Theodore S. Streibert, who also attended White House National Security Council meetings.[16] The USIA became the parent organization of the Voice of America (the beginning of an unhappy marriage for the VOA, which would wage an eternal struggle for news independence) and later would take over from the State Department the administration of international educational and cultural exchanges.[17]

The early 1950s also saw the founding of two additional U.S.-sponsored broadcast services, Radio Free Europe (RFE) and Radio Liberty (RL), which brought local news to information-deprived listeners behind the Iron Curtain. Funded initially by the Central Intelligence Agency, RFE and RL were known as "surrogate" services, with domestically targeted RFE programs beamed to Communist Eastern and Central Europe, and RL home broadcasts aimed at the Soviet Union.[18] The job of the VOA, on the other hand, was to tell *America*'s story in those areas and elsewhere around the world.

In general, State Department foreign service officers have never liked using the media to conduct foreign affairs. They deal with host government officials, then report to their superiors in Washington. Hence, the State Department was slow in grasping the expanding role communications was playing in shaping public opinion and underestimated its impact on the relationships between nations. There was a natural inclination to adhere to more traditional, secret government-to-government diplomacy, as opposed to reaching out publicly to foreign audiences and, through them, to their governments. Indeed, many diplomats felt that public diplomacy hindered or even subverted their efforts. They perceived it as a provocation and meddlesome, liable to unsettle the private, sensitive diplomatic process.

From the moment of its birth, the USIA's activities were guided by Foggy Bottom. Policy was dictated by the State Department, and because the new information agency wanted to produce its own films for audiences abroad, it continued to give Hollywood pictures a bad rap in order to justify its mission. An Agency confidential report stated that "many misconceptions about America—that it is rich, materialistic, lacking in culture, jazz-happy, full of gangsters— have been promoted and prolonged by productions from Hollywood. The United States Information Agency is constantly faced with having to correct this view."[19] USIA officials spent a good deal of time trying to convince congressional funding committees that its documentary films, which provided glowing images of America, had as much influence abroad as Hollywood products.

Judging by the degree to which the Soviets felt they had to dismiss its efforts, the USIA had good reason to believe in its success. In 1963 the Soviet magazine *New Times* devoted three pages to an article entitled "Battle Lost in Advance," suggesting the importance it was attaching by this point to the propaganda cold war with the United States:

> Just as ideological struggle is inevitable in the world we live in, so is your defeat in that struggle. Try as you will, you cannot win the battle for men's minds. All your efforts are doomed to failure. You can complicate, you can retard the triumph of Communism, but you cannot prevent it. Just as you cannot prevent the coming of spring.

President John F. Kennedy had cautioned that the war of words was real. "Our security may be lost piece by piece," said the president, "country by country, without the firing of a single missile or the crossing of a single border." Political propaganda was a key part of Communist world strategy, and both Radio Moscow and the Voice of America played important roles during the Cuban missile crisis of 1962. Because diplomatic communications were so primitive, it took as long as eight hours to get a classified message transmitted between the two world capitals. Nikita Khrushchev and Kennedy had their messages to each other read on their respective international radio services as a way of saving time.

The USIA's effect on foreign policy was in large measure dictated by the personality of its director. Legendary CBS News correspondent Edward R. Murrow, USIA director in the Kennedy Administration, insisted on getting a letter from his commander in chief stating unequivocally the prominent position of the Agency in the administration's foreign affairs activities. Murrow wanted to be certain that the precedent set by Eisenhower, who had placed his USIA director in the mainstream of foreign policy deliberations, would be continued. If the USIA director was there for the landings, Murrow told Kennedy, he ought to be present for the takeoffs. Kennedy complied, writing to Murrow on January 25, 1963, that all government departments and agencies would seek counsel from the USIA "when considering policies and programs which may substantially affect or be affected by foreign opinion."[20] Murrow was then invited to participate in NSC and State Department meetings at which foreign policy was formulated, as a result. The prevailing notion, however, was that the USIA was a place to which you sent ideologues who couldn't be trusted to handle serious issues such as arms control negotiations and similarly weighty affairs of state. One problem was that there were often slightly ambiguous definitions of what constitutes "public diplomacy." Congress provided its definition of public diplomacy in its April 1964 White Paper:

> Certain foreign policy objectives can be pursued by dealing directly with the people of foreign countries, rather than with their governments. Through the use of modern instruments and techniques of communication it is possible today to reach large or influential segments of national populations—to inform them, to influence their attitudes, and at times perhaps even to motivate them to a particular course of action. These groups, in turn, are capable of exerting noticeable, even decisive, pressures on their governments.[21]

Congress was convinced that public diplomacy was an increasingly important element of foreign policy, because the Communists were beginning to use "words, pictures and ideas, in addition to military force and economic weapons—and exploit modern means and techniques of communication, to advance their objectives."[22]

Another 1964 Congressional study bluntly used the word *propaganda* and went on to describe what goals public diplomacy, and by extension the USIA, should have:

- to implant the notion that the future of the world belongs to democratic societies

- to convince underdeveloped areas that the U.S. wants to improve their technological ability

- to knock the myths that capitalism is exploitive and wants to dominate the world, and that Communism is inevitable[23]

News reports should contain the facts, said the report, but the facts should be put together "selectively" to achieve an objective and be tailored to specific audiences. "Hard-hitting advocacy of the American point of view," it said, "would be more successful in winning adherents to American policies than the mere projection of a favorable image." The White House on more than one occasion made it clear that the mission of the USIA should be to "persuade," and not to simply "inform."[24]

But if it wanted to persuade anyone abroad, it was becoming clear that the United States had to clean up its act at home. Foreign correspondents assigned to the States have always been greatly influenced by what they have seen on American TV news broadcasts and what they read in U.S. newspapers. Murrow argued that the United States would be judged on what it did, rather than on what it said. In the tempest-tossed 1960s, violence in the cities and the Vietnam War undermined America's ability to project itself as a role model.

Lyndon Johnson's administration was in the eye of the storm. When Vice President Hubert Humphrey returned from a trip to Western Europe, he reported that the image of America was that of "bombs dropping, riots taking place, crime and corruption." Though the Johnson Administration recognized the problem, it was unable to do much about it. One of its biggest public relations blunders involved the scheduled visit of the carrier U.S.S. *Franklin Delano Roosevelt* to Cape Town, South Africa. Returning to the United States in February 1967, the ship was carrying some 3,800 men, about 200 of whom were black, who had just spent nine months in Vietnam. It was scheduled to dock in Cape Town for four days. The crew, understandably, was longing for shore leave. Revolted by South Africa's apartheid policies, American black leaders vociferously objected to the visit. In a telegram to President Johnson, Roy Wilkins, president of the NAACP, characterized the port of call as "an insult to American Negroes, to the black people of Africa, and to democratic men throughout the world."[25] The NAACP was supported by other civil rights leaders, who urged President Johnson to cancel what the Navy passed off as little more than a "refueling stop."[26]

As a compromise, the ship steamed into Cape Town but shore leave was canceled. It was a no-win situation. The government of South Africa was offended, and so were other African countries, who considered even an offshore visit by the ship as an affront. For four frustrating days, the ship's weary crew watched the twinkling lights of Cape Town from the ship's deck. The ship was opened to the public, however, and in one day 15,000 persons showed up, with women and midshipmen quickly exchanging addresses. Later, some sailors managed to sneak ashore for a few hours but were only lightly disciplined.[27] During the three days the ship was in port, the government of South Africa made an emergency appeal for blood donations, and sixty crew members, both white and black, were permitted to leave the ship for this purpose. The press found out that the blood was marked according to the race of the donor, causing further embarrassment for American representatives around the world.[28]

Near the end of the Johnson Administration, foreign public opinion about the United States was at a fifty-year low.[29] The assassinations of Dr. Martin Luther King, Jr., and Robert Kennedy were devastating blows to America's reputation, and a drastic drop in the confidence of American leadership ensued. The America portrayed abroad through TV shows, news broadcasts, and movies was violent and racist. Images of America's ghettos dispelled those of the American people as generous and open-minded. America's military strength, its high standard of living, and its scientific accomplishments had been long envied—as had the big bucks of American foreign aid. People around the world admired the American people themselves, the freedom of expression they appeared to enjoy, and the rewards of their hard work, but America's overall rating was decidedly mixed.[30]

Disillusioned by the USIA's ineffectiveness, William J. Fulbright, the chairman of the Senate Foreign Relations Committee, recommended slashing its budget by $235 million, which would have severely curtailed Voice of America broadcasts. Fulbright felt the Agency was being run by a band of cold war warriors toiling clumsily and furiously to justify the administration's failed Vietnam War policy. The only Agency programs worth salvaging, Fulbright felt, were those dealing with cultural issues, such as the student-teacher exchange and fellowship programs. In a TV interview, the hawkish director of the Agency's motion picture and TV service, Bruce Hershensohn, made the unfortunate blunder of calling Fulbright "naive and stupid." Several days later, Hershensohn held a news conference at Washington's National Press Club, during which he received an award for outstanding service from Richard Nixon's USIA director Frank Shakespeare—who also accepted Hershensohn's resignation from the Agency (and the position I would hold a decade later).

One of Hershensohn's last projects, a film called *Vietnam Vietnam* was begun during the final year of the Johnson Administration and completed three years later, in 1971, during the Nixon presidency. Directed by Hollywood filmmaker John Ford, the purpose of the film, according to Hershensohn, was to provide "balance" to the view of the war that critics were presenting. Hollywood movies had traditionally been supportive of American military efforts. Some of its biggest box office successes included *From Here to Eternity, The Longest Day, The Dirty Dozen,* and *Patton,* which President Nixon watched twice to psych himself up before ordering U.S. troops into Cambodia.[31] With the Vietnam War, it was clear that if the American government wanted to put a positive spin on things, it had better produce the film itself. *Vietnam Vietnam* went after critics of the war tooth and nail, especially student demonstrators.

The film went through numerous cuts and script alterations over a three-year period, due to the changing political situation in Vietnam, and when finally completed, the documentary managed to offend almost everyone. Critics had a field day with John Ford, comparing his feature movie *Drums along the Mohawk* to the Vietnam documentary, which one reviewer dubbed *Drums along the Mekong.* The good Indians were the South Vietnamese and their American "advisers," he wrote, and the bad Indians were the North Vietnamese and their Soviet backers.[32] Only one American GI in

Vietnam was seen firing a shot. It was doubtful the film would ever be released, and USIA director Frank Shakespeare left it up to U.S. embassies abroad to decide whether they wanted to order it. Only a handful did.[33]

Nixon and his secretary of state and national security adviser, Henry Kissinger, preferred secret diplomacy. Paying little attention to the USIA, Shakespeare was effectively excluded from White House foreign affairs deliberations. But the Agency did benefit from Kissinger's secret trip to Beijing, which laid the groundwork for Nixon's dramatic visit in 1972. Lines of communication were slowly opened with China, creating an expanded audience for VOA broadcasts to that country when jamming was eventually relaxed in 1979.

Jimmy Carter changed the name of the USIA to the International Communications Agency (ICA), because he felt the word *information* denoted a one-way message from the United States. Carter had wanted to call it the Agency for International Communications (AIC), but his advisers pointed out that the acronym was CIA spelled backward, and could be misunderstood overseas. Even so, the ICA was confused with the CIA overseas.

Meanwhile, the Agency continued to pump out a steady stream of general information abroad. The Voice of America was broadcasting in 35 languages, and a radio teletype system carried a wire service directly from Washington to diplomatic posts abroad. Publishing centers for magazines, pamphlets, and posters in Manila and Mexico City distributed printed material worldwide. By 1976 the Agency had established 170 posts in more than a hundred countries to interact with local audiences and government officials. An important part of their mission was to provide feedback to Washington about foreign reaction to U.S. policies by maintaining direct contact with top decision makers and by monitoring media coverage. Voluminous reporting cables from posts worldwide flooded into Washington daily. *New York Times* correspondent C. L. Sulzberger wrote that "all around the world foreign policy [has moved] from foreign ministries to the office of the chief of government information."

The VOA boasted that its listeners included presidents, prime ministers, and cabinet members, and while the United States was revving up its information machinery, other nations were doing likewise, establishing broadcasting stations and press facilities, and beefing up the export of their educational and cultural resources. But it was television technology that ushered in the great age of public diplomacy. Sir Arthur C. Clarke, British scientist and author of *2001: A Space Odyssey,* was the first to envision what he called a geostationary satellite, which would turn at the same rate as the Earth's rotation, thus staying in place over a fixed area and providing full-time coverage to specific geographic regions. Dr. Clarke saw the great potential, though he also wondered how such technology would be used. "The engineering problems of bringing education, literacy, improved hygiene and agricultural techniques to every human being on this planet have now been solved," he wrote. "But of course the technical problem is the easy one. Do we have the imagination and the statesmanship to use this new tool for the benefit of all mankind?"[34]

The USIA was slow to appreciate the value of TV satellite technology as a means of promoting its mission overseas. In its 1972 annual review, the Advisory Commission on Public Diplomacy recommended that the Agency take a leadership role and encouraged it to make international use of space satellites as a way of promoting the free flow of information among nations. It asked the USIA to solicit support from non-dictatorships, which embraced this concept. The USIA hadn't even bothered to respond to the recommendation a year later. Videotape was coming into use in the 1970s, but the management of USIA's TV operation rejected it, feeling that it "lacked broadcast quality."[35]

Although the Americans weren't rushing to take advantage of the technology, the prospect that TV satellites might someday beam programs from space directly into small home receivers filled the Soviets with cold fear. "The Soviet Central Committee was absolutely paranoid about the prospect," remembers Victor Sheymov, a former KGB operative who defected to the West in 1980. "They saw TV satellites as a huge threat."[36] In the early 1970s Sheymov worked in the KGB's cipher communications department, where he reviewed all incoming and outgoing cable traffic. He and his intelligence colleagues in the communications center were astonished one day to see a frantic directive from the Central Committee to the Soviet Space Research Institute, demanding that they find a way to jam TV satellite signals. Sheymov said it was the first time he and his associates had seen the Central Committee "running scared." He quotes Brezhnev as saying, "If they [the USIA] pull this off, all our propaganda efforts will be worthless."[37]

The Soviet Space Research Institute studied the problem and issued its report. Nothing short of shooting down the satellites could be done to stop TV satellite signals from being seen in Soviet homes. The reason: the "footprint" of a given satellite is so vast—blanketing many thousands of miles of the earth's surface—that jamming its signal would be virtually impossible.[38] It would be difficult for government authorities to detect small receiving dishes set up in homes, Sheymov believed, and the units themselves would be easy to obtain.

Now Soviet leaders really began to panic. The whole Communist system was held up by a total control of information from the very top and would only survive if it was sealed off from the rest of the world. Direct broadcast satellites would spread a virus of foreign information throughout the country. It was Lenin who said, "Ideas are more dangerous than bombs." The Central Committee decided to undermine the American initiative through diplomatic channels and by disinformation, but it would meanwhile keep close tabs on USIA's television planning. For more than a decade it had little to fear from an uninspired USIA bureaucracy. John Reinhardt, a career foreign service officer with the rank of ambassador, was appointed by Jimmy Carter as the director of the newly named ICA. Reinhardt visited the Agency's modest television service in Washington in late 1977 as part of a get-acquainted swing through headquarter departments prior to his Senate confirmation. He told the TV staff of his interest in visual communications, but used the term "film" exclusively. After speaking for about thirty minutes, he opened the floor to questions, and veteran videotape technician Stanley Kraft raised his hand. "Do you realize that you're standing in a television studio speaking to a TV staff and you've never used the words TV or tape?" admonished Kraft.[39] Reinhardt apologized for the oversight, and was never seen again at the Agency's TV studios during his four-year term. He devoted most of his attention to cultural and educational exchange programs, which Carter brought into the ICA from the State Department early in the administration.

Years earlier, Edward R. Murrow had shown the remarkable impact a single television program could have on public opinion abroad. In October 1960 he gave a demonstration of America's Polaris missile on the BBC program "Panorama." A USIA-commissioned survey showed that some 8 million British adults had tuned in, 21 percent of whom said their opinion of the United States went up as the result of the program. The same survey showed that only 9 percent reacted negatively. Murrow often claimed that the USIA's budget was "less than the cost of one combat-loaded Polaris submarine, and it is one-fifth of the estimated advertising budget of one armaments manufacturer."

Later, the landmark television series *Roots* was cited as an excellent example of how dramatic television's impact on public opinion could be. The week-long exposure to the series, which depicted the strength and courage of people under slavery, produced a positive change in attitudes of Americans toward blacks. A Trendex report revealed one-third of U.S. viewers indicated a more favorable attitude toward blacks after seeing the programs.[40]

Until Ronald Reagan became president and TV satellites were beaming images behind the Iron Curtain, the propaganda war of words was fought primarily via shortwave radio, but even these were an expensive nuisance to the Communists. To block Western signals an army of some ten thousand Soviets came to work each day to make noise. Their sole purpose was to play electronic babel on the same radio frequency as incoming transmissions, to prevent radio programs, such as those about the persecution of Soviet dissidents, from being heard behind the Iron Curtain. With all the squealing, groaning, and shrieking, jamming noise would frequently provoke the listener to whack the radio, or to rotate it in the hope of boosting signal strength. It generally led to tuning in a clear station or switching off the set altogether.

Perhaps the most inventive international broadcasters were in Beijing. To circumvent Soviet jamming of its Russian-language broadcasts, Chinese radio would broadcast some of its programs backward, making them unintelligible. Soviet censors did not bother to jam these programs, which Russian listeners would tape and then play in reverse. The VOA was not that creative.

The Soviets began to jam Russian-language radio broadcasts by the VOA and the BBC in 1948, the height of the cold war under Stalin.[41] From the outset programs in English were not jammed because few Russians spoke the language. Local-language news broadcasts by Radio Free Europe and Radio Liberty to Eastern Europe and the Soviet Union were jammed virtually nonstop from the second they went on the air. Communist authorities considered such "local" services a provocation and an intrusion in their country's internal affairs.

Jamming was done in two ways. "Groundwave," or local jamming, which was conducted in large urban areas, effectively blotted out incoming signals in populous areas, but the range of jamming signal was limited to about twenty miles. Muscovites who went to the countryside on weekends could often escape local groundwave jamming and pick up the VOA and other foreign radio services. "Skywave" jamming covered broad rural areas, and was less effective. Skywave transmitters were located hundreds or even thousands of miles away, with jamming signals bouncing between the earth and the sky.

Almost every Soviet town with a population of more than 200,000 had a "jamming center," where noise was brewed, then transmitted from another location. By the mid-1950s there were more than 2,000 jamming stations in operation.[42] Each one employed about a hundred, and most employees of the centers who originated the noise were female, members of the "Interference Activity Service." Generally they had little education, usually about the equivalent of the seventh grade or less. Young men just out of the military often took jobs there to further their technical training. But for anyone of education and refinement, the jobs quickly became torture, and most would soon depart. Working in a noise factory was not a privileged occupation. Working at the transmitter sites, where noise generated elsewhere was relayed out into the ionosphere, was a lot more pleasant. Turnover of transmitter employees, who were mostly male, was minimal.

Russian-language programs of the VOA, the British Broadcasting Corporation, and West Germany's Deutsche Welle were jammed selectively on instructions that were sent to the regional centers from Moscow, usually by teletype. When the bosses at headquarters heard something they didn't like, such as news about Soviet dissidents or someone being sentenced in a political trial, they issued a directive to the regional shift leader, who would then bark out, "Masha, switch on the jammers!"

When Moscow sent an order to jam a particular frequency at a specific time, it would stand for no deviation from its instructions. Operators in the field were allowed no leeway to make decisions themselves, even though it would sometimes happen that by the time a jamming directive came in via teletype from Moscow, got decoded, and the noise transmitter was turned on, the offending broadcast had already been made. Program transmissions from Western radios also didn't always run on schedule, and frequencies were changed to make blocking them more difficult. But dutiful Soviet jammers would follow their instructions from Moscow, thus enabling many transmissions to come in unhindered.

The KGB frequently complained about the sloppy job performed by the jammers, particularly those who worked during the night. Many employees would simply turn their teletypes off when they went to sleep, so that messages from Moscow would not ring on the printer and wake them up. Said one former jammer, "Like all other Soviet institutions, jamming stations work very badly. When an operator wants to sleep, she simply switches off the transmitter or else pays no attention at all to it." Few workers were ever fired. When operators were caught sleeping on the job, their wages were merely lowered, or their already skimpy "productivity" bonuses were cut, but such extreme action was rare—not even when shift leaders who also slept on the job filed false monitoring reports, as was common. None of this conformed to the image the West had of the "elite" corps of Soviet technicians who had reportedly built a firewall around the Communist bloc that stifled news from the outside world. Soviet jammers were so inept that they frequently disrupted Radio Moscow programs by mistake.

The sheer size of the Soviet Union, stretching across eleven time zones, made effective jamming difficult under the best of circumstances and increasingly expensive to achieve, particularly as the number of radio and television shortwave signals that would begin to invade that country and those in Communist Eastern Europe began to grow. Radio receivers sold in the Soviet Union were equipped to receive shortwave broadcasts because of the vast distances domestic radio services needed to cover. It was not a crime to listen to Western radio or television broadcasts in the Soviet Union (though it was risky). Soviet law also permitted listeners to write letters to Western stations, so long as communications didn't contain "knowingly false fabrications discrediting the Soviet political and social system." The government read all the mail. A. S. Lakalov sent a letter to Radio Liberty, in which he allegedly said something derogatory about the Soviet government, though exactly what was not clear. Lakalov was convicted for violating a criminal code.[43] In another incident, a Soviet seaman named Boris Grezin sent a letter from the Canary Islands to Radio Liberty. The letter found its way into the hands of the KGB. Grezin was found guilty of anti-Soviet agitation and other charges, and sentenced to four years at hard labor.[44] The Soviet Union, by the way, wasn't alone in opening the mail of its citizens. During the 1970s, the CIA set up shop in a back room at LaGuardia Airport in New York and opened about 1,800 letters a day going to and from the United States and the USSR. The letters were photographed and the envelopes resealed, then placed in the mail the next day. Even special delivery mail was intercepted and delayed. The CIA was especially interested in letters from scientists and students, Soviet and American.[45]

In those areas where jamming was ineffective, it was common practice for people to listen to Western radios at bus stops and in other public places. Victor Sokolov, a Soviet émigré, recalled that in his former hometown near Moscow, "adolescents by the hundreds would stroll along the main streets in groups. . . . And in every group there is somebody who constantly clasps a transistor to his stomach . . . and every transistor is constantly tuned to 'The Voice,' or some other Western station and is sure to be blasting out at full volume." While it was permissible to listen to foreign shortwave radio broadcasts within the Soviet Union in the privacy of one's home, as long as information was not disseminated, a person could be arrested and sent to jail if he or she played a Western shortwave program out in the open, such as on a street corner, so that others could hear it. This the government considered to be a criminal act.[46]

A Ukrainian dissident named Dmitri Mazur listened to a foreign radio station at a bus stop and was indicted for it. He had been listening to an unidentified station for two minutes, during which time a story claiming Soviet troops had committed atrocities in Afghanistan was broadcast. On December 5, 1980, a court in the city of Zhitomir sentenced Mazur to six years of hard labor and five years in exile for his dirty deed. As a dissident, Mazur was particularly vulnerable, since the KGB was cracking down on them following the Soviet invasion of Afghanistan in December 1979.[47] Scribbled notes could also land a person in jail for a very long time. Larisa Lokhvitskaya was tried on charges of circulating human rights leaflets in Kiev. A search of her apartment turned up notes she had taken while listening to Western radio broadcasts, notes she used to write the leaflets. Nikolai Pavlov listened to the Voice of America and other broadcasts and made transcripts of commentaries for his political pamphlet. He was sentenced to five years in a "strict regime" camp. Vladimir El'chin and Lev Shefer were accused of building an audio-tape library, consisting of 750 broadcasts on 66 cassettes, containing VOA and Deutsche Welle broadcasts. They were sentenced to five years of hard labor.[48]

Communist authorities routinely blamed foreign radio broadcasts for inciting civil unrest. On August 31, 1982, as the second anniversary of the founding of the Solidarity movement in Poland approached, Communist officials charged that Western radio broadcasts were responsible for anti-government street demonstrations that broke out throughout Poland. Said the Soviet news agency Tass:

> The radio stations of the NATO countries have recently unleashed an anti-Polish propaganda campaign of unheard-of proportions. The entire arsenal used by Radio Free Europe, the Voice of America, and other radio stations broadcasting in Polish is aimed at destabilizing the situation in Poland. Calls to organize disorders and to unleash fratricidal civil war are being broadcast. In the last month alone, the number of broadcasts with a provocative, anti-Polish cast have increased three-fold.[49]

An article in the Soviet Novosti news agency charged that Radio Free Europe was trying to create "RFE Clubs" for young Poles and "a secret network of informers" in the country.[50]

The Soviets found that their counter-propaganda efforts against Western broadcasts only heightened interest in the forbidden fruit. Some 70,000 lectures were conducted daily in the Soviet Union to counter "alien influences" from abroad.[51] Questions from members of the audience were scrutinized to gauge the effectiveness of foreign broadcasts. In Soviet Estonia alone, more than 16,000 questions put to Soviet officials during lectures were collated and evaluated. Massive public opinion polls were also conducted to assess the impact of foreign broadcasts, and the findings were distributed to those involved in propaganda warfare.[52] The weekly publication *Argumenty i Fakty (Arguments and Facts)*, with a circulation of 656,000, furnished Soviet propagandists and political information officers with advice about how to answer negative questions relating to news in Western broadcasts that might be asked. Some 1,200 lecturers were stationed on Soviet merchant marine ships to deliver talks to military personnel serving outside Soviet borders.[53]

Ronald Reagan and Charlie Wick had an idea up their sleeves that would make Soviet propagandists apoplectic.

↔ **3** ↔

Cranking Up the Volume

SHORTLY AFTER JOINING THE NATIONAL SECURITY COUNCIL STAFF IN the new Reagan White House, Dr. Carnes Lord began to hear horror stories about confusion reigning at the Voice of America. It didn't take him long to realize most of them were true. The VOA, the government radio service that tells America's story abroad, was a chaotic assortment of more than forty foreign-language broadcast services run by dissidents from their homeland, and it was beset by differing agendas and national/ethnic conflicts. Things didn't improve by 1982, when the VOA was to embark on a major foreign policy initiative for the Reagan Administration that would be thwarted by, respectively, flocks of migrating birds in the Middle East, floods in North Africa, squatters in Asian coconut forests, the Iran-contra scandal, and mountains in Central America that seemed to appear from nowhere.

Ronald Reagan's first term was a turbulent but promising period in world politics. The Soviet buildup in Afghanistan, the rise of the free trade union movement in Poland, and the pro-democracy movements in Eastern Europe and the Soviet Union all suggested new opportunities for Western government-to-people public diplomacy.

But the United States was being effectively prevented from reaching much of the world. Resumed jamming of Western radio broadcasts in the summer of 1980, after a seven-year respite, once again made it more difficult to communicate with audiences behind the Iron Curtain.

"In its grandest sense, public diplomacy is preventive diplomacy," wrote Kenneth L. Adelman, a member of the Reagan Administration's transition team. "It can help prevent the peoples and leaders of friendly countries from drifting away, and the peoples of adversary countries from losing all touch with freedom or with America."[1] But if international broadcasting was to become a true player in the conduct of Reagan's foreign policy, it needed top-level attention, and fast. The international radio network Reagan inherited in 1980 was nearing its fortieth birthday, and well into a mid-life crisis. Unremitting management problems and presidents who favored more traditional means of diplomacy meant the VOA was little more than a repository of aging, underpowered transmitters, a relic of the past. Incredibly, an old radio transmitter built in the 1930s and captured from the Nazis was still beaming programs into Eastern Europe and the Soviet Union. Forty-five-year-old Crosley transmitters sent feeble signals into Africa. Coverage in the Middle East was spotty at best, and broadcasts from Castro's Cuba were overpowering VOA's efforts in Central and Latin America.

As a wizened radio performer himself, a former sportscaster who cut his teeth at WHO-Radio in Des Moines, Iowa, in 1932, Reagan recognized how effective the VOA could be. Both he and Wick believed the antiquated radio network could fulfill an important role in U.S. cold war politics were it allowed to speak with a louder voice. One of the first orders of business for the new administration (in addition to changing back the name to the United States Information Agency) was to give "the Voice," as it was affectionately called, a major boost so that it could broadcast clearer, stronger signals to Eastern Europe, the Soviet Union, and Central America, where the major public opinion battles were being waged, and to other areas it had never before tried to reach. The administration had widespread backing on Capitol Hill. "Though U.S. arsenals of defense are stocked with state-of-the-art weaponry," said a 1982 House Foreign Affairs Committee report, "the United States has neglected the technology of broadcasting and has relayed this nation's message on transmitters which were 'state-of-the-art' in 1938."[2]

Ronald Reagan had pledged during the 1980 presidential election campaign to strengthen the Voice. He gave the National Security Council the task of injecting new vigor into the lumbering, antiquated radio network of more than three thousand employees. "We wanted to get our arms around the VOA and shake up this whole backwater of U.S. government policy," said Dr. Lord. "We were disturbed with the lack of fresh thinking in approaching the mission, and its World War II mentality."[3] Through a series of directives from Reagan, the NSC—founded in 1947 to advise the president on matters relating to both domestic and foreign policy—would fold the USIA into its general foreign policy initiatives. On July 15, 1982, the president issued an NSC directive calling for a major five-year overhaul of the VOA, to be completed by January 1988, a year before an anticipated second Reagan term would end.[4] He wanted the government to give the same priority to rebuilding the VOA that President Kennedy had placed on putting a man on the moon twenty years earlier. "We are as far behind the Soviets and their allies in international broadcasting today as we were in space when they launched Sputnik in 1957," said the president, to strengthen the parallel. "Not enough has been done to combat Soviet jamming." In addition to expanding and strengthening its worldwide coverage, Reagan ordered the NSC to increase the number of languages the Voice broadcast, from 42 to 60, and to add more than 400 hours a week to its program schedule. Powerful new transmitters would be installed around the world.[5] "The National Security Council wanted this to be a clear command for everyone down below to salute, get into line, and make it work," said Lord, who drafted the presidential directive. "It was the first time in recent memory that a president got so involved with international broadcasting."[6]

The renewed Soviet jamming of VOA broadcasts to Eastern Europe in 1980 helped mobilize support of Reagan's initiatives in Congress. "There was almost total unanimity in backing the VOA plan on the Hill," recalled Kenneth L. Peel, Republican staff director of the House International Operations Subcommittee. "A lot of people were very excited about the program."[7] Before long, Congress would pour money into the Voice faster than it could spend it. Voice

engineers promised to complete the job at a cost of $1.3 billion.
Sixteen new transmitter relay stations would be added to the sixteen
sites already in operation, and eight of these new stations would have
shortwave facilities, which would enable them to reach audiences behind the Iron Curtain. The other eight stations would be on the
medium wave or AM band in Central America, where transmitters
could be placed nearer to target audiences. Newer and better overseas relay stations were to be set up in the most strategic locations
and equipped with the latest, most powerful transmitting gear, to
bring clearer and stronger radio signals to listeners anywhere on
earth. Existing relay stations were to be outfitted with stronger, more
up-to-date transmitters. The CIA estimated that radio jamming of
Western broadcasts was costing the Soviet bloc more than $400 mil-
lion annually, an amount that far exceeded the Voice's entire annual
worldwide operating budget, and the rebuilding and modernization
efforts would put pressure on the Soviets to spend even more to boost
their jamming capability and to increase the effectiveness of their
own broadcasts to the West.

Setting up a large number of new shortwave relay stations abroad within a five-year period was a formidable task. Locations had to be identified and negotiations initiated to obtain the host
country's agreements. Based on past experience, it would take several
years before such leasing agreements were concluded. Sites had been
sought in Israel and Sri Lanka since the mid-1970s, without success.
The VOA and Greece had been haggling for decades over details of a
formal site agreement, which had still not been signed. Once agreements were reached, site surveys had to be conducted, and technical
and architectural plans developed. Contracts would have to be
solicited and awarded for equipment, including the more than one
hundred massive transmitting towers, each as tall as a Manhattan
skyscraper and wide as a city block, to be spread among all locations.
Finally, these massive towers had to be put in place and tested. The
average length of time to get a VOA relay station on the air, from negotiating a site agreement to actually turning on a transmitter, was
ten years. To sweeten their offers for leasing deals, the United States
routinely spent tens of millions on land development for a host country, to do everything from building highways to digging wells. In
several countries the Voice became the largest local employer, substantially bolstering local economies. At the Kavala relay station in

eastern Greece, the VOA facility pumped $8 million a year into the tiny local economy. The one on the island of Luzon in the Philippines had been the largest local employer since the mid-1960s. More than a thousand foreign nationals were at work worldwide at VOA relay facilities. Stations worth hundreds of millions each were "willed" to the host country when leases expired.

Instead of hiring an experienced construction management firm to take charge of this highly ambitious and complex initiative, Voice bureaucrats insisted on handling everything in-house. A study by the Massachusetts Institute of Technology warned the VOA that it would get in over its head, and questioned whether the VOA had "the ability to coordinate a complex network, plan for the future, develop along with new technology, and attract the necessary skills and talent within the framework of the Federally-funded and operated agency, and do so in a most efficient manner."[8] The record of the Voice's engineering division did not exactly inspire confidence. It had recently suffered through two internal reviews following allegations of mismanagement. Several key officials had been forced to resign, and vacancies were not filled. A General Accounting Office (GAO) investigation reported the engineering division continually "operated in a crisis environment . . . unable to develop long-range plans."[9] Another report, from the Stanford Research Institute, warned that the Voice's record on handling complex engineering projects was "very poor."

The Stanford report also referred to a failed effort by President Jimmy Carter to modernize VOA facilities on a somewhat smaller scale. In 1977 Carter had approved the purchase of seventeen new radio transmitters for multiple locations in Europe, Africa, and East Asia, and Congress appropriated $52.7 million for the project. But VOA engineers couldn't make up their minds what to buy, or where to place the equipment. Contract specifications for transmitters were changed sixteen times, according to a GAO investigation. When some of the transmitters arrived, there was no place to put them, and for nine years they gathered dust in storage. Equipment was found to be defective long after warranties had expired. In the end only two transmitters eventually found their way overseas. The remainder were installed at VOA transmitter sites in the States. "Instead of putting the transmitters in Liberia, where they were supposed to go, they put a couple in the Philippines," concluded a GAO investigator, who wished to remain anonymous. "It took them about five years to decide to put some in California, and then it took another four years to decide to put the rest in Ohio."

Now it was Reagan's turn to see if he could get the VOA back on track. As a first step, the Voice spent more than $23 million for "advanced engineering and technical development studies." One of the major new shortwave stations targeted for construction was in Morocco, from where it would retransmit signals to Eastern Europe and the Soviet Union. A new facility was slotted to be built in Sri Lanka, off the southern tip of India, to beam programs into Soviet Central Asia. A station in Botswana would cover neighboring South Africa and the rest of the African continent. From Thailand, a new facility would take some of the load off an old relay station in the Philippines to expand coverage into China and the rest of Asia. A massive new station in Israel would transmit into Central Asia and the Soviet Union. Medium wave AM stations planned included a facility in Costa Rica, which would relay programs into neighboring Nicaragua to support anti-government contra rebels. This would form part of the Reagan Administration's Caribbean Basin initiative to counteract Cuban and Soviet broadcasts then blanketing the area. Radio Havana carried more than 280 hours of programs per week to Central and Latin America. The Soviets were actively engaged in placing radio and television stories in Colombia and Nicaragua.

Once it got the green light from Congress, the VOA got to work on one of the key parts of its plan: the purchase of giant 70-story, 500,000-watt transmitters, each one ten times more powerful than the biggest transmitters then used by U.S. commercial radio stations. The VOA planned to buy 102 of these huge transmitters at a cost of over $4 million each. Some relay stations would require as much electrical power as it would take to light a city of 200,000—the size of Dayton, Ohio.

To keep construction money flowing from Congress, a team from USIA produced video programs dramatizing the Voice's plight at congressional budget hearings. One of the videos shown to the powerful Senate Foreign Relations Committee depicted antiquated VOA equipment at various overseas locations. "Vacuum tubes, some nearly forty years old, are still in service at our Munich, Germany, facility," said the video voice over accompanying footage showing a technician struggling to lift a mammoth glass radio tube almost half his size. "They could all be replaced by a handful of microchips," continued the narration. The same video showed a man standing on his toes poking a broomstick handle against the ceiling. "A VOA technician still has to close switches in the ceiling by hand, using a broomstick, at our Tangier facility," explained the narrator. "Superpower Soviet transmitters blanket the world from their land mass. The VOA must negotiate for transmitter sites with foreign governments. We are falling further behind."

Senator Jesse Helms (R-NC) of the Foreign Relations Committee was dutifully impressed. He said that it was obvious that the Voice was using the same kind of equipment that "every tank-town radio station in the U.S." had thrown out twenty-five years earlier. "I think it's a tragedy that we do not devote enough funds for the VOA," he declared. On the House of Representatives side, the equally dutifully impressed chairman of the International Operations Subcommittee, Daniel Mica (D-FL), requested a copy of the video-cassette to show visiting constituents.

USIA lobbyists worked their way through congressional offices on Capitol Hill, carrying portable videotape players under their arms, while the USIA's press department churned out stories trumpeting the potential impact the Voice would have behind the Iron Curtain. The VOA's cause became a rallying point. Said the *Los Angeles Times* in an editorial: "The truth is a powerful weapon, but it is only powerful when it can be heard. The Voice of America deserves to be heard more clearly and widely than its present physical and personnel resources allow."[10] James Reston wrote in the *New York Times:* "The balance of radio power between the United States and the Soviet Union is much more favorable to Moscow than the balance of military power."[11]

By 1983, there was unprecedented clutter of shortwave radio services broadcasting from 123 nations in hundreds of languages and carrying nearly 24,000 hours of programming every week: a cacophony of individual tongues and perspectives, each promoting its own point of view and each competing for listeners on fading, scratchy shortwave signals. Even the International Red Cross had a station in Switzerland, from where, at the end of World War II, it broadcast the names—in 17 languages—of more than 600,000 persons who had been released by the Nazis as prisoners of war.[12] Officials of the VOA argued that all this new competition was the main reason to increase the Voice's signal strength. Radio Moscow, of course, was the main competition. In 1983, it was broadcasting in 82 languages, at a cost of more than $700 million per year, according to CIA estimates.

Despite all the new funds heading the Voice's way, television waves were the waves of the future, not radio waves. Charlie Wick's basic instincts told him that television was really the name of the game, not radio. He was convinced it was the most effective way to get America's message out to the rest of the world. The VOA's encrusted bureaucracy became a constant source of frustration for Wick, who couldn't seem to make it responsive. During Wick's eight-year term as USIA director, the VOA's top job would be a revolving door, filled with seven directors or acting directors, most caught in Wick's potato masher.

In the early 1980s, Ted Turner's Cable News Network was still in its formative stage and not yet recognized by the White House press office as an equal participant in the TV network press pool, along with CBS, NBC, and ABC. CNN was still competing in the U.S. market with ABC's Satellite News Channels cable service, which CNN would purchase in October 1983. Turner didn't start full-time service in Europe until late 1985, and it was several years after that before the channel built up any appreciable following. Still, encouraged by the results of "Let Poland Be Poland," Wick envisioned a weekly television news magazine program that would be fed to Europe via satellite and distributed to TV stations on other continents via videocassettes. He believed it would offer a sound platform from which to promote Reagan's foreign policies. The program would attempt to shore up the sagging image of American military strength abroad and to show off the country's moral, political, and technological achievements. Major themes of the program, named "Satellite File," were spelled out in a USIA policy paper:

- Europe. Defensive, intermediate range nuclear weapons need to be placed in NATO countries to deter Soviet aggression. Reach young people and the "successor generation," the target audiences.

- Africa. Emerging African nations have pronounced interest in American education—particularly its universal availability at all levels—and in U.S. medical and agricultural techniques and research. USIA research indicates that emerging African nations are interested in what individual Americans are like and how they succeed in making things work.

- Middle East. The central reality about Arab nations is their dual preoccupation with tradition and technology. Energy is another concern.

- Latin America. It is believed that Latins would welcome program segments demonstrating U.S. respect for their independence and advancement. Audiences there also have a liking for American popular music.

- Brazil. This Portuguese-speaking nation represents roughly half the South American population. It is in the process of revitalizing its democratic institutions. Problems are environmental protection, labor relations, urban growth, and energy supply.

In the fall of 1982 I was named the director of the Television and Film Service of the USIA, whose function was to project U.S. foreign policies to international audiences.

We all agreed that American public diplomacy efforts worldwide should be funneled through Western Europe, which was still the center of a worldwide information system. We believed that once the European opinion makers were persuaded of the value of American institutions and policies, they would radiate the story to the rest of the world with great impact. Also, the USSR was continuing to deploy more missiles targeted toward Western Europe than NATO. To maintain a strong defense, the United States was seeking to convince its NATO allies to allow it to place upgraded cruise and Pershing intermediate range ballistic missiles on their soil. Our program effort was to support this. It was equally important to get information into closed societies, to bring public pressure on repressive regimes there. We wanted to talk about American values as a basis for better understanding U.S. foreign policies. We were looking forward to locking horns with the Communist bloc, which we believed to be far less sophisticated than we in the art of communications.

It was clear to us that the most efficient way of getting U.S. policy positions on European TV news programs and into newspapers was by holding interactive press conferences via satellite. On October 13, 1982, in a memo to Wick, I proposed such a press conference as "a two-way video transmission between a U.S. spokesperson and foreign journalists asking questions from their home base. There would be much better press," I argued, "and TV play in various regions of Europe if we could involve journalists of several nationalities—their key TV and press players—in by-line on-camera situations."

Wick's idea was that cable television would provide an important outlet for us in Europe. Twelve new cable channels were being planned for 1984 in Germany, and our initial discussions with cable operators were promising. They appeared eager to be offered a fresh source of American programs to fill up their multiple cable channels—especially since we would provide our programs free of charge. Other locations in Europe looked equally promising. Everyone was excited by cable TV, catching Wicks's enthusiasm. Jack Hedges, our astute, supportive public affairs officer in Paris, reported, "Hardly a day goes by when there isn't an article in the press about plans for cable TV in France." There were also ambitious plans to introduce cable TV in Great Britain, where a government commission had enthusiastically proposed the rapid construction of cable networks throughout the country. The London *Times* predicted that the TV cable law would amount to "the most sweeping changes in British broadcasting since the formation of commercial television." There would be dozens of new, private TV stations in Italy and Spain within a couple of years.

In May 1983, we mounted our first effort to feed television and print coverage to Europe: coverage of the economic summit meeting of the Western allies being held in Williamsburg, Virginia. We felt it offered a golden PR opportunity, and we pulled out the stops. From the session would come what we thought was a major story—unanimous agreement among Western allied leaders on the placement of updated intermediate range missiles in NATO countries. Three months before the summit, the USIA contracted with the nearby College of William and Mary for space in three campus buildings to house an international press briefing room, as well as areas for support staff from the USIA, the White House, and the State Department. This involved no small effort. Classroom walls would have to come down, for example. The USIA was put in charge of contracting for construction, and wrecking balls soon began to crash into William and Mary's hallowed halls. By the time the dust cleared, the USIA had spent more than $1 million on construction. This included the installation of an improved air-conditioning system and new electrical wiring for the school gymnasium, which was turned into the main international press center. Press staging platforms for camera crews were brought in and powder-blue telephones (to match the new color of the hall) installed for the press. USIA contractors put in a post office, currency exchange, first aid station, message center, and other support facilities to keep the foreign media happy. "Courtesy desks," to be manned by USIA workers, were set up at each of the four hotels where the media were housed to handle personal details—everything from tracking down lost shirts in the laundry to making dinner and airline reservations.

We plugged in everything we had. Our television operation arranged live TV satellite feeds from Europe, so that foreign delegates could see how they were being covered on television news programs back home. USIA's media reaction staff, set up in a boiler room operation in the basement of the international press center, provided up-to-date reports on press coverage of the summit from abroad via a new high-speed computer system. Reports were quickly dispatched to summit delegates and to spokespersons from the White House and State Department to use as background for their briefings and press conferences at the summit. The USIA arranged for a huge circus tent to be trucked in from Florida and put up over the tennis courts, where free food and beer were served up to the press corps. Murray Lender's bagel bakery made bagel bracelets for reporters. CBS won an impromptu contest, stacking empty beer cans more than two stories high.[13]

Our efforts didn't go unnoticed. In the Kremlin, Soviet Premier Yuri Andropov and his top aides closely followed press and television reports from Williamsburg. Andropov was convinced that as a result of the USIA effort a propaganda counteroffensive had to be mounted to marshal public opinion against Reagan's "militaristic" posture and to drive a wedge between North Atlantic Treaty Organization countries, which, so our images were telling him, were gloriously united. Said Andropov:

At the session of the NATO countries that is going on in
Williamsburg, very aggressive speeches are given; and the
very resolution [on missile placement] adopted by the 'Big
Seven' is non-constructive, but aggressive. . . . It seems to
me that on that meeting we should develop, adopt, and
then publish a document that would express our reaction
on NATO's decision. . . . We have to open a wider network
to win public opinion, to mobilize public opinion of the
Western countries of Europe and America against the location of the nuclear weapons in Europe and against a new
arms race that's being forced by the American administration.[14]

Defense Minister D. F. Ustinov agreed. "We should speak out more
widely about our suggestions and expose the militaristic intentions of
the Western countries," he said.

"Of course, we aren't going to change Reagan's behavior,
but we will expose his anti-Soviet, militaristic intentions very deci-
sively," replied Andropov.

"Reagan doesn't react to our suggestions any more,"
said N. A. Tikhonov. "We have to find such a method in our
propaganda."

"Gather the editors of leading newspapers, information
agencies, and tell them about these ideas. Point the sharp end of our
propaganda at Reagan and his aggressive suggestions," declared M.
V. Zimyanin.[15]

But within three months, during the Labor Day holiday
weekend of 1983, the Kremlin's NATO propaganda offensive would
be derailed by events that took place in the air, one black night over
a distant ocean.

↔ **4** ↔

The Five-Minute Tape Gap

WITH ITS 269 PASSENGERS AND CREW, KOREAN AIRLINES FLIGHT KE-007 was cruising on the last leg of its journey to Seoul, little more than three hours away, on August 30, 1983. Its flight crew, giddy from jet lag, was relaxed and chatting drowsily, unaware the aircraft had strayed off course over Soviet territory and was being hunted down by Russian interceptor planes armed with cannons and air-to-air missiles. In his Sukhoi-15 fighter, Major Gennady Osipovich had KE-007 on his radar scope and could see its dim outline through the clouds. He had made several maneuvers to signal that the plane should identify itself and immediately land. There was no response. Soviet military authorities at ground tracking stations believed it was an American spy plane. Major Osipovich locked on to the target with his missiles and prepared to shoot it down.

We now know many of the details of the tragedy from actual verbatim transcripts of conversations. Almost ten years after the incident, the Russians released original tapes and transcripts of conversations between USSR ground centers and their interceptor pilots, as well as ground-to-ground communications between USSR air defense centers. The Russians also made available the black box flight recorder retrieved from the ocean floor, with the voices of long-dead crew members. Tapes were deciphered in neutral territory, a French laboratory, and results turned over to experts at the International Organization of Civil Aviation in Canada, which issued its report.[1]

The Korean airliner, a wide-body Boeing 747-200B Superjet, had started out from Kennedy Airport in New York. After a refueling stop in Anchorage, Alaska, KE-007 continued on its way toward Seoul, eight hours flying time away. When the plane left Anchorage, its flight crew inexplicably had not set the navigational systems correctly, and during the long flight toward Asia the plane arced on a higher path than was planned and went more than 300 miles farther north as it drew closer to the Asian mainland. Navigational checks along the way by an inattentive crew failed to detect the mistake. The plane was now flying over some of the most sensitive Soviet military installations on the high seas. KE-007 veered across the Kamchatka Peninsula, where Russian long-range missiles were tested, across the Sea of Okhotsk, where Soviet nuclear submarines held training exercises, and on toward a major Soviet forward air base on Sakhalin Island, by which point the Korean airliner was 365 miles off course.

When Major Osipovich's missiles slammed into the Korean airliner, it was 2:26 P.M. in Washington, D.C., Wednesday, August 31, 1983. Minute by minute, top secret American military intelligence stations near the Soviet border had monitored Osipovich's pursuit of KE-007, and its destruction.

Deputy foreign minister Georgi Kornienko was given the task of telephoning Yuri Andropov, who lay deathly ill in the hospital. Kornienko explained the situation to the Soviet premier, who asked Kornienko to wait and not hang up while he reached defense minister Ustinov. In a few moments Andropov came back with the answer.

"Ustinov says we shouldn't admit to anything," he informed Kornienko. "Nobody will find out that we shot it down. It is an imperialist provocation."[2]

The official line would be that the plane was intercepted over Soviet airspace, that it continued on its flight, and that there was no word of its fate.

Secretary of State George Shultz first became aware of the incident when he received a phone call at about 6:30 Thursday morning. Shultz had invited friends from California to stay at his home in Bethesda, Maryland, for the Labor Day weekend. When he read that a Korean airliner had been shot down, his first reaction before reading further was that Lebanese fanatics were responsible.[3] Shultz arrived at his State Department office at 7:45 A.M. Because President Reagan was in California for the weekend, Shultz was designated to take the lead for the United States that morning. Undersecretary of State Lawrence Eagleburger gave Shultz an update on the situation. State Department press spokesman John Hughes was next in line. He needed to discuss whether or not to release intelligence information confirming that the Soviets had shot down the Korean civilian airliner, killing all aboard.

"So how do you want to handle it?" Shultz asked.

"If we're right we don't have to massage the story," replied Hughes. "Let's get out everything we have and let it play."

Shultz thought Hughes should break the news of the Korean airliner's fate at his morning press briefing. "Go out and do your number, John," Shultz advised. Hughes replied that because of the magnitude of the story Shultz himself should appear. More information arrived shortly after nine. U.S. and Japanese intelligence had eavesdropped on the Soviet pilot talking to his ground controller who ordered the destruction of KE-007.

Hughes then learned some interesting news. Eagleburger had heard that there might be an audiotape of the air-to-ground communication with the Soviet pilot who shot KE-007 down.

"Tapes? There are tapes of this?" asked an astonished Hughes.

"We hear there is an actual tape recording of the Soviet combat pilot chattering about shooting down the Korean plane. Japanese intelligence has it," said Eagleburger.

"Where did they get it?" asked Hughes.

"It was recorded at a top secret listening post in Hokkaido," replied Eagleburger. "The NSA is also involved out there. The Japanese themselves may not even know about it. So if we make it public, we'll have to say where we got it. It's a tough call."

"This will blow the Russians out of the water!" exclaimed Hughes. "It's overwhelming evidence and we simply have to get it."

Japanese and American intelligence officials had to be

persuaded to release what they had. According to former assistant secretary of state Gregory J. Newell, "They knew if the tape were made public it would expose their intelligence gathering activity in that region. The operation there would be about 90 percent useless."[4]

The Reagan Administration's spin machine began cranking up. And that meant the USIA was getting involved. Thursday afternoon Wick ordered his top Agency aides to form a special task force to devise ways of playing the story overseas. The objective, quite simply, was to heap as much abuse on the Soviet Union as possible. As the USIA's director of television, I was on that committee, which was chaired by senior foreign service officer Jack Hedges. We quickly established contact with the "Korean working group" at the State Department, which was having trouble identifying the passenger list from the downed plane, and was unclear whether any of the passengers with Korean or Chinese surnames were American citizens. USIA overseas posts assisted by checking press contacts and by monitoring local media coverage.

To keep the Soviet's feet to the fire, our task force came up with a list of immediate objectives:

> Reinforce the impact of worldwide reaction against the Soviet shootdown, emphasizing its human and multinational dimensions; stimulate continuing international attention that the issues raised by the tragedy are of concern to all nations, and inform those without ready access to commercial media for political reasons (such as the USSR) or technological reasons (such as the Third World) via Voice of America, and Agency print and TV output.

The Voice of America's radio transmitters were pumped up to maximum power, and the KE-007 story led every news broadcast. Gutwrenching interviews with the families of victims were featured. Transmitters were redirected to beam 56 hours of additional language programs per day into the Soviet Union, whose citizens had not been informed by their government of the KE-007 incident. Special videocassette programs on the disaster, including statements by Reagan and excerpts from a UN debate, were air-shipped to U.S. embassies abroad (not as yet equipped with their own TV satellite receiving dishes to obtain such programs instantaneously). The point of all this was to portray the fighter pilot as a reckless cowboy and the Soviet military authorities generally as a bunch of Keystone Kops with their fingers on the nuclear trigger.

We were all told we had the goods. State Department spokesmen claimed the United States had evidence proving that the Russian pilot knew he was downing a civilian plane.

"I think that it was understood that it was a commercial aircraft," said State Department official Richard Burt. He told newsmen in private briefings that he was *certain* the Soviets knew it was a civilian airliner.[5] Dozens of Soviet-bashing U.S. government spokesmen began telephoning media contacts.

A few hours after Shultz's news conference, the California White House issued a statement by President Reagan condemning the Soviet action: "I speak for all Americans and for the people everywhere who cherish civilized values, in protesting this Soviet attack on an unarmed civilian passenger plane," said Reagan. "Words can scarcely express our revulsion at this horrifying act of violence. The United States joins with other members of the international community in demanding a full explanation for this appalling and wanton misdeed." Reporters wanted to know whether Reagan would cut his vacation short and return to Washington. Press spokesman Larry Speakes said the president would stay in touch with KE-007 developments from his California ranch and leave the next morning for Washington.

The Kremlin was reeling from all the bad press it was beginning to get worldwide. Andropov ordered an emergency meeting of the Central Committee Politburo to consider a public relations plan of action. Those present would include the Soviet premier, the general secretary, the KGB secret police chairman, the foreign minister, and the head of the Russian armed forces, among others. They were particularly angry over Reagan's strident remarks. General Secretary Konstantin Chernenko set the tone for the meeting by insisting that something had to be done about "the wild orgy of American propaganda that has been launched . . . the important thing is that the first step has already been taken—an announcement has appeared in our press." The official news agency Tass had broken a day of silence on the incident, issuing a watered-down two-paragraph item stating only that a Russian fighter had intercepted a Korean airliner that had violated Soviet airspace. It gave no indication that the plane had been shot down. Gromyko expressed his concern over how quickly Reagan had spoken out on the subject, and that now the United States was demanding an immediate session of the UN Security Council. "Clearly we will have to use our veto," said Gromyko. He announced that the Japanese had indicated they had recordings of the conversations between the pilot and ground services. "So," he concluded, "imperialistic propaganda will try to portray our moves as a deliberate attack on a peaceful plane and a violation of all conventions."

Defense minister Ustinov agreed and defended the action. The South Korean plane had flown deep within Soviet airspace and not responded to repeated instructions to identify itself. Ustinov also informed the group, erroneously, that the Korean plane had had no navigational lights, and that the Soviet pilot had fired tracer shells to warn the Korean crew. His contention that the destruction of the KE-007 was justified would be echoed by the meeting's other participants. They agreed that the United States provoked the attack. "This was a well-planned anti-Soviet act, and this must be stated frankly in the press and in our statements, which will reach foreign readers as well as our own," stated V. V. Kuznetsov. The group of aging bureaucrats then turned its attention to what the official Soviet press announcement should say. Gromyko thought they should admit publicly to firing on the plane because its wreckage would probably be found. Nicolai Ogarkov, chief of staff, concurred, feeling that Western propagandists would broadcast tapes of the Soviet airmen's conversations. Everyone was in agreement with Gromyko's idea. The public relations campaign would be done in stages. First, there would be an announcement that the Korean airliner had violated Soviet airspace and had done so for some two hours. Next, it would be stated unequivocally that warning shots were fired. And then it would be firmly asserted that the whole incident was a deliberate provocation by "imperialist forces." They would cap their PR campaign with a charge that KE-007 was actually on a spy mission for the Americans.[6]

From his hospital bed Andropov approved the plan that very morning. Gromyko began to talk to the press, claiming that KE-007 had entered Soviet airspace and that it "did not have navigational lights, did not respond to queries and did not enter into contact with the radio control service. Fighters . . . which were sent aloft toward the intruder plane," he continued, "tried to give it assistance in directing it to the nearest airfield. But the intruder plane did not react to the signals and warnings from the Soviet fighters."

On Friday the Soviet news agency Tass repeated the same line: KE-007 had had no navigational lights; Soviet fighters had attempted to contact the intruder "using generally accepted signals and to take it to the nearest airfield in the territory of the Soviet Union"; and "Soviet aircraft fired warning shots with tracer shells along the flying route of the plane." A spokesman for the Soviet air defense forces maintained that the interceptor pilot had thought the intruder aircraft was a U.S. RC-135 reconnaissance plane. Despite the inaccuracies, the Soviet version of what happened, as we later learned, was a whole lot closer to reality than ours.

However, the Soviets made several fatal public relations blunders. First, instead of letting the story dribble out slowly, they should have gone on the offensive. After all, they had all the evidence in hand, and could have used it to take the initiative, blunting our effort. Had the Soviets done so in cohesive, dramatic fashion, stating precisely what had happened, things would have been different. Blame would have been placed squarely on an inept South Korean flight crew and on the United States, which had been monitoring its flight and done nothing about it. The loss of so many innocent lives was a tragedy of monumental proportions, of course, but the Soviets could have shifted blame away from themselves and toward the United States, citing, among other things, its hard evidence on America's RC-135 spy missions.

Accusing the United States of having used KE-007 as a spy plane was a costly miscalculation. Before returning to Washington from his abbreviated California vacation, Reagan issued his most scathing denunciation to date, accusing the Soviets of advancing its interests through "violence and intimidation" and of "flagrantly" lying about such a "heinous act." With wife Nancy at his side, Reagan read from a prepared statement before boarding Air Force One at Point Mugu Naval Air Station, California. "What are we to make of a regime which establishes one set of standards for itself and another for the rest of humankind?" he asked. Russian citizens lined up at newspaper kiosks and were insulted and bewildered by Reagan's attack. Many were astonished that an American president could be so venomous toward their country.

On Friday morning, Shultz was told by briefers from the Central Intelligence Agency and the National Security Agency that intelligence data suggested the Soviets had thought they were shooting down a U.S. spy plane, not a passenger jet. Shultz dismissed the notion, telling briefers their theory was implausible. The downed plane had been tracked for a long period of time and its design was distinctive, he maintained. Following the briefing, Shultz told his senior staff that intelligence agencies "have no compunction about fooling you."[7] The administration would take the hard line, and everyone in the know, including the intelligence community, would play ball.

The American media swallowed the U.S. government line without reservation. Said the venerable Ted Koppel on the ABC News "Nightline" program: "This has been one of those occasions when there is very little difference between what is churned out by the U.S. government propaganda organs and by the commercial broadcasting networks." Wrote *New York Times* columnist James Reston: "Even if you assume that this whole tragic affair was a case of mistaken identity—which takes quite a stretch of imagination— the Soviet response to it has been so bizarre, so indifferent to the human tragedy and so vicious in its charge against the U.S. and the South Koreans that it can be explained only by the Russians' pathological fear of freedom."

Once media heavies such as Koppel and Reston had weighed in, we at the USIA began to see a major public relations opportunity to link the incident to nuclear disarmament issues. We realized that raising concerns about Soviet trustworthiness in security and arms control areas could do serious damage to the Kremlin's peace campaign to dissuade West European NATO allies from placing upgraded American nuclear weapons aimed at the Soviet Union on their soil. The KE-007 disaster would enable us to put the competence of the Soviet military in considerable doubt. Administration sources had been privately raising this issue with press contacts, but now it was out in the open. Eagleburger said that the Soviet downing of the Korean airliner raises "the most serious questions about the competence of the Soviet air defense system, with all the danger that implies."

The widespread erosion of support for NATO and the alliance with the United States had posed a serious challenge. Our task force received special reports on foreign media reaction from more than two hundred USIA overseas locations to gauge how the KE-007 story was being played out. We looked hard at the ones coming from Western Europe. It made for satisfying reading. Coverage of Shultz's press conference, in which he condemned the Soviets for knowingly shooting down an unarmed passenger plane, was extensive, and there was widespread editorial condemnation of the Soviet act and concern over what it might mean to East-West relations. *Il Tempo* of Rome called the shooting "a deliberate mass murder." West Germany's *Frankfurter Allgemeine* cautioned, "There is no use talking peace if one doubts the basic peacefulness of others and resorts to shooting whenever an aircraft gets off course." Our task force kept up its steady drumbeat in Europe. The USIA office in Lisbon rushed a videotape of a United Nations Security Council session on KE-007 to the biennial convention of the European Airline Pilots Association being held there, and the tape was viewed by some 17,000 members. Our USIA officer in Madrid screened the videotape for NATO foreign ministers who were meeting in the Spanish capital. We directed our overseas public affairs officers to get American ambassadors and embassy spokespersons on television news and talk shows so that they could keep stirring things up. Soviet ambassadors in these same Western European capitals, meanwhile, were summoned to foreign ministries to give a full accounting of the KE-007 downing. The Soviet Embassy in Paris issued a statement lashing out at the United States for whipping up a "hysterical anti-Soviet propaganda campaign."[8] The statement continued, "What is concerned is a catastrophe of an aircraft which, furthermore, twice violated the air space of the Soviet Union. For two hours the crew of the aircraft did not reply to insistent signals addressed to them in ways conforming to the universal international aerial code."[9]

The Soviet statement had its facts straight, but because it was released through the embassy in Paris it had minimal impact. The Soviet information machine still seemed incapable of getting its version of the story out in a dramatic, coherent way. Wick also came under attack, a sure sign of Soviet desperation. These attacks were nothing new. In fact, Wick was attacked so frequently by the Soviets that his staff prepared a weekly summary of Soviet press assaults on him. The Soviet press had recently accused him of operating a "brothel" before coming to Washington (he owned nursing homes) and of being the "maestro of false propaganda, lies and demagogy, hypocrisy and instigation" in running the U.S. government's foreign information programs. The Soviets would later admit that they hated Wick because he did a lot of things that made them feel miserable. And KE-007 was not making them feel any better, particularly when within a few days he would employ his big-ticket item: television.

By late Friday afternoon, noticed *Izvestia* correspondent Alexander Shalnev, every single Russian diplomat in Washington had disappeared from public view. He was told that Russian security officers had issued a special warning advising diplomats to stay inside the embassy compound. Diplomats should not appear on the streets of Washington, the warning read, because anti-Soviet feeling ran so high that it was not safe. Shalnev and Eugeni Igorov, Isvestia bureau chief, received no such instructions, however. They walked around and drank in bars with other journalists to find out what they were saying. They went to every State Department, Pentagon, and White House briefing, listened attentively to every statement, and later attempted the impossible task of analyzing tape transcripts of the Korean airliner attack that they were given by American officials.

That evening, back in Washington, Reagan chaired a crowded National Security Council meeting with top administration officials, including Shultz, Secretary of Defense Weinberger, CIA director William Casey, General John W. Vessey, chairman of the Joint Chiefs of Staff, and Charles Z. Wick. The president was briefed by General Vessey, and various responses—ranging from imposing economic sanctions to a military response—were being discussed. By now it had been confirmed that sixty-one American citizens had been aboard the Korean plane, and that among them was Congressman Lawrence P. McDonald of Georgia.

Ambassador Jack Matlock arrived late. To get to Washington from Prague, he'd had to make several connecting flights. A White House secretary told him brusquely that the meeting had already begun.[10] Matlock slipped quietly into the meeting room, right at the moment when the group began to consider the public opinion aspects of the incident. Reagan agreed with Shultz and Wick that the United States should get its hands on the audiotape of the Soviet air-to-ground communication as quickly as possible. Although he hadn't heard it, Wick recommended that the tape be played at a special session of the United Nations Security Council, which could be convened as early as the following Tuesday, the day after Labor Day. Shultz agreed. As Wick's chief television executive, I would be brought into the loop.

The audiotape arrived at the State Department late Saturday afternoon. Eagleburger and Ambassador Roger Kirk, representing UN ambassador Jeane Kirkpatrick, who was vacationing in Morocco, hurriedly located a recorder to listen to the tape and gauge its usefulness. Even though the tape was larded with static, Russian-language voices themselves would have solid impact, Kirk told Eagleburger. "This is information we can use, and we should put it out." Kirk called Wick to tell him the tape had arrived, and that the National Security Agency had "checked" the translation.

By Saturday, U.S. officials acknowledged that an Air Force RC-135 reconnaissance plane, the military version of a 707 passenger airliner, had flown close to the Korean jumbo jet for a short time over international waters near the Soviet Union two hours before KE-007 was shot down. However, the RC-135 had landed at least an hour before KE-007 met its fate. The military aircraft was already in a hanger 1,200 miles away at the U.S. air base at Shemya in the Aleutian Islands.

Wick telephoned me about 8:30 Sunday morning, asking me to meet him at the State Department at noon. We went through a heavy metal door with a combination lock in its center, and into a conference room. I felt as if I were in a bank vault. I had asked my deputy, Richard Levy, to meet me there, but he was not permitted into the conference room and had to wait in the outer office. Inside the meeting room, Ambassador Kirk was seated at the head of the conference table, the audiotape resting directly before him.

Kirk began by analyzing the tape transcript, which he said covered a period of some 50 minutes, about 30 minutes before the missile firings and 20 minutes afterward. The tape began at 17:56 GMT, and ended at 18:46 GMT. The Korean airliner was struck by missiles at 18:26 GMT. Kirk maintained that comments by the interceptor pilots contradicted several Soviet government statements. "The interceptor pilot saw the airliner's navigational lights and reported that to the ground on three occasions," he said. "Contrary to Soviet statements the pilot makes no mention of firing any warning shots. And there's no indication that the interceptor pilot made any attempt to communicate with the airliner, or to signal for it to land, as the Soviets maintain. The most striking thing," he concluded, "is that it appears that the ground controllers never asked the interceptor pilots to identify the aircraft."

Kirk told us he had played the tape for a couple of U.S. Air Force pilots who told him there was no way the Korean airliner could have been mistaken for the RC-135 reconnaissance plane. The passenger plane is about 50 percent larger than the military craft and has a distinctive hump, the pilots reportedly told Kirk, and the Soviet interceptor was close enough to the Boeing 747 to have eyeballed the difference.

None of us saw any reason to doubt Kirk's story. We agreed that the transcript should be turned into a video document for presentation before the UN Security Council in two days. The most effective format, we felt, would be to identify the voices of the four interceptor pilots as they closed in for the kill, together with an English translation. I suggested that we show the pilots' comments in white typeface against a plain black background without any texture or shadings, so that the attention of the viewer would be riveted on what the pilot was saying and not on extraneous visuals. The tape would be played during Jeane Kirkpatrick's speech at Tuesday's special session of the Security Council.

We discussed contingency plans. What if at the last minute the Russians succeeded in vetoing our plan to play the tape in the Security Council? We decided to have a bank of television monitors set up in the hallway, garden, and lobby, and invite everyone to pile out of the Security Council to watch the tape with us. Kirk slid the tape across the table to me, along with transcripts of its English- and Russian-language translations. "Everything in it is classified," he said. "We don't want any leaks. Anybody who even looks at it should sign a piece of paper."

We didn't listen to the tape. As I leafed through the transcript I noticed it was all in capital letters and that only two-thirds of each page had type. It consisted of a grand total of five pages. "Not very talkative, were they?" I remarked. Kirk again told us that the period of time covered on the tape was just under fifty minutes, from 17:56:58 GMT through 18:46:09 GMT. The first thirty minutes covered the stalking of the intruder aircraft, which was struck by missile fire at 18:26GMT. After that, Soviet pilot 805 broke off his attack through to the tape's conclusion at 18:46 GMT. I asked if everything was recorded. "Everything," Kirk answered emphatically. "Let's see what you come up with tomorrow morning." We agreed that I would come back with a finished program at 8:30 the following morning.

I placed the tape and transcripts in my briefcase, clamped it shut, and went back through the door with the combination lock. Levy was waiting patiently in the outer office. I briefed him as we walked down the hall toward the elevator. Before joining the government, Levy had done publicity for Paramount Pictures and other movie studios, and had handled international marketing for such films as *The Graduate, Rosemary's Baby,* and Jane Fonda's *Barbarella.* With his signature heavily tinted teardrop eyeglasses, wash pants, and open collar shirt, he was far more Hollywood maven than Washington bureaucrat.

Several months earlier, decked out in his Aquascutum leather trenchcoat and silk scarf slung around his neck, Levy had attended a press conference held by Secretary of Defense Weinberger. Levy, a friend of Weinberger's son, Cap Jr., had brought a camera with him to snap some souvenir photos of Weinberger as he fielded questions from the press. Back at the office that evening, Levy and I happened to be watching ABC News when Pentagon correspondent John McWethy did a report on the Weinberger press conference. Suddenly there on the TV monitor was Levy, pictured roaming the perimeter of the room in his dark glasses and leather jacket, taking photos. "In the audience at the press conference," ABC's McWethy intoned, "the Tass correspondent from Moscow. He took no notes, but copiously photographed the event." Before McWethy had finished, Levy was on the phone to ABC News in Washington to demand a retraction. He was told that ABC bureau manager Edward Fouhy was unavailable. "Tell him it's the Tass correspondent from Moscow," Levy snapped. Fouhy got on the line. "You may be interested to know that I'm not a Soviet spy," said Levy. "I'm a U.S. government official." "Oh shit!" exclaimed Fouhy. In a correction the following night, which ran longer than the mistake itself, ABC News anchor Frank Reynolds apologized for the error.

Levy and I headed out the C Street exit of the State Department with our secret audiotape in tow. We gave a thumbs-up to the TV network camera crews and reporters as we walked by them on our way to my car. "They should only know what we've got in here," I said quietly to Levy, patting my briefcase.

Back at our USIA television office, a short walk north of the Capitol, Levy and I met with our production team and briefed them on our assignment. The television and film operation, which had expanded to new studio facilities and added programs during the Kennedy Administration when the legendary Murrow was USIA director, had fallen on hard times after he left. By 1980 budgets had been drastically reduced, and television was being reabsorbed into the Voice of America radio operation, where its potential growth was underappreciated and underused. But given Wick's fascination with television and his access to the White House, morale had picked up, and the group of managers, producers, and technicians I met with on that Sunday afternoon, September 4, were enthusiastic and dedicated. They viewed the Korean airliner project as an unparalleled opportunity to make a real difference. We would be putting together a document that would be shown to the entire world in less than two days. It would be the pièce de résistance in the U.S. government's propaganda campaign against the Soviets.

We paraded into the control room, where our technician Mike Ernst cued up the tape so that we could all listen to it for the first time. Something was wrong. The tape was supposed to run 50 minutes. But the tape segment we had ran only 8 minutes and 32 seconds. Our first reaction was that someone had taken a meat cleaver to it. I telephoned John Hughes at the State Department. "Where's the rest of the tape?" I asked. Hughes said he would check on it.

About 15 minutes later Hughes called back with the answer. "The tape is voice-actuated," he explained. "It went on and off. It ran only when the Soviet pilots said something." "Do I detect the fine hand of Rosemary Woods here?" I asked sarcastically. "Your guess is as good as mine," Hughes responded good-naturedly. John Hughes had been a Pulitzer Prize–winning journalist with the *Christian Science Monitor*, and I trusted him completely. As a press spokesman, he had to rely on information supplied by others, as did we. "What about the guys on the ground?" I inquired. "We don't hear the ground controllers at all. Only the pilots." "You have just what they gave us," said Hughes, referring to the National Security Agency, which had turned over the tape to the State Department. "That's all we've got." Hughes seemed as uncomfortable as I was with the situation.

Time was running short, and we knew production would be tricky. I gave the tape to engineer Arnie Hauser, who ran it through an electronic device that tweaked the audio quality and, by reducing an annoying high-pitched whine, made it clearer. The quality of the pilots' transmissions was still poor, and this slowed us down in our race to complete the video program by morning.

The production technique was simple but time-consuming. Each time one of the three Soviet interceptor pilots spoke, we wanted to identify him by his pilot number, which would be displayed on the screen along with what he said, in both Russian and English. We had no idea at the time that pilot 805 was named Osipovich. The international Greenwich Mean Time when the transmission occurred would also be shown. Thus, the Soviet pilot's exclamation, "I'm closing on the target," would be printed in Russian and English on the screen, along with the time, "18:25:11 GMT," and the appropriate call sign, "Pilot 805." We also planned to provide transcripts to UN Security Council announcers, so that they could give simultaneous translations in every UN language of what the Russian pilots were saying.

I wanted to keep the visuals simple, so as not to detract from the drama of the Russian pilots' own comments. Only a map. No file footage of airplanes or exploding animation. Future tabloid TV shows would no doubt have used canned music and colorized computer-enhanced images. After many years in television I had learned that messages in that medium had to be simple. Television creates perceptions. The perception we wanted to convey was that the Soviet Union had cold-bloodedly carried out a barbaric act. The Soviet pilots' words, by themselves, would effectively drive our point home.

What bothered me, of course, was that our tape would represent only the last thirty minutes of KE-007's flight. What happened prior to 17:55:58 GMT? What had the pilots said? What had the command control centers on the ground said to the pilots? Had anything been deleted from the tape before it was given to us? We simply did not know. For the first time, it dawned on us that our segment would be taken completely out of context. Naturally, no one knew what was going on inside the flight deck of KE-007 during this period.

Because the Soviet interceptor pilots were Russian, we needed language experts to help us match what was said on the tape with what we would show on the screen. I called our project coordinator, Jack Hedges, to request his assistance in locating Russian language experts to help us, and asked one of my top TV producers, Michael Messinger, to go to New York to coordinate our Security Council TV production. I cautioned Messinger that the Soviets might veto our plans were they to learn of them in advance. Showing a videotape as evidence in the Security Council had never been done before. Messinger telephoned the U.S. Mission to the United Nations and reached Irene Payne, a USIA press officer. He asked Payne to get him inside the Security Council chamber so that he could conduct a production survey. Equipment would have to be brought in for the big production, and TV monitors set up in strategic positions.

Payne told Messinger she would make an informal request to the Security Council weekend duty officer, traditionally on a seven-day rotation among member nations, to get him into the chamber. She called the UN telephone switchboard and was transferred to the person in charge, who answered the phone in Russian. "Is this Riverdale?" asked a flustered Payne, referring to the nearby New York suburb where the Soviet diplomatic residence was located. "Yes, yes, who do you wish to speak to?" came the reply in heavily accented English. "Thanks, wrong number," Payne said and hung up. So as not to tip our hand to the Soviet Embassy, she wouldn't be going through the weekend duty officer after all. Messinger went back to the drawing board.

In our Washington production facility we had the capability to do captioned programs in many languages, but Russian was not one of them. Because our electronic keyboard was not equipped with Cyrillic characters, which were not commercially available, we had to find someone who had the software so that we could copy it. It was Sunday and businesses were closed—as they would be the following day as well, since it was Labor Day. Our engineering manager, Ken Boles, started making some calls, and was lucky enough to reach a maintenance man working on video equipment at Voxcam, a

TV production facility in nearby Silver Spring, Maryland. Voxcam specialized in foreign-language captioning and had a Cyrillic alphabet disk. Boles raced out the door to pick up the disk, and by early Sunday evening it had been loaded into our computer. Then came the painstaking task of matching the English-letter keyboard with the Cyrillic alphabet. For the next several hours, a Russian linguist pasted the proper Cyrillic symbol on each keypad. At best, we were looking at a long night of hunt and peck.

Jeane Kirkpatrick had returned home from Morocco to prepare for Tuesday's special session of the UN Security Council. Advised that a videotape was being readied to accompany her speech, she instructed her staff at the U.S. Mission to "thoroughly investigate the precedent for using visual aides in the Security Council."

In October 1962, UN Ambassador Adlai Stevenson used blowups of still photographs in the Security Council to show Soviet missile emplacements in Cuba. Stevenson demanded, "Do you, Ambassador Zorin, deny that the USSR has placed and is placing medium and intermediate-range missiles in Cuba? Yes or no? Don't wait for the translation. Yes or no?" Zorin had responded that he was not in a courtroom and didn't have to answer. "You are in the courtroom of world opinion," Stevenson shot back. "I am prepared to wait for my answer until hell freezes over." It was quite a performance. Although Stevenson's use of visual aids had set a precedent at the UN, putting on a television program was far more complicated than bringing still photographs into a room and propping them up on an easel. Large monitors would have to placed in advance in the Security Council chamber, and cameras needed to be pre-positioned on the floor. At some point, we would have to obtain formal permission from the president of the Security Council to premier our made-for-TV special.

It was midnight Sunday, and in our Washington studios Russian-language experts continued to pore over the translated transcripts to check their accuracy. At one in the morning we were ready to produce our videotape, and the tape machines started to roll. About an hour later, Levy and I went to my office to meet with intelligence officers from the Air Force, who, we were told, had been sent "just in case we had any questions." I suspected they were actually from the National Security Agency, which, together with Japanese military intelligence, had recorded and provided the tape of the Russian fighter pilots to the State Department. There were three men in my office, an Air Force colonel in uniform and two others in civilian clothes. They seemed particularly interested in a map we were preparing, which would show the flight path of the RC-135. It was the only map we would use in our videotape presentation.

The Soviets had still not admitted shooting down the Korean airliner and were simultaneously insisting that the RC-135 was similar in appearance to KE-007 and could have been mistaken for it. We had decided that our tape should start with a map showing the flight path of the RC-135, indicating where it had already landed— 1,200 miles away from where KE-007 was shot down. We got the RC-135's flight information from the Pentagon. Its flight path was illustrated on a large map in my office, the one we would incorporate into the videotape. One of the men in civilian clothes peered at the map.

"The RC-135 flight path is wrong," said the man with the mustache and open-collar, short-sleeve sport shirt.

"That's what we were told," said Levy. "We got it from the Air Force."

"I don't care where you got it. It's wrong," the man insisted.

"So who are you?" I asked.

"Just call me John," the man answered.

"How do you know this is wrong, John?" inquired Levy.

"Because I was on the plane," said John. "Don't worry. I'll get what you need."

A couple of hours later, we received two beautiful, professionally mounted four-color maps by courier. We were also provided poster-size photographs of the Soviet interceptor planes with all their technical specifications, which we would take to New York with us to display at Kirkpatrick's news conference at the U.S. Mission following our Security Council TV extravaganza.

Downstairs in our TV studio, we were wearing out one translator after another. The audio quality of the Russian pilots' tape was poor, and our deadline was getting ever closer. Translators were beginning to wilt under the pressure of accurately deciphering the static. We roused more translators from bed, one of whom showed up in our studio after 4:00 A.M. in a pajama top, scrub pants, and slippers. There was considerable disagreement over one NSA translation in particular. "Yolki palki," said pilot 805, as he locked on the target plane and prepared to fire his missiles. The NSA translated the pilot's words as "Fiddlesticks." Not so, said one of our translators, it means "Christmas trees." Wrong, said another, it means "Oh, my gosh." "Not so," said another, who was Russian-born, "the literal translation is, 'Oh fuck.'" We decided to stay with "Fiddlesticks." Several years later the KGB would accuse us of being prudish for having toned down the tape for the United Nations audience.[11]

We finished the last of 273 video "pages" and the rough-cut version of our tape at 8:00 A.M. We sent a portable TV monitor and a videotape playback machine to the State Department for our scheduled 8:30 A.M. screening. I took the videotape to Undersecretary Eagleburger's meeting room, where about fifty State Department and intelligence-community officials had gathered two rows deep around an immense conference table. Seated at the head of the table was a haggard-looking Larry Eagleburger, who had obviously been up all night, like most of us. Wearing a crumpled safari suit, he sat slumped in his chair, listing slightly to his right, his drooping eyes barely visible above the edge of the table. To Eagleburger's left sat Jeane Kirkpatrick, and Charles Wick was sitting to her left. I gave a brief introduction to the tape. The group sat hushed as we screened the program for the next ten minutes.

Our version left little doubt that the Soviets had shot down the Korean airliner in cold blood and without warning, knowing it was a civilian plane. Soviet pilot 805 had certainly seen the enemy plane clearly—at least according to our presentation of what had happened:

> 18:06 GMT: I'm flying behind.
> 18:10 GMT: The target's [strobe] light is blinking.
> 18:12 GMT: I see it visually and on radar.
> 18:18 GMT: I see it!
> 18:21 GMT: I'm going in closer.
> 18:21 GMT: I see both [strobe light and plane].
> 18:22 GMT: I am going around it, I'm moving in front of
> the target.

From this, one would get the unmistakable impression that pilot 805 had a clear view of the plane from close up. Nothing could have been further from the truth. We now know from complete transcripts and tapes provided by the Russians almost ten years after the tragedy, and from the KE-007 flight recorder retrieved by the Russians, precisely what happened that night.

For starters, the three planes—two SU-15 interceptors and one MIG-23—were airborne by 17:46 GMT. Our audiotape began a full ten minutes later, at 17:56 GMT. Prior to, during, and after this period, according to now-complete transcripts, Russian commanders believed the intruder to be a U.S. military RC-135 reconnaissance plane. The intruder aircraft was heading on a course that did indeed take it smack over the supersensitive Soviet Sakhalin Island military installation. Our tape did not include pilot Osipovich's comment, "Unclear," at 18:10 GMT, in response to his ground controller's question, "805, can you determine the [intruder aircraft] type?" Osipovich had said it was too dark for him to see the intruder clearly. The full transcript would later show that Soviet pilot Gennady Osipovich had circled the intruder to get its attention and tilted his wings to force the aircraft down, after being asked repeatedly by his ground controllers to do so. Osipovich also had reported firing his warning bursts to get the intruder's attention. This comment was also not on the tape we were provided. Our tape *did* include innocuous transmissions from the Soviet ground command post "Karnaval," which by itself belied the U.S. contention that only the Russian pilots' voices were recorded on tape. The tape we were provided did not, however, include those critical transmissions from the "Deputat" (ground) command post where General Kornukov had relayed his instructions to Osipovich, such as "Fire a warning burst with cannons and rock wings to show the direction to Sokol," and "How many jet trails are there? . . . If there are four jet trails, then it's an RC-135." Each of Kornukov's instructions were relayed from the Deputat command post to Osipovich.

Yet the consensus at the Monday morning State Department session was that we had a powerful video document, one that heightened one's feeling of horror at what happened. There was the voice of Gennady Osipovich, pilot 805, as he moved in for the kill: "Missile launched. The target is destroyed." We did a freeze frame on "The target is destroyed," holding the words on the screen so they would be imprinted in the minds of viewers.

Kirkpatrick felt it was important for a narrator to begin the program by making a statement that made clear the RC-135 had landed well before KE-007 was shot down, so that it could not possibly have been confused with the Korean airliner. It was agreed that a voice would make the following announcement while we showed a map of the area on the screen:

> Soviet radar began tracking the Korean airliner at 15:51 Greenwich Mean Time. At 16:35 GMT, Soviet ground controllers noticed the 747 actually was flying over their landmass. At 17:28 GMT, the Korean airliner was flying over the Sea of Okhotsk, at the same time a U.S. reconnaissance flight, RC-135, was landing at a base on the Aleutian Islands. The RC-135 had been flying a routine mission in support of the SALT compliance agreements, off the Kamchatka Peninsula. At 18:26 GMT, a full hour after the U.S. reconnaissance flight had landed, the Korean airliner was destroyed near the Soviet Sakhalin Island, 1,200 miles away. The tape you are about to hear begins at 17:56 GMT, thirty minutes before the Korean airliner was shot down. The communication is from four Soviet fighter pilots, talking to their ground controllers while tracking the Korean airliner.

The group agreed that the United States would press for an 11:00 A.M. start to the special session of the Security Council the following day, Tuesday. We also agreed that we would place TV monitors in the Security Council chamber and in the UN hallways, garden, and lobby as backups in the event we were prevented from showing the video inside the chamber during the special session. In case the electricity failed (we suspected the Soviets might clip some wires), we had a standby generator. We would also have a third video display at the U.S. Mission, across the street from the UN, for a follow-up press conference Tuesday afternoon. It was agreed that I would bring the revised tape over to the State Department and play it for Kirkpatrick early Tuesday morning so that she could give final approval before we left together for New York.

In New York on Labor Day Monday, USIA producer Mike Messinger was meeting with UN television director Joe McCusker to go over the placement of the TV monitors within the Security Council's chamber. Through his own contacts, McCusker had arranged to get Messinger into the chamber without going through the Russian duty officer. Six monitors would be spotted around the floor, the key one placed above the left shoulder of Soviet Ambassador Oleg Troyanovsky, giving news cameras an unobstructed view of the program on the TV screen and the Russian official at the same time. It would be a sophisticated setup, with McCusker feeding the tape to all monitors from the UN control room, as well as directing the cameras positioned on the chamber floor to catch the reactions of delegates. The whole program would be transmitted to the American and international television networks.

Monitors were also needed for the backup positions in the UN lobby and garden and the U.S. Mission, but renting the equipment over Labor Day weekend was not easy. At USIA's midtown Manhattan office, Messinger had to fast-talk his way past a building guard who had stopped him as he lugged TV sets down to his car. Back in our Washington studio, we were still tweaking the video presentation. In Western Europe, the media were giving prominent coverage to the story that the American RC-135 reconnaissance plane was near the Korean airliner when it was downed. London's conservative *Daily Telegraph* said: "The belated American admission . . . is certain to prove a windfall for Soviet propaganda efforts." Lisbon's pro-Socialist *Journal de Noticias* said the disclosure "may change the whole case and ridicule the worldwide accusations." Other Western European dailies carried stories suggesting that the Soviets might have mistaken the Korean airliner for an American spy plane with a similar outline.

At the United Nations, deputy American ambassador Charles M. Lichenstein felt it was time to approach the president of the Security Council and formally request permission to play the tape at Tuesday's special session. The presidency of the Security Council rotates among member nations every month, and it was the turn of Noel Sinclair of Guyana. Because a videotape had never before been shown in that forum, Sinclair wanted to know how Lichenstein would respond to those who might object to playing the tape, such as the Soviet Union. What arguments could be used to persuade those who might see the videotape as being intrusive and overly dramatic? Lichenstein found Sinclair was not being resistive, but cautious. He was, after all, a diplomat, and caution is their byword. Lichenstein replied that what the American delegation had in mind was "a modern version of what Adlai Stevenson did" in the Security Council during the Cuban missile crisis more than twenty years earlier. "Video is simply an updated technology," Lichenstein reasoned. "Why should we be prohibited from using it?" "That's a very compelling analogy," responded Sinclair stiffly. When the word reached the Soviet delegation, it vehemently rejected the idea of permitting the Americans to show a videotape. Ambassador Jeane Kirkpatrick demanded that the Soviet delegation state its opposition out in the open, and not behind closed doors, "because we want the world to know the Soviets are trying to block the showing of the taping." The Soviets knew that if they prevented us from displaying the tape in the Security Council chamber, we would simply play it in the UN hallways. Arguing convincingly for suppression of the tape was awkward. Backed into a corner, the Soviets would eventually relent. To maintain the propaganda offensive, President Reagan went on national television Monday night and during his speech a twenty-second segment of the Soviet pilots' audiotape was played. Reagan then promoted its airing at the UN the following day: "Here's a brief excerpt of the tape which we're going to play in its entirety for the United Nations Security Council tomorrow," proclaimed the president.

Although we had not yet received formal permission to put TV monitors and cameras in the Security Council chamber, Messinger and McCusker went ahead and set up things Monday night. McCusker explained to the Office of Security Council Affairs that once approved the monitors required considerable time to be installed and checked to be ready for immediate use. The equipment could be removed quickly if the council decided against the idea.

We finished the final version of the video at six Tuesday morning. It was up to Kirkpatrick to give final approval, but we were running short of time. I gave our TV production team the go-ahead to strike off multiple copies of the video and audiotapes that Levy and I would then hand-carry to New York for distribution to the media there. Levy and I rushed over to the State Department for our 8:00 A.M. screening with Kirkpatrick. She signed off on the tape immediately. Then, with Kirkpatrick in tow, we hustled down to the State Department garage, piled into the backseat of her black limousine, and headed to for the 9:00 A.M. shuttle to New York. Kirkpatrick's face appeared in the media enough so that she was often recognized. Because of President Reagan's Monday night buildup of Kirkpatrick's UN appearance, people at the airport applauded and cheered. "Give 'em hell, Jeane," they shouted as she walked with us toward the plane. Two seats had been held in the first row of the air-craft, directly behind the bulkhead, for Kirkpatrick and a general from the Pentagon. Levy and I sat in the row behind them, and Kirk-patrick's aide, Alan Gerson, sat behind us. During the 45-minute flight, Kirkpatrick and I reviewed the placement of the tape within her speech, and the exact words that would be used for the "roll cue," so the TV director could call for the videotape to be played at precisely the right moment.

A USIA station wagon, with ample room for our visual material, was to meet Levy and me at LaGuardia Airport and take us into a special secured entrance at the UN, near the TV control room. After dropping us off, the USIA driver was then to deliver the videos and audiotape dubs to the U.S. Mission, where they would be dis-tributed at Kirkpatrick's afternoon news conference following the Se-curity Council session. We landed at LaGuardia, and as we were about to disembark from the plane, I mentioned to Gerson that Levy and I had a USIA car ready to take us to the UN, and that he was wel-come to come along. It would only take a few minutes for us to col-lect our tapes and pictures at LaGuardia, I added. "Thanks, but I'm going right to the Mission," he said. "I'll take a cab."

Levy and I got off the plane, proceeded through the pas-senger tunnel to a nearby freight area to pick up the maps and video-tapes, and hurried out the door to the limousine pickup area to meet our car. It was nowhere in sight. It was the end of New York's rush hour, but the airport was teeming with vacationers returning from the long weekend. Traffic congestion promised to be fierce, Levy and I both knew, having lived and worked in Manhattan for many years before going to Washington. Feeling panic, I ran over to a pay phone to call our USIA New York office.

"A car is supposed to pick me up at LaGuardia, but it's not here," I said breathlessly.

"There's been a snafu," said the USIA dispatcher. He put me on hold. Seconds later he came back on.

"The driver's on the Grand Central Parkway on his way into town with Mr. Gerson."

I was furious with Gerson. Precious time was wasting and we had to move fast. The UN session was slated to begin in an hour. Levy and I collected our boxes and carted them around the corner to the taxi stand, which was at least twenty deep with people waiting in line for cabs. "This won't work," I said. Levy reached for his wallet. He flipped it open, flashing his honorary Lackawanna County, Pennsylvania, sheriff's badge. "Let's go!" he exclaimed. "Emergency, State Department! Emergency, State Department!" Levy bellowed, as we elbowed our way past intimidated people to the front of the line and piled into a taxi-van with ample luggage space.

Traffic was heavy. We were already running late but had to make an unscheduled stop at the U.S. Mission on the corner of 45th Street and First Avenue to drop off our visuals for the press conference. The USIA driver was to have done this for us. Because we were not in an official government vehicle, we were not permitted entry into the UN compound. Instead, our cab had to circle the block to the visitor's entrance, much farther away, wasting more valuable time. We got inside at 10:50 A.M., and ran the equivalent of two city blocks to the escalator to head up to the Security Council area. Levy clutched the videotape bag to his chest with both hands, like a fullback breaking through the line of scrimmage. I was shocked to see Soviet Ambassador Oleg Troyanovsky on the step behind me, on his way to the Security Council.

Mike Messinger was waiting at the top of the escalator. He took the master tape and hustled off to the UN television control room, where he handed it to UN engineer Chuck Rini. On instructions from Messinger, Rini had already unplugged all outgoing video lines from his tape machine to make certain that nothing from the tape was inadvertently fed to the TV networks before the Security Council session began. Rini dubbed the three-quarter-inch master tape onto a one-inch video, which would be used for playback during the session. He then cued up the tape to its starting position and plugged in the video output cables to feed the tape to all the TV networks, both domestic and international.

Inside the Security Council chamber, Levy and I inspected the placement of the TV monitors. There we found Gerson, grinning sheepishly at us from the corner of the room. "You ripped off my car, you moron," I said. "I'm sorry," he replied meekly. "I didn't realize it was your car until it was too late." There was work to be done and I couldn't waste time with Gerson. At 10:55, five minutes before the scheduled start of the Security Council session, I inspected the monitor that was placed directly behind Troyanovsky's position at the round conference table and verified that transcripts of our videotape had been provided to each of the six UN translators. The meeting was finally called to order at 12:10, more than an hour late. Kirkpatrick began her now historic, albeit misleading, speech at 12:21.

In his TV address the night before, President Reagan had roundly condemned the Soviets for intentionally shooting down a civilian airliner. "There is no way a pilot could mistake this [Boeing 747] for anything other than a civilian airliner." Reagan also claimed it was "a clear night with a half-moon," although actually there was less than a half-moon, and in the area of southern Sakhalin Island, where the plane was shot down, there was a low overcast, and scattered medium and high clouds.[12] Early morning frontal weather had placed several Soviet airfields in the area below operational weather minimums. But our good press rolled on, even from the *New York Times,* which said, "What has been so admirable about President Reagan's performance so far is his insistence on arguing from the evidence and tailoring his actions to the problems at issue."[13] The Soviet government had reacted to Reagan's speech by calling him an "ignoramus."

Kirkpatrick would reinforce Reagan's theme in her Security Council speech, claiming the videotape would "spread the evidence" of the Soviet atrocity. "Nothing was cut from this tape," said Kirkpatrick, as she began her introduction to the video. "Contrary to Soviet statements, there is no indication whatsoever that the interceptor pilot made any attempt either to communicate with the airliner or to signal it for it to land in accordance with accepted international practice." There had been no wavering from the administration's position since the preceding Thursday morning, when an angry and emotional George Shultz had gone on television to inform the world of the tragedy. Shultz said he was in possession of evidence suggesting that a Soviet fighter had gotten close enough to make visual contact with his target and said that it was a passenger plane. Shultz claimed there was no evidence that Soviet fighters had attempted to warn the aircraft or had tried to force it to land before shooting it down. "There was apparently no ability to communicate between the two aircraft," Shultz claimed. He said the Soviet plane was in a position "where it had visual contact with the [Korean] aircraft, so that with the eye, you could inspect the aircraft and see what it was you were looking at. . . . I can't imagine any political motivation for shooting down an unarmed airliner," he concluded. Other key U.S. officials echoed the same line in follow-up talks with the media. The Soviets had knowingly shot down a civilian passenger airliner and had killed everyone aboard in cold blood. We were all unwitting participants in the U.S. government's disinformation campaign of the KE-007 tragedy.

"Perhaps the most shocking fact learned from the transcript," Kirkpatrick continued in her Security Council speech, "is that at no point did the pilots raise the question of the identity of the target aircraft." Another whopper, as we know now. She did at least acknowledge that the Soviet attack pilot had said that "the target isn't responding to I.F.F.," the international military request to identify friend or foe. Kirkpatrick claimed the Korean airliner could not hear the military command, since it was on a civilian radio frequency. "At a distance of two kilometers, under conditions prevailing at that time, it was easily possible to identify a 747 passenger airliner." She concluded her introduction by saying that only the Soviet people had still not heard about this attack on KE-007. The tape was then played.

The crowd in the standing-room-only chamber hushed and gazed intently at the TV monitors to watch the horror unfold. The restrained voices of the Soviet pilots could be heard above the heavy static as they narrated the final terrible moments of KE-007. Soviet UN delegate Troyanovsky refused to turn around to look at the monitor directly behind him and stared defiantly ahead. He twirled the wire on his translation headset, his face twisted in a frozen grimace. Troyanovsky looked in every way the perfect heavy—a jowly, arrogant, unapologetic Soviet bureaucrat—right out front for everyone to see and loathe. In photos carried around the world, he was pictured staring icily ahead, his back to the TV screen, while the chilling words of the Russian pilot flashed, "The target is destroyed," and he remained expressionless when Kirkpatrick announced her verdict: "Quite simply, [the tape] establishes that the Soviets decided to shoot down a civilian airliner, shot it down, murdering the 269 persons on board, and lied about it."

It was Troyanovsky's turn to speak. He blamed American and Japanese air controllers for not getting the Korean plane back on course, but said little else. His position must have seemed even to him indefensible. Before he had even finished, reporters were streaming from the Security Council and racing over to the U.S. Mission for copies of the video and audiotapes of our presentation, which we had announced would be available. Within the hour, the Soviet government had issued a statement admitting for the first time that its interceptors had shot down the Korean plane, not realizing it was a civilian airliner. It was accompanied by no apology; indeed, it accused America of having used the plane as part of a spy mission.

Armed with information from its Korean task force, USIA personnel at our 206 posts overseas began appearing on local TV and briefing media contacts, key government officials, diplomats, foreign affairs editors, and anyone else in a position of influence who would listen. We used our tape for all that it was worth, and it was worth a great deal.

How successful the U.S. cover-up of what really happened on the night KE-007 was destroyed became readily apparent. Five days after the Security Council session, the State Department announced a revision of the tape transcript that showed that pilot 805 had fired warning cannon bursts near the Korean airliner almost six minutes before he shot it down. At 18:20 GMT, according to the new transcript, Osipovich radioed that he was firing warning shots at the target aircraft. "I am firing cannon bursts," he said. By early October, National Security Agency experts admitted that further analysis of tapes showed that Osipovich flew behind and below KE-007 while firing warning rockets, and proved that neither he nor the Soviet air command realized the intruder was a commercial airliner.[14] Such information was duly reported in the media, but the deed was done. The Kremlin's own propaganda effort would never fully recover from this defeat.

By my calculations, the National Security Agency, with the apparent approval of the State Department and the White House, had deleted at least five critical minutes of conversation between the Russian fighter pilots and their ground controllers from the tape that we presented as evidence in the UN Security Council. In March 1985, the United States admitted that tapes made at military radar facilities in the North Pacific, which had monitored KE-007's flight, had simply been erased.[15] We had been duped. The extent to which we had been duped became clear when the International Civil Aviation Organization, with all the Russian data now in, issued its complete report on the KE-007 disaster on June 14, 1993. The Russian government had kept squirreled away for almost ten years the black box and other information because it showed that KE-007 had obviously not been on a spy mission. Former U.S. officials involved in the cover-up, who insist on anonymity, confirm that monitoring data was withheld from our UN tape. The short-term objective, they say, was to disgrace the Soviet Union before the world and to weaken the new, hard-line militaristic regime of Yuri Andropov. "Although untrue and unfair," said one former official, "it intimidated the Russians, and probably helped to prevent future such incidents and saved lives. We gave them a beating."

The moral of the story is that all governments, including our own, lie when it suits their purposes. The key is to lie first. *Izvestia* correspondent Alexander Shalnev told me that our media show at the United Nations had been the most devastating propaganda blow his country received from the United States during the cold war. "The most important rule in propaganda is to get the first word out on a given subject," said Shalnev. "Ninety percent of the time the person who takes the initiative wins the battle. You guys said the first word about the Korean airliner. And we lost it completely. It was devastating, terribly devastating." KE-007 was a victim of the cold war, and it proved this war could be very real and could lead to human casualties. Another casualty, always war's first, was the truth. The story of KE-007 will be remembered pretty much the way we told it in 1983, not the way it really happened.

When the news came that the Soviets had shot down KE-007, the U.S. Air Force was asked how it would respond should a foreign commercial airliner invade its airspace. The Air Force responded by saying that under no circumstances would the American military shoot down such an aircraft, even were attempts to communicate with it unsuccessful. Planes would be sent to investigate and the intruder aircraft would be escorted to land, said an Air Force spokesman. "It certainly would not be up to the pilot to decide what action to take. That decision would have to be made at the Pentagon or at an even higher level."[16]

On July 3, 1988, in the Persian Gulf, a U.S. Navy warship mistook an Iranian passenger airliner for a military aircraft and blasted it out of the sky with missiles. All 290 persons aboard perished. No American military planes had gone aloft to identify the aircraft, which the Navy said was flying outside civilian air lanes. The Navy could not explain how a wide-body Airbus A300 passenger plane could have been mistaken for a much smaller military fighter. The Navy said its warship the *Vincennes* sent radio beacon warnings to the intruder airliner before it fired its missiles, but received no response. From his vacation retreat at Camp David, President Reagan issued a statement saying the incident was a tragic but "understandable accident," because officers aboard the *Vincennes* thought they were under attack.

On April 14, 1994, in a no-fly zone over the skies of northern Iraq, two U.S. F-15 jet fighters shot down two American Blackhawk helicopters they had mistaken for Iraqi helicopters. The attack was carried out in clear weather and in broad daylight. Twenty-six American military officers were killed. The two American F-15 pilots had circled the helicopters three times and had established visual contact with them. Both jets and helicopters employed electronic identifying devices. The F-15 pilots, who had extensive training on how to recognize enemy aircraft, said they had sent the electronic "friend or foe" signal but had gotten no response. They made no attempt to contact the helicopters by radio. On June 20, 1995, the Air Force captain in charge of radar operation was found not guilty in a court-martial.

On August 10, 1994, an argument between the pilot and co-pilot of a Korean Air jetliner over who should control the wheel just as the plane was coming in to land caused their Airbus A300 to crash. The plane had skidded along a rainy airport runway on a Korean resort island. All 160 persons aboard were evacuated before the plane burst into flames. The pilot and co-pilot were arrested. "Korean flight crews are not very good," said a U.S. pilot.

↔ **5** ↔

Casting Wide the Worldnet

THE STUNNING IMPACT OUR KE-007 VIDEOTAPE HAD AT THE UNITED Nations showed how dramatically television could manipulate world opinion. It was clear to all of us that it would henceforth influence the way in which America conducted its foreign affairs. Diplomacy would be played out on international television. We began to look hard at how satellite technology could expand the possibilities and extend our range.

Before long, high-powered direct broadcast satellites (DBS) would transmit to receivers the size of a pizza pan, affixed inconspicuously to window boxes, for example. Such technology was rapidly coming of age, and both the United States and Russia knew that soon video signals from the West would be lobbed over the Iron Curtain into Soviet living rooms. *New York Times* columnist James Reston wrote in an op-ed piece in 1983: "There is no way that the Soviet Union can stop the flow of acts or ideas out of . . . the broadcasting stations of the U.S. . . . We are probably only at the beginning of this struggle between political tyranny and modern technology."[1]

Reagan thought television pictures of Americana would have lasting impact on people behind the Iron Curtain. On a helicopter trip in southern Illinois, Reagan looked down at an affluent suburban area. "Look down there," he remarked to his news secretary, Larry Speakes. "I wish every Soviet citizen could see this. That's America. Every house has a car, every house has a swimming pool. If we could just get the Russian people to see this type of thing."[2]

Western Europe, which had been our primary target area, was moving quickly toward transmitting television, using cable systems. We liked the idea of programming via cable because it meant there would be multiple channels looking for free material, material we would be only too happy to provide. Our embassy personnel abroad, particularly those posted in the more advanced media markets, were simply not trained to place our programs on television. Satellites meant that we could do it directly from Washington. By 1983, cable programming reached more than 25 million homes in Western Europe.[3] Research predicted an explosive growth for cable TV in Europe by mid-decade. Cable systems would receive distant signals via satellite and transmit them directly into the homes of subscribers. It seemed likely that cable growth would be fueled by pay-TV movie channels, and that the USIA could go along for the ride.

Reagan Administration officials continued to feel their policies were being distorted by the European media, and that a special effort needed to be mounted to offset this.[4] Wick was particularly annoyed with the extensive coverage the Soviet Union was getting in the world media, evidence of which he read daily in the Central Intelligence Agency's Foreign Broadcast Information Service (FBIS) summaries. "The FBIS reports are voluminous," wrote Wick in a 1983 memo. "I think we should have a major effort to suggest that State and/or the White House grind out information to the world every time a Soviet defector leaves, there is a crop failure, or whatever daily intelligence we can get just as *Pravda* and Tass are parading all of our warts and/or distorting our beauty into warts. The least we can do is try to find out where their warts are and make a pictorial presentation around the world."[5] What he had in mind was satellite television, a massive infusion of information via TV satellites. It was up to us to figure out a way to make a hidebound bureaucracy fulfill Wick's vision.

From a technical standpoint, a worldwide television program service was not a difficult proposition. There were, however, serious financial and political considerations. Satellites were already in place over the Atlantic and ready to transmit our programs, but using them at a rate Wick wanted and paying retail rates would be too costly. We had to come up with a cost-effective way to make it work. On the political side, the vast majority of diplomats at our embassies were too self-preserving to appreciate the prospect of policy-related material from Washington going over their heads and direct to local government and media contacts. Finally, there was also concern within the USIA that a burgeoning television operation would siphon money off from the big-ticket programs, such as the Voice of America and the educational and cultural exchange programs.

Getting a TV signal into one of our embassies in Europe was much like placing an overseas telephone call. To reach the other party, one went through the local communications carriers (usually the PTT or post office) of each European country. They exacted costly "down-link" fees to take the signal from the international Atlantic satellites into their large receiver dishes. From there, the signal needed to be transmitted to our embassies via a land cable or microwave relay. Each country charged its own down-link fee, and this meant costs would quickly escalate, since we envisioned having hundreds of satellite locations broadcasting programs around the clock.

We were fortunate that by 1983 a new and powerful regional satellite was to be poised over Europe, owned and operated jointly by several Western European countries. Soon after I came aboard as USIA's TV director in October 1982, I visited with officials throughout Europe, and went home convinced that we could strike an affordable deal with them. (From November 3 through 20, 1982, I visited London, Geneva, Rome, Vienna, Munich, Wiesbaden, Hamburg, Cologne, Frankfurt, Brussels, and Oslo.) From the European Communications Satellite (ECS), a signal could be received by using a relatively small backyard dish that could be placed right on our embassy grounds. What especially interested me was that the Western European countries that owned and operated this satellite were also using it to pump out quality programs, and these were being picked up by a growing number of European cable systems and transmitted directly into people's homes. Each country was assigned a channel, called a transponder, on the satellite. Because satellites don't distinguish borders, French or Italian or Belgian programs could be picked up throughout Europe. If we could gain access to a transponder on that satellite, our programs would reach not just our embassies, but cable subscribers throughout Europe. Within a year, a second ECS satellite was to be launched, and it would be trained on Eastern Europe and the Soviet Union.

Nothing would happen, of course, if we failed to get the cooperation of our foreign service officers in the field. An uncooperative bureaucracy could certainly kill the plan, or at the very least drag out interminably its realization. As a follow-up on my European trip in the fall of 1982, I sent my top career foreign service officer, Stephen Monblatt, to a number of European cities to explain to nervous embassy officers what we were up to, and to convince them that the new system would provide them with an invaluable new communications tool. Monblatt was a true believer and was convinced television would assist U.S. diplomats abroad in furthering their policy objectives. As a foreign service officer himself, he was the right point person.

What should we call this new international TV network? Monblatt, my deputy Richard Levy, and I brainstormed. Levy suggested "Omnicon." "It means we're all over the place," he said.

"Sounds too much like a conglomerate," said Monblatt. "We should have regional networks, like Afro-Net—'"

"That's a hair spray," Levy remarked, in all seriousness. "What about 'Eye on America?'"

"Too much like a spy satellite," I replied. "If this is a worldwide network, why not just call it Worldnet?" That's what it would be. Worldnet.

We already had a number of program topics in mind, most of them designed to maintain allied solidarity in the face of the Soviet aggression in Afghanistan and pressure on Poland. We also wanted to project images showing American commitment both to allied defenses and to a process of consultation among NATO countries, and play up the military strength of the Warsaw Pact nations in order to drive home the necessity that even the smallest NATO countries contribute to its defense program. It was critical that the United States not appear to be advocating arms control by pushing NATO defenses. We needed to show that an adequate deterrent and strengthened allied security would make détente possible and therefore provide continuing evidence of our peaceful intentions, stressing American participation in negotiations in Geneva and in other arms control initiatives.

We wanted especially to reach those born after World War II—the younger "successor generation" of European movers and shakers—for they didn't share the previous generation's special bond with the United States, a bond formed by a common victory over a Nazi enemy. This was a generation that had not lived through the rebuilding of Western Europe under the Marshall Plan.

Our public opinion research indicated that many Western Europeans felt that NATO was essential to meeting the Soviet challenge as a unified military group, but that there was little enthusiasm for undertaking security initiatives, especially if they came at the expense of social services. The European public was still opposed to the deployment of the new Cruise and Pershing nuclear weapons on their soil, even though their leaders had endorsed the concept at the Williamsburg Economic Summit. Our job was to turn this around. Europeans were most concerned by heightened superpower tensions, the possibility the Soviets might cut Western access to Middle East oil, and the possible Soviet invasion of Poland, but they also didn't want NATO to overreact.[6] Our TV initiative would fit in nicely with Reagan's desire to engage more vigorously in a peaceful "competition of ideas and values with the Soviet Union," and not with "bombs and rockets."[7] The Reagan Administration felt more strongly than ever that the time was ripe to show the U.S. commitment to Europe, and to use the medium of television to help improve relations between America and its allies.

Through his National Security Council, the president directed the USIA to conduct a vigorous campaign to project a positive image of America abroad. The public relations component that grew out of this was called "Project Truth," an all-American, flag-waving, anti-Communist effort to carry on the war of ideas with the Soviets. Well-organized demonstrations were being held throughout Western Europe protesting American plans to beef up NATO nuclear forces on the Continent. Project Truth was to explain American objectives to European allies and to strike back at Soviet propaganda. Its television component, however, was flimsy—conceived by Reagan hardliners who had little understanding of how to manipulate the international media to achieve their objectives. Their plan was only to acquire and distribute a Canadian film entitled *The KGB in North America* and an Italian show called "Soviet Military Power." And the lone USIA news and feature print service available was called "Dateline: U.S.A.—What's Good about America." A monthly "propaganda alert" was put into place to combat Soviet disinformation, and regional themes were identified. The task before United States information specialists was formidable, and Project Truth, with a budget of $65 million, would not be up to it, particularly if a wire service called "What's Good about America" was the best it could come up with. We believed our satellite television programs would be far more effective, and shortly after the United States invaded the Caribbean island of Grenada on October 25, 1983, only a month and a half after the KE-007 airliner disaster, we had a chance to find out.

Early in his term President Reagan had warned the Organization of American States (OAS) that the Soviets were attempting to destabilize the security of Caribbean nations, including the former British colony of Grenada, a picturesque island 90 miles north of the Latin American mainland. The Organization of Eastern Caribbean Nations had requested the United States to intervene to prevent the Soviet, Cuban-dominated government that was emerging in Grenada from terrorizing the general area.[8] They pointed out that since 1980 the number of Soviet and Cuban military "advisers" in Grenada had been growing rapidly, and that an airfield that would facilitate Communist military activities expansion throughout the Caribbean and Latin America was under construction. Civil war broke out on Grenada in early October 1983, raising fears about the thousand Americans there, about half of whom were students at the St. Georges University Medical School. Reagan sent in the Marines to evacuate the students and to restore a democratic regime on Grenada.

In their effort to rally support for the invasion, American officials had not disclosed that the military regime in Grenada had offered to allow the United States to evacuate the students. Having suffered through the Vietnam War era and failed miserably to rescue American hostages in Iran a few years earlier, the Pentagon had to show that it still knew how to fight and win. The enemy would be mostly Cuban construction workers in Grenada. The American students were quickly rescued and began arriving back in the United States on the afternoon of October 27, suntanned and in shorts, carrying guitars and tennis racquets.[9] One of the students, in full view of news cameras, strode down the airliner ramp, then got down on hands and knees to kiss the tarmac.

It soon became clear that the rest of the world didn't see the Grenada invasion the same way as the United States. Prime Minister Margaret Thatcher was furious that we hadn't tried applying economic sanctions before launching a full-scale military operation. She had telephoned Reagan before the invasion to dissuade him from taking such action, claiming British lives would be endangered by U.S. military intervention. The United States was being roundly criticized not just in the British press but throughout the rest of Europe and in Latin America.[10] The Kremlin condemned the "bloody" U.S. aggression against such a small and defenseless neighbor, and set about to use the incident to discourage Western European countries from fulfilling their promise to deploy U.S. medium-range missiles.

A Pentagon-imposed news blackout made it difficult for anyone to get the complete story. It was not reported that the Marines had stormed the Soviet Embassy in Grenada, killed several civilians, and confiscated records, including films. By official count, there were 19 American casualties; 71 Cuban construction workers; and 110 Grenadian soldiers.[11] Also unreported were some of the spoils of war: hundreds of canisters of Soviet and Cuban films that were confiscated and secretly transferred to a military base warehouse in the Washington, D.C., area. Our film acquisition department was asked to review its contents. Foreign service officer David Seal was dispatched to bring back the haul from the military warehouse. Before he left he was given some words of caution from Robert Earle, an assistant to Charles Wick.

"Stop your van in front of the Soviet Embassy and kick those cans out the back door," Earle advised. Seal thought otherwise. He picked the canisters up, drove back to our television studios, and lugged them down to a basement storage area, where he proceeded to pry open the containers. Several held Soviet and Cuban passports, and others films on terrorist training, sabotage, and how to make explosives. Film narration was in Spanish and done by announcers with Cuban accents. There was also microfilm showing Soviet missile designs, and the operation of Soviet missile batteries. Even though disclosure of what we found would have bolstered the U.S. case for invading Grenada, we decided it would be better not to break silence, because doing so would have raised questions about how the canisters were obtained in the first place. The boxes were resealed.

The drumbeat of world criticism over the American invasion of Grenada continued steadily. Wick was passing through London at the time and was stunned by the hostile reaction we were getting from our European allies. He felt the time had come to see if we couldn't turn things around with a smart television initiative, and directed me to set up a media teleconference with participants in the United States, the Caribbean, and Europe. I sent USIA producer Tom Mullins to Barbados, which is near Grenada, to coordinate our first Worldnet telecast from there. Two East Caribbean prime ministers, Tom Adams of Barbados and John Compton of St. Lucia, were to be interviewed via satellite. In New York, Ambassador Kirkpatrick would be broadcast live from the United Nations, and in our Washington studio two State Department officials, Craig Johnson and James Michael, were on hand to present the American point of view. We arranged satellite feeds into our embassies in Bonn, London, The Hague, Rome, and Brussels, where our public affairs officers hurriedly sent out invitations to a bewildered press corps for the November 3, 1983, event. Reporters tramped into our European embassies with their notebooks and TV cameras.

Our program used the distinguished *Christian Science Monitor* Washington correspondent, Harry Ellis, as our anchorman. At 9:50 in the morning, executive producer Hugh Foster gave the cue to start the one-hour program, and as it progressed we knew we had a winner. Our embassies in Europe were packed with hundreds of journalists watching the program on large projector TV monitors. With great dignity, prime ministers Compton and Adams responded to questions from journalists overseas and talked in detail about the flow of Communists into the East Caribbean—Cubans, Bulgarians, Czechs, East Germans, North Koreans—all heavily armed. Compton recounted how he had warned Washington that there was no army in the Caribbean—just policemen, about five hundred of them. "We need help desperately before this whole area goes up in flames," he said he had told Washington. It was all very convincing. Wick leaned over to me in the TV control room and whispered, "Al, we're on a roll. Keep that satellite up." We extended the time an additional hour.

Jeane Kirkpatrick was, as usual, tough and glib. She

didn't wilt or give an inch. From Bonn, a German reporter asked her how the American invasion of Grenada was any different than the Soviet invasion of Afghanistan. "That's a really outrageous question," she retorted, proceeding to spell out the difference between the rescue of students and the killing of innocent peasants by Soviet troops in Afghanistan. She reminded participants in Europe that in World War II "a good many governments and peoples were rescued from tyranny by force," a comment that must have had a telling impact on German journalists. Another reporter wanted to know how the United States thought it could justify the invasion of Grenada under international law. Kirkpatrick responded that fear for the safety of the thousand Americans on the island was justified. "We have not put the whole Iranian hostage situation behind us yet," she responded. "The memory is still vivid and we were very deeply concerned about those Americans."

The program received major media coverage throughout Western Europe. The British Independent Television Network carried eleven minutes of what the news commentator called "an experimental broadcast" from America on its half-hour prime-time news that evening. Large segments appeared on other TV news broadcasts throughout Europe, and the program was headlined in newspapers across the Continent. In addition to the eleven-minute segment on Britain's Independent Television's 7:00 P.M. news, there was a Worldnet story on the BBC's main evening TV news, a lead editorial in the *Times* of London, a front-page story in the London *Daily Telegraph*, news clips on several German and Dutch TV news broadcasts, and newspaper articles in Belgium, West Germany, the Netherlands, Denmark, and Italy. "We could never have afforded to buy that time," Wick told a reporter.[12]

What the broadcast had done was afford TV and print journalists the opportunity to ask questions themselves, then to use the information in their own stories. Interactive TV, which is essentially what this was, meant we weren't talking *at* people, we were discussing issues *with* them in a no-holds-barred format. But we also retained a great deal of control, choosing when these sessions would take place, who would be invited into our embassies to ask questions, and who would answer them. Criticism of the Grenada invasion evaporated overnight. An even bigger surprise was that State Department officials gave Worldnet full credit. We had arrived.

The Communist government in Poland was nonplussed. The Worldnet program would later be featured in the Warsaw newspaper *Poznan Daily Gazeta,* which called Worldnet a "gigantic propaganda machine." The Grenada broadcast, it said, "wildly succeeded in brainwashing the public on the airwaves and in hundreds of publications. Front-page headlines and follow-ups in Western Europe softened a wave of criticism to the Grenada invasion."[13] Our Moscow embassy told us that Soviet officials privately expressed their fear that the TV satellite service would be global in a few years and would include Russia. The Brussels newsletter *Western World* stated in a November 19, 1983, editorial: "In the long run, this communication link-up between Western Europe and the U.S. may prove more important to the Alliance than the 'coupling' of the defense of two continents by stationing of the American Pershing II and Cruise missiles in Europe." In an awards speech Reagan said the Grenada operation proved that the American military was "now standing tall" after the dark post-Vietnam days. "Our days of weakness are over," he maintained proudly as he awarded hundreds of Bronze Stars and other decorations.

The Worldnet television operation was establishing itself as a major news source in Europe. Following our satellite telepress conference on the Grenada invasion, we began producing two Worldnet programs each week for the five U.S. embassies in Europe at which we had satellite facilities. In the comfort of American embassies, the best local journalists from the TV, radio, and print media could sip good wine, light up cigars and Marlboros (all courtesy of the embassy), and chat over live TV satellite with top policymakers in Washington. One week, Kenneth Adelman, director of the U.S. Arms Control and Disarmament Agency, discussed upcoming U.S.-Soviet talks in Geneva. A few days later Undersecretary Eagleburger answered questions about U.S.-Soviet relations. Two days after that, Secretary of Commerce Malcolm Baldridge chatted with journalists about America's trade relations with Europe. The *Wall Street Journal,* in a lead editorial, announced that it was dazzled by the technology:

> We recently attended press conferences held in Washington by National Security Adviser Robert McFarlane and (nuclear arms) negotiator Edward Rowny. Big deal? Yup. We

were in Brussels at the time. This electronic magic is part of a new U.S. shot at getting its policies better understood abroad. The U.S. Information Agency has gone high-tech to allow European journalists to reach out and touch U.S. officials.[14]

European TV satellite dish vendors would soon be displaying live feeds of Worldnet at shopping malls to dazzle potential customers.

But a core of resistance to Worldnet was steadily hardening within our embassies in Western Europe. To a suspicious bureaucracy that disliked change above all else, Worldnet was no easy sell. For starters, participating in a program was work. Scores of guests had to be invited, and organizing involved several days of advance planning that had to be done by staffers who had other assignments. It was also a strain on a post's somewhat limited entertainment, or "representational," allowance, because broadcasts came around the lunch hour in Europe, and media representatives expected to be fed. The real cause for the resistance was the fear that new communications technologies would render the function of diplomats assigned abroad obsolete. Since it was now possible for officials to speak directly to audiences anywhere in the world, why did America need such a large cadre of diplomats abroad?

London was probably our most popular foreign location for Worldnet during its formative period, and Wick expected the embassy there to participate in every program. Sig Cohen, a USIA public affairs officer in London, made the mistake of turning down a request for the embassy post to participate in a program with Commerce Secretary Malcolm Baldridge, who had visited London only a week before.

"I don't want to drag people in to the embassy to see the Commerce Secretary on satellite TV," Cohen complained to associates. "Administration spokesmen come through London like water." He then sent a cable to Washington saying London would be too busy to take part in the Baldridge program. "Where's London?" Wick asked, as he was going over the program lineup. "The post said Baldridge was just there last week and it wants to pass," I replied. "They'd have to drag people in."

"Who's in London?" Wick bellowed. He was not happy. "Sig Cohen," I replied. Cohen's job as information officer at the London embassy entailed liaison with the international media. He also had responsibility for Worldnet. "Well, I want him out of there," Wick shot back, as he grabbed the phone to call London. I remained in the room as he read the riot act to Cohen's boss, chief London public affairs officer Phil Arnold.

Cohen went home that evening and told his wife to call the packers. They were going back to Washington. Actually, Wick had no intention of firing Cohen. He just wanted to teach him a lesson and warn others. Cohen was suspended for five days. London participated in the Baldrige program. Several years later Cohen admitted to me that there was some initial skepticism "as to the value of talking to someone in Washington from a studio." It didn't take long for the word to spread among USIA foreign service officers that opposing Worldnet could be dangerous for one's career, but we were still getting flak from all sides; in particular from skeptical public affairs officers abroad and from U.S.-based European correspondents who saw Worldnet as a problem.

Everyone seemed to feel threatened, and not just USIA personnel. Martin Bell, the BBC's Washington correspondent, was one of the earliest and most vocal critics of Worldnet, which he felt would undermine the role of foreign correspondents in America. If a secretary of state or defense could talk directly with the BBC's anchor in London via satellite, correspondents like Bell would be so much excess baggage. He had, of course, a valid point. Many foreign correspondents also viewed Worldnet as a controlled format, and felt that Washington would set the agenda. Right again. The BBC, in fact, lodged a formal protest and at first declined invitations from our London embassy to participate in programs. We pulled together a meeting in Washington with the disgruntled European correspondents and invited White House press secretary Larry Speakes and State Department spokesman Charles Redman to attend. Redman made clear to the correspondents that the administration understood their concerns and assured them that their access to the secretary of state would not be impeded. Speakes made a similar promise on behalf of President Reagan. To keep the peace, Wick suggested to administration officials that when they did a Worldnet program, they should also hold a news conference for the foreign press corps assigned to Washington. The foreign press got over their jitters. The BBC, like Britain's commercial Independent Television Network

(ITN), began to use Worldnet material on news broadcasts, or "bulletins," as they called them after being scooped by ITN's Worldnet interview with Secretary Shultz, which the BBC boycotted. Neither news organization informed its viewers that the video interviews were being made available from the U.S. government. Said a spokesman for ITN, Norman Rees, "I would not have thought it necessary."[15]

One of the first programs to capture the attention of Europe was called "Astronet," which linked President Reagan in Washington and West German Chancellor Kohl—in Athens that day—with German and American astronauts in the orbiting Spacelab. Journalists in seventeen locations around the world asked them questions during the program, which Reagan called "one heck of a conference call."

The show almost went off without a hitch. At the very end, just as we were signing off, the smiling pudgy face of Gary Coleman, from the sitcom "Different Strokes," suddenly filled the screen. A technician at AT&T had thrown the wrong switch. It was, a German daily proclaimed, "a demonstration bound to startle even a public that has forgotten how to be surprised." *TV Guide* reported, "There were no policy-changing pronouncements . . . but no matter. The medium was the message that day."[16]

Before long, Worldnet began to transmit Reagan's speeches in their entirety to our embassies overseas. Important journalists and VIP guests were invited in to watch the live transmission on a large projection TV screen. One could see an entire speech, unedited and free of media post-speech commentary, instead of brief clips that would later be carried on a news broadcast. The system was not fail-safe. One of the president's speeches to the Veterans of Foreign Wars was fed live via satellite to invited diplomats and press at the U.S. Embassy in New Delhi, India. "The speech went on for about ten minutes or so, then we began to receive 'The Price is Right,'" recalled public affairs officer Jim Magee. "I called TV [in Washington] to tell them. They said, 'We'll look into it,' but it continued for about twenty minutes."[17] The audience in New Delhi started to play along, trying to beat "The Price is Right" contestants. We also started testing the Worldnet system in Latin America, where we linked Henry Kissinger from Washington with audiences at embassies and TV stations in Brazil, Venezuela, Mexico, Costa Rica, and Argentina. The subject was Kissinger's Central American Commission report. We were now able to do programs with multiple simultaneous translations. Surprisingly, the dour George Shultz turned out to cut a surprisingly firm and authoritative figure on TV and became a regular on Worldnet. Each time he did the international TV news conference it was a major media event. European journalists were happy to have access to Reagan's top policymaker. The mass circulation *Algemeen Dagblad* of the Netherlands said that Shultz's performance proved he was "the boulder in the surf."

We trotted out just about every one of the administration heavyweights for Worldnet interviews, including Vice President George Bush, who talked to journalists via satellite in eight European capitals on a program commemorating the thirty-fifth anniversary of NATO. Bush put on a convincing show, usually calling journalists by their first name, which added to the informality and credibility of this satellite event.[18] But our pièce de résistance on NATO was a satellite linkup of fourteen alliance countries. We flew in one of Britain's top TV anchormen, Sandy Gall, of Britain's ITN network, to moderate the two-hour NATO hype, which included live interviews with a number of world leaders. Eleven young Soviet political leaders who visited Washington's Worldnet studio took particular interest in the empty chair to be occupied that evening by Secretary of Defense Weinberger, and gathered closely around it. Iceland's largest daily, *Morgunbladid,* summed up the general reaction of papers all across Europe in its extensive coverage of the Worldnet program. It was the message we sought to convey: "The television program," said *Morgunbladid,* "confirmed once again that NATO is the strongest peace movement that has been established since the end of the Second World War and even further back in history." Cables from our embassies in Europe carrying transcripts of the glowing press coverage flooded into our Washington headquarters. Wick himself recruited the guests to appear on Worldnet, and he made certain their egos were properly massaged so they would return. Right after the program aired, a videocassette and full transcript were sent to the guests, along with a personal thank-you letter from Wick. The following day we sent them what was called a "preliminary media usage summary" plus reaction from our foreign diplomats, and within a week, we provided them with a final media reaction assessment. We usually found them willing to return for another appearance. Our spokespersons became regulars abroad on such news interview programs as "Face à la Presse," "Confrontatie," "Madagascar Matin," and hundreds of others we would soon get to know.

I was frankly astonished by the impact the Worldnet satellite format was having on jaded veteran newsmen, who were so dazzled by the technology that it actually influenced their work. It seems I had underestimated the size of many journalists' egos. They liked sitting back and chatting one-on-one with some of the world's most influential people. It seemed to soften them up. An example of how the foreign media could be influenced involved a program in which Reagan's national security adviser, Robert McFarlane, talked via satellite with newsmen in Bonn, The Hague, Brussels, Madrid, Geneva, and Tokyo. From Bonn, the radio network Westdeutscher Rundfunk-2 carried the McFarlane program. Anchorman Klaus Juergen Haller noted that it was just one day after Ronald Reagan's State of the Union address, and already there was an especially interesting talk in progress with McFarlane. Haller said that he had participated in many press conferences "but never in one like this." Although this was the thirty-eighth program of its kind, he was still amazed that you could see a leading American politician, sitting in a Washington studio, "in color and hear him loud and clear." Haller reported that a colleague had asked McFarlane about the Pershing missile accident in Heilbronn, and that McFarlane had replied, "We share your concern and express our deepest regrets. We still believe that the Pershing system is a very reliable system." Haller's conclusion was that this was "a really good show." Another Bonn participant, Hilde Purwin, correspondent for the newspaper *Neue Ruhr Zeitung,* was also awestruck just by being there. She wrote as her lead, "We were able to admire the latest progress in technology at the U.S. Embassy. Six German journalists were there to ask questions of the U.S. president's national security adviser McFarlane, located in far-off Washington. They saw him on the television screen as clearly as though we were sitting with him in the room, and with the same ease colleagues in The Hague, Madrid, Brussels, and Tokyo asked him questions." Our embassy post in Brussels reported that many journalists remained after the program was over to discuss with officers and embassy colleagues some of the issues it raised. In Tokyo, anchorman Taro Kimura of the national NHK network opened and closed his program with his McFarlane interview from earlier in the day, and it was seen by an estimated 12.3 million viewers in Japan.

It was soon apparent that we had gotten the Soviets' attention. Whenever I made a speech or held a news conference about our television operation, I could usually spot the correspondent from the Soviet news agency Tass in the audience. He followed me all over town. When I was invited to talk at a National Press Club newsmaker breakfast in March 1984, I saw him standing at the back of the room. Not wanting to disappoint him, I said, "The technology for transmitting television to Eastern Europe is here for those who know how to harness it. Our intention is to broadcast television into the Soviet Union." Press attention was mounting, including a page-one story in *Variety*, headlined "Uncle Sam Eyeing Global TV Web."

"Worldnet will not be simply a high-tech program delivery system," I told *Variety*. "It will be a regular full-time TV system. It is the beginning of a regular television service from the USIA." Our plan was to set up five regional networks: Euronet (Europe), Arnet (American Republics—Latin America), Pacnet (Asia and the Pacific), and Afnet (Africa), the latter of which we would produce in English and French.[19] The Russians knew one feature on television was worth a thousand words, and they viewed a concerted effort by the U.S. government to enter international television at the peak of the cold war with great trepidation. "We saw a lot of future in your Worldnet," Tass correspondent Alexander Shalnev told me in 1992. "There was a fear that within a few years this program would be entering the homes of the Soviet people. So we did everything we could to knock it out from the very moment of its existence. We were more concerned about this than about your radio broadcasts."[20]

While our TV operation was garnering praise and attention for administration policies, a major problem was growing: we were running out of money. At retail rates in 1983 we were paying about $21,000 for a one-hour program broadcast to six European embassies.[21] Then, of course, there was that "down-link" fee we had to pay to the local telephone and telegraph companies (the PTTs). The more locations we added to a program, obviously, the greater the cost. We had projected employing some three hundred satellite locations around the world on a 24-hour-a-day schedule, so we had to strike a quick deal for some kind of cost-efficient, permanent arrangement. The only reasonable course of action was to seek permission from the PTTs for direct reception from the satellites by installing our own receiver dishes in our embassies. Obtaining such permission from the local authorities would be tricky, since it would bypass their own equipment and avoid tariffs. Some sort of cooperative venture had to be established. We also needed to get the cooperation of the State Department, which ran our embassies, to put permanent satellite installations on embassy premises. Usually this meant the roof. Since the State Department and other U.S. government agencies, such as the CIA, had eavesdropping gear of their own in those locations, no one was too eager to have local workmen tramping around on embassy rooftops installing satellite dishes. Word would eventually have to come from Reagan himself if anyone was to cooperate with us.

Word came. Wick and I flew to Paris in November 1984 to brief PTT officials from eight Western European countries on our requirements. With us came my top staff satellite engineer, Dr. Robert Rostron. Through the European Space Agency, the PTTs had launched their second satellite in August, this one aimed at Eastern Europe, the Middle East, and the Soviet Union. Here was our chance to get behind the Iron Curtain. Although private satellite dishes were outlawed there, we knew resourceful people would find a way to put them up. Our plan included inviting guests to American embassies and libraries in Eastern Europe to watch our satellite programs, and putting TV sets in embassy windowboxes along the sidewalk so that passersby could watch. A growing number of cable systems in Western Europe were down-linking the first European Communications Satellite (ECS), launched a year earlier, and sending its programs directly into viewers' homes. Should we arrange a cost-effective contract to lease a transponder on the ECS "bird" aimed at Western Europe, our programs would be not only accessible to our embassies, but delivered along with other European television broadcasters directly into the homes of cable TV subscribers throughout the continent.

Rostron and I briefed the Europeans about our satellite requirements, and in the end Wick worked out a co-venture deal by which all the European PTTs would share in a contract with the USIA, administered on their behalf by the French telecommunications agency. We got what we wanted: access to both ECS satellites and an unlimited number of satellite down-links for a flat yearly, and affordable, fee.[22] Secretary of State Shultz passed the word that no one was to impede the construction of satellite dishes on embassy premises. A few months later, Rostron and I visited the huge French satellite transmission center at Berceney, outside Paris. There we decided that we would simultaneously transmit the European programs to Asia and the Pacific via the Indian Ocean satellite, a cost-effective routing.

Our plan was to send out a mixture of news, public affairs shows, and movies on our daily feed—in addition to the interactive press conferences—and thereby establish a full-fledged new American government network service. Wick felt that viewers behind the Iron Curtain would be interested in watching our programs, and it would help cheer them up. "During the Depression when people were selling apples and factories were still and guys were jumping out of windows because they lost everything, people would go to the movies," he said.[23] Wick was ecstatic about the new TV service because he thought it would give people behind the Iron Curtain a contrast to what they had been told to believe. He asked us to put together a briefing for NASA, focusing on ways our new network capability might be shared government-wide. About fifty United States officials, many from intelligence agencies such as the CIA, listened intently as Wick explained his idea. "We could provide you the use of our satellite free of charge," said the ebullient Wick. Eyes began to roll in the heads of intelligence community representatives, who spent much of their time explaining to Congress why billions of dollars were needed for additional spy satellites. The last thing they wanted was a free ride. Wick's generous offer to share free satellite time received a lukewarm reception.

In April 1985 Wick and I traveled to the French Riviera and held a news conference at the Cannes annual international television marketing convention to announce that Worldnet had just begun a daily global TV satellite service. With some twenty French and American security police and assorted aides in tow, Wick swept unannounced into the Soviet radio/television exhibition booth. "Hi," he said, glad-handing everyone. "I'm Charlie Wick, U.S. Information Agency." The Russians manning the booth were stunned. "Come on, let's take some pictures," Wick said to press photographers, grabbing the Russians by the arms and getting them to line up and face press cameras.

Within a couple of weeks, Hungarian state television had agreed to receive a two-week test of Worldnet, making it the first Eastern European nation to sign on. That fall, we did our first full-blown two-way video teleconference with the Eastern bloc, with President Reagan's Hollywood cardiologist, Dr. Eliot Corday, chairing a panel of leading American heart specialists in a discussion with their Eastern Europe Communist counterparts. The success of the program in Bucharest and Budapest ended with backslaps, hugs, and the delights of peach brandy.

By 1985 Worldnet had become Ronald Reagan's chief foreign public opinion weapon. It was, as the *Washington Post* described it in a page-one story, "the jewel in the crown" of the Reagan Administration's overseas "propaganda" effort.[24] The reaction from Soviet leaders was even more flattering. The general secretary of the Soviet Communist party, Konstantin Chernenko, warned that the West was launching "an information-propaganda intervention against us." He added, "We must increase our persuasiveness, timeliness, attractiveness, and interest of our materials intended for foreign audiences, effectively revealing the concrete substance of our peace-loving international policies."[25]

When the Soviets began to build their powerful domestic television network in the 1960s, they had intended at first to develop the capability to transmit directly into small, inexpensive satellite dishes. The idea was dropped when it was understood that if Soviet citizens could receive USSR programs on a small satellite dish, they would also be able to receive programs from other countries. The Soviets did not pick up television coverage of the 1960 Olympic Games in Italy because they were concerned about the effect seeing well-dressed spectators in the stands would have on their people. Programs were therefore transmitted to a fixed government receiving station, and then sent terrestrially to individual households, to provide total control over what viewers could see.[26] In the mid-1970s, Soviet authorities submitted documents to the United Nations, proposing that a country should have the right to destroy satellites being used to transmit programs into another country whose government may not want them. "Every state has the right to take whatever countermeasures are available to it, not only on its own territory, but in space," said the Soviet Union.[27] But the Kremlin was in a bind. The Worldnet programs denounced by Chernenko were being carried by the International Telecommunications Satellite organization, known as Intelsat, which was formed in 1964 and designed to carry the telephone, data, and television traffic of countries around the world. If a Soviet missile destroyed such satellites, with their telecommunications traffic from the world's most highly industrialized nations, it most certainly would have been considered an act of war.

Conceived and fostered by the United States, Intelsat membership roll call voting rights are based on the share of international satellite usage. America, the largest user, currently holds 19 percent ownership, with the other 135 nations sharing the rest. But from the outset, even the smallest shareholder enjoyed sizeable profits from this enterprise. Had it joined up, the Soviet Union would have held only a one percent share, so it set up its own organization, Intersputnik, with other founding member nations: Bulgaria, Czechoslovakia, Cuba, East Germany, Hungary, Poland, and Romania. More than thirty countries used the facilities. Whereas the Intelsat consortium owned its satellites, the Soviet Union owned all Intersputnik satellites, and leased them to member Communist nations.[28] While Intelsat satellites covered the lucrative heavy communications routes of the United States, Europe, and Asia, and produced excellent revenue for member nations, Intersputnik served low-density routes and traded in rubles. Intersputnik's major customer was the Intervision News Exchange. The News Exchange, headquartered in Prague, comprised the Communist Warsaw Pact countries and provided a handy mechanism by which the Soviet Union could control news distribution to Eastern Europe, since the Kremlin owned the satellites on which program material was transmitted.[29] Employing Intersputnik's array of satellites, the Kremlin's International Service broadcast TV programs that could be picked up practically anywhere on Earth and gave the USSR the power to cast wide its own net of disinformation.

↔ 6 ↔

Brilliant Pebbles, Ethnic Guns, and Baby Parts

HERBERT ROMERSTEIN'S JOB WAS KEEPING THE SOVIET UNION HONest by publicly denouncing its officials every time they lied. He was a very busy guy. People who wanted to verify the authenticity of documents they suspected might be Soviet forgeries usually turned to Herb, who would carefully examine each page with the eye of a diamond appraiser. Herb was a born-again Communist basher. A former member of Communist Youth, he had later become disillusioned and repented by spending sixteen years on Capitol Hill as chief investigator for the House Un-American Activities Committee. He joined the USIA in 1982 to expose Soviet disinformation. The *Washington Post* asked Romerstein to authenticate a letter it suspected was a Soviet forgery. "That's a fake," he asserted without hesitation. The letter was signed "Herbert Romerstein, U.S. Information Agency."[1]

      The art of forgery had become so refined in the Soviet Union's propaganda hierarchy that forgers had their very own department within the KGB. Known as "Service A" in the KGB's First

Directorate, it was a high-class cut-and-paste operation: cut off the top of a White House letterhead and the bottom with the president's signature, then paste them on a forged letter and photocopy it (a little out of focus and reduced in size, if you please, so as to make forensic analysis difficult), and you've got an authentic-looking document that's hard to bust. Forging something was a lot harder when documents were written in pen and ink. Word processors and copying machines had made life a lot easier for KGB forgers. Herb's response was to put special markings on important U.S. documents. By doing so he exposed one forgery after another—from an alleged White House memo about American plans to nuke the Soviet Union to an alleged plot to assassinate Indian president Rajiv Ghandi.

Nothing pleased Romerstein more than debunking the assertions of top Soviet propagandists in face-to-face confrontations. One day, he noticed a letter in a newspaper from a reader who claimed Ronald Reagan was lifting quotes from an old Nazi propaganda booklet and using them to slam the Soviets. The slogan had accused the Soviets of believing that "Promises are like piecrusts—they are meant to be broken." Reagan cribbing Nazi propaganda? The accusation deeply upset Romerstein. He felt the letter could embarrass the country. "The Soviets will pick this up," he warned his deputy, Todd Leventhal. Leventhal thought this was silly. "Who's gonna notice that?" he asked. "The Soviets will notice it and they'll use it," replied Romerstein, who proceeded to lecture Leventhal on the importance of being finicky. "You have to check every minute detail." Herb could pick up on the smallest issue and see something everyone else missed.[2]

He vaguely remembered a Lenin quote that involved something about breaking promises. He asked Leventhal to look it up in Lenin's collected works at the Library of Congress. Leventhal went to the Library of Congress and, sure enough, found the quotation in a large volume of Lenin's writings. And, sure enough, a couple of weeks later, Soviet spokesmen started blasting Reagan for using Nazi quotes about piecrusts and broken promises. An item was run by the Soviet news agency Novosti, which consisted of a special department of about forty employees on assignment from the KGB to produce disinformation.[3] Romerstein was scheduled to meet Novosti's chief editor, Valentin Falin, during a forthcoming visit to Moscow to discuss issues involving a broad range of information disputes dividing the two countries. Romerstein's style was to come out swinging. And he was always prepared. Falin was an astute intellectual and a complex apparatchik with a piercing gaze who had worked his way up in the Soviet bureaucracy to become one of its top propagandists. A hard-liner who prospered under Leonid Brezhnev, he was still a force to be reckoned with.

"You insulted us last week, insulted our president," said Romerstein, wagging his finger at Falin. "You claim we are using Nazi propaganda, and we are insulted by this."

Falin was prepared. He had a notebook filled with nearly thirty pages of points he wanted to make. He thumbed through his notebook and stopped at a tabbed page.[4]

"Our researchers have found that the 'piecrust' quote was in fact based on Nazi propaganda," he said confidently. "The quotation was drawn from a Goebbels propaganda booklet, *The Ten Commandments of Lenin,* published during the Second World War. We know of no other source."

"You're wrong," Romerstein replied, opening up the volume of Lenin's works that Leventhal had checked out for him and spreading it on the table. "Lenin made the remark, not Hitler. Lenin said, 'As the British saying goes, promises are like piecrusts—they are meant to be broken.' This quote was taken verbatim from this compilation of statements by Lenin, published by a Soviet publishing house in Moscow, and a Nazi propaganda booklet was never utilized by the U.S. for this quote."

Falin was too taken aback to respond. A flustered aide popped up. "Let me explain what Comrade Lenin meant," he stammered.

"It doesn't matter what Comrade Lenin meant," Romerstein interrupted. "The question is, did Lenin say it or not?" The Soviet team was silent. After the meeting, an aide to Falin approached Romerstein and admitted the Soviets were dumbfounded because Falin was one of their Lenin experts. "We were trumped," said the embarrassed aide.[5]

Romerstein had proved another point. That it paid to get worked up over a quote about piecrust. By tracking down the source, Romerstein had ended the Soviet attempt to capitalize on a figure of speech and engage in disinformation. Such attempts seemed like pedantry, but they could add up to trouble. Ladislav Bittman, former deputy chief of the disinformation department of the Czechoslovak secret service, compared disinformation with poison: "One drop may not be a problem," he said, "but together a dose could be fatal." The Soviets would keep up a steady drumbeat during the entirety of Reagan's presidency. Reagan's public comments, especially those about Lenin, were always carefully scrutinized by no less than the Central Committee of the Communist party of the Soviet Union. In a secret 1985 memorandum, the committee instructed the Soviet Embassy in Washington to lodge a strong protest with the State Department over some comments Reagan had made about Lenin. Said the Committee, "During one of his recent statements, Reagan attributed to Lenin plans to seize Eastern Europe, China, Latin America, and the United States. . . . We demand the American administration end such antagonistic attacks against the Soviet Union and the gross falsification of Lenin's works."[6]

The war of words was unending and the stakes were high: to sway world opinion. Soviet leaders were very good at distorting reality, for every single day they needed to convince their own people that they lived in a land of freedom and plenty. Not an easy sell in a country where the average family had to stand in line for nearly three hours a day to buy bare necessities. The Soviets relied on the same approach to convince the outside world that Western democracies were decadent and that the USSR was the only working democracy. One of their favorite tools was *aktivnyye meropriyatiya,* meaning secret operations in support of Soviet goals, which the U.S. government translated as "active measures."

The Soviet disinformation desk divided its activities into three primary categories. "White" propaganda efforts involved overt activities, such as those by Radio Moscow, the Tass and Novosti news agencies, and overseas information offices at Soviet embassies.[7] "Black" propaganda was covert: the KGB, the circulation of forgeries, and the planting of false and embarrassing stories. "Gray" activity involved various front groups, such as the World Peace Council and the World Federation of Trade Unions, which actively demonstrated against the placement of the allied NATO missiles in Western Europe.[8] Members of the gray group included scientists, doctors, journalists, and students, among others. By the mid-1980s the Soviets were spending nearly $3 billion a year on their various disinformation activities, which required the services of more than 70,000 people, according to CIA estimates. But the U.S. was spending more. The combined annual budgets for the USIA and Radio Free Europe/Radio Liberty totaled more than $1 billion annually, while the CIA's yearly disinformation activities were estimated at about $3.5 billion.[9] Meanwhile, Romerstein and Leventhal occupied shoebox-size offices in a dingy federal office building near Capitol Hill crammed with yellowing newspapers and overstuffed, dog-eared file folders. Black and gray disinformation didn't do all the damage. "White" propaganda could also sting. Quoting "legitimate" news sources, state-controlled Soviet media had carried stories that the U.S. military had developed an AIDS weapon targeting only blacks; that America was butchering babies and selling their body parts for medical research; that the FBI murdered Martin Luther King, Jr., and that the CIA had assassinated Swedish prime minister Olaf Palme and Indian prime minister Indira Ghandi. A Soviet disinformation campaign even accused the American government of attempting to kill Pope John Paul II, possibly to counter a USIA-publicized article by American journalist Claire Sterling suggesting that the KGB had engineered the assassination attempt on the pope through a Bulgarian connection. The accusation carried by Soviet media that the United States had attacked the Grand Mosque in Mecca and murdered worshipers led to the sacking of the American Embassy in Islamabad, Pakistan. An American serviceman was killed in the attack. The Soviet Union's successful campaign against U.S. plans to develop a neutron bomb in the late 1970s showed how effective a combined white and gray disinformation program could be. A neutron bomb would kill people, but leave buildings intact. The Soviets' slogan, "Kill the people, save the buildings," spearheaded a campaign that was estimated by the CIA to have cost more than $100 million. Worldwide rallies held during a "week of action" by Communist front groups and media coverage of their activities helped to convince President Jimmy Carter and Western European NATO allies in 1978 to back off from plans to develop the neutron bomb. *Aktivnyye meropriyatiya* could indeed influence public opinion and alter government policies.[10]

American equivalents relied on the same dirty tricks, and had for years. Thomas Jefferson himself once approved a plan to smuggle arms to rebels in Tunisia so that they could overthrow one ruler and replace him with one more cooperative to American interests.[11] Benjamin Franklin, considered by many the father of American disinformation, in an effort to embarrass the British government after the Revolutionary War once planted a newspaper story that American Indians were scalping children who had been "ripped out of their mothers' bellies," and sending their scalps to London to impress the government.[12] During World War I, the American government appealed to the patriotism of citizens with propaganda slogans such as "Make the world safe for democracy," and by calling the conflict "The war to end all wars" (a gross distortion, to say the least)—slogans that became hollow memories. During World War II, because American newsreels were such an effective means of conveying American interests, the government formed and bankrolled the "United Newsreel Company," which culled pro-American story segments from the five major American newsreel organizations and then sold them worldwide. After the war, the UNC continued to distribute commercial newsreels to theaters until the show business weekly *Variety* printed a story blowing the government's cover. After World War II, in an effort to counter Soviet disinformation, the CIA began engaging in disinformation activities of its own to influence the world media. This included setting up book-publishing facilities and financing newspapers and wire services.

In the postwar years, the most flagrant disinformation campaign—a decidedly "black" activity—involved President Allende in Chile. Although the United States was a signatory to the Organization of American States charter, which prohibited one country from interfering in the internal or external affairs of another country, in the 1960s through the early 1970s America did its best to undermine Allende's government, in part because he had decided to establish diplomatic relations with Communist Cuba. In an attempt to swing popular support behind anti-Communist political parties and organizations, the CIA funneled money into commercial TV stations and newspaper wire services that bribed reporters into writing favorable stories about opposition parties. The major Santiago daily *El Mercurio* ran CIA-promoted editorials almost daily.[13] In addition to putting pressure on the media, the CIA paid for posters and signs plastered around the countryside, showing that an Allende victory in the 1970 presidential election would mean Stalinist repression with firing squads and an end to religious freedom and family values. American-subsidized right-wing women's groups and others opposed to Allende weighed in with propaganda scare campaigns.[14] International Telephone and Telegraph was also reported to have offered the CIA a million dollars to keep Allende out of office.[15] The TV station that received CIA payoffs aired USIA-produced film stories showing "pro-democracy" students demonstrating against Allende. The station also carried a USIA program about anti-Castro Cuban exiles in Miami.

Disinformation is a feature of every administration, even those supposedly unsympathetic to it. During the Jimmy Carter presidency, the CIA set up a secret project to pay off European journalists to write favorable stories about U.S. plans to deploy neutron bombs. The CIA later admitted that it regularly indulged in such practices,[16] and a study by Harvard's Kennedy School of Government in October 1984 showed that these efforts had some impact. "It does appear that the combination of public statements by European officials, along with the covert action program, had a marked effect on Western press coverage," concluded the Harvard report, although Carter decided not to deploy the bombs anyway.[17] So long as disinformation worked, it was used, whether white, black, or gray.

By the time of the Reagan Administration, disinformation, particularly as it involved manipulating the foreign media, was thriving. When the U.S.-funded National Endowment for Democracy shuffled some $100,000 to the opposition newspaper La Prensa in Nicaragua, no one was surprised to learn that the paper's coverage became more sympathetic to America's interests.[18] Use of disinformation was even gaining credibility among intellectuals and academics, who formerly would have been quick to condemn its use. The line between "truth" and "black propaganda" was blurred. Stanford University political scientist Angelo M. Codevilla argued that "there is nothing inherently wrong with spreading the truth by black propaganda, and, so long as this is aimed at foreign audiences, there is nothing illegal about it."[19]

The primary reason propaganda worked in foreign countries was because it paid well. Everybody, to put it bluntly, was on the take. During his first year and a half as the leader of the Solidarity labor movement in Communist Poland, Lech Walesa took in more than $1 million from the West, most of it from U.S. trade unions, that he salted away in private bank accounts outside Poland.

KGB operatives also paid handsomely to have stories run in African or Indian publications, stories that the Soviet media then picked up and broadcast to the home front. Bribes to reporters, editors, and publishers usually were made in cash, but sometimes took the form of paid vacations, tuition scholarships, subsidized cars, and duty-free goods. In Bangladesh, the owner of the daily *Sangbad* reportedly became enormously wealthy from his business dealings with the Soviets. His paper ran several articles suggesting American involvement with the assassination of India's Prime Minister Indira Ghandi. Publishers were also bribed not to print stories from Western news services. Articles friendly to Soviet policy views were sometimes written under false names, although using the name of a known local journalist gave the report more credibility.

Bruce Koch, USIA's public affairs officer stationed in Lagos, Nigeria, designed a computer program to track Soviet press disinformation. During a 30-month period, from mid-1985 through the end of 1987, he identified twenty Nigerian and twelve non-Nigerian writers who admitted lending their names to stories distributed by the Novosti news agency. Nigerian writers admitted that they had received "bonuses" for putting their names to ghost-written articles. Koch found that even the larger, more established newspapers were running stories planted by the Soviets. Nuclear disarmament was the most popular Soviet theme. Seventy percent of the stories on this subject, Koch discovered, could be tracked back to Soviet ghost writers. In all, Koch came up with more than 1,250 articles from the Nigerian press that contained disinformation placed by the Soviets. Even pro-American Nigerian journalists were on the take. In 1987, twenty of a total of twenty-eight articles suggesting America was sending toy bombs into Afghanistan to maim children were Soviet-written. So heavy was Soviet influence in the Nigerian press that it was nearly impossible to know how it viewed the outside world. Koch later reflected that even the Nigerian journalists who knew what the Soviets were up to and were not on the take were nonetheless influenced by the disinformation campaign. "The Soviet line dominated the Nigerian media," said Koch, "and hardly anything else was coming from other sources. The honest journalists began to feel that they were not getting the full story from the U.S." Koch said the average person began to feel that the AIDS ethnic weapon was true, and further proof that America was the new colonialist power trying to exploit

Africa, and that any time there was a coup in an African nation, the United States was blamed for it. Koch said that in such an environment, it was easy for Soviet disinformers to plant absurd stories that would quickly spread.[20] It is a basic tenet of all disinformation campaigns that stories gain credibility by being repeated often. At some point, we no longer disbelieve the story about alligators in New York City sewers, or about the nun whose car was dented by a falling elephant and was arrested for drunk driving after trying to explain this to a policeman, or the dog owner who nuked his pet in the microwave in an effort to dry him off. The mythology spun by Soviet disinformers was that capitalism was doomed and that a classless Communist world society, with plenty for all, would prevail. To attain their goal, Communist mythologists knew they had to spin some pretty tall tales, and to have them repeated often enough so that they might be accepted as fact.

Because they exercised total control over their media at home, the Soviets had a distinct advantage in spreading disinformation abroad. Tass was both a domestic and foreign operation and had offices in 126 countries. The CIA estimate was that as many as 70 percent of Tass's correspondents were KGB agents. There were also 260 Tass correspondents in 67 developing countries.[21] Part of Tass's success was that it was much cheaper to subscribe to than Western news agencies. As a result, by the mid-1980s the authoritative voice of the Soviet government could boast over 600 clients—newspapers, radio and TV stations—many of which were in cash-starved developing countries. Novosti was the so-called "unofficial" news agency, specializing in feature reports and regional and local coverage. Novosti employed many foreign nationals in its target countries, and relied heavily on photographs to supplement text. It served up the most blatant Soviet pap to the developing world. The writing style was somewhat livelier than that of Tass, but Novosti, no less than its official counterpart, carefully tailored its material to specific countries and objectives. It also published a large number of books and pamphlets, in more than fifty languages, and used a massive grant program to bring thousands of journalists and government officials to the Soviet Union each year.[22]

American officials were so alarmed by the scale of the Soviet disinformation effort that a special high-level USIA public relations group, the International Information Committee (IIC), was set up to gauge the impact of Soviet propaganda around the world. The committee set out to "investigate developments in Soviet public diplomacy approaches, programs, and techniques which serve as conduits for propaganda." Radio and television were not, of course, the only media utilized by international propagandists. USIA research showed that in Latin America, for example, a variety of programs aimed at influencing public opinion abroad. The USSR was placing emphasis on its student scholarship program. In a four-year period, the number of students from Central America receiving study grants in the Soviet Union more than doubled to 7,600, despite the fact that a Soviet academic degree was not recognized in many parts of Central America, and returning students often had to settle for low-paying government jobs. The IIC also found that the Soviets were making a big push in their book program: by the early 1980s its textbooks were widely used in Central American universities. In a report dated March 22, 1985, the IIC said the impact of Soviet publications was increasing in Nicaragua, "especially among youth who have no way to evaluate them and who are strongly influenced by Sandinista educational programs that include heavy doses of Socialist and Communist ideology." Soviet-sponsored exhibits were also on the rise. Music, dance, and circuses were popular and played to packed houses.

Most of the Soviets' efforts in the 1980s, in Central America and elsewhere, were geared at striking back at American accusations of human rights abuses in the USSR.[23] This didn't play well in such countries as Venezuela, Colombia, and Argentina, to which large populations had fled from the Soviet Union and Eastern Europe—precisely because of Communist human rights abuses. Almost a million Jews from the Soviet Union and Eastern Europe had settled in Argentina, for example. USIA's research concluded in 1985 that the Soviets' campaign was having minimal impact in Central America, where its appeal was limited mainly to left-wing sympathizers.[24] The Russians were countering U.S. human rights charges by proclaiming that American dissidents were regularly being put in mental hospitals when they protested too actively over American policies. According to *Pravda,* the White House had even ordered the construction of "concentration camps" for dissidents: "The President's instruction leaves no doubt on this account" that such camps were being used "for illegal immigrants, for political opponents of the official line, for people trying to evade military service, and also for open critics of the administration. In short, for unreliable people."[25]

While this might seem like the blackest of all white disinformation, such charges were not unexpected, given how heavy American criticism of Soviet human rights violations had been. All shades of Soviet disinformation cast shade on all aspects of the American ideal of itself, including freedom of the press. "There is no independence of the mass media in the United States," insisted Radio Moscow. "Is there any difference between the *New York Times*, the *Daily News*, the *Chicago Tribune*, the *Boston Globe*, and other newspapers? Only a symbolic one, reflected in the placement of similar news material in different columns and slightly different emphasis on one event or another. In all other respects, bourgeois American newspapers are as alike as peas in a pod."[26] When Russian writer Andrey Sakharov went on a hunger strike to protest Soviet human rights violations, drawing sympathetic attention in the West, the Soviets trotted out four other Soviet Nobel Prize laureates, who in the mid-1980s rose to the defense of Leonard Peltier, the Native American imprisoned for life for killing two FBI agents. The Soviet press and therefore newspapers throughout the developing world portrayed him as a human rights martyr.[27] The MOVE disaster in May 1985, when the members of the Philadelphia cult were bombed on orders from the city's mayor, inspired the Soviets to launch a counterpropaganda campaign portraying members of the cult as poor people who simply couldn't afford to pay their rent, and who made the fatal mistake of criticizing City Hall.[28]

By 1985, the Soviets had stepped up efforts in the gray disinformation area to induce independent and third parties to promote their policies. USIA studies found that Soviet journalism training was being stepped up with more than three hundred young Third World journalists going through programs at various media training centers in Russia and Eastern bloc countries at any given time. They were being taught print media journalism at the Werner Lamberz Institute in East Berlin, and radio and TV instruction at the Center of Professional Education of Journalists in Budapest as well as at the Julius Fucik School of Solidarity in Prague. Journalists in agricultural and economic reporting also studied there. In Latin America, apprentice journalists were getting Soviet training at the Jose Marti International Institute in Havana.

The theory behind some of the Communist instruction in journalism was actually sound. Students were generally (and rightly) reminded by their Soviet instructors that Western news sources were not the only ones in existence. Listen to the BBC, they told students, then to Radio Moscow, and then weigh what each has to say. Relying on a single, Western news source would skew perspective. Young journalists and other potential opinion molders were regularly invited to the USSR, usually for three-week stays to correct misperceptions.[29] India was the focus of Soviet Union's largest disinformation operation outside the Warsaw Pact. As the world's most populous democracy, home to nearly 21,000 newspapers and magazines, it provided a valuable propaganda resource. Industrial accidents provided ready-made subjects for disinformation. After the tragedy at Bhopal's Union Carbide plant in 1984, killing 2,000, Tass alleged that behind it all was a cynical American experiment to get scientific data on gas poisoning. Several publications carried accusations by an Indian spokesman that the United States had been experimenting with a chemical bomb that blew up the facility. Tass, of course, ran the story worldwide.

Probably the most bothersome Soviet press fabrication of the entire cold war, charging the American government with developing the AIDS virus that would kill only blacks—an "ethnic weapon" as it would later be labeled by the Soviets—initially appeared in India's pro-Soviet daily newspaper, *Patriot,* in 1983. The accusation hit a nerve because the CIA did maintain unauthorized stockpiles of paralytic shellfish toxins, cobra venom, and other biological poisons at an army laboratory at Fort Detrick, Maryland. One ounce of shellfish toxin was enough to kill at least 14,000 people. Gary Powers, the American U-2 spy plane pilot shot down over Russia in 1960, carried shellfish toxin concealed in a drill bit and a silver dollar. He had the option of using it if he was captured. He opted not to do so. A U.S. Army laboratory had also developed hand-held dart guns filled with poisons, capable of hitting a human target at a distance of 100 yards.

In 1969 Fort Detrick engineers introduced a nontoxic chemical into a water fountain at the Food and Drug Administration building in Washington, D.C., to see if this kind of covert activity would be feasible under real conditions. A similar test was carried out on the New York City subway. Again, the idea behind it was to assess the threat of infection to subway passengers. The toxins used were developed with funds from federally supported public health services.[30]

The United States was doing so much damage to itself that Soviet disinformers could sit back and watch the news stories about the CIA Senate investigation about Fort Detrick run in the major media outlets. KGB bribes to journalists weren't required in order to obtain media coverage. A decade later, public disclosures from the Senate hearings relating to toxins produced and stored at Fort Detrick would lend credibility to the "AIDS ethnic weapon" campaign, one of the blackest, most intensive, and most bizarre Soviet disinformation operations since the KGB had formally established its disinformation directorate in 1959. Because it paid scattered attention to combating Soviet disinformation until Charlie Wick came on board in 1981—and Herb Romerstein a year later to focus full-time on the subject—the United States would have to get its act together, fast.

Because the AIDS disinformers had accused the United States of attempting to annihilate the world's black population, their prime target audience would be black Africa, fertile ground, as previously noted, for finding journalists on the take (and fertile ground, too, for other disinformation pranks, as we would later discover). The best defense is, of course, a good offense, but the USIA was far from being battle-ready. Voice of America signals to the African continent were spotty at best, and Radio Free Europe and Radio Liberty did not transmit there at all. The sad truth was that well over half of all American broadcasting was trained on only 10 percent of the world's population, in Eastern Europe and the Soviet Union. We needed to isolate the major policy issues that meant something to our target audiences in Africa and had policy value to us—in other words, follow the Soviet's example. For Africa this meant covering such subjects as hunger relief assistance, the treatment of hypertension, and AIDS research. These and other substantive issues would be our message to Africa. Since the Soviets had a tight hold on the African print media, and since radio broadcasting opportunities were limited, we needed another route.

The beauty of a television satellite was that you could rent it like a car, by the hour, day, or week or longer. We could turn it on virtually within minutes of when we wanted it. Because a satellite signal beam, like a giant spotlight from space, can cover enormous areas, we would be able to fit both Europe and Africa within the satellite's cone of coverage, so that audiences on both continents could see the same program simultaneously. While Europe remained Worldnet's number-one-priority area, the same programs we beamed to it would be picked up via satellite dishes throughout most of Africa. By putting dishes on our African embassies and giving satellite receivers to local television stations there, which were eager for programming, we anticipated widespread use of our material. For a portion of the broadcast day, we could also do programs designed specifically for Africa. To counter Soviet disinformation themes such as the AIDS story, this was critical. To get the audiences in the first place, we needed to provide quality entertainment programs. The first African Network (AFNET) program was held on April 9, 1984, and publicized American famine-relief efforts in Africa. M. Peter McPherson, head administrator of the Agency for International Development (AID), was linked by satellite from our Washington studio to Dakar, Lagos, Nairobi, Lusaka, and Kinshasa, as well as to Paris and London. For the next hour, McPherson talked with journalists in all those locations about American foreign aid objectives. The program was as big a hit as it had been in Europe. Nigerian TV, which carried the program live, heralded it as "a major demonstration of Nigerian TV's new capability to reach out across the world for answers to topical questions."

The Soviets, of course, also tuned in. Moscow Radio's broadcast to Africa a couple of days later commented that "the White House's real policy in Africa is quite different from the beautiful picture presented by AFNET broadcasts, and people in Africa are more aware of this than anyone else." We had their attention. They knew as well as we did that we would be capable of handling Soviet disinformation stories, not by responding to them directly, but by putting their subjects into a larger context, thereby diminishing them. So instead of directly refuting Soviet charges that America was selling baby parts for medical research, for example, we could overwhelm it with television programs on children's medical research and adoptive procedures. The AIDS story was one of the first topics. Rather than being defensive over charges that the United States had developed the AIDS virus in a laboratory to commit genocide, we could do programs raising public awareness of the AIDS problem, and suggest specific measures that could be taken to prevent the spread of the deadly disease.

Until we were able to dispatch satellite dishes to Africa, we did the next best thing. We invited African journalists stationed in Europe to our embassies there, to participate immediately in our Worldnet telepress conferences. There were a large number of African journalists in Europe, especially in Paris, where they reported for newspapers and TV stations in French-speaking Africa. African journalists came to our facilities in London, Paris, Bonn, Rome, The Hague, and elsewhere in Europe to take part in almost daily live satellite press conferences with U.S. officials in Washington.

Within weeks we were doing programs for Africa in both English and French on a multitude of subjects. Our satellite news conference, which carefully explicated American assistance programs for Ethiopia and other drought-stricken areas, received extensive coverage on African television stations and in newspapers. A satellite congressional hearing on hunger in Africa, involving both Washington legislators and a panel of Nigerian agricultural officials in Lagos, was a technical and programmatic "tour de force," according to our embassy in Nigeria. The program provided the Nigerians "with an opportunity to speak about a subject of immediate and pressing interest to them, directly to U.S. congressional leaders. It showed a sensitivity to their concerns and respect for their opinions which made an obvious impact . . . not only on the Minister of Agriculture and his colleagues but on the fifteen reporters and fifty other spectators present." The program was also carried in full by Nigerian television. Said a leading newspaper in the West African country of Gabon: "If the ambitious goal of Worldnet is to help Africans better understand American society, internal and foreign policy, Africa for its part will be able to contribute to mutual understanding between the two continents by participating in world dialogues."

We scored another coup by obtaining 31 hours of video sports programming for our African posts, ranging from National Basketball Association games to the Rose Bowl football classic to track events and rodeos. Through the generosity of the NBA and film distribution companies, we received the package free of charge, and with full broadcast rights for TV stations in Africa.

The Soviet disinformation campaign in Africa had its moments of success, but AFNET, when it was up and running in 1985, was something the Soviets simply could not match. Because our programs involved both print and TV journalists from abroad, they struck directly at the Soviet "strength"—its virtual lock on providing newspaper syndication services to the Third World. The reason was, as I've mentioned, cost. In Liberia, the annual fee for the French wire service Agence France Presse was $23,000, compared to $1,000 per year for Tass. A typical Tass package for Third World countries also included other features, such as equipment installation, maintenance, and journalism training for reporters.

Worldnet was an even better buy. It was free. It also put African opinion-makers in direct contact via live satellite television with American officials. The Soviets chose the 1984 Summer Olympics in Los Angeles as the vehicle for avenging a number of wrongs, including the new American hegemony in Africa. Four years earlier, in protest over the Soviet invasion of Afghanistan, President Jimmy Carter ordered a U.S. boycott of the 1980 Moscow Olympics. In retaliation (although Afghanistan was not mentioned specifically), the Soviet Union announced on May 8, 1984, that its athletes would not attend the world Olympic Games in Los Angeles that summer. Commentaries in the Soviet media denounced the event as being organized by the FBI "to further the sinister aims" of America.[31] Then leaflets purportedly written by the Ku Klux Klan started to show up, warning African athletes of bodily harm if they attended the games. "We have been training for the games by shooting at black moving targets," the leaflet read. "Blacks, welcome to the Los Angeles Olympics. We'll give you a reception that you'll never forget."[32] Another flyer claimed that any blacks competing in the games would "be shot or hanged. All Olympic gold medals to the white only." The Soviet press and TV carried the texts of the forged leaflets. Tass charged that the KKK was an organization where "thugs operate under the open or thinly veiled patronage of the U.S. authorities," and that America was not a safe place for either Asian and African athletes because authorities would not be able to protect them. Tass ran a story suggesting that the KKK "expressed in an extremely base

manner what the architects of American policy have in their minds."
Another Tass dispatch claimed that an Israeli Mossad intelligence
unit would be handling security at the sporting event. "It is feared,"
read the dispatch, "that under the pretext of combatting terrorism,
the 'security department' can stage repressions against the 'unreliable
elements' on the eve of the Olympics. These include . . . activists of
progressive public organizations and fighters against racial discrimination in the U.S."[33]

African, Asian, and European publications picked up the
Tass commentaries. Wick and I saw the stories on a trip to Brussels
in the spring of 1984. Our public affairs officers in Africa felt that the
disinformation was so effective that many athletes might be persuaded not to take part in the Olympic Games. Wick asked me to call
Peter Ueberroth, who was president of the Los Angeles Olympic Organizing Committee. "See if he'll do a Worldnet," Wick said. It was
Saturday morning on the West Coast, and I reached Ueberroth at his
home. I told him that we could link him up via TV satellite from Los
Angeles with journalists around the world to defuse the propaganda
offensive the Soviets were whipping up against the Summer Olympics. It would be particularly effective in Africa, I told him. Wick also
thought it would be a smart move to put Ueberroth on Worldnet
with the black mayor of Los Angeles, Tom Bradley. Ueberroth liked
the idea. "I'm in," he said without hesitation. Wick called Tom
Bradley, who also accepted the invitation on the spot.

We produced three separate one-hour Worldnet press
conference telecasts with Bradley and Ueberroth. Local media in
twenty countries in the Far East, Latin America, Africa, and Europe
joined in. Bradley was especially impressive at assuring Africans they
would be entirely safe in Los Angeles. The programs were carried on
television in Korea, the Philippines, Nigeria, the Ivory Coast, and
Kenya, and long excerpts were used elsewhere. An estimated 52.4
million viewers tuned in in the Far East; 81.6 million viewers in Latin
America; and 28.2 million viewers in Africa. South China Morning
Post in Hong Kong commented that Ueberroth ("the man with perhaps one of the most unenviable jobs in the world") "oozed goodwill
and honest endeavor." At the television station in Lagos, Nigeria,
staff members burst into applause when Ueberroth, answering the
last question on the 90-minute program, told the questioner that
Nigeria could telecast as much of the games as it wanted without

paying "one more penny" than previously negotiated for limited usage. The world was impressed with Ueberroth's breadth of knowledge and by the technical mastery that tied together the five participating continents. The program played a significant role in stemming the potential boycott of the games by Asian and African nations. In an article published in *Le Monde* entitled "U.S. Worldnet Starts a Crusade," Daniel Lageron wrote that "Worldnet really shines when it transmits live and direct its interactive programs."[34] But to drive home our point, USIA's Meyer Odze produced a half-hour documentary, called *Hello, Los Angeles,* and distributed it to audiences worldwide to quell fears about safety in L.A. The film's narrator assured that the security of everyone would be guaranteed by the Los Angeles Police Department, "by common admission the best trained and most highly disciplined police department in the world. So don't worry about a thing. We want you to come to Los Angeles and have a good time."[35] (Had the Olympic Games been scheduled following the Los Angeles riots of 1992, they would have been a much harder sell.) Again, Worldnet had gotten the attention of the world's media, and the Soviets weren't alone in seeing us as a growing threat. In a feature article in the March 1985 issue of the Algerian newspaper *Algérie Actualité,* writer Lofti Maherzi made a prescient comment about the Olympic program in particular and the use of satellite television in general:

> The purpose is in fact an ambition of astronomical proportions: the conditioning of billions of human minds, through direct access to their television screens. This is the new empire of the superpowers, no longer territorial, but audiovisual and informational. Whoever controls information governs the world. It is a battle which takes place in the skies, with blows struck by satellites. The message is no longer obvious; instead it is impressively seductive.[36]

The Soviet newspaper *Literaturnay Gazeta* called our new TV capability the creation of "ideological saboteurs" entrenched around the White House, from whom it receives its protection and long-range plans.

As before, convincing American diplomats abroad as well as the U.S. Congress of the value of modern technology in America's foreign affairs effort was no easy matter. The old way was better, they thought, and a lot less risky. A group of congressional staffers traveled around Europe on a Worldnet fact-finding mission and were largely negative in their report.[37] They wondered whether the USIA could find a market for U.S. official policy pronouncements in the competitive European media markets, given that "a press conference format can only hold the viewer's interest for a half-hour." Voice of America shortwave radio engineers held fast to the view that satellites were too expensive and unreliable. It was tough to do new things within the bureaucracy.

The Soviets, meanwhile, flattered us with an imitation and produced a documentary about the homeless in New York City entitled *The Man from Fifth Avenue.* Called a "scathingly critical" film by the *New York Times,* it was aired on Soviet television. The program centered on an unemployed New Yorker by the name of Joe Mauri, who gave Soviet cameras a guided tour of Manhattan. The film showed the homeless man and a child break-dancing in New York City's Times Square. In another scene, Mauri was pictured standing in front of the swank Plaza Hotel. "If you don't have money, forget it," Mauri said. "If I try to go in there, they'll throw me out like a dog."[38]

Our diplomats felt the film would be very damaging, and one described it as "one of the most scurrilous attacks in recent memory on life in the U.S."[39] Interestingly, we learned it was not perceived negatively by Soviet viewers, bringing to mind the story of a politician who didn't care whether the story about him was good or bad so long as he got his name in the paper and it was spelled right. Just getting pictures of life in America on Soviet TV, even if unflattering, was a plus. Although the *New York Times* correspondent said the film "portrayed New York as a modern Gomorrah, focusing on the misery of the homeless, the squalor of Times Square and the presence of prostitution, drug addiction, pornography and poverty,"[40] Soviet viewers saw other things: the gleaming Trump Tower skyscraper in the background and plentiful consumer goods.

These were not easy days for Soviet disinformers. The Soviet line was not being bought in Third World countries the way it used to be. A USIA survey of the world press showed overwhelming disapproval of the Soviet presence in Afghanistan. The Kremlin stressed that it was in Afghanistan at the invitation of that country's leadership, and that outside interference from the United States and others just prolonged Soviet presence there. Soviet media portrayed anti-government Mujahideen rebels as CIA-funded bandits, and the United States as anti-Islam. But it was that AIDS story, lovingly nurtured by the Russian disinformers after lying dormant for more than two years, that constituted one of their last and greatest weapons. A major article in the Soviet weekly *Literaturnaya Gazeta* entitled "Panic in the West or What is Hidden Behind the Sensation About AIDS," cited details from the "well-respected Indian newspaper, *Patriot.*" The Soviets had updated the *Patriot* story, now offering more details about how Americans had first developed the AIDS virus at its infamous biological warfare research center in Fort Detrick, Maryland, and warning that the virus was being tested on humans (the same story announced that killer mosquitoes were being bred by the U.S. government at a secret laboratory in Pakistan).[41] Radio Moscow quoted from the *Patriot* story and beamed it to areas where the United States had military bases, such as Turkey and Japan, stressing that American servicemen were carriers of AIDS. Then Western European media picked up the story, and the propaganda crusade began to build. Most American officials believed the campaign was designed to discredit the United States to create pressure for the removal of U.S. military bases overseas.[42] By the end of 1985, North Korea had started its own AIDS disinformation campaign against the stationing of U.S. troops in South Korea. The campaign was seen as an attempt to counter U.S. claims of Soviet "yellow rain" environmental pollution from nuclear tests. Kremlin authorities also were attempting to scare its citizens into limiting potential harmful contacts with foreigners, since the USSR was just beginning to admit to a domestic AIDS problem.[43]

By early 1986, the story seemed to have run its course in the highly skeptical Western press. Only parts of the Third World and the leftist press kept the ball rolling. Soviet propagandists were then ordered by the Kremlin to turn up the heat on Ronald Reagan. On July 31, 1986, the Central Committee of the Soviet Communist party issued a "SECRET" directive entitled "On Measures to Strengthen Our Opposition to the American Policy of 'Neoglobalism.'" Led by Ronald Reagan, right-wing groups bent on world domination had come to power in America, and the Central Committee specified that coalitions, especially in the developing world, should be put together to oppose American "neoglobalism." The directive demanded that

Soviet "foreign policy propaganda" be intensified to damage American credibility and that the KGB implement countermeasures as well.[44]

Radio Moscow picked up the cue and carried a report to South Africa in the Zulu language introducing the latest and most potent AIDS angle: it was an ethnic weapon that would kill *only* blacks. "Lately there has been growing talk in Africa about the presence of biological weapons in South Africa that can discriminate on the basis of race," said the broadcast. "These are meant to selectively kill the black race and leave out the white race. Such diabolical weapons are being researched and manufactured with the aid of the United States." Tass claimed that the white South African government had joined with the United States in refining the AIDS strain so that it would be "harmless to whites but fatal to Africans, Asians, and other people of color." It also claimed that Israel was experimenting with the AIDS virus on Arab prisoners. The last and biggest spark of all was provided by a trio of pseudo-scientists from Communist East Germany who presented a paper at a summit meeting of nonaligned nations in Zimbabwe. The paper, written by professor Jacob Segal, his wife, Dr. Lili Segal, and Dr. Ronald Dehmlow, seemed to lend an air of academic legitimacy to allegations that the AIDS virus was artificially developed at Fort Detrick from the existing viruses, VISNA and HTLV-1. Within months, Segal's allegations blanketed the media in more than fifteen African countries. London's *Sunday Express* ran the story, which was picked up by Western wire services and sent around the world. The Soviet media then ran the story, liberally quoting Western news sources and adding that the U.S. had invented the virus to wipe out African populations. American claims that AIDS originated in Africa were further proof of racism.[45]

Herb Romerstein and Todd Leventhal were doing their best to punch holes in the story, and they had their hands full. A new, bizarre angle would surface almost daily. A Kuwait newspaper, *Al-Oabas*, carried a picture purporting to show an ethnic weapon actually being fired. The story was subsequently carried worldwide by London's Reuter news agency and run on the "CBS Evening News with Dan Rather," March 30, 1987. Leventhal got a tip that the Soviets were lifting quotes about the AIDS ethnic weapon from a gay publication called *New York Native*, which had run its story years earlier, when the facts about AIDS were not yet known and there was a great deal of speculation.[46] Romerstein was preparing to leave for Moscow to confront some of his adversaries over disinformation stories such as this. On the cover of *New York Native* was a picture of three guys in drag; one in a long gown and cowboy hat, and the other two in cowboy boots and jockstraps. "Why don't you take them with you to Moscow?" Leventhal suggested to Romerstein. "I can't use these in the meeting," Romerstein replied. "Take them with you," insisted Leventhal. "You never know."

In Moscow, Romerstein went to his meeting at the headquarters of *Novosti Military Bulletin,* a publication that carried all sorts of nonsense about U.S. biological warfare. Romerstein watched as several men in overcoats entered the meeting room. One didn't need to be Sherlock Holmes to figure out they probably didn't work in the press building. Romerstein assumed they were KGB agents. "I wanted to go to the United States and it denied me entry," one of the men complained. Romerstein replied that it was U.S. policy not to let foreign intelligence officers in. "What are you so afraid of KGB for?" asked one of the men, with a grin. Others, without overcoats, joined the meeting. Herb got to the point, complaining that the *Novosti Military Bulletin* had carried stories that the AIDS virus was created as a biological weapon by the United States and that AIDS was also caused by U.S. nuclear testing.[47] "We've seen this crazy story," said Herb. "Stay away from it because it's not true."[48]

"We didn't create this AIDS disinformation story," said one of the men. "It was in your press."

With that, Herb opened his briefcase, pulled out the *New York Native,* and held it up so that they could see its cover. "This is your source," said Romerstein. "Now, we want to save you embarrassment. We don't want you to be known for quoting this as your source. It's not good for your image. Anytime you have a question about a source in America, you can call us and we'll give you help."

"Since you do us a favor," said one of the Soviets, "we'll give you a year's free subscription to *Novosti Military Bulletin.* It normally costs $200."[49]

In a later session with Romerstein, Novosti news editor Valentin Falin defended use of the story. He maintained that the article responded to repeated accusations that it was the USSR that had invented the story about the artificial development of AIDS and merely provided a synopsis of American publications on this subject.

He also denied that the USSR had taken special actions to encourage other countries to publish the AIDS story. "We did not, and will not take such actions."[50]

Herb Romerstein was a known quantity to the Soviets—the former Communist who became an effective anti-Communist—but Russian disinformers were by now also able to take the measure of their nemesis Charlie Wick, as Gorbachev's policy of Glasnost (openness) began to emerge. They would also feel the heat of Wick's bluster. He happened to be in Moscow on the morning the Novosti news agency ran yet another of its anti-U.S. AIDS stories. Since part of his visit to Moscow was to open an exhibition on information technology, Wick was scheduled to meet with Soviet editors and publishers in order to discuss the exchange of journalists between the two countries. Falin, who would soon rise to a key propaganda post of the Communist party, was the senior editor at the meeting with Wick.[51]

The Novosti article said in part: "The Langley [CIA] agents widely use war gases in the developing countries. One of the latest strides in this field is the ethnic weapon, Plus Morbific Plus, which is lethal for the Africans and harmless to those of European extraction." The Novosti story also claimed the Reagan Administration had "unleashed large-scale terror and subversion against national liberation forces in Asia, Africa, and Latin America," and concluded by claiming that the CIA used war gases in developing countries and that terrorists were being trained in some 160 camps in the United States and elsewhere.

Ray Benson, public affairs counselor at the American Embassy in Moscow, showed Wick an English-language translation only minutes before the scheduled meeting with Falin. Wick, who had a law degree, digested every word of every document that was staffed out to him. Falin would have to wait. Wick read the Novosti piece carefully, pausing several times to underline passages. His cheek began to twitch in anger. "This is the worst kind of Stalinist cold war nonsense I've ever seen," Wick said, as he headed over to Novosti press agency headquarters with his entourage. Nervous aides trailed behind as he entered the meeting room. Noting fire in Wick's eyes, Falin closed a notebook on the table in front of him. "I am willing to discuss whatever the director has in mind," Falin offered. Wick said he wanted to cite a blatant area of Soviet disinformation, and proceeded to read the entire article aloud, then looked at Falin squarely in the eye, and asked him for an explanation.[52]

Falin didn't mind at all playing bad cop with Wick. In fact, he appeared to enjoy it. The tall, athletic Falin fixed his eyes on Wick and claimed that he hadn't seen the article, but that it was probably based on a story that had already been run in the Western press. "And given the U.S. treatment of American Indians, putting smallpox blankets on them, and the placement of Japanese-Americans in detention camps during the Second World War, the development of an ethnic weapon by the U.S. sounds pretty logical." He continued that it was no secret that the United States had been working on various "exotic" weapons, including the so-called ethnic ones. These, he said, are biological and chemical agents with selective action against people of different races, populating the same areas yet having different genetic susceptibility to these agents. Falin also claimed that by charging that the Japanese had used bacterial weapons against American prisoners of war, the U.S. Defense Department was guilty of disinformation. He concluded by saying that an epidemic affecting cattle and people was sweeping Cuba and Nicaragua, and that even American scientists admitted not being able to find natural causes for it.[53]

"Is the epidemic connected with AIDS?" Wick asked. Falin shook his head no, but continued to take the offensive. He said he had not charged the United States with spreading false rumors about Soviet use of toxic weapons in Southeast Asia and Afghanistan, though he would "not be wrong" if he accused the USIA of spreading these rumors. Wick was furious, and charged Falin with using "nonresponsive, polemical, cold war, Stalinist, irrelevant responses"[54] to disrupt their meeting, which Wick believed could have resolved the issue of the AIDS disinformation story. "Perhaps," concluded Wick, "the time has not yet come for us to have a useful discussion." With that, Wick got up from his chair, collected his papers, and stomped out of the room.[55]

A few days later, Falin was quoted in the *Moscow News* daily as saying that once you start an exchange on a sharp note, you must be prepared for sharp words, and not just weak smiles in reply. He reiterated that the United States used biological and chemical agents with "selective action against people of different races, populating the same areas yet having different genetic susceptibility or vulnerability to these agents." The Soviet press would soon pick up on a report that American nuclear testing was also causing AIDS.

Falin hadn't heard the last on this issue from Wick. He had just earned his very own color-coded slot on Wick's disinformation tracking chart. Falin and his cohorts would find out what it was like to get caught in Wick's potato masher, like the Marine guard who had attempted to stop Wick from entering the American Embassy in Belgrade a few years earlier.

The second most enduring and most damaging pieces of Soviet disinformation during the 1980s centered on America's alleged sale of baby parts. A grisly "black" story was making the rounds that Latin American children were being kidnapped and butchered, and their organs sold for medical research in the United States, Western Europe, and Israel. The Soviet daily *Sovetskaya Rossiya* carried a story claiming that human hearts were being sold in America for up to one million dollars. The baby parts story first surfaced in Honduras, where in early 1987 a government official was quoted in a newspaper as saying he had heard the United States was carrying out this barbarous activity. The fable has ancient roots. Christians were accused of the ritualistic murders of children in ancient Rome, and Jews have suffered such accusations throughout history. In eighteenth-century France, children were said to have been abducted to supply body parts to kings or princes maimed in battle.[56] The medical truth is that organ transplantation requires a series of highly sophisticated procedures, including donor and recipient compatibility tests, the storage of organs, and the complex operation itself, making it impossible for any of this to be carried out in secret makeshift facilities.[57]

The story was based on a statement by Leonardo Villeda Bermudez, from the Honduran National Council on Social Welfare, who said: "Several years ago, some social workers told me that foreign parents were coming to adopt children. They [the parents] would say, 'It doesn't matter to us that a child has no eye, or has a physical defect; it doesn't matter that he may have a bad heart. I'm going to take him with me to the U.S.' And what would happen? These children would be taken to be sold for parts. This is also a crime. This has been largely stopped." Bermudez's comments were run in the Honduran newspaper *La Tribuna* and circulated worldwide by the Reuter news service.

A children's defense fund based in Geneva carried the baby parts story in its quarterly publication, *International Children's Rights Monitor*. "In view of the wide echo given to this affair, we felt it necessary to publicize the information in our possession," it read. Several leftist papers in Mexico City, Guatemala, and the Netherlands had picked up the story. A radio talk show on the Canadian Broadcasting Company carried an interview with a Dutch member of the Council of Europe. Apparently referring to comments attributed to Leonardo Volleda Bermudez, the Dutch parliamentarian said that "a person in Honduras" had said there had been an export of physically handicapped children to the United States for the purpose of using their organs.[58] The gates were open.

Delighted that it now had a Western European source, Tass circulated those comments worldwide. An article in *Pravda* embellished the story with unsubstantiated speculation. Thousands of Honduran children, even cripples, it said, were being butchered for "eyes, kidneys, hearts—in short, everything that can be used for transplants." The French Communist party newspaper *L'Humanité* ran a long story entitled "Child's Heart for Sale: Children in Honduras, Guatemala, and El Salvador Abducted and Sold to Secret Laboratories in the United States." The Cuban and Nicaraguan news picked up the *L'Humanité* story. Radio Moscow then jumped in with the most sensational treatment of the story to date. In its Spanish-language service to Latin America, it claimed that "fattening centers have been established in Central American countries to feed the children properly before they are used by organ-transplant centers in the developed countries." The official Soviet government newspaper *Izvestia* managed to embellish the story even further: "In Guatemala, for several years in a row, the international mafia has bought up children with physical disabilities and sent them to the United States for 'treatment.' There, the butcher medics cut out their hearts, kidneys, and eyes—whatever was required for saving U.S. children." It continued: "There is only one step from American arrogance, from racist contempt for the Latin American peoples, to cannibalistic total license." The newspaper also quoted an official at an organization identified as the International Defense for Children. "Yes, the facts are screaming out," she supposedly said. "We must not remain indifferent, we must shout about this at the top of our lungs." Although the group claimed it had been misquoted, the comment was further circulated in the media in the Dominican Republic, Switzerland, Canada, Morocco, and elsewhere.[59]

The Council of Europe, when few members were in attendance, passed by hand vote, without debate, a resolution sponsored by the French Communist party. Entitled "On the Trafficking in Children in Central America," it claimed that 170 children from Guatemala had been sold abroad for body parts. Moscow Radio carried the story, which now had a thoroughly legitimate air about it (despite efforts by Romerstein and the USIA's public affairs officers overseas to repudiate it). Chief Soviet press spokesman Gennadiy Gerasimov defended the use of the story by saying the Soviet media—naturally—was merely reporting what others were saying. "The Soviet Union had nothing to do with this story," said Gerasimov. *Literaturnaya Gazeta* claimed the U.S. government was becoming paranoid about the subject. "Ultimately, what has the U.S. administration got to do with it?" mused the paper's editorial. "After all, no one has hinted anywhere that the child dealers have official blessing." By this time, charges had been repeated so often by so many people that no one seemed to question the story's authenticity. The lines between truth and fiction and between the various kinds of disinformation had been hopelessly blurred.

USIA research showed that the Soviets scored heavily with their baby parts disinformation effort.[60] It was being blared across Western Europe despite Romerstein's monumental attempt to call as many international newsrooms as he could. When Swiss TV eventually realized that the story was a hoax, it ran a piece on the evolution of rumors as disinformation.[61] U.S. Embassy personnel were interviewed by an embarrassed Swiss reporter who was trying to set the record straight. A Viennese monthly picture magazine also picked up the baby parts story. After much prodding, a letter to the editor from the U.S. Embassy debunking the story was finally printed in the publication.

Soviet disinformation was carried mainly by the print media, not by television, the latter of which would have reached the greatest number of people and had the greatest impact of all the media overseas. According to a secret CIA report of March 1985, developing countries treated TV and radio as "more valuable political resources" than newspapers and "reserved them for their own use." Arab and African countries, said the report, "even ban Soviet media from using their radio and TV but will allow them to print stories in local newspapers." The CIA said the Soviets weren't trying very hard to gain access to TV systems of other countries, where competition from American entertainment programs made access especially difficult.[62] The CIA also warned that "lengthy visa hassles" would continue to plague access to many Third World countries by Western reporters. With satellite television we could sit in the comfort of our modern TV studios in Washington and beam programs anywhere in the world we wanted, without a visa. While it may have seemed that the United States was helpless to deflect such Soviet disinformation thrusts as AIDS and baby parts, we were, in fact, gaining unprecedented access to foreign television systems with our gray disinformation, reaching huge audiences within credible, locally produced program formats with carefully crafted, U.S. policy–laden messages.

As damaging as Soviet disinformation was, when it came to heavy-duty disinformation with the biggest "return on investment" (in crass, commercial terminology), no one could top the American government. Ronald Reagan was a firm believer in the adage, "If you grab them by the balls, their hearts and minds will follow." Borrowing an idea from the movie *Star Wars*, the former actor made his grab and the Soviets snapped to attention. In a nationally televised speech in March 1983, he mused how wonderful it would be if free people "could live secure in the knowledge that their security did not rest upon the threat of U.S. retaliation to deter a Soviet attack, knowing that we could intercept and destroy strategic ballistic missiles before they reached our own soil and that of our allies."[63] Star Wars, America's disinformation pièce de résistance, had been hatched.

Throughout the 1980s, the Soviets lived in mortal fear that the United States would launch a nuclear first strike because it could deter a counterattack through Star Wars technology. The main Soviet propaganda line at numerous KGB-funded World Peace Council meetings in various world capitals was "Say no to Star Wars," because it would heat up the arms race by spreading it to outer space.[64] During the 1960s, Soviet Premier Nikita Khrushchev had boasted that his missiles could "hit a fly in the sky," ostensibly to scare the United States from defending the divided city of Berlin. The

Soviets attempted to convince American intelligence services that it had "tested a superpowerful thermonuclear warhead, along with a system of detecting and eliminating the adversary's missiles in the air."[65] At about the same time, during an intelligence debriefing on Soviet intercontinental ballistic missiles, Soviet defector Colonel Oleg Penkovsky was telling the CIA, "We don't have a damn thing." In fact, there was a vodka shortage in the Soviet Union, because the government had restricted its sale to make more alcohol available for missile fuel.[66]

Reagan's Star Wars, or the Strategic Defense Initiative (SDI), as it was known formally, was no less of a hoax. But it hit a nerve. The USSR's military analyst, Sergei Rogov, saw SDI as a no-risk effort for America: "If we respond to the U.S. challenge, the Soviet economy will collapse in trying to compete with the stronger economic, scientific, and technological potential of the United States and its allies. If we do not follow suit, the U.S. will gain an overwhelming military superiority."[67] Initially the Soviets charged that the development of Star Wars technology would be too costly for the United States, that such a system could not work, and that all the United States was doing was escalating the arms race. The head of the U.S. Arms Control and Disarmament Agency (ACDA), Kenneth Adelman, called the charges "spurious."[68] Adelman coyly teased the Soviets by saying on a Worldnet program that if they were so sure Star Wars wouldn't work, why were they so upset about it?

The Kremlin had to adopt a more conciliatory approach, because its nuclear strategy was built on a heavy offensive, first-strike capability aimed at wiping out U.S. military installations. The Soviet military had limited nuclear defensive capability, and felt particularly vulnerable to a Star Wars "leak-proof Astrodome," as the new system was being called by the United States. The fear was that if the country felt secure under its "Astrodome," it could feel secure in launching a first strike. Soviet foreign minister Eduard Shevardnadze pleaded to be cut in on Star Wars technology to combat terrorism, among other things. "We must cooperate, share technologies and scientific achievements," he said. Elements of the plan, he went on, could be used for the solution of such global problems as "ecological monitoring, early warning of natural calamities, and an effective navigation system."[69] Deputy national security adviser to the president Robert McFarlane knew Star Wars technology was a long shot. He saw it as a ploy to scare the Soviets into reducing the number of its land-based missiles. McFarlane would later contend that the program was not deceptive.[70] Secretary of Defense Frank Carlucci, an advisor to the president for national security affairs, knew it was a silly idea, but went along with it anyway. The Pentagon questioned whether Secretary of State Shultz, who felt Star Wars technology was being oversold,[71] had the proper clearances for a top secret Star Wars briefing.[72]

The SDI con job came at a critical time. The CIA's top secret estimates of Soviet nuclear capability were apocalyptic. It was feared that the Kremlin had no fewer than 1,300 nuclear warheads capable of reaching targets within minutes, and that the Soviets were adding an average of three new warheads each week. The CIA estimated that the Soviets could produce as many as 21,000 nuclear warheads by the end of the decade. Something had to be done. To work, Star Wars technology had to appear flawless. To deceive the Soviets, as well as the U.S. Congress, which would eventually ante up $35 billion for Star Wars research and development, a colossal gray disinformation campaign got under way to get nongovernment groups, including the news media, to help sell the SDI concept (the media would be willing, albeit unsuspecting, contributors). The Pentagon planned to put bombs aboard the missiles that were to be hit by incoming Star Wars projectiles, so that the explosion would prove that test firings were "successful," thereby conning the Soviets into thinking that American missile technology was more developed than was actually the case. A target was launched from Vandenberg Air Force Base in California, and an interceptor sent aloft from the Kwajalein Missile Range in the Pacific. The idea was to simulate a Soviet nuclear missile coming from space. According to an investigation by the General Accounting Office several years later, "The plan was to set off an explosion if the interceptor flew by without hitting the target, which was to fool Soviet sensors expected to monitor the test. The target's explosion was to simulate the effect of a strike by the interceptor."[73] Bombs were duly placed aboard the target missiles in the first three tests, but the interceptor missed the target by such a great distance that detonating the bombs would have been ludicrous. For the fourth test, which took place over the Pacific, an incoming Minuteman missile was artificially heated and special heat-seeking sensors were placed aboard the interceptor, so it could more easily find its target. A radar beacon was also placed on the target, which was turned sideways to make a broader bull's-eye for the interceptor. The GAO report concluded that this doubled the likelihood of success. And, indeed, with the help of the many "enhancements," the fourth and final test firing was right on target.

The Pentagon had pulled it off. Neither Congress, which approved funding for the hugely expensive program, nor those of us who were grinding out propaganda abroad to garner support for SDI, were in on the secret. We put an array of Reagan spokespeople on Worldnet and this generated headlines abroad about the successes of Star Wars technology. On our programs, Defense Secretary Weinberger told Congress and the NATO allies in Europe that the Soviets had laser weapons capable of blinding spy plane pilots and that the U.S. had to keep pumping funds into high-tech defenses to stay ahead. "Soviet Lasers Blind Spy Plane Pilots" blared a headline in the London *Daily Telegraph*. Said the independent *Le Soir* of Brussels: "A most serious reason of concern . . . is the technological breakthroughs coming out of the Soviet Union. The most dramatic development . . . is probably the laser weapon capable of blinding its victims—a weapon which will perform beautifully in 'Star Wars.'"

To enhance the Weinberger show, we had produced a music video with rock music and colorful animation of the alleged new Soviet laser weapon, which we transmitted before the start of Weinberger's satellite TV press conference—during which he alleged that the Soviets were using the laser against Afghanistan rebels. The music video was widely played on television systems abroad, such as the prime-time coverage on NOS-TV, the national network of the Netherlands. Said the Dutch announcer introducing the piece: "The presentation . . . was typically American, with reporters receiving a fast montage on the Soviet challenge along with disco music and fighters as good as Western F-16s and old bombers equipped with new Cruise missiles." Following the successfully rigged fourth Star Wars tests, we produced an international TV press conference with the director of the project, Lt. General James Abrahamson, linking him live from Washington with hundreds of reporters in London, Copenhagen, The Hague, Paris, Geneva, London, Oslo, Bonn, and Tel Aviv. The American Embassy in Oslo reported a "highest-level audience of

57 persons" drawn from parliament, political parties, labor, media youth groups, defense, think tanks, and academic institutions.

Abrahamson's comments generated major stories around the world. "I am particularly satisfied with the test," he told reporters on the program. He also assured Europe that test results proved Star Wars would protect the Continent from Soviet attack. The young, affable Army general was a deft TV performer. "A cherubic Luke Skywalker . . . the complete antithesis of the caricature image of a Pentagon hawk," the London *Times* described him. *Paris Match* also ran a feature story on Abrahamson's Worldnet interview. The Norwegian ambassador to the United States, a special guest in our Washington studio, compounded his delight with Star Wars by learning of General Abrahamson's Norwegian ancestry. In a page-one story in Israel, Abrahamson gave convincing evidence that Star Wars would provide protection against tactical missiles "of the type threatening Israel and other U.S. allies."

Reagan also appeared on Worldnet, and the Tass correspondent in Washington, Igor Ignatyev, reported that the president repeated "his known views that SDI offered the promise of a 'safer world.'"[74] On one Worldnet program between Washington, Moscow, and Stockholm, Soviet scientists debated Star Wars with some of the top American experts in the field. A technical glitch developed during the program, causing the video from the Soviet Union to be in black-and-white, while participants in Washington and Stockholm were seen in blazing color. Several media accounts about the program said Moscow's black-and-white picture placed participants there at a disadvantage. On the program, the American participants forced the USSR scientists on the defensive by calling attention to extensive Russian ballistic missile production. The United States added another hoax, "Brilliant Pebbles," to the Star Wars mix. We produced several TV programs showing how thousands of tiny satellites, with their brightly lighted heat shields armed with their own rockets, would seek and destroy enemy missiles over a broad area. The *Wall Street Journal* loved Brilliant Pebbles. "This vindicates Ronald Reagan's judgment," said the newspaper. "He understands . . . science advances in ways we don't expect."

In the end, our Buck Rogers stories did more damage than the "ethnic guns" or "baby parts." "You accelerated our catastrophe by about five years," said Ambassador Vladimir Lunk, chairman of the Supreme Soviet Foreign Relations Committee during the Star Wars salad days.[75] Gorbachev was convinced that no one country could win a nuclear war, because each side would annihilate the other.[76] The Soviets were spending over one-third of their gross national product on the military,[77] compared to 7 percent by America, and Gorbachev felt Russia's "supermilitarized economy" could withstand no further strain.[78] SDI made the Russians think a lot about the next generation of military technology, how hopelessly they were falling behind the United States, and the toll it would take on the Soviet Union and its citizens to stay in the race. Gorbachev was convinced that the technology gap between the United States and the Soviet Union was widening rapidly and would lead to Russia's "strategic defeat."[79] American officials involved in promoting SDI during the Reagan years equate their disinformation campaign to the "missile gap" of the 1950s and 1960s, when the United States had claimed the Soviets had many more nuclear warheads than America. John F. Kennedy ran on the theme when he defeated Richard Nixon for the presidency in 1960. The missile gap did not exist. And the U.S. government's bluff about Star Wars was part of another round in the high-stakes propaganda poker game. Eventually, the Russians would fold their hand.

↔ **7** ↔

Antenna Towers and Asparagus Stalks

GERMAN TELEVISION PRODUCER GERHARD BESSERER ASSIGNED A reporter and a video camera crew to do a story about an issue that was making a lot of Berliners angry. It seemed the city's streets were filling up with dog poop. Peter Kendall looked at the videotape when it was brought back to the Berlin studio. The pictures showing a dog defecating, in tight close-up, made him wince. Kendall, a former CBS News executive who was acting as consultant to our TV station and to Besserer, suggested the story be left out. Besserer defended using the story. It would upset his viewers and that was good for ratings. Kendall replied it was a question of ethics. "I couldn't imagine anyone ever using something like this on CBS News," he said with an air of superiority. "I've seen a lot of shit on CBS News," Besserer retorted. Besserer knew his audience. The story ran.

Besserer knew that Berlin was a weird place—a "free" zone where young West Germans flocked by the thousands to legally dodge the military draft (in 1985, almost 23,000 persons filed applications for political asylum in Berlin).[1] Berlin was a city with a large intellectual subculture, made up of many who had fled staid, bureaucratic West Germany (the capital, Bonn, was jokingly referred to as half the size of a Chicago cemetery and twice as dead).² It was a city of glitzy boulevards as bright as Times Square, cozy little clubs, art galleries in backyards, and a Free University bursting with anti-establishment young people. It was definitely a place where dog shit could help topple the Berlin Wall.

It was business as usual at the German-American television station in West Berlin, RIAS-TV, a cooperative venture between the two governments to bring news and information to viewers in East Germany. A story about dog doo would strengthen the case for the freedom of captive nations by getting viewers to tune in. Then they could deliver the freight. Some forty years earlier, the thunderous allied pounding of Berlin had leveled almost everything in sight. Miraculously, Radio Berlin, the city's only station and the former voice of the Third Reich, was only slightly damaged. On May 2, 1945, the Soviets captured the city, and within days they had the station on the air again. When the Western Allies arrived in Berlin two months later and divided the city into four sectors—run by the Soviet Union, the United States, Great Britain, and France—the Soviets refused to turn the station over to the British, in whose sector the station was located. The Soviets wanted the Americans and the French to keep their hands off as well. Although it had neither trained personnel nor broadcasting equipment, the American military government decided to open a German-language station of its own so that it could tell residents about curfews and explain other occupation policies. Since there was no transmitting antenna available, to get on the air quickly programs were sent directly into home radio receivers via existing telephone lines. The station would be known as RIAS, Radio in the American Sector. In addition to news and information, the daily seven-hour RIAS program schedule included music and light entertainment programs.

Before the end of 1945 a captured Nazi Wehrmacht transmitter, nicknamed "Lili Marlene" after the wartime song, was erected near Berlin's Tempelhof Airport to expand RIAS's coverage. Unemployed musicians were hired to form the RIAS Symphony Orchestra, which would grow to become one of Europe's finest. A youth orchestra, a chamber chorus, and a dance band were added over the years, helping to make RIAS a formidable cultural force right in the middle of East Germany. During the Soviet blockade of Berlin in 1948–49, RIAS began broadcasting around the clock, and the radio signal doubled as a homing device during bad weather for Allied planes landing at Tempelhof bringing in food and other supplies from the West. Because of power shortages, RIAS had to reduce its program schedule to twelve hours a day. Loudspeakers were placed on old, beat-up Dodge pickup trucks to broadcast the day's news. During the 1953 uprising in East Germany, RIAS reporters covered the rioting, capturing the sound of gunshots crackling in the background, and the station earned its reputation as an alternative to East German stations. Communist authorities accused RIAS of fomenting unrest (their acronym for it was "Revanchism, Intervention, Anti-Bolshevism and Sabotage"), and jailed anyone caught listening to the station.[3]

In 1955 RIAS became part of the USIA, and by the end of the decade it was broadcasting from eight powerful transmitters on AM, FM, and shortwave bands throughout Germany, and reaching into parts of Poland and Czechoslovakia. Requests for music could be mailed to constantly changing locations, making it difficult for Communist postal authorities to trace who sent them.[4] Children's programs and soap operas also became popular. Within a couple of years RIAS had a larger audience in Berlin and in Communist East Germany than old government standby Sender Freis Berlin (Radio Free Berlin) and was much larger than the Voice of America. Three-quarters of East Germany's population had some exposure to USIA media, and information from the West was beginning to have an influence on fashion, music, movies, and plays.[5]

By the 1980s RIAS had more than 800 employees and was by far the most dominant radio station in Berlin, with a program schedule on its second channel specifically designed for younger audiences. To listeners in a decaying East Germany, it was a beacon of hope from garrulous, westernized Berlin. "We gave the East Germans a window to the world," said Patrick E. Nieburg, former head of RIAS Radio. "We would carry debates of the West German Parliament that also affected East Germany. We would have discussions with young people in schools about their concerns. We would have interviews with intellectuals and artists who fled from East Germany." People over the age of sixty-five were permitted limited visits to West Berlin by the Communists and would come into RIAS to have breakfast in the studio, listen to a popular morning show, and then return home. East German radio did not carry weather forecasts because

Communist authorities considered this military information, so RIAS did. Another program, featuring political satire, attracted a large following and ran for more than fifteen years. Books banned by Communists were read aloud on RIAS. Travel programs seemed to be more important to the East Germans than bread. "Radio was a social, cohesive force between Communist and free Berlin," said Nieburg. "It gave people something in common that they could discuss with each other."[6]

RIAS became a popular source of news because it presented evenhanded coverage of the most controversial subjects. During the 1980s the Russians had proposed a gas pipeline that would run into Western Europe. The American government was dead-set against the idea, concerned that if Western European countries endorsed the plan they would become energy-dependent on the Soviet Union. To its dismay, West Germany did endorse the plan. RIAS, a German-American enterprise, was caught in the middle. "We ought to treat this story as professional news people," Nieburg told his staff. "What we will do is present both sides of the story. We will not endorse it either way. People aren't dumb. They will make up their own minds if we'll give the story a fair shake." The station picked out newspaper editorials that were both for and against the pipeline.

"Most of the time we heard nothing from Washington—nobody could give a damn—and it was a blessing," said Nieburg. But when Charlie Wick became USIA's chief, he decided to visit RIAS. Nieburg wanted to make the visit as painless as possible for himself. Remembering that Wick was a jazz musician who had once had his own band (and was later Tommy Dorsey's music arranger), Nieburg went to the conductor of the RIAS big band, Horst Jankowski, and asked him if he would play Glenn Miller's "In the Mood" when Wick walked into the control room. And, indeed, when Wick walked into the control room, Nieburg nodded to Horst Jankowski's dance band and they started to swing. Wick's eyes grew misty. "Won't you come down and try the piano, Mr. Wick?" asked Jankowski. Wick jammed with them for more than an hour. He told Nieburg that "RIAS plays the right kind of music." Nieburg lugged Wick's lead-lined coat out to the limousine, bade farewell to the director, then sighed. Another Washington visit was over.

RIAS enjoyed a whopping 50 percent share of Berlin's radio audience for most of its existence, but by the mid-1980s radio had fallen under the shadow of television. The charismatic young mayor of West Berlin, Eberhart Diepgen, had an idea. Diepgen and his ruling conservative Christian Democratic Union (CDU) political party felt West Berlin's public TV station, Sender Freis Berlin, was too liberal and that they favored the opposition Social Democrats. Diepgen wanted a second TV outlet in the market that would be friendlier to his own politics. Diepgen, the only Berlin-born mayor in the divided city's brief history, was interested in wooing new business and encouraging American investment. He was also interested in using his office as a springboard for national office.[7]

Diepgen sprung the idea of a TV station when Wick and I visited Berlin in April 1984. He proposed that the two governments collaborate on a television version of RIAS. He noted that the TV signals would be picked up by viewers in nearby Communist territory as well. Wick was still smarting over West German TV's decision not to air his "Let Poland Be Poland" special two years earlier, and Diepgen knew it. He also knew that the idea of the United States controlling its own TV station deep within Germany and behind the Iron Curtain would have its obvious appeal, particularly since, as he admitted to Wick, West German TV did such a poor job representing Western values to the East. He also added that RIAS-TV would act as a counterbalance and reflect the United States in a positive light to audiences in East Germany and would be important to U.S.-German relations. Wick nodded. "TV is the way to go," he agreed. We both knew that the CNN broadcasts were of limited value in Germany because they were done in English and their content was directed toward an American audience. Worldnet programs were dubbed into German and had a decided U.S. policy spin on them. The deal was sealed with a handshake.

Later, on the plane back to Washington, Wick and I discussed the RIAS idea and how to proceed. Our dream was to make it a superstation, right in the heart of Communist Eastern Europe, one that would carry freight from the Atlantic Alliance to viewers behind the Iron Curtain. An exciting prospect. We would run it like RIAS radio, with a resident general manager dispatched to Berlin from the USIA in Washington. He or she would have overall supervision of the station, although on paper it would be set up as a joint U.S.-German cooperative effort.

Back in Washington, Wick discussed the project with the

USIA's senior foreign service officer, Stan Burnett, who agreed that American foreign policy interests in the region were overwhelming, and that an American presence in Berlin was central to our political and military objectives in Europe.[8] I drafted a letter on Wick's behalf to President Reagan's national security adviser, Robert McFarlane, telling him of the RIAS proposal and enlisting his support. "Because of the potentially vast viewing audience in East Germany," I wrote, "and what is felt as a need in Berlin for American programming, Mayor Diepgen would like the U.S. government to consider the proposed RIAS-TV. Most important, RIAS-TV could serve as a model for our direct broadcast of Worldnet programming to Europe, and throughout the continent via cable." An audience survey from a Hamburg consultant suggested that RIAS-TV would reach approximately 5 million persons; 2 million in West Berlin and 3 million in East Berlin and the rest of the Communist German Democratic Republic.[9]

Patrick Nieburg back at RIAS in Berlin felt no enthusiasm for the project. He thought that a TV counterpart would compete for funding with his operation. As the head of a hugely successful radio enterprise, he had every reason to be concerned that an expensive television operation might siphon off valuable resources. Nieburg got together with Mayor Diepgen's aide from the Berlin Senate, Winfried Fest, and came away with the feeling that neither Fest nor his boss Diepgen had a handle on the size and complexity of the RIAS-TV idea. In his report to the American Embassy in Bonn, Nieburg said Fest left him with the impression that the RIAS television idea had been "inspirational rather than premeditated." He was not convinced that Diepgen was "wedded to it on a do-or-die basis." The new concept required further study and "dispassionate judgment."[10] In government, "further study" frequently means slow death.

Both Wick and I knew that an idea similar to this one had been shot down during the Carter Administration. An American entrepreneur named Paul Bartlett had proposed that the United States sanction private radio and television stations in Berlin, but he was brushed off by then-deputy secretary of state Warren Christopher, who felt that the Berlin government had to make that call.[11] Bartlett, a broadcasting consultant from California, was shuttled from one Carter aide to another, and despite persistent efforts spanning several years, he never got to first base. Eventually, the State Department issued a single-spaced, seven-page study listing several dozen reasons why the idea was unworkable. And that was that.[12]

Hans Tuch, the U.S. public affairs minister-counselor in Bonn, knew Wick well enough to realize that when he grabbed hold of a project he wanted, he wouldn't let go. He offered Wick a blueprint showing how to proceed. Tuch informed Wick that what we should do was indicate to Bonn that the U.S. government would be in favor of, and would support, a joint effort to establish RIAS-TV. Tuch also felt it was important for us to move quickly. He said any decision to back the RIAS-TV concept should be made official, recommending that this decision be conveyed directly to the chancellor himself.[13]

Tuch's advice to Wick was to structure the deal along the same lines as RIAS Radio. The United States had built the station, but over the years an arrangement had been worked out by which the Germans paid for its operating costs. The USIA on-site manager remained the station's top executive, however. U.S. sovereignty over the RIAS TV station would be represented first by its having an American director and second by controlling the TV signal. A German "intendant," or "supervisor," would be the chief operating officer, reporting to the USIA station head. Tuch suggested we should make a substantial one-time capital investment in plant and equipment to give us a major stake in the station, but let the Germans be responsible for the operating budget. By not assuming operating budget responsibility, Tuch wisely concluded we would avoid having to involve ourselves in the "uncertainties of the yearly congressional appropriations procedures and the hanging priorities which occur when U.S. administrations change."[14]

The price tag? $12 million. Where would we get $12 million? Wick suggested finding a private entrepreneur to fund and run the station as a commercial operation. USIA's general counsel, Thomas E. Harvey, advised against it. He added, however, that persons could make tax-deductible "gifts" to help put the station on the air.[15] Ernst Cramer, a top official at the powerful Springer Publishing Company of West Berlin, told us that his organization supported the concept of RIAS-TV and would endorse the idea in his publications' editorials. Cramer said his company had planned to get into cable TV, and that they would consider paying some RIAS-TV programming costs in exchange for access to the programs for their own cable use.

A few attempts at private fund-raising were made, but

were unsuccessful, so it was decided I would head a USIA task force that, together with our German counterparts, would come up with a business plan.[16] Before I had even started, however, we were cautioned by Ambassador Richard Burt that our German allies were already very sensitive about the American military presence and increasingly uncomfortable about the idea that the security of West Germany depended on America. Tact was critical.[17]

We hired Lee Hanna, a former NBC News vice president and TV station owner, to check out potential Berlin building locations and to make suggestions about programming. My feeling, shared by Hanna, was that the RIAS-TV program schedule should be built on an American model. You provided top entertainment programs to attract audiences and fast-paced, comprehensive news to lure viewers away from the more staid European program fare. In October 1985 we met with the two top RIAS radio officials, General Manager Peter Schiwy and his boss, William Marsh from the USIA (who had succeeded Nieburg as head of the station; station chiefs rotated periodically), and began to scout possible studio locations. I had met Schiwy a couple of years earlier when he was television news director at Norddeutscher Rundfunk (North German Radio) in Hamburg. An affable man, a native of Berlin, Dr. Schiwy studied law and East European history in Berlin and Cologne before beginning his journalistic career at Springer. At RIAS, Schiwy specialized in political broadcasts to East Germany. The plan was to have Schiwy and Marsh run RIAS TV, as well as RIAS Radio.

Schiwy was convinced that there would be a huge audience for RIAS-TV in Berlin, because there was already great curiosity about the project. "People will tune in," he predicted, adding that what was critical was to do the news in a way that appealed to young people. The younger generation in Germany, he explained, needed a new form of journalistic approach. A generational split marked not only the music German youth listened to but also the kind of reporting they watched. German TV announcers (who usually read the news) looked like funeral directors. "We have to change that to get new viewers." Schiwy also said there were very few qualified television producers, writers, and technicians available, and not much in terms of management personnel. It was critical to find a highly trained, experienced television producer. Hanna suggested that we bring the German broadcast personnel to the United States for training at major market TV stations and networks and bring American consultants to Berlin to help organize the management of the facility. Hanna concluded that the facility would require at least 20,000 square feet. He laid out a blueprint for a newsroom, production facilities, and offices.

By this point, Wick wanted RIAS-TV badly and looked to his top foreign service counselor, Stan Burnett, to help him articulate its importance to U.S. foreign policy before Congress, which would decide about funding. Burnett was a diplomat with many years of experience abroad, and he wrote the pitch for Wick with consummate skill: "Let's not forget [Berlin's] special place in our history and in our consciousness," Wick told a subcommittee. "The Berlin blockade, the Wall . . . and President Kennedy's speech bring it all back." Support for Berlin through television is especially important, he said, "since television is, like Berlin, a link to the outside, to the United States—a crucial consideration, given Berlin's isolated position within East Germany."

On April 2, 1985, one year to the day after our first session with Diepgen in Berlin, we met with him again, this time in Wick's office in Washington. Diepgen reported the sad news that he still could not get a commitment to fund the operation of a TV station. The finance ministry had some problems with the idea, he stated, noting that time was growing short. "Cable TV planning is moving rapidly in Berlin, and decisions will have to be made soon about holding channels open for RIAS-TV." But Diepgen was still optimistic. He felt that ultimately the West German government would come up with the funding if the United States matched it.[18] Wick replied that it would not be easy to pry the money loose from Congress, but that he would give it his best shot. Jerry Campbell, his trusted assistant, went to work on the project. He solicited letters of support from Chancellor Kohl and Secretary of State Shultz, among others, to send to Congress. RIAS director Marsh was in Washington the week of January 13, 1986, and Campbell arranged more than a dozen appointments with key staff members of the House and Senate. Campbell arranged a trip to Germany for eleven members of Congress during the Christmas recess, so that they could be briefed on RIAS-TV by Diepgen.

Momentum toward our side was starting. A television study about the power of TV in Germany released in early 1986 provided more ammunition for RIAS-TV. According to the survey, television was by far the most influential medium among West Germany's young people. Television was perceived as more credible than radio, newspapers, and magazines. It was the primary source of information, considerably more influential even than videos, phonographs, and books.[19] And a report by the German Academy of Sciences found that television had also become the most important leisure activity in East Germany. The majority of East Germans preferred spending "all or most" of their leisure time with their family watching television.[20] A West German media scientist was commissioned by Peter Schiwy to conduct a survey that concluded that young Berlin professionals would be attracted to a RIAS-TV station if it provided a mixture of sports, artistic movies, and political information.[21]

East German officials, meanwhile, were scurrying around trying to learn as much as they could about RIAS-TV planning. Peter Vincenz, chief press officer of the East German Embassy in Washington, kept in close touch with his counterpart at the USIA, Ralph Ruedy, a foreign service officer assigned to USIA and a veteran Europe specialist. Vincenz invited Ruedy to lunch at the Pier 7 restaurant along Washington's Main Avenue waterfront to see what he might learn. Vincenz talked about the plans to expand his country's press contacts in America and about additions to his staff. When lunch was almost over, he suddenly raised the issue of RIAS-TV. Ruedy realized immediately that this was the reason for the lunch. Ruedy was privy to the plans for RIAS-TV and knew that every word he uttered would be reported back to East Berlin. Vincenz asked if it was true that the United States planned to establish a TV station in West Berlin. Ruedy replied it was. "How would your government view this project?" he asked Vincenz. "Our foreign ministry doesn't like the idea," said Vincenz. Ruedy said the new station would be administered following the same guidelines as other agreements that affect Berlin, and that plans were going forward to put the facility on the air as soon as possible. Vincenz was visibly upset.

Diepgen for his part was urging his opposition not to turn RIAS-TV into a political tug-of-war. Members of the opposition Social Democrat Party replied they would support the station were it to be controlled by some form of public council, to ensure it did not become a mouthpiece for Diepgen. The mayor reported this to Wick. Schiwy met privately with SDP chairman Juergen Egert, who said the party was divided on the issue of RIAS-TV. He added that he, for one, would rather have the available frequency assigned to RIAS-TV than to a commercial station. "Better RIAS-TV than Springer or Luxembourg TV." Egert also said he would agree to a loosely structured RIAS-TV advisory board, rather than formal public control over the station.[22] He suggested that Schiwy also meet informally with a small group of influential SDP leaders in Berlin, which he did.

Now that plans for RIAS-TV were receiving widespread newspaper attention in Germany, the Soviets began to mount a sophisticated, multifaceted public affairs campaign in Berlin involving arms control and other peace initiatives. Russian press aides were seen at lunch with union leaders, journalists, and church groups. A television appearance by Red Army General Cherov turned out to be particularly effective. He was interviewed on state-run SFB television from Allied West Berlin, on a program broadcast throughout East Germany. Cherov, in civilian clothes, set no prearranged conditions for the interview. USIA officials in Berlin watched the wide-ranging discussion about cold war East-West tensions and felt that Cherov handled himself with skill. He was a model of the new, relaxed and informal Soviet propaganda technique.

Wick was appearing in European TV interviews. He was asked by a BBC interviewer if America might want to set up its own TV station in Great Britain, as it was planning to do in Berlin. "I don't think we really need it," said Wick, adding that there were already a multitude of stations and information services. The FRG (Federal Republic of Germany) was a less pluralistic government, having been "made up artificially" after the war. "Let me put it another way," he said. "We will not undertake in any country anything that is not welcomed by the people and its government."

"Lucky England," commented one West German television reporter after the Wick interview. "It [England] has a well-functioning democracy and, therefore, does not need such a station. At the risk of being misunderstood as anti-American . . . what I'm hearing here is the voice of some big brother."[23] Wick's comments were cited during the Berlin Senate's debate over RIAS-TV. Diepgen was concerned that the opposition might attempt to prove that America was planning to use RIAS-TV as a propaganda station. There were no newspaper reports on the Wick statement, and

Ambassador Burt advised us to let the matter drop without a clarifying comment. Nothing further surfaced.

Along with fear of propaganda, there was fear of competition. Broadcasters and cable operators in West Germany were concerned that RIAS-TV would go into their area via cable and compete for scarce advertising revenue. They thought RIAS-TV would seek "institutional" advertising from American firms such as IBM and Exxon. A West German television documentary in December 1986 claimed the Americans would use RIAS-TV to propagandize German citizens and questioned the legality of using public funds for this. To make its point, the documentary accused our Worldnet service of being "America's propaganda mouthpiece."

Still, there was local enthusiasm for RIAS-TV, based principally on the great popularity of RIAS Radio, which over the years had become part of the fabric of West Berlin. The Berlin tabloid *Bildzeitung* recalled that RIAS Radio had rallied the city's spirits in times of stress, and that citizens had shown their gratitude by making the station number one in popularity.[24] It was the strength of local sentiment that had encouraged German politicians to offer to cover the annual operating cost of RIAS-TV, estimated to be more than $20 million per year, and to earmark start-up costs of more than $3 million once a final commitment came from the American side. Our request for $12 million to build the station, and for an additional $2 million to cover annual transmission costs, was still pending in Congress.

Mayor Diepgen flew to Washington to lobby Congress on our behalf. "Berlin is not only a city of walls," Diepgen told lawmakers in February 1986. "It is also a lively city that needs to be protected—economically, politically, and militarily." Congressman Barney Frank (D-MA), was dubious, wondering if it was appropriate for the U.S. government to be operating a TV station in Berlin. Diepgen responded that it was important to have an American radio station located in Berlin, but even more important to have a TV station. "TV represents the future," he said. "Radio is the past. RIAS-TV would be a major symbol of America's commitment to Berlin and its freedom." He pointed out that the media scene had changed in Germany, and that if ever there was a time to move on RIAS-TV, that time was now. "For a small cost you have an incredible opportunity to play a role in European media policy at a crucial stage." Afterward Diepgen went to USIA headquarters to brief Wick, who was not optimistic. He asked how soon a funding commitment from the American side would be needed. Diepgen replied that German funds wouldn't become available until a favorable decision came from the American side. "Opposition could build in Germany, and it would be best to avoid protracted discussion by acting quickly," he added somewhat ominously.[25]

Jerry Campbell, who was Wick's key liaison with Congress, drafted a resolution of support for RIAS-TV. It was signed by several dozen key members of the House and Senate and helped pave the way for final congressional budget approval October 24, 1986. Tass greeted the news by calling RIAS-TV "large-scale . . . sabotage against the European Socialist countries."

It was time to get things moving. The USIA's director of European affairs, John Kordek, helped orchestrate an intricate and carefully timed exchange of letters between the Agency and various German bureaucracies proposing that Channel 25 in Berlin be used to transmit RIAS-TV. Kordek endorsed the appointment of Peter Schiwy as the new intendant of the station. Schiwy, in turn, wanted to bring in Gerhard Besserer, who was then program director of RIAS Radio, to head up the TV operation. Besserer knew how to get the attention of the East Germans, especially young people. One way to stir things up was to carry open-air rock concerts live on RIAS from the Western side of the Berlin Wall. In June 1987, RIAS Radio promoted a three-day-long "Berlin Wall Concert" by the British rock group Genesis, among others, that took place at the West Berlin side of the wall. More than 1,000 East German youths, gathered at the other side of the wall to hear the concert, chanted, "The wall must go" and "Long live freedom and democracy." East German police used batons to quell the disturbance and to drive people from the street leading to the wall.[26] On a visit to Berlin, Wick dropped in to meet Besserer, about whom he had heard a lot from Schiwy. Besserer was surprised that Wick knew so much about him. They chatted briefly about Besserer's background, then Wick cut to the chase. "Okay, you're it," he told Besserer. "How fast can you get this TV station on the air?" "This will take some time," responded a surprised Besserer. Wick looked down at his watch and smiled. "You have nine months," he said.

We turned down an offer from the Berlin city government to use its abandoned old Congress Hall, a dilapidated structure that had begun to crumble under its own weight years before (when it had been in better shape, West Berliners called it the "pregnant oyster"). The posh estate of a German film director, located in a beautiful setting on the banks of Berlin's Wansee River, was available for lease at a reasonable price, but it would have required extensive renovations to build broadcast studio facilities. In the end we selected a site that was already housing a Berlin community cable television operation, meaning that broadcast lines and a satellite receiving dish were already in place. Perhaps best of all, the building had been designated a historical site by the city, which would donate space for RIAS-TV. Located in the French-occupied sector of Berlin, the building needed a lot of work. Many of its windows were broken, and bullet holes from World War II still pockmarked the exterior. But it was rent-free.

Our top engineer/architect, Barry Malko, soon found shortcuts for building studios and offices. Normally it would have taken a year or longer to get construction permits, but Malko discovered that though he was dealing with a historical building he didn't have to go through regular channels. Construction could be started immediately without the usual permits. The second he had finished the architectural and engineering plans, Malko began tearing down walls. Cameras, lights, videotape machines—everything had to be purchased, but it was important to keep USIA's bureaucracy out of the picture as much as possible to avoid costly delays. Malko contacted John Klein, the American Embassy's chief business officer and a crackerjack operator who knew how to cut corners. Klein's only request was that Malko keep Washington off his back. Malko called the USIA's chief contracting officer in Washington, Phil Rogers, to tell him how many problems there were in Berlin, and how much of his time would be required to sort things out. Malko was trying his best to convince Rogers to give up control of the project. Rogers agreed.

German labor laws required that every office have an outside view and a large number of "tea kitchens" for staff use. Malko made sure all his bases were covered. Experience in managing large government projects had taught him that the first couple of months were critical and that before you started anything all of the key ingredients had to be gathered. He worked 16-hour days. Walls went up; crates of camera and editing equipment began to arrive. There was the problem of hiring a staff of some two hundred, then getting them to focus on the content of the programs. Gerhard Besserer felt that the material could be quirky but, above all, it had to be credible. "If anyone knows what propaganda is, it's the people who live under communism," Besserer pointed out. Although Besserer had done amazing things with RIAS Radio, he lacked TV experience, so we hired Peter Kendall as a consultant, and CBS News director Robert Camfiord was brought in to train the technical production staff.

German television was not known for its glitz. It was not uncommon for a German TV news anchor to stare blankly at the camera and say, "Where am I going next, to sports or weather?" Kendall felt it would be necessary to raise the energy level and to give things more polish. He therefore introduced the "telex," a hidden earphone through which instructions to the anchor are barked from the director in the control room. Kendall looked at the cramped control room. He noticed there was no seat for Besserer, the broadcast's producer. "Where are you going to sit during the news?" he asked Besserer. "In my office," replied the young German. "No you're not. You're going to be in the control room," replied Kendall, who then ordered that the control room be expanded in size.

A major dress rehearsal was scheduled for the weekend before RIAS-TV's inaugural broadcast. A few days prior to the rehearsal, Kendall noticed that Besserer was not in his office. Besserer's secretary explained that her boss had taken the week off. Kendall was furious, but he was powerless to reprimand Besserer, who was protected from being fired as a German government employee. As such, Besserer was entitled to six week's vacation per year, and every three years could take an additional four-week "cure" at a sanatorium or spa. Besserer returned in time for the Saturday rehearsal, but went to a cocktail party instead. The next day, Kendall got together with the staff to watch a tape playback of the on-air rehearsal, but Besserer decided not to attend because he was watching TV coverage of a soccer game between West Germany and the Netherlands. While Besserer displayed the typical German civil servant work ethic, he knew his audience, and how to communicate with it. He felt he didn't need any rehearsal time. He already knew what to do. He would communicate with his audience of quirky Berliners with such things as dog shit and, as we shall see, phallic-looking asparagus stalks.

Directors of the United States Information Agency.
ROW ONE (LEFT TO RIGHT): Theodore C. Streibert, Arthur Larson, George V. Allen. ROW TWO: Edward R. Murrow, Carl T. Rowan, Leonard H. Marks. ROW THREE: Frank Shakespeare, James Keogh, John E. Reinhardt. ROW FOUR: Charles Z. Wick, Bruce S. Gelb, Henry E. Catto. ROW FIVE: Joseph Duffey.
(PHOTOS USIA WORLD; PHOTO OF HENRY E. CATTO BY BILL FITZ-PATRICK; PHOTO OF JOSEPH DUFFEY BY DAVID BURNETT)

ABOVE LEFT: John Houseman, director of the Voice of the America, 1942-1943; ABOVE RIGHT: Robert Bauer delivering the Voice of America's first broadcast on February 24, 1942, in German. "The news may be good," he said. "The news may be bad. But we shall tell you the truth"; BELOW: Edward R. Murrow, USIA director, 1961-1964. (COURTESY VOICE OF AMERICA)

Emergency session of the UN Security Council after the Soviet downing of Korean Airlines flight KE-007. Pictured on the screen is a transcript of the pilot's words: "The target is destroyed." Note the expression of the Soviet ambassador to the UN, Oleg Troyanovsky. Seated at far right is Jeane Kirkpatrick, U.S. ambassador to the UN. (COURTESY UNITED STATES INFORMATION AGENCY)

Author discusses plans regarding Worldnet's TV program on the American invasion of Grenada with Prime Minister Eugenia Charles of Dominica, chairman of the Organization of Eastern Caribbean States, October 1983. (COURTESY UNITED STATES INFORMATION AGENCY)

Author showing USIA director Charles Wick (both at far left) how the Worldnet system operates. (COURTESY UNITED STATES INFORMATION AGENCY)

CLOCKWISE FROM UPPER LEFT: Ambassador Jeane Kirkpatrick being briefed before a Worldnet broadcast; President George Bush being prepared for a broadcast; an Italian journalist in Rome posing a question to Secretary of State George Shultz, on the screen, in Washington; Charles Wick in the Worldnet control room.

(WORLDNET PRESS PHOTO, COURTESY UNITED STATES INFORMATION AGENCY)

Conference to promote exchange of information between the Soviet Union and the United States, October 1986. FROM LEFT: USIA director Wick, Alexandr Yakovlev, and Valentin Falin, chairman of the Novosti news service.
(USED BY PERMISSION OF CHARLES Z. WICK)

UPPER RIGHT: RIAS (Radio in the American Sector, a joint U.S.-German radio service started after World War II) utilizes a U.S. Army weapons carrier equipped with a rudimentary loudspeaker system to broadcast the news during the Berlin Airlift, 1948.
LOWER RIGHT: Forty years later, Peter Lamy, a technician at RIAS, demonstrates a microwave mobile radio unit.
(COURTESY RIAS PRESS OFFICE)

A group of Mujahideen sitting atop a captured Soviet armored vehicle.
(COURTESY AFGHAN MEDIA RESOURCE CENTER)

Haji Sayed Daud, director of the Afghan Media Resource Center, interviews an
Afghan militia commander in the Kandahar province, September 1988.
(COURTESY AFGHAN MEDIA RESOURCE CENTER)

Jorge Mas Canosa, the driving force behind Radio and TV Marti, with President Reagan.
(PHOTO BY ENRIQUE MUÑOZ, COURTESY CUBAN-AMERICAN NATIONAL FOUNDATION)

Fat Albert, moored at Dujoe Key in Florida.
(COURTESY TV MARTI)

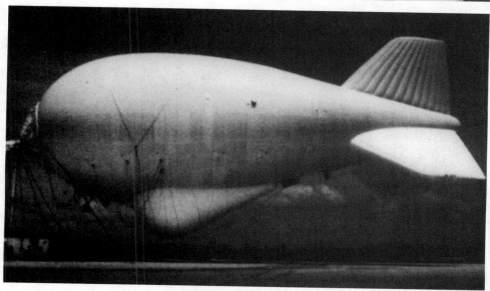

A Cuban MI-17 helicopter equipped with TV antennas and transmitters used to jam TV Marti's transmissions to Havana. Photo taken at La Cabaña air base outside Havana.
(COURTESY TV MARTI)

President Ronald Reagan awarding Charles Z. Wick the
1988 Presidential Citizens Medal.

The station debuted with a nightly news broadcast, followed shortly thereafter with a breakfast show, from 6:00 to 10:00 A.M. weekdays.[27] As expected, East German television lambasted the new RIAS-TV service, but Besserer saw this as proof that his operation was making an impact. "The failings of RIAS Radio are notorious" said a government official on GDR-TV, who went on to describe RIAS-TV as "perverse." Others, even on the other side of the wall, were soon to think it might have a purpose.

Besserer's news was meant to appeal to young viewers, and youthful anchors were used regularly. The program was fast-paced, with lots of visuals and flashy computer graphics. Besserer also had to be mindful to stress a U.S. connection, not just because it was a joint German-American enterprise, but because America was, he said, still a symbol of freedom for East Germans. Besserer wanted stories that affected people. He wanted to be controversial, to get people involved, to make them angry, to give them something to remember—to give them dog shit, if necessary. Above all, he wanted to continue to attract large numbers of viewers, especially from the other side of the wall. Kendall had earlier lost his battle to Besserer over the dog story, and the result was that phones at the station had rung off the hooks. Most of the calls came from irate viewers. Besserer wanted to get people angry and involved, and he was succeeding. Kendall would soon have another problem with Besserer, who wanted to show tape of a musical called *Lulu*, which featured a nude and well-endowed young woman gyrating wildly holding two large stalks of asparagus. Kendall pleaded with Besserer, who reluctantly dropped some of the more revealing of Lulu's parts, but not all. The asparagus stayed. The phones again rang off the hooks.

RIAS-TV was taking off. It was reaching an audience of 3 million East Germans, dwarfing the size of the audiences of state-run TV stations in East and West Berlin. A new Saturday morning rock music program, from 9:00 A.M. to noon, soon became a favorite of young people in Berlin and East Germany. The program was done in music TV (MTV) style and featured lots of video clips, interviews, music, and news, as well as art deco sets that changed every week. A year later, GDR-TV as copied it with a program of its own in an attempt to lure young viewers back. Mimicking their anti-establishment West Berlin counterparts, the young producers of the East German program "11-99," who were often critical of the

Communist government establishment, became a problem for the regime. Another popular RIAS-TV youth-oriented magazine show, "High Live," was cloned by GDR-TV.

RIAS Radio and TV, I am convinced, did their part to bring down the wall. RIAS-TV and radio programs provided a window to the West for young people in the dreary GDR. Older people saved their money to buy a little piece of land somewhere in the countryside with a little hut on it, and they would flee to their "dachas" for the weekend. But escape for younger people meant listening to radio stations and watching television, and the impact of media in the GDR was incalculable. Hundreds of miles from Berlin, nearer to the West German border, young people in Communist-held areas watched television beamed in from the free part of Germany, from Sweden and Finland, and via satellite. "Sesame Street," "Bonanza," "I Spy," and other shows provided East Germany with a surrogate social and cultural background that their official state-run media didn't supply. RIAS-TV tailored programs for East Germany that would resonate with its population. Each morning dissidents from East Berlin called RIAS-TV on the telephone, and interviews were played daily on RIAS-TV's morning breakfast program. The airspace between East and West had been broken, and the wall would follow.

↔ 8 ↔

That's Entertainment!

AT CHRISTMASTIME IN 1957, USIA TRAINEE RALPH HINES WAS TAKEN by a Lapp driver and his reindeer to thirty-seven isolated Norwegian communities to show films and hand out pamphlets about America. A few years later, in Africa, USIA public affairs officer Merton Bland drove around the bush country in a pickup truck showing pro-American movies. His trip was generally a success. "But one day my twelve-year-old son Bruce set up the projector on a fire ant hill," recalled Bland. "The place cleared out pretty fast." In time, rather than messing around with reel-to-reel films, Hines and Bland settled into cushy embassy easy chairs and dealt in videocassettes.

Videocassette recorders first began to be smuggled into Eastern Europe from the West beginning in about 1980. There weren't very many of them, and they were expensive, so a few venturesome individuals with entrepreneurial flair held illegal screenings in their homes, or the homes of others, to raise money.[1] Caught by Moscow authorities, one received a jail sentence of three and a half years for taking videocassettes from house to house and charging for showings. Another was sentenced to a three-year jail term for dubbing and selling pornographic tapes.[2] Indeed, until the late 1980s, videos were still considered precious novelties. In April 1984, Wick and I went to Amman, Jordan, for a meeting of USIA public affairs officers from the Middle East. As we drove into town one evening, we noticed people patiently waiting in a line that stretched for well over a city block. They were waiting to get into a video rental store. "We've got to get our PAOs [public affairs officers] into this business," said Wick as we scanned the scene. The USIA already ran more than a hundred libraries and cultural centers worldwide. Wick thought they should also run video clubs.

The videocassette trend was an exciting prospect. Like the developing technology of direct broadcast satellites, videocassettes would provide a fundamental change in the delivery of propaganda, which would now be available in the privacy of one's home. Although there were laws forbidding the copying of videotapes in Russia, the ban would not be enforceable, predicted Arkady Vakssberg, media critic of the Soviet weekly *Nedelya*. "Nothing is sweeter than forbidden fruit," he wrote.[3] As soon as I got back to Washington, my deputy Richard Levy and I met with the USIA foreign service officers in charge of our regional offices around the world. We selected ten countries in which to conduct test marketing, to see if an American-style video club would work at our information and cultural centers there. From the results we would determine whether or not to establish permanent video libraries. The sample run, we decided, would include feature and entertainment films, in the same way that our overseas libraries included popular fiction. We appointed Merton Bland to be our Captain Video, the man responsible for managing the operation from Washington. Bland had seen his share of ant hills (his résumé also included a Ph.D.) and was enthusiastic about the idea of using VCRs as part of our overseas information programs. He began by publishing a newsletter that went to USIA offices abroad, which, it turned out, were eager to stock embassy libraries with videos.

To the test countries selected we sent out an 80-title video starter kit. These countries represented a cross-section from developing to sophisticated societies, from the smallest one-person USIA operation in Gabarone to one of the largest in Bonn.[4] Word got out fast. Within days, so many people were coming into our libraries and cultural centers to view and check out the tapes that we increased the catalogue to 231 titles and expanded the number of test areas. In some locations, people would check out anything they could get their hands on because local government TV programming was usually so bad. Many had access to only a single state-run television channel, which might be on only during daylight hours, so videotapes filled the void. In Pakistan, for example, it was (initially, anyway) a lot more interesting to watch a Jane Fonda exercise video, or even an old USIA propaganda film about mechanized farming, than a black-and-white close-up of someone meditating directly into a camera lens. In addition to feature films, we stocked public television programs, such as Alistair Cooke's thirteen-part "America" series, a tape collection on "The Black West," seventeen episodes of "American Short Stories," and "The Writer in America" videos, among others. We encouraged TV and film producers to donate their tapes to our library, and a few did, in part because it gave them a chance to introduce their material to international audiences. In many parts of Africa, for example, there was no broadcast TV, and videocassettes were being purchased for home entertainment. Videos were inexpensive, reusable, and effective. Although we offered films such as *Star Wars* and *Raiders of the Lost Ark* as a come-on, Bland reminded our libraries and cultural centers abroad not to lose sight that "your mission is to influence people," and not to order only movies and rock videos.

Wick felt there was nothing wrong with our USIA posts becoming entertainment centers, if by doing so they could attract more visitors to the embassies. He thought there was a unique opportunity to enhance America's image abroad by personally bringing the resources of Hollywood to bear on public diplomacy. Most public affairs officers felt Hollywood films could sweeten relationships with top government officials, by increasing ambassadorial influence and opening the door for more serious programming. But foreign service officer Robert Nevitt, who was in charge of USIA's public affairs operations in Asia, told me that works of fiction that weren't "sociologically sound or historically accurate" could lead audiences to draw the wrong conclusions about American society and values. Nevitt felt that many films, such as *Kramer vs. Kramer* and *The Texas Chain Saw Massacre* would be seen by foreign audiences as "representing the truth about the United States." He thought it would be best to have stars travel with films and speak about them with audiences after screenings. Nevitt suggested to me that Gregory

Peck could travel to Asia with the war film *Twelve o'Clock High,* to talk about American attitudes toward war and threat of war, after audiences screen the movie.[5] Such a plan was hardly feasible, and, fortunately, Nevitt's dim view was not shared by his other foreign service colleagues who were in charge of USIA's public affairs activities in other areas of the world. American films were by far our most popular export. Soviet films, meanwhile, could not compete commercially with U.S. and European products because of their poor quality and lack of money-making prospects. In Latin America in 1984 (even in pro-Marxist Nicaragua) fewer Soviet movies were being distributed than in previous years, and even among those shown, their impact was insignificant, according to a USIA study.[6] American films could open doors for us overseas, Wick agreed, by bringing us increased contact with people abroad. Political restrictions and lack of hard currency limited commercial distribution in many countries. Wick felt that distributors could make videos available to us for use in such countries with little commercial loss. He had asked me in May 1983 to go with him to Hollywood to meet with several of his friends who were influential in the entertainment industry. There, we met first with agent Bill Hayes, who suggested that the best person to head up a Hollywood committee to help the USIA would be Leo Jaffe, chairman emeritus of Columbia Pictures. Jaffe was a Hollywood icon, having spent more than fifty years at Columbia, starting out as a junior accountant and working his way up to the top of the corporation, where he was responsible for such blockbusters as *Lawrence of Arabia* and *Bridge on the River Kwai.* Wick quickly approved the idea of approaching Jaffe and Bill Hayes, and John Mitchell (then president of the Academy of Motion Picture Arts and Sciences) proceeded to enlist Jaffe, who was enthusiastic about the project from the outset and agreed to head what we would call a private sector "Motion Picture and TV Committee," which would obtain, free of charge, the best Hollywood films and TV programs to show at USIA centers abroad. Jaffe rolled up his sleeves and immediately got to work to recruit committee members, who included, among others, Mike Frankovich, chairman of Screen Gems; Irving Felt, chairman of the board of Madison Square Garden; Milton Rackmil, former president of Universal Pictures and Decca Records; and John Mitchell. Soon to be added was Aaron Spelling, producer of some of the most popular TV series and sitcoms, including

"Charlie's Angels," "The Mod Squad," "The Love Boat," and "Dynasty." Jaffe, who worked several hours a day cajoling his high-level show business friends to make their programs available to the USIA free of charge, later recalled our first approach to him: "I was told my duties would entail no more than one hour a week," said Jaffe. "I would get no salary, and would be expected to pay for any expenses incurred. Financially, opportunities like this don't come too often, and I accepted."[7]

President Reagan took personal interest in the committee and greeted its members in the Oval Office on July 21, 1983, to formally launch the committee's activities. It was the biggest concerted patriotic effort on the part of Hollywood to help its government since World War II. Following the meeting with Reagan, my staff and I coordinated committee activities, often by Picturephone, with participants in New York and Los Angeles, so as to avoid sensitive problems regarding travel of committee members, whom we could not reimburse for such expenses. Considering the important potential benefits that Jaffe's committee could bring the USIA, we were convinced that paying a few thousand dollars for a ninety-minute, three-way Picturephone meeting was certain to be a good investment for the government.

Perks were doled out in other ways, Mo Rothman a case-in-point. Rothman was a high-powered agent who administered the rights to the Charlie Chaplin movies on behalf of Lady Chaplin. The comedian's silent classics (*City Lights, Limelight, The Gold Rush,* and others) were immensely popular overseas, especially in areas such as Sanaa in the Middle East, where English was not spoken. To get access to the films, Jaffe signed up Rothman to become a member of our film acquisition committee. Rothman, who lived in England, stipulated that he would cooperate with the Agency if we paid his round-trip, first-class air travel to the United States, where he would attend his daughter's wedding. Only then would he sign over the rights to the Chaplin films. The Agency's director of management, Woody Kingman, aware of Wick's interest in the private-sector motion picture committee, approved Rothman's ticket to New York, where Wick, Jaffe, my deputy Richard Levy, and I met him for the contract signing. The licensing fees for these films would have been many times more than the first-class air fare for Rothman, who later requested follow-up trips every six months to "oversee" how the

Chaplin films were being used by our embassies overseas.[8] Rothman also requested that our embassy in London obtain tickets for him to the Ascot races in June 1986. Complicating things was that Rothman was a Canadian citizen, and our embassy did not wish to contact British authorities on his behalf. Robert (Bud) Korengold, our public affairs officer in London, and three of his assistants worked for days in an unsuccessful effort to get the tickets for Rothman from personal contacts.[9]

I suggested to Wick that enough was enough, and Rothman's subsequent requests for perks were turned down. Still, Chaplin's silent films proved to be excellent "communicators" in areas where English was a problem, such as the Middle East. Posts felt unanimously that the popularity of these films gave them an opportunity to maintain contact with key foreign officials in an apolitical social setting. Jaffe's committee gathered momentum and acquired more than 500 hours of free programming, or about 18 days' worth,[10] at a book value of several million dollars, according to Agency estimates. Timing couldn't have been better. Jaffe's committee was revving up in 1984, just as our video clubs were being put in place at our embassies abroad, and films could be dubbed onto videotape.

We featured packages that included everything from feature films, music, and sports to the arts, business, medicine, and health. We were light years ahead of everyone else in education and training videos. English-language instruction videos were especially in demand.

Within a few months our experiment had become mainstream, and almost one hundred USIA posts were on board. Bland asked them to write us about their experiences, so that they could share information. "We want it all," said Mert in his newsletter. "We won't change the facts or hide any warts."

Our officers at the embassy in Islamabad replied that it was featuring the screening of "a tape of the day" and that this was drawing large audiences. The USIA cultural center public affairs officer in Riyadh said they were keeping requests for tapes in a shoe box. Not exactly high-powered propaganda strategy, but one of their major preoccupations was video theft, which became a growing problem. Bland shared such information with other posts. "To avoid theft," he advised, "many video outlets with open shelves remove the cassettes from the cases and substitute pieces of wood." Generally, however, the news was good. Our U.S. cultural center in Kuala Lumpur cabled that the number of visitors coming into the center had doubled since the video club was introduced. One problem was getting videos on the shelves. Each tape had to be approved in advance by the Malaysian censorship board. The average video was borrowed nine times as often as the average book.[11] Our tape duplication center in Washington became swamped with requests. Posts were ripping open their mail pouches looking for tapes, and then panicking when they didn't arrive, because we could not keep up with the demand.

Life in the video club business was not without its embarrassing moments. At the conclusion of a video screening of new plowing techniques, in Nairobi, members of a high-level, invitation-only audience were startled to find themselves looking at pornographic scenes. The video technician had not expected to see anything else on the tape and let it run. I immediately received a scathing cable from a mortified public affairs officer, and proceeded to try and find out what happened. Our Washington tape center maintained that it was supposed to have been a blank tape and could not explain what happened. We never did find the culprit.

In some countries in Eastern Europe, where authorities did not permit citizens to enter our centers, videotape programs were displayed in window boxes so that they could be watched from the street. Large crowds would gather. In the fall of 1986, authorities in Prague finally dismantled a protective barrier that had surrounded the American Embassy for ten months. Almost immediately, a stream of humanity started pouring into the embassy library. In one month alone, more than 5,000 people attended video screenings. Over 330 tapes—mostly Hollywood movies—were loaned from our Prague video library, and approximately 150 people came in each day to watch feature films. Foreign-made VCR machines were selling on the black market for as much as $4,300, more than the average Czech worker made in a year. Our office in Sofia, Bulgaria, reported that in a single month, 4,100 people watched the video schedule of news, documentaries, and feature films. One day the cultural deputy from the Soviet embassy in Sofia walked into our video library and signed up for a membership.[12] Said our officer in a cable: "Attendance figures reinforce our view that Bulgarians maintain a strong, if somewhat superficial, interest in American culture despite their government's attempt to limit access to it."[13] Our public affairs officer in East Berlin said that the video club was pulling in a new, young audience. The library audience had nearly doubled. The Hungarian ministry of culture permitted people to use our video club collections, including teacher-training programs, at seven of its universities. In Jordan, tapes of *Chorus Line* were snapped up, and young men said they particularly liked the cheerleaders on NFL football highlight tapes. Thousands of U.S.-educated Jordanians checked out tapes on American football, and films on American art and artists, to maintain cultural and intellectual ties with America. "Will it be possible to expand these offerings?' our post in Amman cabled us.

Video libraries had succeeded in getting through to young people where other forms of propaganda had failed. Our posts reported that they had been able to increase contact with youth through political groups, schools, and other organizations. VCRs furthered their knowledge and interest in a wider range of aspects of American life and policies. It enabled posts to reach members of its elite list of foreign contacts who, under normal circumstances, were too busy to attend film shows or other cultural presentations in the embassy. In Warsaw, video customers were predominantly from clubs, schools, and other organizations. English-teaching and student-counseling videos were especially popular, but feature films topped the list. Hollywood films personified what the American dream was all about. Our embassy in Warsaw thought that the films gave more dimension and depth to the American cinema, and American society, than that "offered by the limited number of films selected by Film Polski to present to Polish audiences." Jackson Diehl, Warsaw bureau chief of the *Washington Post,* recalled that the availability of Western feature films in the mid-1980s, and their duplication by the Polish underground, caused a massive run on videocassette players, which could then be purchased openly in currency stores. "You could watch all kinds of features on Western lifestyles and affluence, and this had an effect on a broad audience," said Diehl. "When the regime was ready to collapse for economic reasons, not for political reasons, there was this organized opposition that still exists in Warsaw, disciplined and ready to take over."[14] We provided feature films for Poland's New American Film Festival in 1987, including *The Color of Money, Hannah and Her Sisters, Children of a*

Lesser God, Crimes of the Heart, and *Brighton Beach Memoirs,* all of which "visibly reasserted the American cultural presence in Warsaw," according to our embassy. Soviet features had little appeal. "There was no such thing as a Soviet video in Poland," said Diehl. "You couldn't get a video with a Soviet movie on it."[15]

One of our most popular and affordable video offerings was a special series of every Academy Award–winning film since 1927 (the 1927 winner was *Wings,* with Gary Cooper). During our first full year of operation, our top five bestsellers in the classic film category were: *Mr. Smith Goes to Washington* (1939), *It Happened One Night* (1934), *On the Waterfront* (1954), *Born Yesterday* (1950), and *A Man For All Seasons* (1966). In the sports and exercise category, the most popular tape was *Dr. J's Basketball Stuff.* In second place was *This Is American Football,* and third was *Jane Fonda's New Workout.* Before long we had become the world's largest international video club, with more than 150 locations overseas, a catalogue of more than 1,000 titles, and some 20,000 videotapes in circulation. Our video libraries were flourishing everywhere, but especially in Bucharest, Prague, Sofia, and Warsaw.

Our tapes also found their way onto the Russian black market. Although authorities had imposed strict laws forbidding copying of videocassettes, it was a law that simply could not be enforced. Video dubs began to circulate on the black market by the tens of thousands. Soviet authorities were fighting a losing battle, and by 1985 the ban on videocassettes was lifted. The first Russian video rental stores were opened outside Moscow, but others quickly followed. There was nothing authorities could do to stem the flow of pornography, violence, or anti-Soviet themes. Videos of Tina Turner, the Live Aid Concert with Mick Jagger, and others featuring music previously banned in the USSR began finding their way in through the unchecked luggage of tourists and diplomats who had visited the West.[16] In 1985, it took the average Soviet worker about six months to afford a Soviet-made VCR, which was priced at $1,700. There were still thousands of people on the waiting list and Soviet manufacturers could not keep up with the demand. Foreign-manufactured VCRs were better-made and more popular than the Soviet brand, despite their higher cost. Poland and other Eastern European countries were slower to capitalize on the new video technology, and for many years practically all tape machines were purchased from Asia and the

West. VCRs were soon to become the number-one consumer demand item in the Soviet Union.

Engineers who manned state-run TV satellite ground stations in the Soviet Union copied movies and other programs beamed from the West, and then sold cassettes of them on the black market. There were unconfirmed reports that in Moscow and Soviet Armenia astrophysicists were using receivers in their observatories to record programs from Western TV satellites, which they then sold.[17] Despite their incredibly high cost, as many as 2,000 people might be on a waiting list for pirated tapes. A fast-growing videotape black market was headquartered in Soviet Estonia, on the Finnish border. Western programs on Finnish TV were taped in nearby Estonia, dubbed into Russian, and then spirited off to Moscow and other major Soviet cities. When the Soviet deputy minister of film visited the United States, he realized, said his host Greg Guroff, a USIA Soviet expert, that just about everyone had a VCR at home. "He looked around here and began to understand that the threat of video piracy was big-time, and that the problem would only get bigger in the Soviet Union." What he realized, perhaps for the first time, was that video piracy would be more successful than decades of live-broadcast propaganda.

The USSR wasn't alone. A video news magazine, showing a summary of Western news events, made the rounds in Czechoslovakia. Anti-Communist fantasy films like *Rambo II* and *Rocky IV* were wildly popular. In Poland, films that had not been released publicly found their way as videos. Among them was a documentary entitled *Witnesses,* which was about a pogrom in the city of Kielce in 1946.[18] One of the most explosive and disturbing motion pictures about Communist human rights violations was a Polish film entitled *The Interrogation.* It had been banned and put under lock and key by government censors in 1985. It was forbidden even to mention the film in the government-controlled press. When the active cultural underground seized a copy and released the videocassette, it became the film sensation of Poland. Thousands of video dubs were made of the film, which showed the brutal treatment of a young Polish woman in a Stalinist-type prison.[19] This and other underground films became powerful weapons for Polish government opposition leaders. No longer did it matter that certain films were banned from theaters, for they could be easily acquired and screened in the comfort and privacy of one's home, in secret, on videotape. A whole video underground grew up. When a Warsaw church announced after mass that *El Cid* would be shown that night, it really meant that an underground videotape would be screened in the church basement.[20] Polish law eventually permitted video shops, which were filled with pirated dubs of Western movies and video games. By 1986 there were some 250,000 videocassette recorders in Poland, mostly imported from the West.

By the following year, there were 30,000 videocassette recorders in Leningrad alone,[21] about 2 million VCRs in the six Soviet bloc countries, and even though Soviet propagandists were doing their best to keep pace with their Western counterparts, Kremlin disinformers were fast becoming relics of a bygone era, so they tried to produce their own spy thrillers. The world premier of *Can-Can in an English Garden* took place at the Eighteenth All-Union Film Festival in Minsk, in the Soviet Ukraine. The counter-propaganda story of intrigue at Radio Liberty headquarters opened with Hollywood-type publicity fanfare. In the picture, an anti-Soviet spy is discovered at Radio Liberty and dealt with harshly. A review in *Sovetskaya Rossiya* stated, "Against the background of one-dimensional cardboard caricatures of villains who flash across the screen, the particularly noble and positive Rutkovsky [the spy] looks so outstanding that you wonder why the professionals from the CIA do not realize that he is a Soviet agent."[22] *Can-Can* was the first Soviet feature film on the ideological sabotage being conducted against the USSR by Western radio, which had become a major theme of the Soviet counter-propaganda offensive. The film had an experienced director and a cast of Soviet stars. More interesting than the film were the reviews. In former times, Soviet arts critics would never have dared to fault a Soviet propaganda film.[23]

The video revolution obviously played a part in the critics' increasing boldness, and the Kremlin's information blockade was being breached by a host of other electronic gadgets, including, of course, the home computer and copying machine. Copiers were kept under lock and key by security officers from the Soviet ministry of interior affairs, which scrupulously monitored the number of documents copied and by whom.[24] But technology was rendering efforts by the Soviet government to control information useless. A little printer for a home computer could easily be hidden and thousands of documents reproduced in a matter of hours. The joke going around

Moscow was that Marx's *Das Kapital* wouldn't have made it through a computer program check, because it would have been found invalid.[25] Solzhenitsyn's books were copied to computer disks and distributed. *Samizdat,* or self-published newspapers and magazines, began to spring up overnight throughout Russia.[26] The Soviet government tried pathetically to argue that people really didn't need computers. Great writers, scientists, and composers throughout history hadn't had computers, and they managed pretty well. It would be bothersome to creative writers, being hurried by the electronic gadget to work faster, the government argued.[27] Said the Russian émigré writer Vladimir Voinovich of the computer age: "In the course of its history the Soviet state has successfully dealt with many enemies, but I'm afraid it's not going to be able to cope with this one."[28] Voinovich had visited a friend in Chicago in the early 1980s and was fascinated to see a computer in operation firsthand. "And what would such a computer cost in Moscow?" asked his friend. "Well, as you know," said Voinovich, "prices in Moscow are all very stable, and this applies to computers as well. A computer like yours would cost you no less than three and no more than ten years in jail."[29]

↔ 9 ↔

The Faustian Bargain

BY 1987 INFORMATION WAS STREAMING OVER THE IRON CURTAIN. Most of East Germany was being buffeted by television signals from its neighbors.[1] Realizing that joining was better than fighting, East German officials arranged to bring Western TV programs via cable signals into Dresden, located in the "valley of the blind," so called because it was an area too distant from the West to receive programs transmitted over the air. To dissuade workers from moving out of Dresden and into areas where they could watch West German television, the authorities sanctioned cable transmission from Western stations.

Elsewhere, Bulgarians could pick up channels from neighboring Yugoslavia, which in turn was bombarded by TV signals from Italy and Austria. Swedish television was popular in Poland. Liberalized Hungarian television, which included commercial programs from the United States picked up via Austria, was being received in Czechoslovakia. Albanians could pick up programs from Yugoslavia and Greece, and parts of the Soviet Union were being bombarded by programs from neighboring Finland. In Soviet Estonia, where the Finnish TV schedule was published in the local newspaper, the most popular show was "Kojak," which was taped by Estonians and sent to their friends in Russia.[2] There were complaints from Ukrainian authorities that religious programming was coming in from Czechoslovakia. Communist authorities were at a loss as to what to do about the information invasion—not only from ground transmitters, but from TV satellites hovering overhead. Wallace W. Littell, the USIA's public affairs officer in the Soviet Union, had predicted in 1981 that satellites beaming directly into home dishes "would present the Soviet authorities with their most vivid nightmare." By 1987, it was a nightmare about to come true.

The increasing accessibility of images, ideas, and information, facilitated by the rapid development and deployment of communications technology, presented closed societies with a Faustian bargain. On one hand, the new technology provided totalitarian governments with a new tool with which to control and manipulate public opinion, on an unprecedented scale. On the other, using the new technology meant those same governments would be subjected to greater domestic and international scrutiny, reducing their ability to control what their citizens saw and heard. Soviet officials knew that information coming in from the West would quickly debunk their own version of events. They feared that people would get angry when they learned how much they had been deceived, and that government-controlled media would lose what scant credibility it had. Television pictures from the affluent West were certain to generate discontent.

The Kremlin announced not only that it was illegal to receive foreign TV signals on a home satellite dish but that it was virtually impossible to do so in the first place. "This would require," reported one government-controlled newspaper, "special antennas with a diameter of four to six meters, as well as other receiving equipment that cannot be manufactured at home."

But resourceful Soviet hobbyists would have none of this. Although sensitive electronic components were difficult to come by, and those lucky enough to acquire them had to register the parts with military authorities, thousands of tiny home satellite dishes were being built to capture signals from space. A thriving black market trade developed in electronic parts that were either stolen from or rejected by the military. Even screen doors were being fashioned into satellite dishes, and one resident of Tashkent built a miniature satellite-receiving antenna that was about the size of a carton of cigarettes.[3] We at USIA knew that electrical engineering was a popular pastime in Eastern Europe, and that many people there would have the skills to assemble the components required to receive the signal (a "low noise amplifier" and a "down converter") in addition to the satellite dish itself, which could be as small as 1.5 to 2 meters in size. A new generation of more powerful satellites, capable of being received by even smaller satellite receivers, was coming to Europe. Satellite TV reception was on its way whether state authorities liked it or not. In January 1986 I cabled our posts in Eastern Europe, asking them to inquire about the availability of children's sleds, which we would then tell people how to use as TV satellite dishes, via Voice of America broadcasts. In response, our post in Romania advised me that TV satellite dishes were readily available to the public in that country and that "sleds would not be necessary to take down the Worldnet signal."[4] In East Germany, neighbors would pool money together to buy satellite dishes, which were connected by wires strung to dozens of apartment buildings. Homemade dishes sprouted on rooftops throughout Prague. Czech government officials on a trip to Vienna bought a dish there, strapped it to their car, then sped back to Prague.[5] Satellite parts were being smuggled in from the West, or hardware was fashioned locally in Czechoslovakia. One Czech built his own antenna from an old radio telescope; he turned it using an ingenious system of pulleys.

Just to be sure the word was out, Wick directed the Voice of America to offer instructions about how to build dish antennas, then position them to receive Western TV programs. The VOA received hundreds of requests for instruction manuals, which the USIA printed up. This made Polish authorities hit the panic button. An article in the influential Polish Communist party newspaper *Polityka* expressed alarm over the impact of new technologies, including videocassettes, satellite television, cable TV, and computers. "We still do not know what to do to counter the offensive the West is mounting with the help of the new technologies," said the paper, noting that the Soviet bloc continues "to ponder . . . how to counter U.S. television programs coming to us via satellite."[6] The Polish army daily *Zolznierz Wolnosci* called Worldnet and other Western satellite programs a "kind of SDI in information warfare" designed to undermine socialism.[7] A regional Communist party daily warned darkly that "the United States Information Agency intends in the very near future to encompass the globe—with a 24-hour program, using to this end three satellites that will work simultaneously. Test programs can already be seen on Polish territory daily." The story described Worldnet as the "jewel in the crown of the U.S. government, which is fascinated by technologies of aggressive propaganda." American propaganda masters, it said, had turned the hitherto colorless foreign information activity into the biggest and most sophisticated propaganda vehicle in the world.[8]

The USIA's European director, John Kordek, was also convinced that technology was, as he put it in a memo to Wick, "the most serious challenge to Communist control in Eastern Europe since World War II." Kordek argued that Polish citizens, in particular, were hungry for new information sources because of the credibility lost by state media when martial law was declared in Poland in 1981. "The uniquely independent, industrious Polish character," Kordek wrote to Wick, "always will find some way to evade official constraints, a form of resistance the Poles have practiced for centuries against different occupying or repressive regimes."[9] Signals from four Western satellites were capable of being picked up in Poland. Although satellite dishes were banned, their manufacture was not, and dishes began to appear on rooftops and in backyards in Poland, too. The government announced on February 20, 1986, that all satellite dishes had to be licensed with the approval of the internal affairs ministry and were legal so long as they did not interfere with regular antennas. Licenses would be granted to any "honest individual." By "honest individual," the Polish police meant that viewing would not be possible for groups that might benefit politically, such as the Solidarity labor movement, whose members might gather to watch "subversive" programs.

The Polish press began to ridicule the government decree, suggesting that licensees would need to ask guests to leave the room before a satellite channel was turned on.[10] Solidarity leader Lech Walesa had his own TV satellite dish. "The monopolistic system cannot win," he predicted.[11] And he was right, of course. By the end of 1986, some 1,500 individuals had applications for satellite dish licenses pending in Poland, and by February 1987, more than 2,000 homes had satellite dishes.[12] Licenses were granted usually within 4 to 6 weeks, and with the approved certificate an individual could purchase the satellite equipment. In downtown Warsaw, the PEWEX hard currency store, about a ten-minute car ride from the American Embassy, had a satellite dish prominently displayed on the side of the building. It sold satellite packages costing from $1,300 to $2,200, the more expensive extras consisting of motors, remote control, and better quality receivers. One manufacturer, the Svensat company, produced about 4,000 dishes a year (most of them distributed to Western Europe), each one costing about $1,500.[13] Svensat, one of the largest private companies in Poland and the biggest producer of satellite dishes in Eastern Europe, projected the production of 20,000 satellite dishes annually by 1987. Other satellite dish manufacturers were preparing to move into the Polish market, including Fuba of West Germany and the Tesla organization, a Czech company.

Still caught in its Faustian bargain to build its technology and risk its misuse in receiving Western propaganda, the Soviet Union urged its Communist allies to "use new media techniques" to promote its own propaganda counteroffensive. Those allies were embracing the first part of the equation; *Polityka,* for one, felt that Poland ought to become a part of the technological revolution or risk being left behind: "We should start getting used to this change and without delay," it pronounced boldly. Yugoslavia was unimpressed by the Soviet's counteroffensive and simply wanted to receive European and American satellite programs and then to distribute them to viewers. There would be no turning back to the old isolation. Bulgarian authorities sponsored a symposium called "Children in the Information Age," which discussed, openly, the sociological impact of the media revolution. For their part, Czech officials permitted local manufacture of satellite dishes and videocassette recorders that would be capable of playing tapes using both the Eastern European SECAM technical standard and the Western European PAL standard.[14] Hungary, which received clear TV signals from neighboring Austria, upgraded the quality of its own programming in an effort to compete for viewers.[15] Hungarian officials came to an agreement with a consortium of Western European countries that operated the European Communications Satellites, so that they could broadcast their programs directly into homes. Hungary also became the first East European country to officially welcome a Western satellite network, when it signed an agreement to retransmit the British-based Sky Channel, owned by media baron Rupert Murdoch.[16]

Innovative entrepreneurs in Budapest were even using Western computer hardware to invent their own software programs. The Hungarian firm Novotrade was the first Communist business to export video games to the West.

The Soviet Union had little choice. It had to speed up its efforts to participate in the international satellite television market. In the summer of 1986 it began satelliting TV programs to Africa, and in early 1987, to Asia and twenty countries in Latin America, adding to the services it had set up a couple of years earlier to Western Europe, North America, and the Middle East.[17] At issue, therefore, was whether this technology would give totalitarian governments the ability to advance their goals more effectively, while also forcing them to permit an increasing openness. Soviet policy statements illustrated this dilemma. In response to broadcasts on Worldnet, Radio Moscow editorialized that TV was allowing "Washington's ideologists to break into other people's homes without knocking, and to fish for the naive and gullible in the muddy torrent of disinformation relayed via its Worldnet TV satellites."

A week after the broadcast, the Soviet ambassador to West Germany invited Western journalists to his villa in Bonn to view a Soviet satellite TV program that was modeled on a Worldnet format. The program showed Mikhail Gorbachev announcing an extension of the nuclear test ban treaty. The Soviet ambassador's residence was luxurious and stocked with Russian caviar, German Pilsner beer, and Marlboro cigarettes.[18] Correspondents watched Gorbachev's speech while munching on caviar and sipping red wine at marble tables poolside (the Worldnet studio at the U.S. Embassy in Bonn was a cramped facility). The correspondents watching Gorbachev were not permitted to ask questions afterward, although they did get to chat with their host, ambassador Yuri Kvitsinsky, a former Soviet arms negotiator.[19] The Kremlin announced that its television effort was "a force for understanding."

About a week after its Bonn television foray, the Soviet Embassy in Rome also announced plans for a satellite news conference. Moscow diplomats were now being called "information managers." "We have changed a lot," said the deputy chief of the Soviet mission, Valentin Bogmasov, adding that he and the other information managers would "show the world a new image in Soviet diplomacy." The new password was "dynamism." Bogmasov proudly displayed a live satellite picture from Moscow showing a Tom and Jerry cartoon being played on a large projection TV. He said that Gorbachev's press conferences would henceforth be held regularly, instead of "spasmodically," as in the past.[20]

By 1986 the Soviet Union had launched almost 150 communications satellites at a cost of approximately $150 million each. The technical quality of Russian satellites was poor, having a life span of only three years, compared to more than seven years for U.S. satellites. Russian satellites, therefore, had to be replaced regularly, an expensive proposition. The Soviet press reported that about 10,000 government satellite receiving stations were in use throughout the Soviet Union, and that each one cost some $220 million per year to operate. It could cost as much as ten thousand rubles or more (about $60,000) to reach each inhabitant of a small, faraway village in the high latitudes of the Soviet Union with a satellite TV signal, according to Russian estimates in the mid-1980s.[21] It was immensely expensive, but there was no turning back. Television had become, overwhelmingly, the number-one source of information in the Soviet Union. There were 100 million TV sets in use in 1986, indicating almost total penetration (not as many as in the United States, however, where there were 157.5 million TV sets in use, in 98.1 percent of American households).[22] Not only was TV the primary source of information in the USSR, it was also the central focus of leisure time. In fact, TV had become a major weapon in the government's war against alcoholism. It kept people occupied when they weren't working. Indeed, Soviet authorities viewed television as a major force for unifying and controlling its domestic population, which was spread out over eleven time zones. In 1984 the Soviet Politburo had reported that the lack of television reception in some parts of the USSR "was a serious loss in the quality of life of Soviet man and in the development of his personality." Television was "a major medium in the people's political, aesthetic, and moral education."[23] Television, it felt, exerted a certain stabilizing effect on a population that might otherwise become restive. A Soviet Communist Politburo communiqué in August 1984 called for "the development of multi-channel color broadcasting and the significant elevation of its quality." Broadcast schedules were expanded; new transmitting towers began to spring up in outlying areas.

Because it had become impossible to prevent Western

broadcasts from invading the Soviet Union, the challenge facing authorities was to make Russian television more appealing to domestic viewers. Music and dramatic programs were added to the usual fare. When viewers complained that they were watching ten-year-old reruns, more than 25 percent of central television programming was replaced.[24] A new breakfast news TV program was introduced, as were late-night news and entertainment shows. Soviet TV official Leonid Kravchenko boasted in March 1987 that the programming would put life into the TV schedule, which he openly admitted had been "pompous and dull."[25] TV was to be the vehicle for Perestroika, the other Faustian bargain Gorbachev was striking in an effort to keep the USSR going. He himself fussed over every detail of his appearances on the big evening news program "Vremya," broadcast across the USSR. He frequently telephoned producers of the program to make certain things were being set up properly.[26] Viewers were urged to send in suggestions about how to improve programs. News broadcasts became more aggressively topical. "Telebridge" programs (as the Soviets called them) with the West introduced Soviet audiences to American-style television talk shows. The first such program combined America's Phil Donahue and Soviet commentator Vladimir Posner, and it was seen as a plus for Soviet propagandists. One Soviet newspaper commented that the program proved that the country could "enter into a debate and offer the platform even to those who do not share our views."[27] Donahue's questions to the Soviet audience were not felt to be very tough, and more to the point, questions from American audiences might "induce immunity to a free flow of information from the West," read a letter to the editor of the Soviet newspaper *Izvestia*.[28] An avalanche of mail was generated to show that such immunity could be induced.[29] A letter from one "average" viewer sought the protection of the KGB from such telebridges, which were rife, in his words, with "gangs of anti-Soviet and anti-Russian 'denouncers.'" V. Bochevarov of Leningrad felt the telebridges were nothing but "dirty anti-Soviet shows," and they couldn't help but provoke "patriotic anti-American feelings."[30] One Soviet commentator said the programs strengthened negative perceptions of American materialism and urban violence.[31]

While Soviet television became the primary vehicle by which the government relayed information to own citizens, it was also reaching into other parts of the world. The Molniya (lightning) satellites, which traversed the Soviet Union, arced across North America as well, where their signals were picked up by U.S. universities and used as part of Russian studies. One such location was Columbia University's Harriman Institute for Advanced Study of the Soviet Union. "We have opened what is essentially an untapped scholarly resource," said Harriman's assistant director Jonathan Sanders. "We see time-urgent material quickly. In the process we will learn more about how Russian is spoken . . . we see how the Soviets define news itself, and how they use television for didactic purposes. We hear their book reviews and literary discussions and see their plays. It is a very broad exposure, from a speech by Chernenko to the Million Ruble Movie."[32] Between the Molniya and Gorizont (horizon) satellite systems, television programs from the Kremlin were capable of being picked up almost anywhere on earth, although the satellites were wobbly and had less than one-third the life span of their Western counterparts. Soviet-manufactured TV sets were also of inferior quality. Some 18,000 TVs caused fires that killed 927 people in a six-month period. Neil Hickey reported in *TV Guide* that one morbid joke in the Soviet Union had it that the "principal suspense in watching Soviet TV is whether or not your set is going to explode."[33]

↔ 10 ↔

Clearing the Voice

BY MID-SEPTEMBER 1986, ONE MONTH BEFORE THE SUMMIT BETWEEN Reagan and Gorbachev was slated to take place in Reykjavik, Wick had made up his mind to pressure the Soviets to stop jamming the Voice of America. He directed his top foreign service counselor, Stanton H. Burnett, to set up a task force, which was to include representatives from the State Department and White House, to develop a plan of action. Wick was anxious to rally the support of Secretary of State George Shultz and national security adviser Admiral John Poindexter.

The American position had always been that Soviet interference with U.S. radio broadcast signals violated international agreements to which the USSR was a signatory.[1] Officially, the Soviets refused to admit they were jamming broadcasts, but at the same time had to come up with a legal loophole should they choose, officially, to justify their practice. They dusted off a 1936 League of Nations document sanctioning jamming under certain conditions, such as when foreign broadcasts incited violence and posed a threat to national security. The document had been written to curtail Hitler's propaganda broadcasts. Prior to the outbreak of World War II, Austria jammed broadcasts from Nazi Germany, Italy interfered with programs from England and Ethiopia, and Germany routinely jammed broadcasts from Moscow. The Soviets interpreted the document as guaranteeing their right to "defend resolutely the national sovereignty of countries in the fields of information and culture."[2] The United States agreed with a 1972 United Nations resolution that stated jamming was a human rights violation,[3] and the State Department took the position that the content of Western broadcasts was not negotiable.[4]

Soviet jamming usually coincided with periods of rising world tensions. It resumed after the Soviet invasion of Czechoslovakia in 1968; in 1979, when the Soviets invaded Afghanistan; and again with the rise of free trade unionism in Poland in 1980.[5] In the mid-1980s new jamming stations were being opened on the borders of several countries in Eastern Europe, and there were plans to put facilities in Syria because of American intentions to build a short-wave radio relay station in Israel.

Burnett met with the State Department and the White House and sent Wick a secret memorandum in which, ironically, he cautioned that it might not be in the United States' best interest if the Soviets were to stop jamming the VOA: "It would undercut Voice of America efforts to obtain additional radio frequency assignments from the International Telecommunications Union (ITU)," wrote Burnett. He added that the Soviets were not about to dismantle their jamming facilities, and would have the capability of throwing the jamming switch on again whenever they wanted. He was concerned, too, that the cessation of jamming would "exert subtle, but strong, daily pressure to moderate VOA reporting and programming to avert Soviet resumption of jamming." Burnett was convinced there was a real risk of inadvertently giving the Soviets the means to influence our programming: "Is this preferable to increasing our technological capacity to blast through or circumvent Soviet jamming?"[6] The government was pumping hundreds of millions of dollars into a program to build stronger stations for the VOA, which did not wish to see this funding dry up. At congressional budget hearings, VOA and Radio Free Europe/Radio Liberty officials emphasized that Soviet jamming was a measure of their effectiveness.

The "evil empire" kept the USIA alive and healthy, and this did not go unnoticed by Soviet propagandists who earned their livelihood slamming the United States. Georgi Arbatov, who appeared frequently on American television to provide a Soviet perspective on a variety of subjects, picked up on the theme. "The United States needs the Soviet Union to satisfy the American psychological need for a villain," he said. "In this way, Americans can see themselves as a shining city on the hill." Arbatov was right. The Soviet Union was critically important for American propaganda. As U.S. government broadcasters would discover when the cold war was over, it would be a lot harder to justify their existence when the Soviet Union wasn't there to kick around anymore. In 1986, the American broadcasting organizations—the VOA, Radio Free Europe/Radio Liberty, and Radio Marti—were broadcasting 2,411 hours per week; the Soviet international radio networks 2,229 hours per week.[7]

The Soviets were beginning to think jamming might be more trouble than it was worth. There was no question it violated the so-called spirit of Geneva that Reagan and Gorbachev announced at their first meeting in late 1985. It was also difficult for Gorbachev to proclaim a new era of Glasnost while his jammers continued to block the free flow of information from the West. Most of all, jamming was horrendously expensive. More than 3,000 noise-generating transmitters were working up 600 megawatts of power a day, at a cost of some $1.2 billion a year for electricity alone. And electricity was in short supply in Russia. The disaster at the Chernobyl nuclear power plant on April 28, 1986, had further depleted the Soviet Union's energy supply. It couldn't have come at a worse time for Soviet propagandists, for not only did they have to handle radio signals—there were more than forty foreign radio stations directing programs specifically to the USSR, broadcasting 200 hours a day in 24 Soviet languages, but, for the first time, foreign television signals as well. A decision needed to be made as to whether electricity would be used for industry or for generating radio static. Soviet citizens were ordered not to use electrical appliances at certain times of the day so that radio jammers could generate their noise. Aside from the cost of jamming, which was running about twice as high as the VOA's entire annual budget, the Russian overseas information service was a huge financial burden. The Soviets were outspending us five to one. In 1986, the Soviets spent $3.2 billion on radio and television broadcasting; the USIA's broadcasting budget was $600 million.

For those reasons, State Department Soviet experts felt the USSR could be persuaded to stop jamming the VOA. What was less clear was whether they might also stop jamming the more strident Radio Free Europe/Radio Liberty broadcasts behind the Iron Curtain. The United States had to decide whether to de-couple the VOA from RFE/RL in its approach to the Soviets by pushing for the cessation of VOA jamming only. The Soviets had been keeping close watch on the USIA's congressionally appropriated budget since Reagan had come into office, and watched its yearly upward spiral in horror. By 1986 hundreds of millions were being plowed into the project for new and more powerful VOA stations. If jamming was expensive for the Soviets now, it would only get much worse. There was no way out. Some accommodation with American propagandists had to be reached, for this and other reasons, as we shall see.

Meanwhile, Glasnost was supposedly in full flower. The year 1986 had begun with an exchange of televised goodwill messages between Reagan and Gorbachev. An estimated 60 million American viewers saw Gorbachev's address; in the Soviet Union 150 million watched Reagan on the sole nationwide TV channel. Said one Muscovite, a twenty-seven-year-old factory worker named Larissa: "We have a Russian proverb that goes, 'After forty years of life, you start paying for your actions in your face.' The lines in [Reagan's] face reflected good—not the evil that we'd been led to expect. Seeing him for three minutes was worth more than hearing about him for thirty years." Naturally, we used this in all of our promotion. But as 1986 wore on, relations between the two superpowers began to deteriorate. Just before the October 11–12 Reykjavik summit, Soviet diplomat Gennadi Zakharov and American journalist Nicholas Daniloff were arrested for espionage. Thankfully, they were hastily released and sent to their respective homes. The summit could go forward, but brows were furrowed. For one thing, there was still debate about whether to raise the issue of Soviet jamming. Wick had carefully weighed the points Burnett had set forth but decided to press the issue at Reykjavik. The White House and State Department agreed. Jamming was normally argued as an ideological issue, but now it was even being attacked by the International Frequency Registration Board, an organization under UN auspices and chaired by a Soviet national. Because of that Shultz felt it was possible to approach the issue from a less cold-war position.

The USIA sent a cadre of almost forty public relations specialists to Iceland, and they outnumbered the State Department and White House negotiators being sent to discuss arms control issues with their Soviet counterparts. Reagan himself was prepared to raise the VOA jamming issue with Gorbachev. Those of us in the American delegation assembled at Andrews Air Force Base outside Washington on Friday, October 10, 1986, to await our early-morning flight to Iceland. I had driven to the airport with John Kordek, who directed the USIA's European public affairs efforts. Kordek was an astute career foreign service officer whose skills would earn him an ambassadorship a couple of years later. We were sipping coffee when the Soviet ambassador to the United States, Yuri Dubinin, walked by. Dubinin had come to see off the American delegation as a courtesy. After an exchange of pleasantries, Kordek seized the opportunity.

"You know, Mr. Ambassador," said Kordek, "it might be productive if Director Wick and Mr. Yakovlev met in Reykjavik. They both have overlapping responsibilities for information and culture." Dubinin nodded in agreement. "I will send a message to Moscow when I get back to my office," said Dubinin. Alexandr Yakovlev was widely regarded as the second most important person in the Soviet Union. As Gorbachev's confidant, and as the man in charge of *all* Soviet media, Yakovlev could make things happen. He had also become an outspoken advocate of change, even though his roots went back to earlier cold war days, when he played a major role in shaping Soviet propaganda policies. He was now the architect of the new Soviet reformation—a process that Wick distrusted.

Yakovlev was no stranger to the West. He had been one of the first Soviet exchange students in the United States in the late 1950s, when he attended Columbia. Young Alexandr was living the graduate school life on a tight budget and kept pretty much to himself. He found his Americans classmates "cliquish." He observed some of the failings of the democratic system, and saw America's social problems—poverty, racial inequality, and crime—firsthand. He was familiar with America, but not enamored of it. Following the Soviet invasion of Czechoslovakia in 1968, Yakovlev became the acting head of the propaganda department of the Soviet Central Committee. He stoutly defended the invasion, engaging in a carefully planned propaganda offensive that he himself had designed. Yakovlev reported to the Central Committee that as part of this propaganda effort he had prepared more than 2.5 million leaflets, which his department printed and distributed in the United States and Europe, all glorifying the valiant Soviet effort to suppress the anti-revolutionary movement in Czechoslovakia. Yakovlev was also Soviet ambassador to Canada for ten years and helped orchestrate Gorbachev's successful visit there in 1983. An impressed Gorbachev brought Yakovlev back to Moscow, where he quickly rose through the ranks to become the chief of propaganda.

As Gorbachev's top propagandist and one of the principal architects of Glasnost, Yakovlev was the guardian of the newly emerging freedom of the press and mindful of the huge impact television would have when it communicated Russia's new image to the world.[8] Yakovlev also realized that with satellite technology becoming more sophisticated it would also become increasingly difficult and expensive to jam Western broadcasts. Both Moscow and Washington hastily approved Wick's meeting with Yakovlev.

In Iceland, Charles Wick, John Kordek, Rick Ruth (Kordek's Soviet expert), and I were scheduled to meet with Yakovlev at 7:00 P.M. on Saturday, October 11, in a private conference room at the Hotel Saga, where Soviet officials were staying. Ambassador Arthur Hartman warned Wick that Yakovlev was "tough and wily." Aides cautioned Yakovlev that Wick was a rabid cold war warrior who, like Reagan, despised Communists. Indeed, by this time, Wick was well known in the Soviet Union, where the press for the past several years had portrayed him as something akin to an ax murderer. We were met at the entrance to the Saga Hotel by Vitaliy Kobysh, an expert in American affairs, who escorted us upstairs to Yakovlev, propaganda official Albert Vlasov, and an interpreter. Yakovlev, a short burly man who resembled former Soviet premier Brezhnev, had just come from a meeting with Gorbachev. His face was flushed with excitement.

"I am not trying to exaggerate," said Yakovlev enthusiastically, "but after the second round of talks between the President and the General Secretary [Gorbachev], no one was in a bad mood; everyone was smiling." He spoke in Russian through an interpreter, but punctuated some of his comments in idiosyncratic but understandable English for emphasis. It was true that the Reagan-Gorbachev talks on nuclear disarmament had gotten off to a promising start, but the air of cordiality was getting more chilly by the day. With congressional elections only weeks away, Reagan was not about to back away from his pledge to develop Star Wars technology.

Our meeting area at the hotel was in a long, narrow room with a wall of opaque glass at one end, behind which I assumed were Russian observers and probably a video camera. We sat facing each other and would remain there for more than two hours discussing a wide range of issues.

"I have heard you are a very sharp man," Yakovlev began, looking at Wick. He smiled. "Maybe to improve relations we should invite you to work for two years at the International Information Department."[9] Wick returned the compliment: "I have read your biography and am impressed with your wide responsibility for information and propaganda," he told Yakovlev. "Culture, too, please," responded the Russian.

Wick made the first thrust. "The United States and the Soviet Union have two ideologies, and there is plenty of evidence of name-calling on both sides," he observed. "Incidents such as Three Mile Island, Chernobyl, and the sinking of a Soviet nuclear submarine in the Atlantic clearly show the realities of the nuclear threat, and that no one can hope to derive an advantage. We must now level with each other." Wick then raised the issue of Soviet jamming of the Voice of America, which, he noted, violated international telecommunications accords to which the Soviet Union was a signatory nation. "You may not like what the VOA is saying, but so long as the VOA is telling the truth, Soviet jamming isn't justified," said Wick.

"You are wrong if you think we are afraid of your criticism of our society," replied Yakovlev. "We criticize ourselves even more strongly. What bothers us is that the VOA deals in marketplace rumors. For example, the VOA reported that there were attempts on the General Secretary's life, and that he has had differences with his military leaders. Hitler created rumors of Soviet generals disagreeing with Stalin on policy and this resulted in the death of many military men. This is provocative."

Wick noted wryly that Yakovlev's remarks about the Nazis and the Soviet military must have referred to Stalin's purges of the Soviet officer corps, which were worse than anyone could have imagined. "If you find an error in a VOA broadcast," said Wick, "I promise to you that we will correct it."

"There have been many occasions when the word 'barbarian' has been used by the VOA to describe the USSR," Yakovlev continued. "We have never used that word to describe America."

I had expected Yakovlev to raise complaints raised previously by Soviet commentators about Hollywood movies such as *Rambo* and *Rocky* and television commercials mocking Soviet society being insulting to Russians. Hollywood and Madison Avenue loved to stereotype Russians, and Yakovlev could have put Wick on the spot by pointing out examples. One American commercial, for example, showed fat Russian babushkas walking along a beauty contest ramp carting their mops and pails. But Yakovlev stuck to general ideology, accusing the VOA of waging a campaign over human rights in the USSR. "Our patience is running out," Yakovlev said darkly. "We will start a campaign of our own and it won't be pretty."

"We are not afraid of any Soviet campaign against the United States on the issue of human rights," replied Wick. "We have also asked Soviet authorities to send us verbatim transcripts of alleged inaccurate VOA broadcasts, but have heard nothing in reply." He repeated his pledge to correct inaccuracies.

Yakovlev and Wick each took copious notes while the other was talking and being translated. On the issue of radio jamming, Yakovlev pointed out that the United States had transmitters in territories close to the Soviet Union, such as Greece and Germany, so that most of Russia was within reach of U.S. radio. "We cannot reach your borders as effectively being so far away," he said. Then, Yakovlev beat us to the punch. "So let's do this. We will stop jamming and you let us rent a transmitter on or near American territory."

What Yakovlev was saying was certainly true. VOA broadcasts reached the Soviet Union from shortwave transmitters in West Germany, Greece, the United Kingdom, and the Philippines, and Radio Free Europe and Radio Liberty beamed in signals from Germany, Spain, and Portugal. The Soviet Union used far-reaching shortwave signals to reach the populations spread across its vast land expanse. But most radios in the United States were tuned to AM or FM frequencies, which do not carry over great distances. The Soviet Union needed transmitters closer to American borders, whose signals would be carried on AM or FM frequencies. Wick noted that Radio Moscow, relayed from Cuba, already came in loud and clear in the

United States, and that in fact it was interfering with American stations broadcasting on the same frequency.

Yakovlev said his proposal to end jamming was a "fair deal." Each side would present its point of view without insulting the other. Wick agreed. "You've got a deal," he told Yakovlev. Vlasov leaned over to whisper in Yakovlev's ear. "This only applies to the VOA," Yakovlev added. He needed to be certain we understood he wasn't including the more strident Radio Free Europe and Radio Liberty in his offer.

Wick summarized the verbal agreement, to avoid any misunderstandings. The government would be willing to help the Soviets obtain transmission time on a U.S. radio station if the Soviets provided VOA access to a local Soviet radio facility. Yakovlev banged the table with his fist and shouted "OK!" The wily Russian and the U.S. information czar stood up and leaned across the conference table to embrace.

We all knew that the danger of Soviet broadcasts attracting a sizeable following on American radio was practically nil. Radio Moscow dished out dull, heavy-fisted propaganda, and it wouldn't find too many takers among U.S. radio stations. The best part of the Soviet program service, in my view, was the Red Army marching song, the Soviet national anthem—which was played throughout the day and evening. A steady dose of Radio Moscow would win few converts to communism, even if it were available on the popular AM and FM bands. Wick had nothing to lose by agreeing to Yakovlev's deal. The two men also agreed to another exchange of television messages by Reagan and Gorbachev on New Year's Day to increase the number of cultural exchanges between the two countries and to involve the U.S. private sector.

Wick couldn't let the meeting end without citing his statistics showing how low was the number of U.S. officials who appeared on TV in the Soviet Union. National security adviser Robert McFarlane had urged Wick to prepare the numbers for the Reykjavik summit. "We would like greater access for U.S. journalists and officials to the Soviet media," Wick said. He pointed out that between January 1984 and April 1985 there were 155 substantive Soviet appearances on American television. In roughly the same time period, there were four perfunctory American appearances on Soviet TV. Yakovlev gave as good as he got, reminding Wick that only a month earlier, the United States had turned down an offer to have debates between Russian and American officials on Soviet and American TV. NBC had initiated the idea, and the Soviets accepted it. The State Department defended the American position, saying it would be "inappropriate" for cabinet officers to engage in one-on-one, on-the-record debates about issues while preparations were going forward for high-level, confidential meetings in Europe. "The problem with the proposal was one of time," said State Department deputy spokesman Charles Redman.[10] Soviet propagandists quickly seized the initiative. Georgi Arbatov accused the American government of engaging in a "conspiracy of silence." Soviet commentator Vladimir Posner claimed the United States was striving to keep the American public uninformed.[11] The United States also turned down a Soviet offer to put President Reagan on Soviet TV to answer questions submitted in advance from Russian viewers. Yakovlev could not let the opportunity of tweaking Wick on the issue go by. "This is an example of control over the media," he concluded triumphantly.

Yakovlev's main rebuttal to Wick concerned the availability of Soviet culture in the States, versus that of American culture in the Soviet Union. "We publish many times more American books than you do Soviet; we show many times more American films than you do Soviet." He said that the ministry of culture had told him that on any given day as many as fifty-four American plays were being performed on Soviet stages. Very few Soviet plays found their way to American stages.

The disparity, as we all knew, was in large part due to the appeal of the American media and the lack of interest in Soviet films, plays, and books in America. Wick replied to Yakovlev that the number and kinds of films shown in America is dictated by the marketplace. The Soviets can send any film they wish to the United States or even rent an American theater and show whatever they wanted. "I doubt that we would be given any such right in the USSR," Wick concluded. (In 1986 the Soviet Union ran ten American feature films that reached an audience of 64 million persons. Only three Soviet films were shown in the United States in five cities for a period of one to two weeks.)

As we were leaving, Yakovlev sent over a parting shot to Wick. "Many Jews have emigrated from the Soviet Union and the American media always reports their departure from 'Communist hell,'" said Yakovlev. "The Soviet Union now has one thousand applications from Soviet Jews who wish to *return* to the USSR. If we give them return visas, which we probably will, will the American papers report it?"

"If the Soviet embassy calls such a press conference I am sure American reporters would cover it," replied Wick. "I'm certain you are aware of this." They shook hands and departed. We walked down a flight of steps into the Saga Hotel lobby. Dozens of reporters immediately surrounded Wick and began firing questions at him. Both sides had agreed on a news blackout, so Wick offered them no comment.

When we cabled a summary of the meeting to the State Department, officials there reacted immediately and angrily to Wick's having negotiated a deal over what they saw as "Moscow's illegal jamming." They were convinced that once the Soviets got access to the American medium-wave radio market, they would renege on their agreement and start jamming again. In answer to press inquiries about Wick's Reykjavik meeting, the State Department responded that jamming was an illegal activity and "is not negotiable or tradeable." However, said a State Department spokesman, on the question of providing access for the Soviets to a radio transmitter in or near the United States, "We are willing to explore various possibilities on the basis of reciprocity."

The State Department, which had endorsed the idea of raising the jamming issue in Reykjavik, was obviously piqued at not having been invited to attend the meeting with Yakovlev. So were Radio Free Europe/Radio Liberty chiefs. The cable we had sent to Washington detailing the session was promptly leaked to the press. William Safire wrote in the *New York Times* that Wick had been "tricked" by Yakovlev, who had limited his offer to stop jamming to the VOA.[12] The *Washington Post* and several other newspapers slammed Wick for not consulting with the State Department or anyone else at a high level, saying Wick had been had. We were also chided by conservative Republican groups, who initially opposed the idea of giving the Soviets any kind of soap box in or near American territory. The Heritage Foundation criticized Wick for agreeing to help the Soviets find airtime on U.S. stations. The Soviet agreement to end jamming was aimed at heading off reported punitive actions against the USSR recommended by the Conference on Security and

Cooperation in Europe, and the International Frequency Review Board. "This Soviet proposal is contrary to U.S. interests," said a Heritage Foundation spokesman. According to a UPI report, an official at the Radio Free Europe/Radio Liberty organization said that Wick had doublecrossed the stations; the State Department claimed he'd been suckered.

Shultz asked his State Department advisers to put together a list of negotiating options on Soviet jamming. An interagency meeting was called, chaired by the State Department, bringing together representatives from the USIA, the Board for International Broadcasting (the parent organization of Radio Free Europe and Radio Liberty), and the Federal Communications Commission. As Burnett had forewarned Wick, there was a strong feeling that an end to Soviet jamming would not be in America's best interests, since in order to counter jamming the United States planned to request additional international radio frequencies at the upcoming meeting of the World Administrative Radio Conference. Wick's agreement would undercut plans to expand Voice of America language services and build new shortwave stations, and take the Soviets off the hook at international telecommunications meetings. The U.S. government was engaged just then in sensitive negotiations with Cuba over the Mariel immigration agreement, which Cuba would consent to if granted an AM frequency for Radio Havana. State Department officials felt these negotiations would be harmed if the Soviets got a better deal than the Cubans. In classic bureaucratic fashion, the Federal Communications Commission said "thousands" of existing radio frequencies would have to be reassigned were the Soviets given access to its own AM frequency. And it would take special legislation from Congress to boot. Tass didn't help matters when it said the Kremlin should not be required to purchase airtime. The Soviet Union wanted nothing less than the assignment of a U.S. radio frequency for Radio Moscow.

Back in Moscow, Yakovlev was getting the same kind of flak as Wick from his own bureaucracy. Shortly after returning from Iceland, Yakovlev warned a meeting of skeptical Soviet ideologists that the information revolution was going to challenge the Kremlin. New ideas would be coming in from the outside world, and Russia would have to rise to the occasion. The world is getting ever smaller and ever more interconnected, Yakovlev warned. "To think that it is possible to be cloistered, cut off from external influences and to sit in timid resignation is not only to indulge in illusions but also to doom ourselves to defeat. What was needed now was action, an offensive stance that guarantees not only absolute priority in our own house but also a steady strengthening of our . . . influence on the outside world."[13] In the meantime, Wick succeeded in getting agreements from two U.S. radio networks—the Westwood One hookup of former NBC stations and the Mutual Broadcasting System—to take the Soviet program signal from the international satellite. They would then "uplink" it to the American domestic satellite Satcom 1R for transmission to ground receivers at radio stations, and from there Moscow's programs could be retransmitted to home radios.

There were an estimated 3,500 radio stations in this country capable of receiving signals from this satellite. The stations would have to decide themselves whether or not to take the signal down and use it. The head of Westwood One, Norman Pattiz, was enthusiastic about lending support, for which he expected no compensation. Taking down and retransmitting Soviet satellite signals for distribution to an American audience was regulated by the Federal Communications Commission. The FCC, in turn, would need to defer to the White House and other political agencies of the executive branch to determine whether it would be in "the public interest" to permit the Soviets to use a U.S. domestic satellite. One problem was represented by the so-called Fairness Doctrine regulation, which required American broadcasters to provide reasonably balanced presentations on controversial issues of public importance. Would Radio Moscow's programs be balanced? It was not likely. A further complication was that the Justice Department would also enter into the picture. Would stations carrying Soviet programs have to register as agents of a foreign government? The most logical offshore location for a Radio Moscow transmitter would be Cuba. The FCC argued that because of the high density of American radio stations broadcasting in this country, powerful signals from Cuba would interfere with many of these stations on the same or adjacent frequencies, as they had in the past.

In short, the U.S. bureaucracy was inventing every reason it could to support its entrenched belief that Soviet jamming should be allowed to continue. The irony that seemed to escape everyone, including Wick, was that the Soviets were going to stop jamming Western radios whether anyone liked it or not. American diplomats in

Moscow were hopelessly out of touch with what truly motivated the Soviets, who desperately needed to blunt Reagan's propaganda offensives. Putting an end to jamming VOA broadcasts in order to gain an audience in the West for programs from Moscow was a small price to pay. The American ambassador to the Soviet Union, career diplomat Arthur Hartman, was especially clueless about the turmoil in the Kremlin brought about by Reagan's propaganda initiatives. In an effort to downplay the impact of Wick's session with Yakovlev, he sent a confidential cable to Washington shortly after the Iceland summit arguing that the impact of the Chernobyl nuclear plant accident on the USSR's winter energy supply would likely result in the elimination of Soviet jamming. Hartman quoted a professor at the Soviet Central Committee's Academy of Social Sciences who said as much. Hartman wrote that Tass had carried an interview with Dimitry Protsenko, a member of the Soviet Electric Power Ministry, who said that the USSR would experience a power shortfall of 6 million kilowatts as Russia headed into the winter of 1986. Cuts would have to be made. Soviet newspapers were paying special attention to the electrical power shortage, according to Hartman. Wick passed the information to Reagan in a confidential memorandum.

What was being said behind the Kremlin walls, however, told a quite different story. The Soviet's willingness to end jamming stemmed from its desire to extend its broadcasts into North America, and the initiative came directly from Gorbachev. Gorbachev was still livid about the Reagan Administration's unyielding position at Reykjavik on nuclear disarmament, and about the expulsion of Soviet diplomats from the United States. But Gorbachev's overarching obsession was Ronald Reagan himself. He knew he was losing the battle of public opinion. Power shortages in Russia had nothing to do with Gorbachev's sour mood. "It's impossible to expect any constructive actions or suggestions from the U.S. Administration," Gorbachev told his Politburo on October 22. Washington and Moscow were continuing to kick out alleged spies from each other's country. Things were very tense. He needed relief. "In this extremely complex situation we need to win some propaganda points, to continue to carry out offensive explanatory work oriented towards Americans and all international society. Washington politicians are afraid of this. Materials featuring my speech at the Reykjavik press conference and appearances on Soviet television have been delayed at customs for three days."[14] Yakovlev replied that it was his understanding that this material was being held up at American customs. But Gorbachev persisted in believing that they needed to put more pressure on the administration to show the world that the Americans were responsible for the breakdown in the Iceland negotiations over the questions of reduction and liquidation of nuclear weapons.

KGB chief V. M. Chebrikov suggested that details of American espionage should be made public. They had discovered 150 eavesdropping devices in Soviet offices in America, he told Gorbachev, and a press conference needed to be called at which there could be a demonstration of American espionage's eavesdropping devices. Foreign minister Andrei Gromyko asked how many Soviet eavesdropping devices were found in U.S. offices. "One," replied Chebrikov. "The numbers are in our favor." "This should be emphasized," agreed Gorbachev. "When should our announcement be made?" asked V. M. Shevardnadze. "As soon as it is ready," replied Gorbachev, who added that what was key was that the revelation should be transmitted over television. Gromyko was concerned that it should be done in a way so as to fence off Reagan himself. Gorbachev agreed that Reagan should not appear as a liar. "The appropriate formulation should be found."[15] That formulation involved sidling up to Charlie Wick.

On October 24, 1986, less than two weeks after Reykjavik, Ambassador Hartman sent a confidential cable to Washington advising the State Department that the Soviets had signed a decree calling for an end to their jamming of the VOA as a good faith gesture toward America. They expected reciprocal action. The Soviets announced that they would cease jamming the British Broadcasting Corporation's programs, because they "refrained from criticisms of Soviet society and Soviet policy and concentrated on presenting information about the U.K."

Soviet officials at the highest levels believed that their nemesis, Hollywood huckster Wick, was their hot ticket to get their story before Western audiences. Everything was to be done to court Wick's favor. The session between Wick and Yakovlev in Iceland led to "information talks" between the United States and the Soviet Union on a wide range of media issues. One of Wick's harshest critics, Viktor G. Afanasyev, editor-in-chief of *Pravda*, came to Washington to take part in the first of what would become a series of sessions on ways to improve the flow of information between the two countries. Afanasyev, the all-powerful editor of a newspaper with an estimated readership of 50 million, had once boasted that he decided what was published in *Pravda*. Afanasyev was also an active party member and had served in the USSR Supreme Soviet (legislature) since 1979.

Wick began the December 16, 1986, meeting by joking that what bothered him the most about the personal attacks on him in *Pravda* was that "much of it is true." Afanasyev retorted that *Pravda* had criticized Wick very little because "I didn't know you. Now that we have finally met, criticism of you will be stepped up." Afanasyev also said he would be doing a general housecleaning of *Pravda*'s staff in order to make the paper more interesting. While in America, he said, he hoped to arrange a series of teleconferences between members of the Supreme Soviet and the U.S. Congress, "even on your beloved human rights." Wick was ready for this and fired off several ideas in rapid succession, proposing that *Pravda* publish a regular column in which American officials could write whatever they wanted on any subject. In return, he would find an American publication willing to carry articles by Soviet officials. Wick also suggested an exchange of Voice of America and Radio Moscow scripts. Thousands of hours had been devoted to discussing arms control, but "there has never been comprehensive discussions of information and the media." Said Afanasyev, lightheartedly, "You are making so many proposals that my head is swimming." He thought the suggestions were worthy, however, and promised to discuss them with his colleagues back home. Among them was the exchange of Soviet and American journalists.

The year 1986 was the turning point in Soviet-American relations, with nonpolitical cultural activities breaking the ice. Reagan appointed Wick, along with his other duties, to be his personal representative in fostering American private sector initiatives with the Soviet Union. The year marked the return of world-renowned pianist Vladimir Horowitz to his native Russia for the first time in six decades. His concerts drew a thunderous response in Moscow and Leningrad, and wafted over the airwaves of both the VOA and Radio Moscow. In March 1987 Soviet TV asked Wick to help produce a TV special by supplying films of American jazz stars in concert, such as Benny Goodman and Louis Armstrong. The Soviets also invited the

United States to send a delegation, a full-length feature film, and a program of short films to the International Film Festival in Moscow in July 1987. The Soviets felt that the more Wick could help them look more like the West, the greater credibility their propaganda would have in the outside world, and the more immune ordinary Soviet citizens would be toward American propaganda aimed at them.[16] The Soviet economy and society were in desperate straits, and Gorbachev had to convince his countrymen that things were changing for the better.[17] The Soviets couldn't beat Charlie Wick, so they put the Hollywood huckster to work for them.

By the time of Gorbachev's first visit to America in December 1987, Glasnost was in full flower, and the breaking of the ice of the cold war continued. Yet Wick, reflecting the view of his old friend Ronald Reagan, was still suspicious of Gorbachev's Glasnost, which he saw as "a political offensive aimed at resurrecting the credibility of Marxism-Leninism, achieving political legitimacy in the West, and bringing about the rupture of the Western alliance."[18] Wick liked to call it "gloss-overnost" in his speeches, and cautioned his audiences against Gorbachev's real motives, which were to further socialism.

As Gorbachev worked the crowd after a State Department speech, he spotted Wick, and pulled him aside. "No more disinformation," Gorbachev promised expansively. "I don't want politicians and bureaucrats creating all these tensions any more, disinformation and all that. It's going to be a new day." Wick agreed and suggested that there should be regular meetings between Yakovlev and him "for the purpose of improving communication, reducing conflict, and putting our information relations on a basis of truth, fact, and reciprocity."[19]

Over breakfast the next morning, Wick briefed Reagan on his conversation with Gorbachev. "Just as arms negotiations are leading to weapons elimination," Wick told Reagan, "perhaps information talks will do away with Soviet disinformation."

After Gorbachev came to power in the summer of 1985, disinformation became a sensitive topic, sensitive because there was a disparity between intention and reality. The Soviets were continuing to spread the malicious tale of how the United States had developed an AIDS ethnic weapon that killed only blacks and had added one about how the United States deliberately microwaved antiwar demonstrators in Britain, resulting in miscarriages and hair loss.[20] Said USIA disinformation expert Todd Leventhal, "If they could spread nasty lies about us in the Third World and smile at us in front of the camera, and we didn't call that incongruity into focus, they could have gotten away with it. But we didn't let them get away with it. Our strategy was to let people know the nasty things they were still doing. It hurt them in the eyes of the Western media."[21]

The disinformation about AIDS had become increasingly embarrassing. AIDS was now sweeping through the USSR, and Russian officials didn't wish to jeopardize joint AIDS medical research with the Americans. Charles Horner, deputy assistant secretary of state for science and technology, had seen all the paperwork on a proposal from the Russians to do cooperative AIDS research with the United States. Horner became a top USIA policy official during the Reagan Administration and took the position, one with which the State Department and the Surgeon General agreed, that while America was in favor of scientific cooperation with the Soviets on AIDS research, it would not be willing to let it go forward unless the Soviets stopped their disinformation campaign. U.S. embassies overseas tracked each crude Soviet propaganda effort, and information was passed back to government agencies in Washington involved in scientific and medical AIDS research with the Russians. Surgeon General C. Everett Koop objected to the Kremlin's use of a "grave international public health problem for base propaganda purposes." Soviet authorities lamely maintained that newspapers in their country were free to print anything they wanted.

At Wick's insistence, a series of informational and cultural exchange talks were held during 1988 in both Washington and Moscow in an attempt to cool the rhetoric and improve communications. Both sides agreed upon a "disinformation early warning system" to keep complaints about one another out of the media. The Soviets again stressed that they particularly wished to see the State Department and the USIA put an end to publishing detailed reports about Soviet disinformation activities. The Soviet embassy press counselor in Washington, Igor B. Bulay, found these "very thick" yearly reports particularly objectionable. He claimed they inhibited the improvement of relations.[22] Old-line Soviet publisher Valentin Falin, having decided to go down swinging, continued to take the hard line, charging that there were reputable scientists who felt there was no proof as to the natural origin of AIDS. "This is not to be construed as meaning it is artificial in origin," said Falin. "The scientific fact is simply that there is no proof it is naturally occurring." He also charged there was no basis for the American claim that Soviet nuclear tests and chemical warfare had produced so-called yellow or acid rain. "I have been personally assured by Ministry of Defense representatives in a Politburo meeting that there is not the least justification for the American yellow rain charges," he concluded.[23]

USIA disinformation gurus Romerstein and Leventhal were invited to the Soviet Embassy to meet with Bulay, who assured them that the theory that AIDS had been caused by U.S. nuclear tests was not officially endorsed. Bulay claimed that the Novosti news service had raised it "as part of an effort to explore all avenues in search for a vaccine against the disease." Bulay was clearly embarrassed over Falin's recent remarks. "We have some wild men on certain newspapers," he said. "I'm begging you, don't overplay this."[24] Victor L. Karasin, the young managing editor of *Soviet Life* magazine, believed the difficulty in getting the Soviet media to back off the AIDS story lay with old-line editors and publishers in the USSR such as Falin.[25] We all saw pleadings to suspend disinformation programs as a clear sign that America's efforts to embarrass the USSR were working.[26]

Alexandr Yakovlev laid out his government's official position at the 1988 Moscow bilateral information talks:

> All of us want to hear the truth about ourselves, but the realities of the past few decades are such that the energy and intellectual potential of thousands of people are being expended in fabricating untruths. . . . A great deal of sophistication goes into this, but the amorality of deception is becoming increasingly clear. Satirists in propaganda establishments are sharpening their pens to the point where they run the risk of exhausting their physical and moral resources. There have been many debates and speculations in the West over our policy of Glasnost and its contents and limits. I must say bluntly that Glasnost means abandoning the lie and all its forms.[27]

The President of the USSR Academy of Medical Science, Dr. V. I. Pokrovskiy, gave an interview to *Sovetskaya Rossiya,* which set out the definitive word. Pokrovskiy said that "not a single Soviet scientist, not a single medical or scientific institution, shares this position" that American research and institutions were responsible for AIDS.

By September 1988, Wick and Yakovlev had had four conferences since the Iceland summit two years earlier. At the fourth conference, Yakovlev told Wick lightheartedly that the Soviet Union was becoming so democratic that they were losing control over the mass media. "Soviet officials have more complaints about what the Soviet press says than do American officials," Yakovlev said with a smile. Despite the occasional shot at Wick in the Soviet media, relations had indeed improved markedly. Reciprocal book centers were about to open in Washington and Novosibirsk as part of the joint "Year of the Young Reader" agreement between the two countries, and a major U.S. bookstore was about to open in Moscow.

At the meeting, however, Wick decided it was still not time to let the Soviets off the hook. The Voice of America was given permission to open a news bureau in Moscow, although Wick noted that the project was running into bureaucratic delays. The VOA was having problems finding an apartment and office. "Are they real problems or are you reluctant to let them open a bureau here?" Wick inquired. "A VOA bureau here would demonstrate to the world your tangible commitment to new thinking." He urged Yakovlev to look into the problem. Wick was also unhappy about what he saw as a continuing inability of Americans to get access to the Soviet media. Wick peppered Yakovlev with more irritants: the United States was pleased that Soviet jamming of the VOA had ceased, but was distressed that the Soviets were still jamming Radio Liberty and Radio Free Europe. VOA programs to Afghanistan were also jammed, said Wick. Finally, he complained that Moscow Radio broadcasts carried from Cuba on AM medium wave interfered with domestic U.S. broadcasts on the same or adjacent frequencies, in violation of international law.

Finally it was Yakovlev's turn. "All these minor things will pass into oblivion," assured the grandfatherly figure. "We can feel that we have accomplished our duty, even though occasional disinformation stories may arise. I get up in the morning, brush my teeth, dress, and read *Pravda* during breakfast," he continued. "I do not control what *Pravda* publishes. We have more grudges against the Soviet press than you do."

"I could provide enormous documentation that would prove the contrary," Wick countered. "I could shower you with detail but that would be counterproductive." Yakovlev tried to deflect Wick's anger. "Don't pay too much attention to the media," he counseled Wick. "We have to follow the path of a general, step-by-step improvement of relations. We can't get bogged down exchanging charges."

Then followed a string of old folk sayings. Soviet politicians loved them. "If we swim all the time in cold water, we will get cramps. We should advance the general issues and the rest will take care of itself," said Yakovlev. "You have to decide whether the glass is half-empty or half-full," he concluded, adding, "Woodpeckers can hit their head all the time on a tree and not get a headache, but we can't."

During all this time our Worldnet satellite TV network was broadcasting full-time in five languages. One of the most popular programs was an English-language teaching series that carried its not-so-subtle messages about the good life in the West. One of the segments, shot in an American supermarket, showed a modern electronic cashier check-out facility. There were no lines, at least not in our program. The show's host pointed out that while a shopper was buying food he could also get his suit dry-cleaned and his shoes fixed in the store. The program generated a surge of mail from interested viewers, especially in Eastern Europe. Our two-hour morning breakfast program, "America Today," filled with news and interviews especially for international audiences, was especially popular, "with its politics, its style, its fashions, its technology and science, its culture, high and low," according to *Broadcasting* magazine's Leonard Zeidenberg.[28] In the United States, *National Review* claimed that Worldnet was forcing Great Britain's government "to end its cozy, theoretical discussions about the future of television and come to grips with this question: Is it any longer possible to control broadcasting in an era of global communications? Good. Let the frontiers fall."[29] Wick was fond of saying, to the chagrin of USIA veterans who had spent their careers at the Agency, that "Worldnet has generated more international media coverage in its brief history than the entire Agency was able to place during its previous thirty years of existence."[30] While Worldnet was the good cop, the VOA was the bad cop. A Voice of America editorial had claimed Soviet soldiers in

Afghanistan, as they were withdrawing from the country, were planting new trip-wire mines shaped like toys to maim women and children. The VOA also reported, citing as its source the U.S. ambassador to Pakistan, Robert Oakley, that Soviet soldiers were poisoning Afghan food. The Soviets agreed that land mines did exist, but claimed they were placed there by Afghan Mujahideen guerrillas, and not by Russian soldiers. The Kremlin continued to justify the jamming of Radio Free Europe and Radio Liberty broadcasts because of similar diatribes. Said Valentin Falin, "If the United States were the target of daily, directed propaganda broadcasts regarding its internal affairs it would not be so philosophical about the issue. Nobody gave the United States the right to examine the internal problems of the Soviet Union and try to solve them."[31] Perhaps not. We would allow the victims of Soviet aggression to do that for themselves.

↔ 11 ↔

VOA Follies

THE SINGER ROD STEWART COULDN'T HAVE HAD ANY IDEA WHEN HE recorded his album *Foolish Behavior* that it would be used to send a secret message to a spy overseas. In the summer of 1982, VOA broadcaster Alan Silverman was ordered to play any song from Stewart's album, at specific times when the program was beamed to Europe. He was told to tell no one of the directive, because it came from the top.[1] In April 1985, VOA editor Nodar Djin was ordered by his supervisor to play a certain Georgian folk tune, "Suliko," Stalin's favorite. He was directed to say that the song had been played at a concert in Washington the night before, and that it had been requested by a listener in Soviet Georgia. Neither was true.[2] "It was like a tasteless scene from a cheap Soviet spy film," recalled Djin, who reluctantly did as he was told.[3] When he complained, he was fired and wound up driving a cab. Wick later said he couldn't remember the incident, but that the Agency's duty was to do what's best for America.[4] Although the Voice of America operated under a congressional mandate to report the news accurately and objectively, it made exceptions, such as when it transmitted cloak-and-dagger codes to U.S. spooks abroad.

Of course, sending coded messages on government radios was nothing new. During World War II, to alert French resistance fighters that the Normandy D-Day invasion was under way and to start their sabotage, the BBC French-language service recited three lines from Paul Verlaine's poem "Chanson d'automne" (Autumn Song).

> *Blessent mon coeur*
> *d'une langueur*
> *monotone*
> (Wound my heart
> with a monotonous
> languor)[5]

BBC chimes from Big Ben were also used to send coded messages. But when it came to intrigue and even sheer lunacy, the Voice of America was in a class by itself. With its 46 language services broadcast to more than 70 countries, the VOA in the mid-1980s was a mini-United Nations—a labyrinth of distinct cultures and historic rivalries—housed in a large gray sandstone building on Independence Avenue in Washington. Although its employees work for the U.S. government, many are not American citizens, the VOA being one of the few government agencies permitted to hire foreign nationals—many of whom had been high-ranking officials in their native countries. The former defense minister of Afghanistan, for example, became a lower-rung GS-11 civil servant broadcaster at the VOA. As former VOA chief of staff Michael Schoenfeld recalls, "They were college professors, college presidents, intellectuals, people with very strong views, people with a great deal of ambition and aggressiveness. Pour two thousand of those people into the VOA building in Washington and you have a recipe for constant turmoil."[6]

And turmoil it produced. When word processors were installed in the Russian-language service, rumors suddenly spread that the screens would cause sterility, brain damage, and breast cancer, and that it was all an anti-Semitic plot. On one afternoon, a VOA Bulgarian broadcaster stabbed his Romanian counterpart in the VOA's men's room. A fight broke out in the Armenian and Azerbaijan language-services office. Angry employees started flinging heavy metal tape reels at each other from behind huge stacks in the tape room, and the fight lasted a few hours.

Moslem employees had been spreading newspapers on the floors so that they could pray until someone suggested setting aside part of a utility closet as a prayer room. The General Services Administration estimated the rental value of the space, which offered enough room for one prayer rug angled toward Mecca, at $750 per year. One day an unsuspecting employee, who wanted to get water from the sink for coffee, entered the room by mistake and interrupted a prayer session. He was promptly chased away. Rumors quickly spread throughout the VOA that non-Moslem employees were being harassed.[7]

"If they came from Afghanistan they were tortured by the Khads and wanted revenge," said Richard Carlson, who served as VOA director in the Reagan and Bush administrations. "They are immersed in a world of ethnic politics of old wounds and deep grudges. Nothing that has occurred by way of 'ethnic cleansing' surprises me in the slightest. It was everyday life at the VOA."[8] The Soviet desk was the worst, said Carlson, a portly, affable man who sports bow ties. "I used to get anonymous notes over the transom and late-night secret phone calls. Someone with an East European accent would usually get on the phone and tell me some unbelievable story about an employee being in the Nazi party, or that someone was a Communist or an intelligence agent. Sometimes they were on the mark."[9] Carlson lent much-needed stability to the VOA, which had gone through nine directors or acting directors in the six-year period from 1980 to 1986.[10] He was a compromise candidate during the Reagan Administration, when it was difficult to find someone to run the VOA who could pass the conservative political litmus test, and then stay put.

During Reagan's second term, ex-NBC news correspondent Gene Pell had served briefly as VOA director and abruptly resigned to take over as head of Radio Free Europe/Radio Liberty. Former ABC News president William Sheehan was a candidate to take Pell's place, and the veteran broadcaster looked like a shoo-in to head the Voice. Sheehan had met with Wick and Edwin J. Feulner, Jr., president of the conservative Heritage Foundation, and afterward the word went around that Sheehan was "OK." As a final test, Sheehan was to meet with a group of leading political conservatives including Republican fund-raiser Richard Viguerie, Reed Irvine of the watchdog group Accuracy in Media, and Roy Cohn, the notorious former aide to the late Senator Joseph McCarthy. Cohn had personally endorsed several previous VOA directors, including Kenneth Y. Tomlinson of *Reader's Digest,* who headed the VOA early in the Reagan Administration when the radio service was pressured by ultraconservatives to take a more vigorous stance against communism. Bill Sheehan was now being interrogated for the job. Sheehan and the group met for lunch in a private room at the Ritz-Carlton Hotel in downtown Washington.

"Would you be willing to call the Afghan rebels 'freedom fighters'?" Viguerie asked.

"Yes, if that's what they call themselves," Sheehan replied.

"Did you vote for Reagan?" Cohn asked.

"I don't think it's anybody's business who I voted for," replied Sheehan, visibly annoyed at the question.

"It's our business if you're going to be a political appointee," said Cohn. "I think it's a legitimate question. Did you vote for Reagan?"

"I don't think I should have to make a blood oath for this job," responded Sheehan.[11]

The lunch ended abruptly. When told of how the meeting had gone, Senator Jesse Helms sent word to Wick that if Sheehan were selected for the VOA position, "his nomination will be hung out to dry." Wick got the point, and Carlson got the nod. Richard Carlson, I should add, was not your average USIA bureaucrat. At age two, he was adopted from an orphanage in Boston, the Home for Little Wanderers, by the Carlson family. Before coming to the USIA, he had been at various points in his life a Marine, a cop in Ocean City, Maryland, a TV reporter in Los Angeles, a bank president, and an unsuccessful candidate for mayor of San Diego. Carlson had met Wick several years earlier at a party at the Hollywood home of Ozzie and Harriet Nelson.

Carlson became VOA director when the organization was still mired in its disastrous campaign to put up new, more powerful overseas radio transmitters capable of breaking through Soviet jamming. With a parade of nine directors and acting directors heading the Voice for a six-year period, there was an obvious lack of direction from top management. The Voice was telling America's story abroad, but its program service was dull and old-fashioned, lacking the bite and relevance of Radio Free Europe/Radio Liberty broadcasts, which brought local news to information-deprived listeners behind the Iron Curtain. While Worldnet was taking off, Reagan's $1.3 billion, five-year plan to modernize the Voice of America had gotten nowhere. It had taken the VOA more than eighteen months to reorganize its present technical staff. It would take still another year to write job descriptions and several more years to hire 140 highly skilled engineers—ostensibly to help put more powerful stations on the air, thereby breaking through Soviet jamming.

There was no comparable effort to improve the VOA's program service. Money began flowing in from Congress faster than the VOA could spend it. By late 1983, a surplus of some $90 million had built up in the VOA radio construction account. In an effort to jump-start the VOA, the United States was furiously negotiating with other governments to lease land for transmitter sites, and by year's end an agreement was signed with Sri Lanka.[12] In March 1984 an agreement came through with Morocco, where a new station was to replace a smaller, older station in Tangier (which had been operating since the early 1950s) on a tract twice the size of Disneyland.[13] But there was a problem. The location, a 1,147-acre site one mile from the Atlantic Ocean, was underwater; in fact, it was located in the floodplain of a tidal river. Chief VOA engineer Maurice Rafensperger had seen the area during the dry season when there were lovely spring flowers in bloom. Rafensperger and his technical team advised Wick that the location proposed by the kingdom of Morocco was a favorable one, because it was close to heavy-duty power lines, seaports, and railroads, so that supplies—including fuel to help supply power to the station—would be readily accessible. It was also only a mile from the Atlantic Ocean, offering an unobstructed path for the radio signals (and flood waters).[14] Barry Malko, the VOA architect, traveled from Washington to Morocco to inspect the site. When he drove up to the edge of a lake he assumed he must have been given the wrong directions by his superiors in Washington. "This can't be right," he told his supervisor. "I need a snorkel and rubber suit." "You think we're gonna get prime real estate for radio transmitters?" asked the official. "Besides, water is a good conductor of electricity to boost the radio signal."

Malko was ordered to start mapping the location, which was to be one of the largest Voice of America shortwave radio facilities ever built. It was a ludicrous situation. "Ladies and gentlemen, you just bought yourself a lake," he told headquarters. And indeed, in a mostly arid country the United States had incredibly selected a location that was underwater—at an annual rent of $1.3 million. Wick had relied on his VOA technical experts, who approved the location in Morocco, which he later observed from a dry hilltop overlooking the waterlogged site.

USIA negotiators, meanwhile, tried frantically to strike land deals with other countries, and in April 1984 an agreement was signed with Thailand, and construction started immediately. Wick and other dignitaries, wearing hard hats with Voice of America insignias on them, broke ground with a chrome-plated shovel. Villagers were presented awards for donating their land to the 1,300-acre site.[15] Negotiations with Sri Lanka had been going on since 1977, despite a stern warning from the State Department that Sri Lanka was not the safest location for an expensive relay station because of the country's political instability. Nonetheless, the VOA agreed to the location and had to pay the Sri Lankan Broadcasting Corporation $500,000 for relocation of squatters and for—no joke—coconut development. The money was spent, but the squatters remained, so the VOA looked for land elsewhere in the country.

Soon the VOA had invested $30 million in technical studies, which it had commissioned for its proposed new shortwave stations. One of the completed studies (cost: $4.4 million) did not address any of the fifteen tasks stipulated in the contract. Another contractor was paid to fly a team around the world to take an inventory of technical equipment at VOA relay stations.[16] "Why can't the VOA get this information from its people in the field?" asked senior analyst John Butcher from the General Accounting Office. "One hundred thirty people are assigned to the relay station in Greece where all they have to do is look at meters. Why do they have to pay somebody else to tell these people what equipment they have on the shelf?"[17]

So many consultants' reports flooded into the VOA that managers lost track of them. A consultant was hired to concoct a tracking system for the consultants' reports. He studied the problem and recommended a "document tree," from which to hang lists of various study components in one place. It was implemented but discontinued when it became too unwieldy.[18] An inspector general sent by Congress asked the VOA's engineering department for a list of all the major studies it had commissioned, but it was unable to produce the information. The inspector general persisted and determined that the VOA had been stashing its technical studies in seventeen different offices. The VOA rejected an inspector general's suggestion that a system be established to follow up on recommendations made in consultants' reports. The VOA said this might be "nice to have," but that it "did not directly contribute to the work at hand."[19]

In order to review the studies, I filed a Freedom of Information request with the USIA for a "computerized listing of major reports written by outside consultants on the VOA modernization program." Privacy Act officer Lola L. Secora responded: "I am sorry to inform you that the Office of Engineering and Technical Operations was unable to locate the listing of major reports written by outside consultants that you requested."[20] Here was a group of government managers who would eventually spend $60 million in taxpayer money for engineering studies, yet they had no idea where the important technical research documents were located. They had, in fact, been discarded.

By 1986, three years into Reagan's five-year plan to modernize the VOA, no new transmitting stations had been installed overseas. VOA engineers didn't want to buy the high-powered, monster-size transmitters until they could test them. Instead they bought four 70-story-high transmitters at $4 million each, and began to read the instruction booklets. They proved very slow readers. To complicate matters, the big transmitters were designed and built in Europe. This raised the hackles of a "Buy American" Congress. The Senate Appropriations Committee even complained that domestic manufacturers of radio transmitters were running into "anti-American bias" from the VOA's purchasing department. "How can we remind these VOA officials," asked a committee member, "that it is not Brown Boveri of Switzerland, Telefunken of Germany, and Marconi of England that supply the taxes that pay their salaries?" In the end, the VOA was forced to stipulate to foreign manufacturers of the big transmitters that they had to have an American partner.

Barry Malko witnessed a high-powered transmitter being tested at the VOA relay station in Greenville, North Carolina. "I went into an office at the transmitter site," Malko recalled, "and noticed a fluorescent tube hanging from the ceiling on a string. It wasn't plugged in, but it was lit just from the radiation in the room." Malko felt as if he were entering the Twilight Zone. "I looked out the window and sparks were flying from the antenna," he recalled. "Then I heard a woman's voice about two feet over my head, but no one was there. She was speaking Ukrainian, and I could have sworn it was my grandmother who used to come into my room when I was a boy and tell me stories in Ukrainian. I looked up and said, 'Grandmother, is that you?'"[21] It turned out to be a young broadcaster from the Voice of America studio in Washington. The radio signal was so strong at the test site that it had reflected off the metal zipper on Malko's winter jacket and reverberated throughout the room, giving the impression of a disembodied voice floating over him.

The impressive displays notwithstanding, the clock was ticking and not a single new VOA station was close to being put on line. American commercial broadcasters who served on voluntary USIA advisory committees were aghast at the VOA. "It's the first time I ever heard of someone buying a radio transmitter first, and then testing it to see if it works," said Lee Hanna, a USIA-TV consultant. Skeptics on Capitol Hill and in the Office of Management and Budget questioned whether the project should continue. VOA confidence in itself began to get whittled away. To help fend off its critics, the VOA commandeered two small, low-power portable transmitters from the Defense Department and hurried them into Central America on flat-bed trucks. One went to Costa Rica and other to Belize (former British Honduras). The Costa Rican transmitter was to reach into neighboring Nicaragua and harangue the pro-Marxist Sandinista government. But first the VOA had to come up with $3.2 million to bribe the Costa Rican government into relaxing its ban on foreign ownership and operation of a radio station. Wick decided he had had enough of the incompetent VOA engineering managers, and wanted the more experienced U.S. Army Corps of Engineers to take over the modernization program to get it moving. But he deferred to his telecommunications consultant, Henry Hockeimer, who was lobbied hard by VOA engineers to remain in control. Hockeimer expressed to Wick his general support for the VOA engineers, who continued to mismanage the program.[22]

On April 25, 1986, the USIA's inspector general wrote to

Carlson: "Our survey of VOA's modernization program has developed information which indicates that the engineering approach VOA is using will not meet the time requirement mandated by the National Security Council [and is] more costly and time-consuming than necessary." The VOA's engineering division responded to the inspector general that because of the "complexity of the negotiations," plans for relay stations had run into "considerable difficulty and delay." International agreements take time, said the VOA, because countries do not exactly welcome VOA relay stations with open arms. In its 1986 report, the U.S. Advisory Commission on Public Diplomacy wrote that it was "deeply troubled that the VOA continues to be surpassed by other major international broadcasters in facilities, equipment, personnel, signal strength, and broadcast hours." A 1986 report by the National Research Council claimed the radio network didn't even know whether its modernization program would result in larger listening audiences.

The site for the new VOA shortwave facility in Morocco was still underwater. Millions were being spent to dredge the area, and preparations were under way to bring in thousands of tons of landfill. VOA engineers had another major problem in Israel, where a $300 million radio facility was to be constructed in the Negev Desert. Migrating birds flew across the 2,500-acre location—one of the major intercontinental bird migration routes in the world—on the way to and from the warm waters of the Mediterranean.[23] Local environmentalists were worried that the 500-foot electrified radio towers that were planned for the site would endanger the birds, some millions of which, including endangered species such as rare raptors, pelicans, white storks, and many songbirds, flew over the area during migration.[24] Locating the towers in the Negev was a ridiculous idea to begin with. Radio transmitters work best when put on high elevations, on top of mountains, for example, enabling signals to reach farther. The Negev Desert is next to the Dead Sea, the lowest point on earth.

In all fairness, the Negev site had been a last resort. The United States had been attempting since the Carter Administration to place a major shortwave radio facility in the Middle East. The shortwave radio transmitters in Germany, Portugal, and Spain could not transmit a signal strong enough to reach Soviet Central Asia, the target area. The Middle East was the perfect location. Arab countries were approached first (to blunt anti-Israeli reactions), and Egypt's President Sadat approved a site south of the Gaza Strip. Mubarak, who took office after Sadat's assassination, was cool about the project, because he felt it would destabilize the region by antagonizing Egypt's former allies the Soviets, and plans were cancelled. Turkey, Saudi Arabia, and Oman were then approached, but none of them wanted anything to do with the facility. (Turkey did not wish to alienate its neighbor, the Soviet Union; Oman had already permitted BBC radio towers to be built on its territory; and Saudi Arabia didn't want to be caught between the two superpowers.) Jordan, Greece, and the United Arab Emirates also did not want U.S. transmitters on their soil. Finally, Israel was approached. There was major opposition from the outset, despite the close ties between the two countries. Many Israelis worried that antagonizing the Soviet Union would jeopardize Jewish emigration from behind the Iron Curtain. Others, particularly kibbutzim, felt that the massive structures would destroy the pristine beauty of the desert and disrupt their way of life. Environmentalists demanded assurances that the giant desert facility, with its fifty-three gigantic transmitters and skyscraper-size antennas, would not have an adverse impact on the area. The Israeli military, which had an air base nearby, was concerned that the antennas would interfere with aircraft training exercises. The concept also had its supporters. Israeli contractors would build the station, which would create at least 600 full-time jobs and pump an estimated $25 million into the Israeli economy. For Israel there was also the prestige of having the largest shortwave radio facility in the world located on its soil. Finally, the prospect of entering into a huge, bilateral venture with America was appealing, especially one with such a worthy cause. An agreement was finally signed on June 18, 1987. The Reagan Administration decided that the facility would be shared jointly by the VOA and Radio Free Europe/Radio Liberty for transmissions into Eastern Europe, Asia, and North Africa. The Board for International Broadcasting, the parent organization of RFE/RL, was designated to manage the project. To prepare the site, land was graded, power and sewer lines were run, and flood water around the area was diverted. A highway needed to be rerouted and more than seven miles of new roadway built.

The American government agreed that construction of the station would depend on the approval of a "National Outline Scheme" by Israel's National Board of Planning and Building. While preliminary work at the site was proceeding, the United States spent more than $2 million on an environmental-impact study. It failed to turn up any evidence that the station posed substantial danger to birds, but agreed to take extraordinary precautions to protect them from harm. For example, windows in buildings on the site would be fitted with dark drapes or shutters to block out light that might attract birds. The United States also agreed to spend $20 million for special shielding that would prevent birds alighting on transmission lines from electric shocks. An elaborate $1.5 million monitoring system would be installed to gauge electromagnetic fields emitted from the station, so that operators could take immediate corrective actions.[25] And a bird-monitoring device would be installed to detect new migration patterns, so that preventive measures, including the sounding of recorded bird call warnings, could be taken whenever necessary.

Despite all these assurances and precautions, the Society for the Protection of Nature in Israel (SPNI), was not assuaged. The nocturnal habits of birds, it maintained, had not been adequately addressed, since most birds fly at night and would be more prone to fly into the 70-story structures, or be microwaved if they flew too close to the powerful transmitters. Actually, the $2 million study had included limited observations of nocturnal flight patterns with observers using infrared goggles of the type that would later be used by troops during the Persian Gulf War, but critics thought the subject had not been covered in sufficient depth. SPNI petitioned the Israeli Supreme Court to order a halt to further construction while additional environmental-impact studies were conducted. The court agreed. "No one really thought that some dingbat birds would become such an issue," said National Security Council official Walter Raymond.

The new study was to be done under the supervision of the Ben-Gurion University of the Negev in Israel and would cost $1.2 million. A renowned Swiss ornithologist, Bruno Bruderer, was contracted to coordinate a radar survey of the nocturnal migration of birds flying over the radio relay station site. Dr. Bruderer, head of the migration department of the Swiss Ornithological Institute, measured how many birds flew at night over the site area and at what altitude over three migratory seasons. The study also measured the impact of the antennas' electromagnetic rays on birds flying over them, "bird collisions with various manmade structures in different conditions of weather and lighting," and the effect of radio waves on bird navigation. Bruderer said most of the millions of birds that migrate from Europe to Africa each autumn prefer to fly over land rather than water, and that the Negev Desert was a major flight path.[26] "All flapping fliers, mainly passerine, waders, and waterfowl fly at night," he said. "As many as fifty thousand birds per night during the autumn fly near the vicinity of the proposed shortwave radio facility."

There was, however, some good news. Bruderer concluded that the station facility would have minimal impact on the environment and bird migration. The radar study revealed that over 90 precent of the birds would fly well above the radio transmitters. Bruderer found that nocturnal flyers use air currents above sea level, and since the site was 480 feet below sea level they would clear the towers with ease. Fewer than thirty birds per night would be in danger of colliding with the structures. The report also pointed out that since conditions in the desert are almost always dry and clear and because birds have acute vision, the chances of colliding with the brightly lit towers was minimal. And as far as radioactive hazards were concerned, the study showed no detrimental effects to birds, or humans, for that matter.[27]

The reports were turned over to Israel's National Board of Planning and Building. By this point we had already prepared the site, which now had 16 miles of power lines and 7 miles of road. Designs for the radio facility were completed and paid for, and a prime contractor had been selected to install transmitters and antennas. Everyone was afraid that the Israelis were going to back out of the deal. Instead, it was the American government that decided it had had enough and pulled up stakes, lighter by $64 million.

Meanwhile, in North Africa, more than seventy VOA engineers outfitted in heavy rain gear were dispatched to the Moroccan relay station site to deal with the flooding problem. An exasperated Wick ordered the VOA to call in the Army Corps of Engineers to help supervise construction. Many VOA engineers had come from the Corps, so the move simply shifted some responsibility for the management of the modernization program to another government agency, and added a 15 percent overhead charged by the Corps. The VOA official in charge of modernization, Morton Smith, advised Wick that the rainy season was causing some slippage in the schedule. "Progress was very satisfactory until the rainy season began. However, significant weather delays have been experienced during the last three weeks. Landfill placement will be slowed, but not stopped, during the rainy season; this situation was expected and planned for." Smith cautioned that a visit by Wick to the site would be inadvisable during the rainy season, because he would have to get around in a four-wheel-drive vehicle and view the site from a hilltop, as he had during ground-breaking ceremonies earlier in the year.[28] It would take more than three years to dump enough dirt (2 million cubic meters of landfill were required) into the Moroccan site to raise the level of the land above sea level, at a cost of $15 million.[29]

The problem, said one government investigator, was that "they had to excavate and build the whole area up above the hundred-year floodplain. Trouble was, they got going before they had their layouts for all their antennas and everything and they excavated a lot more than necessary." The USIA's inspector general found that the unnecessary work increased the project's cost by almost $2 million.[30] "Every time a shovelful of dirt was turned over we were charged ten thousand dollars," admitted VOA architect Barry Malko ruefully. The VOA had decided to act prematurely because it wanted to show the Moroccan government it was making progress on the project, which was already at least four years behind schedule. Estimates of the Moroccan station's cost skyrocketed from the original 1984 budget submission of $175 million to an estimated $225 million, an increase of 28 percent. There were more nightmares when transmitting equipment began to arrive in Morocco. The VOA had failed to issue proper customs documents to its contractors, and Moroccan customs officials were overwhelmed by thousands of tons of communications equipment coming into the country, which caused more delays. The VOA also missed out on getting a value-added tax (VAT) refund of $1.45 million from the Moroccan government, because it had filled out forms improperly and submitted them past the deadline.[31]

The VOA was still ill-fated and suffering another crisis, this time in Costa Rica, to which the VOA had moved a portable Defense Department transmitter in a hurried attempt to get something on the air so that it could justify its modernization program. Local residents in Quesada, a town in northern Costa Rica, were highly suspicious of the new kids on the block. There were no signs on the building in which the new people worked. A double chain-link fence—a rarity in the Central American country—had been installed around the perimeter. There are relatively few firearms in Costa Rica, and local residents were also concerned about the armed guards toting shotguns and handguns who escorted workers to and from the building each day. They weren't any less alarmed when the guards underwent an intensive four-week firearms training session on the premises. The security force protecting workers at the Voice of America's radio station at Quesada was larger than the armies of many Caribbean nations.[32]

The station was desperately trying to drive its weak signal from a low-power, jury-rigged transmitter northward into Managua, Nicaragua. Diesel engines powered by generators coughed out only a minimal amount of electricity to run the station. The radio signal, with programming in support of the anti-Sandinista Contra rebels, unfortunately could not be heard in the densely populated capital. The VOA's weak signal was not the only problem. There was also a rugged mountain range located between the transmitting antenna and Managua effectively blocking the signal and keeping it from reaching the city. A radio station in Managua, with a powerful signal broadcast on the same frequency, could have overridden the VOA signal easily, had there been a VOA signal to override. Even if there hadn't been mountains and stronger competition, the VOA interrupted its broadcast schedule for two hours each day in order to perform equipment maintenance.[33] The hours it chose, 1:30–3:30 each afternoon, were peak listening hours. The station was off the air during the time when most Managuans listened to the radio, during lunch and siesta periods.

Exasperated, the USIA's deputy director, Marvin Stone, testified before Congress that the United States had "a white elephant" on its hands. The Costa Rica station was taken off the air. The ill-conceived project had cost taxpayers more than $12 million.

The State Department's official explanation was that Costa Rica, which took a position of neutrality in Caribbean politics, did not wish to have U.S. broadcasts transmitted to Nicaragua from within its territory.

The state of VOA affairs in Costa Rica, Morocco, and Israel meant that by 1987 Ronald Reagan and Charles Z. Wick had all but given up on expanding the Voice. Wick, with Reagan's full backing, focused attention on his pet project, Worldnet. The VOA continued to enjoy general support in Congress, whose ethnic constituents were rallied when needed to prevent budget cuts that would eliminate or curtail transmissions of certain VOA language services. In five years, more than a hundred Worldnet satellite dishes had been installed at American diplomatic facilities in eighty countries and were receiving a stream of U.S. government programs. "Hopefully," Wick told Congress, "we will be able to complete the [radio] modernization, but the beauty of this television technology we are harnessing through Worldnet is that we don't have to build two- and three-hundred-million-dollar stations around the world that are subject to the various vicissitudes of host nations." To buy and install a satellite dish cost $27,000, he pointed out; a radio transmitter cost $4 million. And TV dishes could be put into place within days, not decades.[34]

But the VOA modernization program slogged on. In Thailand, construction of the new transmitting site was plagued by lengthy delays and cost overruns. By 1987, three years after an agreement had been signed with Thailand, land was cleared and foundations for antennas put in, along with storm drainage systems, water lines, sewers, perimeter roads and fencing, a guardhouse, and landscaping. But, as in Morocco, VOA engineers had acted prematurely and begun construction before receiving a technical consultant's report. Three months after the antennas had been erected, an engineering study surfaced showing that the VOA had installed them in the wrong places. They had to be taken down and relocated. "These antennas are as big as office buildings," said a supervisor at the Thailand site. "You need a large amount of space underneath the antenna to service it. It's like a big basement level, with cabling and generators. You also have to build roads to get to each antenna." Revised architectural plans had to be developed and approved, and a new construction contractor selected. Said a consulting architect, "This was a lifetime project. You could have started and ended your career trying to get this station together." The projected cost of $99 million rose to $137 million, a 38 percent hike.[35] For all his efforts, Morton S. Smith, a competent government executive who managed the VOA's relay station projects and served as acting director of the VOA for a few months during Reagan's second term, received the President's Distinguished Service Award as Deputy Director of Modernization in June 1988. He had been selected with the consent of Wick, who had learned a lot about how to get along with USIA bureaucrats.

Things were no better at home, at the VOA's Washington headquarters, where renovations were at least five years behind schedule and monstrously over budget. The centerpiece of the modernization effort was to be a fully automated network control center. According to plans on the drawing board, the chief engineer would be able to monitor his worldwide network of transmitters and antennas from his command post. Computers were to automatically control transmitters around the world, so that programs could be relayed immediately into crisis areas. Construction was painfully slow. New equipment had been purchased but not installed. Unopened packing crates were being stacked in offices and hallways, waiting for construction to begin. Equipment warranties were expiring. "We used to snake visiting VIPs and tours away from the storage cartons," admitted a VOA employee. When construction on the facility finally started, 1950s wiring dripped toxic PCBs into tin cans on the floor, and asbestos-lined acoustic tiles had to be painstakingly removed. The VOA's luxuriously appointed Washington control center was finally completed eight years after it was begun.[36] Projected to cost $2.6 million, the cost of renovations had soared to $21 million. The money spent on new computers that had been purchased "to analyze and respond to listener mail with a rapidity unprecedented at VOA" turned out to be a waste: the General Accounting Office later found that the VOA was throwing out listener mail without reading it.[37] The VOA accumulated about 100,000 unanswered letters in one year, and most were discarded without even being opened. The GAO report noted that this had apparently discouraged listeners from writing because there was a 22 percent decline in incoming mail over a three-year period. The VOA claimed the problem was due to a funding cut in its central audience mail program and the loss of several staff positions. Critics appealed to the Voice to read its mail. They faulted it for putting so much effort into trying to strengthen its signal and so little into improving its program service. The GAO was right. By mid-1985, the engineers had seized virtual control and almost succeeded in stilling the Voice.

↔ **12** ↔

The Mujahideen Go to School

MASOOD FARIVAR WAS A YOUNG AFGHAN JOURNALIST, STUDENT, AND guerrilla fighter who carried an AK-47 into battle along with his minicam videotape camera and his textbooks. "When war broke out, I was part of the troops," Masood recalled. "Then I'd report on it. I worked with an artillery battalion firing missiles and mortars, then I'd do interviews and take photographs." After that, presumably, he would go home and do his homework.[1]

When the Soviets invaded Afghanistan in December 1979 to shore up its pro-Marxist government, Masood fled his native country before he could complete his education. He enrolled as a journalism student at the Afghan Media Resource Center (AMRC) in Peshawar, Pakistan, a U.S.-funded facility established to train reporters to cover the Afghan war. "I was in Afghanistan on assignment, covering a major battle in which the rebels were going to launch a huge assault against the government," said Masood. "And I was there with my SAT study guide. The battle hadn't started yet, and I was getting frustrated. I rushed back to Pakistan two days before the test was given and took it."[2]

The war in Afghanistan was the American government's "made-for-TV" movie. It was the first war in which both AK-47s and video minicams were standard infantry issue. It was a war in which media coverage was purchased from a mail order catalogue, and Uncle Sam owned the warehouse.

Afghanistan was called "'Moscow's Vietnam without reporters.'"[3] A country about the size of Texas, it is surrounded by Russia, Iran, Pakistan, and China. The Soviets' occupation of the remote, mountainous nation, requiring ten thousand Soviet troops, was hugely expensive, costing Moscow an estimated $12 million a day. In addition to being a severe drain on the Kremlin's fragile economy, the war was not helping the Kremlin's public relations image, either. As in Vietnam, innocent villagers—women and children—suffered the most. One and a half million Afghans would lose their lives in the war. About five million were forced to flee their devastated homeland, migrating mostly into neighboring Pakistan and the border city of Peshawar, headquarters of the Afghan resistance fighters, the Mujahideen. It was a public relations nightmare for Moscow; for Washington it was a public relations dream come true.

The problem for American propagandists was that the conflict was getting scant media coverage. Between 1982 and 1985 the major networks devoted fewer than one story per month to the war in Afghanistan. During all of 1983, NBC carried a grand total of only 3.2 minutes about Afghanistan.[4] During all of 1986, the combined American TV network coverage of the war totaled less than one hour.[5]

As a war zone, Afghanistan was more difficult to cover than Lebanon or Vietnam, to which one could get by plane. Whereas news reporters and photographers could stay in hotels in Saigon and Beirut, there were no hotels or restaurants in the mountains and valleys of Afghanistan, where the war was being fought. Covering the conflict was extremely dangerous and expensive. Newsmen trekking over vast, hostile, mountainous regions frequently took months to complete assignments. Thousands of land mines made travel perilous. Soviet jets would suddenly come screaming out of the sky between mountain ranges without warning, which meant that fighting was done mostly under the cloak of darkness by ragtag groups of resistance fighters, mostly illiterate farmers.[6] The Soviet Union, which obviously didn't want coverage of the conflict, warned that newsmen traveling with Afghan rebels would be considered the enemy as well. The former Soviet ambassador to Pakistan, Vitaly Smirnov, minced no words at a news conference. "I warn you, and through you all your journalist colleagues," he cautioned Western newsmen. "Stop trying to penetrate Afghanistan with the so-called guerrillas . . . the bandits and so-called guerrillas will be killed."[7] He meant that the Soviets wouldn't hold their fire simply because Dan Rather might be in the vicinity. An American newspaper reporter, Charles Thornton of the *Arizona Republic,* was killed in Afghanistan in November 1985 when a Soviet helicopter fired on his Jeep.

In an eight-year period, seven foreign journalists were killed while covering the war.[8] It was easier and a lot safer for news organizations to purchase stories from journalistic mercenaries than to send in their own reporters and camera crews. "Gunga Dan" Rather of CBS News amused foreign journalists when he whispered into the microphone and, decked out as a shepherd, stepped across the dividing line into Afghanistan to shoot an on-camera report. "The hardest part of our Afghanistan coverage was living down the dumb Rather thing," said former senior CBS News executive Gene Mater. "It was like Mike Dukakis with his head sticking out of a tank during the presidential campaign. He wished he hadn't done that, either."[9]

The journalists who covered the Afghanistan war with any consistency were mainly the French, Brits, and Germans—although there were some Americans—all combat journalists with extensive military experience, not soft-palmed TV anchormen. There were also intelligence spooks, undercover as journalists, and a smattering of twenty-something would-be adventurers who wanted to make names for themselves. Since there were no more than a handful of journalists in Afghanistan whose special interest was covering the war, and who did so with any regularity, there was a wide-open market niche for any organization supplying newspaper stories, videotape, and stills from the front. Other Muslim countries (99 percent of Afghanistan is Muslim) paid as little attention as the rest of the world.

In the summer of 1982, USIA shot a TV special called "Thanksgiving in Peshawar" with Kirk Douglas, whom we had sent to Pakistan with our producer Ash Hawken as host. The program was intended to condemn the Soviet occupation of Afghanistan and reveal the plight of the 4 million refugees who had fled to neighboring

Pakistan. Douglas became ill while on assignment, and although smartly produced the program, when it finally aired in the fall of 1982, met with limited success. In early 1983 I met with European TV journalists who had reported from Afghanistan and enlisted their participation in an hour-long special featuring their stories. They were joined by reporters from Venezuela, Tokyo, Turkey, and Australia. The program was distributed worldwide and did much better than "Thanksgiving in Peshawar" because it had combat footage and reports by professional journalists. But what was really needed was sustained daily coverage. The Voice of America did frequent editorials on the plight of Afghan refugees, and the USIA produced a color pamphlet on the subject, but overall the USIA effort to embarrass the Soviets in Afghanistan was getting nowhere.

On March 18, 1985, I sent a memorandum to Charlie Wick on an idea called "Operation: AFCAM":

> Television networks have been trying to cover the Russian occupation of Afghanistan, but the business of getting camera crews in on a regular basis is both dangerous and costly. We have sent out own producers around the world attempting to round up any and all available footage for use in our clip reels.
>
> The Agency should purchase a few hundred small mini-cams (cost: approximately $1,500) with tape and supply them to the Afghan freedom fighters. Imagine the pictures they will be able to get! Imagine the publicity! Imagine the Soviet reaction!
>
> Not only could this possibly yield outstanding visual evidence [of Soviet atrocities], but the publicity of such a move could be incredible. Just as the Russians could not face the "video document" we presented at the United Nations to expose them on KE-007, they would again be in a position to have to dispute proof positive of the horrors they inflict on Afghanistan.
>
> If you concur with the idea, I would like to arrange a meeting of key Agency officers with relevant officials at State and NSC to discuss it further.

Wick loved it. There had been a proposal to set up a print wire service that would be run by Afghan refugees, but the concept was fuzzy and left out television, the medium I felt would have maximum impact. Yet another proposal had come from Senator Gordon J. Humphrey (R-NH), who had been complaining that the Reagan Administration was not doing enough to assist anti-Soviet Afghan rebels through public diplomacy. Humphrey had pushed legislation authorizing a "Radio Free Afghanistan" through Congress. He also got an exception from Congress allowing the USIA to distribute its films about Afghanistan inside the United States, circumventing the Smith-Mundt Act. Humphrey's idea of a radio station broadcasting back into Afghanistan of course made no sense. What could a radio station tell the Afghans that they didn't already know? That the Russians were killing innocent people? The objective, those of us in TV emphasized to Wick, was to get out the word to the rest of world, and not back into Afghanistan. And what good would it do to show a U.S. propaganda film about Afghanistan to American college students? But a TV news syndication service to fill a void in the world marketplace—with combat and human interest stories from inside Afghanistan—would generate material that might find its way onto highly rated TV newscasts everywhere.

Needless to say, Wick approved the idea and the White House National Security Council signed off on the broad concept of an Afghan media project. NSC official Walter Raymond met with Senator Humphrey, who agreed to push legislation through Congress earmarking $500,000 to set up a journalism school for Afghan rebels. Congress passed legislation directing the USIA "to promote an independent Afghan media service" and to "train Afghans in media and media-related activities." It would be up to us to work out the details.

I asked one of my senior producers, Robert Butler, to participate in an Agency-wide task force that was to get things moving, and then I sent him to Afghanistan to oversee the project's startup. On August 26, 1985, an announcement was placed in the Federal Register soliciting concepts from private-sector groups that would like to run the training program. The notice said the project was meant to "overcome substantial obstacles" in reporting the war and "to develop an independent, self-funded media organization." We were looking for the right kind of group, first to train TV and print journalists, and then to distribute their material. The Kremlin read the ad, too, as did the pro-Soviet press. Wrote the editor of the KGB-funded *Patriot* newspaper of India, "Their [USIA's] major task is to

gather information and prepare photo and movie documents com-
promising Soviet and Afghan military personnel whose roles, more
often than not, are played by the rebels themselves in Afghan and Soviet military uniform."

Wick sent a newspaper wire service consultant to Pak-
istan to keep a sharp eye out for opportunities for the print side of the
operation. John O. Kohler, a retired Associated Press executive, visited the area in the fall of 1985. He met with Afghan rebel leaders
and received their assurances that their people would participate in
the program. While he was there, Kohler also learned that the independent British film and video distributor *Visnews* had given ten
camcorders to the Mujahideen rebels to take into battle. Results had
been poor because the rebels had not been properly trained to operate the cameras, nor in television producing or news-writing. The
USIA project would address these shortcomings. James Thurber, director of the USIA's Near East offices, met with Pakistani government
officials in Islamabad in December 1985 to review the Afghan Media
Resource Center (AMRC), as it would officially be named. Thurber
wanted to see how the seven Afghan resistance sects planned to select
one of their own number to run the center. Thurber sent a confidential cable back to Washington urging that the Afghans must at least
appear to be in charge.

The USIA received twenty-three responses to its ad in the
Federal Register. A few of them were pretty bizarre. A Polish para-
trooper felt that with his "skills and experience, combined with those
of my wife" he could cover the Afghan conflict. Another proposal
involved setting up an "Undercover News Service" in the Midwest
to pump out Afghan news. "Unlike most news services," said the
proposal writer, "UNS will get most of its news illegally." King
Features/Hearst Metrotone News won the contract to set up an
Afghan news wire service and to distribute stories generated by
it. Boston University's College of Communications was selected to
train Afghan students in print and still photo journalism, and in video
photography and news writing.

Hearst ran into trouble from the outset. King Features,
which distributed stories each day to more than 3,000 papers, started
to get heat from some subscribers who didn't like receiving their
news from a syndicator in cahoots with the U.S. government.
Michael G. Gartner, then president of the American Society of News-

paper Editors and editor of the *Louisville Courier-Journal,* wrote a letter to Hearst. "How can I rely on a syndicate that is in bed with the U.S. propaganda agency?" he asked. John Siegenthaler, publisher of the *Nashville Tennessean* and editorial director of *U.S.A Today,* threatened to stop using King Features if it didn't drop the Afghan project. Hearst decided to call things off after only six months, before it had fulfilled distribution agreements for the Afghan news service with clients in Europe and the Third World.

Boston University's President John R. Silber was also under attack—from his own faculty. Silber had hotly pursued the Afghan training contract, but it soon became a contentious issue on campus. Ten senior faculty members vehemently objected to the training center being located in Pakistan and not in Boston, where it would be shielded from "the turmoil of a refugee center awash with secret agents, rival political factions, and intense emotions."[10] Setting up a training facility in Boston, almost 8,000 miles from Afghanistan, never made any sense to begin with. First, it was hugely expensive for Afghan journalism students to travel and live in the States. Second, the major Afghan resistance groups were headquartered in Peshawar, and their participation was vital to the success of the project. Peshawar was the ideal location. There were major highways between Peshawar and Afghanistan, so once journalists had finished their training and were ready to go report on the war, access to the Afghanistan border would be relatively easy. Finally, Peshawar was close to Pakistan's capital, Islamabad, providing vital access to that metropolitan center and its communications with the outside world. Bernard Redmont, dean of Boston University's College of Communications, was one of the ten professors who demanded that Afghan students come to Boston's Back Bay to be trained. The university promptly made him a "dean emeritus" and sent him packing to London, where he was to supervise an internship program.

Redmont was replaced by H. Joachim Maitre, a former East German MIG pilot who defected to the West in 1953. A hardline anti-Communist, he kept a sign above his desk that read, "Command Post—Cold War Sector." Reporting Maitre's appointment, an article in the *Wall Street Journal* suggested that because he had managed to escape from East Germany to the West, academic skirmishes should seem "like child's play."[11] Maitre selected three instructors to go to Peshawar to set up shop: project director Nick

Mills, associate professor of film John Kelly, and Seattle journalist Chullaine O'Reilly.

The city of Peshawar was like a throwback to the Wild West. Horse-drawn carts kicked up dust on unpaved streets. Pistol shots cracked at night like fireworks. Millions of refugees streamed across the border from Afghanistan, clogging Peshawar's streets and overwhelming utilities and services.

The Boston University program was to be located in a small, one-story house in suburban University Town. There would be rooms for instruction in video, and print and still photo journalism. The Boston University training team decided to appoint an Afghan with media experience to head the daily operation of the center and chose Haji Sayed Daud, a former producer at Kabul Television in Afghanistan. His appointment was cleared by the seven Afghan resistance parties, which meant that the low-key Daud was a compromise choice whose main job would be to keep the peace between the "independent" AMRC and militant Afghan fundamentalist resistance groups.[12] Soon after the Soviets invaded Afghanistan, Daud had organized an underground journalist's association to report what was happening inside the country. When he learned that the Soviet KGB secret police were about to pounce on him in 1985, he fled into neighboring Pakistan. Only a year later, he was chosen for the Boston University project.

When the center opened its doors in February 1987, more than 100 students flocked in. Amid the din of gunfire and exploding bombs—street warfare closed the school down for one week—classes began, in Farsi, with translation into English. After six weeks of training, students were given their diplomas and sent out to cover the war. A second wave of 100 students came in to be trained. During the first six months of its existence, the center received more than 600 training applications from throughout Pakistan. Said one of the Boston University instructors, "I think they're more motivated than our students."[13] The center was running out of space, so a second building next door was leased to handle overflow classes.

Soon, there were on average twelve media teams inside Afghanistan at any one moment. Each team consisted of a cameraman, a still photographer, and a print journalist. Each crew was assigned to a Mujahideen commander and equipped with walkie-talkies that covered some 150 miles. The best writers were kept back in Peshawar, where they took information from the field and turned it into professional scripts, though sometimes unedited video was sent directly from the battlefield to subscribing news agencies.[14] It was not uncommon for a news team to walk for two months with cameras, tripods, and supplies strapped to their backs, and when they got to their destination, they often stayed three months or more. Then they walked back with their film footage to Peshawar, from where it would be distributed.

The AMRC policy manual specified that every employee should be obedient to the Islamic faith and "must honestly and generously sacrifice for Holy Jihad and take an active share in Afghanistan's independence struggle." Salaries were determined by the candidate's achievement in class, and by the dangerousness of the area to which he would be sent. Haji Daud made a list of twenty-nine geographic locations in Afghanistan, and for each location he indicated the number of days required to complete the assignment was specified. An assignment to nearby Nengrahar would take only 10 to 25 days. An assignment to the more distant regions of Faryab or Jauzjan might require from 80 to 110 days. One photographer was in the field for over a year and came back with over 12 hours of videotape showing battle scenes. To be paid, a student had to return from Afghanistan with the goods. Paid rest days were given, and reporters and cameramen were entitled to 20 rest days after completion of a one-month assignment. After a two-month assignment, they got a month. Bonuses were given to those who returned with exceptional material.

Students were also responsible for bringing back their cameras. Excuses, such as the camera was broken, or it was stolen, were not acceptable. Everyone was under an obligation to be truthful, "knowing that Almighty God, Islam and their dear motherland is there always present and checking," according to their instruction manual. Only one camera was ever lost. It had dropped thousands of feet into a mountain valley. Its operator risked his life trying to retrieve it. One videographer returned to Pakistan through Iran, where his camera was confiscated, so he went out to a Peshawar bazaar and bought another.

What these courageous men brought back was gripping. There was footage showing a triumphant freedom fighter atop a Russian tank. The Afghan man waved his rifle overhead as an

AMRC cameraman videotaped the scene, when a rifle shot rang out and a bullet wiped away half of his face. Another sequence showed a nine-foot-long rocket being loaded onto a camel, whose knees buckled from the weight, crushing the animal beneath. Others showed Afghan children rolling empty Soviet land mine casings in the dirt, and a mother and her children who had been buried alive in their home following a Soviet bombardment.

Within a year, more than 500 hours of original videotape shot by AMRC camera crews inside Afghanistan had been annotated and referenced in the center's video archives, along with reports by foreign TV networks. The USIA's Near East director, Kent Obee, gleefully reported to Washington that during a two month period 450 press releases had been distributed in every major language, plus 33 video news reports, which concentrated on the heaviest areas of Soviet military activity. Several thousand still photographs were already on file. The Afghan Media Resource Center sent a printed sales brochure to news organizations throughout the world. The striking color brochure contained samples of the Center's work and informed the recipient that a videocassette would follow under separate cover.

Boston University, and Maitre in particular, continued to take heat from the academic community over the school's involvement in the Afghan training program. In interviews Maitre stressed that he had been asked by the American taxpayer, as represented by the U.S. Senate, to train people in the art and skill of journalism. "We are teaching our journalistic virtue of a free press to the Afghans," said Maitre, who also always stressed that he had been born in Germany after World War II and was trained in the American journalistic tradition, financed by the American taxpayers. He pointed out that Boston University had been running a program in South Africa to train black African students and had heard no protests over this.

There was no shortage of stories about Afghanistan crying out to be heard. The Soviet occupation had shattered the country's entire infrastructure. Schools and health care systems were shut down. Bridges, roads, and tens of thousands of homes had been destroyed. Thousands of Afghans had been maimed or killed by land mines. More than 80 percent of the country's forests had been cut down for fuel or destroyed by bombs. Soil had washed away, and farmland had become barren. Drug addiction was a growing problem. Poppy and narcotic-plant farming was a staple in Afghanistan, and during the war, with limited agricultural land and irrigation, it offered a fast source of cash. Drugs spread from the villages and cities in Afghanistan into lucrative world markets.

Chris Nation was a British photography instructor assigned to the AMRC under a grant from the Swedish Relief Committee. He encouraged photographers, when not shooting combat footage, to wander around the countryside and film how people were going about their lives during times of war. Nation found that mediocre combat photographers often made excellent feature documentarians. "Although combat pictures will always be needed as long as the conflict continues," he wrote, "I feel that a picture should be built up of what Afghanistan is like, as a place to which the refugees will return, as a place that those who have stayed have to deal with, of what has been destroyed, what has survived, what needs to be done." His students supplied superb material to the world media, he said, "as the military activities gave way to political and economic aspects of reconstruction."[15]

Boston University stayed with the AMRC during its formative period, after which the USIA did not renew its contract, because the Afghans had taken over the entire management of the center at the beginning of 1988.[16] Haji Daud remained on board with a new set of instructors under the general supervision of the USIA. Soon, AMRC's camera crews were operating in twenty-five of Afghanistan's twenty-nine provinces, and more than eighty news teams were on assignment inside Afghanistan providing news footage to American and foreign journalists.[17]

Among the regular clients were the worldwide syndicator Visnews, the BBC and Independent Television in England, the Associated Press, Agence France Presse, and the Sygma photo agency in Paris.[18] Footage supplied to Visnews alone reached hundreds of its client stations worldwide. Stories by AMRC print journalists regularly got picked up by the major syndication services, such as the worldwide Reuter news agency of London. One major story the AMRC broke (picked up by Reuter) was that the Afghan government had used Soviet SCUD missiles against the freedom fighters when the rebels were closing in on the government cities of Kabul and Jalalabad.[19] Because the AMRC had direct access to Afghan political and military leaders, it regularly put visiting journalists in touch with valuable news sources. "The work of the AMRC is marked by professionalism that meets Western standards," said Kurt Kistner, military editor of Munich's *Sueddeutsche Zeitung.*

Field journalists were always at risk. One AMRC newsman was killed in action, another died of heat prostration, and several more were seriously injured during aerial bombardments and by ground fire and land mines, which were capable of being spread by new long-range rockets launched from Soviet bases some 50 miles away.[20] The Soviets were also starting to make nocturnal raids using new night-vision devices, which Mujahideen forces did not have in their arsenal. Moreover, camera crews and journalists from the AMRC now had become high profile, and were at greater security risk from anti-U.S. factions. It was important for cameramen to get their equipment to their next assignment as quickly, efficiently—and safely—as possible. They were still getting around Peshawar in rickshaws and tongas, horse-drawn carts. The center's staff had hoped for permission to obtain approval for two Toyota vans. They settled for two Suzukis, and were happy to get those.[21]

We at the USIA did not in any way manipulate the news that came out of the AMRC, though I must say our editors had to sharpen their pencils when Mujahideen scripts were submitted. Militant Afghan resistance groups thought nothing of killing individuals they perceived as too soft on the Soviets, and student writers and editors were mindful of this. Journalist Frank Jossi, an instructor at the AMRC, wondered about the objectivity of several student reporters who had been given special allegiances to one of the seven mujahideen refugee parties. One senior reporter kissed the ring of a mujahideen leader before doing an interview with him.[22] Despite this, Haji Sayed Daud managed to preserve the journalistic integrity of the organization. Mujahideen battlefield commanders would visit the AMRC from time to time to look in on things.

As word of the AMRC spread, some of the more vocal female immigrants from Afghanistan, where women were somewhat more emancipated than their counterparts in Pakistan, said, "Well, we want to become photographers, too." In Afghanistan, these women had worked alongside men in offices, but in Pakistan they had become live-in housekeepers. Some wondered why there were no women trainees in the AMRC. Haji Sayed Daud was soon being pressured by a newly formed group, the Afghan Women's Media

Project. Daud stated his support for the education and employment of Afghan women, although privately he considered the group a "millstone around his neck," because he had to send some of his best employees to Islamabad to meet with the group, and this was taking a lot of time.[23] The truth was that Daud would not dare hire women at the AMRC because Arab fundamentalists objected to the idea.

U.S. Embassy personnel agreed with Daud that Afghan women should be barred from the AMRC. "In a normal Western setting," said USIA official John Dixon, "there would be no reason to make these programs or our objectives gender specific. This, unfortunately, is not the case in Peshawar. The sexes are strictly separated in all sections of life and women rarely leave the family compound unless they can do so in separated, unobserved conditions."[24] Dixon said that since women were "so far out of public life in Peshawar," the United States should fund a separate training facility for them, as this would further the continuation of women's education and would be very important someday.[25] Daud hit upon a solution. There were hundreds of thousands of land mines in Afghanistan, and the United Nations was trying to locate and defuse as many as possible. Daud told a UN representative that these ambitious women could be trained to do it, adding that they could make and distribute posters and pamphlets as well as explain how the mines work, so fewer people will be hurt. "When they finish," said Daud, "maybe these women can work with radio, television, and newspapers." He informed the women's group director that the wife of the Canadian ambassador in Peshawar was involved in a mine safety project. USIA's public affairs officer in Peshawar agreed.

Public affairs officer Richard Hoagland thought it was perhaps the best solution to solving the "problem of doing something for the Afghan women while at the same time absolving the Afghan Media Resource Center of the political problems that the [women's] project has engendered."[26] The deflection worked. The AMRC remained all male, and nearly a hundred women were trained to deal with mine safety.

In January 1988, the Soviets sent more than 12,000 troops to the southern part of the country. The Afghans sent some 10,000. Haji Daud dispatched eighteen camera crews to cover the massing of troops, and a videotape was sent back to London where Visnews distributed the material to its television clients worldwide.

Because the AMRC was now covering the war, Soviet camera crews were sent to document the fighting in each of Afghanistan's twenty-nine provinces. This was the first time Russian television had showed Afghans fighting Soviet troops. Prior to this, Soviet propagandists insisted that American troops and those from other countries were fighting in Afghanistan. Now Czechoslovakia, Poland, Hungary, and other countries could see that Soviet troops were involved.

By 1989 the AMRC was grossing about $18,000 a month in income from its best video customers. One of the biggest users, Visnews, had been bought by NBC News, which was now regularly using the Afghan Center's footage on network news broadcasts. Ironically, the new president of NBC News was Michael Gartner, the newspaper editor who complained that King Features was "getting into bed" with the government by handling distribution of AMRC news material. Gartner became strangely silent about the Afghan project after joining NBC. By March 1989, non-USIA monetary support of the center had risen from about 5 percent of its annual budget to nearly 40 percent.[27] And because the center was becoming more financially independent, government attorneys determined that the domestic ban imposed by the Smith-Mundt Act should not apply to AMRC videos and publications, which could therefore be freely distributed in the United States.[28]

Meanwhile, CBS News, which had a policy against using AMRC videos, used several on Dan Rather's evening news broadcasts without realizing it. One showed a Soviet convoy being blown up by the Mujahideen. It was billed on the air as CBS News footage, but it was the work of AMRC student Mohammed Salaam, who had given the tape to a Mujahideen commander, who in turn sold it to a CBS News representative in Afghanistan, who passed it on to New York falsely as his own. One CBS News contract producer in Peshawar was also on our USIA payroll, and he provided glowing accounts of the Mujahideen's exploits on the CBS "Evening News with Dan Rather." Video cameras were routinely provided by the AMRC to Mujahideen commanders, who shot tape of battles and sold it to news representatives back in safe Pakistan.

The idea of using video shot by the USIA may have bothered CBS News, whose news audience was on the decline, but it didn't bother Ted Turner's Cable News Network, which was rapidly building viewership and prestige. Our Afghan Media Resource Center signed a contract with CNN, whose news management had called one of the AMRC videos as its best international tape of the day. CNN regularly used AMRC tapes and invited its public relations director to Atlanta to attend CNN's annual meeting of foreign TV journalists who contributed to the cable network's "International Hour."

One of the AMRC stories CNN carried showed a young Afghan boy whose legs had been shattered from the knees down by a Soviet land mine. On tape, the boy said he didn't want to live without his legs and asked the doctor to give him some medicine to help him sleep. A wealthy American viewer in Tennessee wanted to help. AMRC officials scurried about trying to locate the lad, and a general announcement went out throughout Peshawar. A boy named Allahuddin came forward to claim he was the one in the videotape, but because the boy's face had been obscured on the videotape it was difficult to tell for sure. It didn't really matter. There were so many young people from Afghanistan whose legs had been blown away that the boy in the news tape represented them all. Whether he was, in fact, the boy on the tape or not, the USIA officers in Peshawar decided to make a positive identification. They had found Allahuddin. Washington instructed the U.S. Embassy in Peshawar to have a doctor look at the boy to determine whether he could be properly treated in Pakistan or flown to the United States. The diagnosis: the boy should come to America to be fitted with a prosthetic device. Allahuddin traveled there on an American military flight at no cost to his family. The American benefactor pledged $4,000 to help pay for Allahuddin's medical expenses, but by this time there were several other government agencies besides the USIA in the act, including the Office of Humanitarian Assistance at the Department of Defense. The story of Allahuddin's rehabilitation reverberated around the world.

Kent Obee reported that the level of the Afghan center's income was climbing steadily and the facility was almost in the black. Saudi Arabia kicked in a one-time $500,000 grant. The United Nations funded five documentaries about Soviet land mines, which continued to maim innocent Afghan women and children. The films were part of "mine-awareness" efforts and targeted for women and children, who made up most of the population of the refugee facilities.

Haji Sayed Daud turned out to be anything but a low-key compromise selection as AMRC director. AMRC journalists were supposed to be "independent," but not so independent as to offend the radical Afghan fundamentalist parties by making them feel that reports were too soft on the Soviets. Daud turned out to be a tough, objective news director and was highly popular with his journalistic associates. He was also getting squeezed by both sides. When AMRC stories began to appear on television and radio, Daud got threats from the Soviet KGB and Afghan security people in Kabul. He was being tailed wherever he went. At the same time, despite his efforts, Arab fundamentalists believed many of Daud's reports were too soft on the Soviets. They also did not like the idea that America was supporting the AMRC with money and equipment. As a result, Daud constantly received death threats from several quarters. Bodyguards were assigned to protect him. Daud realized he could be killed at any time. He expressed his fear frequently to associates, whom he was also training to take his place should the need arise.[29] Kent Obee observed that Daud had made sure the program would continue if something happened to him. "As we all know," said Obee, "Daud has hand-groomed [some associates] for nearly two-and-a-half years in the tenets of objective, nonpartisan journalism and in the tricks of tap dancing through political mine fields."[30]

One evening, the center received a telephone message from an anonymous caller who said Afghan institutions associated with the United States had no business remaining open in Peshawar. The caller said if the AMRC did not close, "those who believe that America and its lackeys have no place in the Afghan community would have to take appropriate action." The AMRC was given three days to close. Haji Daud informed the police of the threat but did not tell his staff. It was part of an increasing tempo of threats circulating in Peshawar from Afghan radical fundamentalists as well as foreigners, and although the warnings were taken seriously, thankfully nothing had ever materialized at the AMRC.[31] Richard Hoagland told me that Arab fundamentalists felt Daud "wasn't preaching the resistance party line that was backed by Pakistan's intelligence operation, which was allied with the CIA. We had a real problem during the Afghan war by getting so close to Pakistan's intelligence that it was hard to tell the two apart." Inadvertently, admitted Hoagland, the United States might have ended up supporting the very worst factions in the resistance.[32] A comment made by Prince Sadruddin Aga Khan when he visited the AMRC one day made officials there shudder. The prince, then United Nations Special Coordinator for Afghan Repatriation and Reconstruction, said he had seen the center's tapes and press reports at his base in Geneva and they were keeping him informed about the Afghan war. But, he added, he felt that one report was "harmful to innocent Afghans." The prince didn't elaborate. Nervous AMRC officials huddled and decided he had to have been referring to one of their stories about a resistance group stopping a UN convoy on a road outside Kabul. Could AMRC students remain objective and stay alive? the prince was asked. Yes. The prince was all praise, but he had gotten his point across. The slightly jittery AMRC staff vowed to remain independent. But it was clear that their work was being scrutinized very carefully.[33]

AMRC's archives continued to grow and soon boasted 130,000 still photos and some 300,000 hours of videotape. The photos were exhibited at the prestigious gallery of the Association of Fashion, Advertising and Editorial Photographers in London and elsewhere in Europe. Haji Sayed Daud had run the media training center with loving care. His meticulousness meant that the center's priceless products could be preserved for generations. Catalogues of the tapes and stills contain complete details, down to a frame-by-frame description and an assessment of the story's quality. Clandestine AMRC camera crews found their way into Kabul and videotaped for posterity the final withdrawal of Soviet troops.

The AMRC presented images of the Afghan war to the world's media, and heightened everyone's awareness of the war. U.S. authorities felt that the center contributed to the "monumental achievement of reversing the Soviet occupation of Afghanistan."[34] It marked the introduction of photography into a society in which a documentary tradition had not existed before, and showed the Afghan people how they could document themselves and create a remarkable national archive of injustice and human suffering.

When it was all over, student freedom fighter Masood Farivar decided he wanted to continue his education in America. Western journalists and AMRC officials in Peshawar, impressed with the bright and engaging young man, gave him encouragement. He entered Harvard on a full scholarship, and later became a journalist. In 1992, after the Kabul government fell, Haji Daud, ever the media warrior, began producing TV documentaries about the reconstruction of his homeland.

↔ **13** ↔

The Caudillo of Miami

AT 1:00 P.M. SUNDAY AFTERNOON, AUGUST 6, 1989, A U.S. RECON-naissance aircraft on a secret mission took off from Homestead Air Force Base in southern Florida in the direction of Cuba. It flew along the 23 degree 30 north latitude line, about 25 statute miles north of Havana. The plane's crew aimed their sensitive electronic devices at the Cuban capital, then swung them over to the east toward Matanzas and Santa Clara provinces, and finally around to the west and Pinar del Rio.[1] After dark, Coast Guard cutters from the Florida Keys cruised so close to Cuba's shore that the crew could see streetlights along Havana's boulevards. The cutters circled the entire island of Cuba, homing in on their targets. From Powder Springs, Georgia, and from Alligator Alley, Marathon, Turtle Key, and Key West in Florida, high-powered electronic eavesdropping devices drew beads on various sites inside Cuba. Not since the Cuban missile crisis and the Bay of Pigs invasion of the early 1960s had so intensive an American reconnaissance effort been aimed at the Communist nation.

An invasion was only months away. But this time, troops would not land at the Bay of Pigs or anywhere else on the island. No blood would be shed. The invaders would be American television programs. The ships and planes and spy stations were monitoring Cuban television and measuring its capacity with field-strength meters, spectrum analyzers, and waveform monitors to determine how a TV signal beamed from Washington could best penetrate homes in Havana. In essence, we were preparing an electronic Bay of Pigs, an invasion of music videos, "Lifestyles of the Rich and Famous," and "Alf," all of which would enlighten the masses in Cuba about the virtues of democracy and motivate them to kick out Castro. The figure behind all this effort, Jorge Mas Canosa, a resident of Miami, was planning to become the next president of Cuba, with the help of the American taxpayer.

Several months later, initial testing now completed, "Fat Albert," as it was affectionately called, fluttered high over the Florida Keys, brushing lazily against wispy clouds. The giant helium inflated airship, looking like a Macy's Thanksgiving Day float dangling at the end of its 10,000-foot tether, was pointed in the direction of Havana, about 140 miles away. Fat Albert was on a mission to sap the Communist spirit by slowly zeroing in on the Cuban capital, then beaming down television programs from a transmitter in its nose. These programs would show America at its very finest: a lineup of soap operas, game shows, cartoon programs about bright green frogs, episodes of "Cheers," and a Spanish-language version of "The Gong Show," all paid for by some 20 million American tax dollars a year. There was just this one thing: no one in Cuba would watch what Fat Albert was selling.

Fat Albert began transmitting to Cuba at 1:30 A.M. on March 27, 1990. While most of Havana snoozed, the blue logo of the U.S. government's new program service, TV Marti—named for Cuba's independence hero José Martí—appeared on Havana's Channel 13, announcing that a new program service would be broadcast every night from 3:30 A.M. to 6:00 A.M., not exactly prime time. The handful of Cubans watching the TV broadcast saw it fizzle and disintegrate into snow. The TV announcer's narration also cut out. A rainbow-colored test pattern appeared. Castro had knocked TV Marti off the air even before it began. The Cuban dictator was jubilant, boasting that "the main technological power on the planet" couldn't prevent Cuba from successfully jamming Marti's picture. Havana's insomniacs missed out on some old music videos, a

Spanish-language version of the sitcom "Kate and Allie," a travelogue about New Mexico, and highlights of the 1971 World Series.

The following night Castro's jammers again zapped TV Marti's signal before viewers could watch the Fine Young Cannibals perform "I'm Not Satisfied." Before it was snipped, a promotional announcement said the evening's fare would include "Fama y Fortuna," a Spanish-language version of "Lifestyles of the Rich and Famous," and "Wrestlemania," among other favorites. Alas, nothing would elude Castro's jammers, who aimed video and audio static at Fat Albert's television signal from helicopters and airplanes, and from microwave dishes in backyards and on telephone poles. Squiggly lines overwhelmed the picture, and a nerve-grinding buzz saw noise overrode the sound. By broadcasting old sitcoms for heavy insomniacs in Cuba, the "Peter Sellers–inspired plan to overthrow Castro," as it was called by critics, would soon become an international joke.

The driving force behind TV Marti (and, a few years earlier, Radio Marti) was Jorge Mas Canosa, the caudillo (dictator) of Miami. A multimillionaire Cuban expatriate, he makes things happen. Concerned that Castro might send a hit squad after him, Jorge Mas packs a .357 Magnum and drives around Miami's Little Havana in a bulletproof Mercedes-Benz.[2] He is undeniably the most influential anti-Castro expatriate in the United States. Born on September 21, 1939, near the Sierra Maestra on the eastern coast of Cuba—the mountains from where Fidel Castro would wage his battle against dictator President Fulgencia Batista—the son of an army veterinarian, Jorge Mas Canosa fled Cuba twice because of his political activism, once when he criticized Batista in a radio interview and later as a law student, when he confronted Fidel Castro during a university visit over holding the free elections he had promised.[3]

Jorge Mas arrived in Miami as a destitute refugee in 1960, and worked as a shoe salesman, dishwasher, milkman, and longshoreman to help support his brothers and sisters. Although he took part in the Bay of Pigs invasion, he never set foot on shore. From the deck, his boat captain had seen the plight of those who landed there earlier and beat a hasty retreat.[4] Focusing his energies on entrepreneurism, Jorge Mas took out a bank loan in 1971 and bought a small, faltering Miami construction firm called Iglesias y Torres. Changing its name to the English equivalent, Church and

Tower, within a year he won a million-dollar contract with Southern Bell to install telephone lines. Church and Tower grew to become Southern Bell's prime contractor in Miami's Dade County, employing more than 600 people. By 1990, it was one of the country's largest Hispanic-owned companies. In a two-year period, Jorge Mas did $80 million worth of business with metropolitan Dade County through some 35,000 public construction projects, which consisted mostly of paving roads and filling potholes. It became a *Fortune* 500 company, and Mas's personal fortune in 1995 exceeded $100 million.

Jorge Mas is a fierce competitor. He once challenged a Miami city commissioner to a duel in a dispute over a downtown construction project. The commissioner defused the situation by whipping out a water pistol.[5] At one point he accused his younger brother, Ricardo, of attempting to steal a quarter million dollars from Church and Tower. Ricardo retaliated by charging that his older brother had tried to bribe Southern Bell's officials with cash and cases of whiskey. Their sister tried to reconcile them, but at a meeting to get them together Jorge and his son allegedly beat up Ricardo, threw him against a pane of glass, and stole his Oldsmobile 98.[6] Ricardo set up his own company and competed against Church and Tower for Southern Bell's business. Jorge Mas wrote two letters to Southern Bell, in which he claimed his younger brother was guilty of fraud and extortion. A Miami jury found Jorge Mas guilty of slander and awarded Ricardo $1.2 million in compensation and punitive damages.[7]

Jorge Mas's entry into big-time politics was aided by Frank Calzon, when he was still a young anti-Castro firebrand political science major at Georgetown. Calzon envisioned what ultimately was to become Jorge Mas's influential lobby group dedicated to the overthrow of the Cuban dictator. A political agitator with a flair for public relations, Calzon attended Jimmy Carter's presidential inauguration ball, where he distributed leaflets that looked like authentic government documents, describing human rights violations in Cuba. Later he proposed a Cuban-American Foundation whose mission was "to destroy Castro's first line of defense: the image he has nurtured throughout the years." He sold the idea to Jorge Mas and two other wealthy Cuban-Americans in Miami, developer Carlos Salman and banker Raul Masvidal, who became the first directors of the foundation. Jorge Mas was the enforcer. "He got the thing going by telling people to put up or shut up," said former aide David Rivera. "He told them if they wanted in, it would cost at least $10,000 each."[8]

Jorge Mas saw a potential ally in the newly elected Ronald Reagan. "Jorge Mas felt Reagan's hawkishness on Communists was made to order," said Rivera. "And he knew the conservatives around Reagan would love to have their very own point man to get Castro."[9] Top Reagan aides in the new administration saw the value of having a political power base in the influential, moneyed Cuban exile community in Miami. Richard V. Allen, Reagan's first National Security Council adviser, suggested to Jorge Mas that the administration would actively support such a Cuban-American group, which was formally established in 1981.[10] "Just like President Kennedy said that we're going to the Moon, we're going to Washington," proclaimed Jorge Mas.[11] Mas's "godfather" in the U.S. Congress was Senator Ernest F. Hollings (D-SC). Masvidal, a Democrat, would later bolt the organization because of a dispute with Jorge Mas over political contributions to Republican candidates. Salman, a Republican, became angry about the foundation's donations to Democrats, and would also bow out. Jorge Mas liked to play both sides of the political spectrum.

The Cuban-American National Foundation sought advice about how to structure itself from one of the most powerful lobby groups in Washington, the American Israel Public Affairs Council (AIPAC), after which it was modeled. Thomas Dine, the head of AIPAC, met the group at a meeting held at the Breakers Hotel in Palm Beach, Florida. Dine was immediately impressed with "the handsome group of Cuban leaders." They were young, successful looking, and asked good questions. Dine lectured the group on the fundamentals of lobbying and gave them advice about how to make an impact on the American political system. "AIPAC is successful because we run a textbook operation; just basic fundamentals and nothing fancy," Dine said. "You cannot be successful if you look for personal aggrandizement. You must have a clear cause which reinforces American democracy and values here and abroad." Dine had an opportunity to talk with Jorge Mas and to size him up: "He for sure was the leader," Dine concluded.[12] The foundation's Washington lawyer, Barney Barnett, who was active in pro-Israeli organizations, helped the Cubans set up a tax-exempt organization with political action and lobbying branches. To help it get started, Jewish leaders also provided the foundation with inexpensive office space in a downtown Washington office building.

The sole objective of the Cuban-American National Foundation was to overthrow Castro, but it soon became a quasi-political party. It even drafted a proposed constitution for Cuba after Castro, designating Jorge Mas as a potential candidate for transitional president. An economic growth plan for post-Castro Cuba was also undertaken. Jorge Mas asked a Wall Street firm to underwrite a $500 million bond issue for the island nation, where he predicted the "next California Gold Rush" would take place. He claimed to have met with the "inner circle" of Cuban government officials and discussed future directions for the country.

By 1981, the foundation had lined up more than a hundred "directors," each pledging to donate at least $10,000 per year, and another hundred "trustees," who anted up at least $5,000 annually. They were joined by more than a dozen corporate sponsors, several of which began developing plans to jump-start the post-Communist tourist industry in Cuba, such as Hyatt Hotels, Bell South, and Royal Caribbean Cruise Lines. Each donated $25,000 or more.[13] Within a few years, the foundation had helped bring in almost 10,000 Cuban immigrants to the United States. A program to sponsor Haitian immigration was begun. Donors thought Jorge Mas might some day be president of Cuba, and they wanted a piece of the action. During the 1980s more than $2 million was doled out by the foundation's political action committee, Free Cuba, Inc., to the campaigns of friendly politicians of both parties, and to the opponents of those who were not friendly, also without regard to party affiliation. Jorge Mas played hard ball, and politicians were well advised to stay on his good side.

During the 1984 congressional elections, Jorge Mas contributed more than $200,000 to candidates, liberal and conservative, who supported setting up a proposed facility for broadcasting into Cuba. The idea behind Radio Marti, the concept of which was stoutly supported by Reagan and Wick, was to report the news that Castro suppressed from government-operated media. Wick headed an interagency group to bring Radio Marti to fruition, and in December 1981 Wick telephoned Kenneth Giddens, the former director of the VOA under the Nixon Administration, who agreed to come to

Washington to run the "Radio Broadcasting to Cuba" project, to guide it through its initial stages and get the station ready to go on the air. As a formality to get congressional legislation passed, on May 30, 1984, Reagan appointed Jorge Mas to be chairman of a nine-member bipartisan commission looking into the establishment of Radio Marti, which went on the air thirteen months later. This gave Jorge Mas even greater access to those shaping America's foreign policy toward Castro.

"*Buenos dias, Cuba,*" began the breezy announcer at 5:30 A.M. on May 20, 1985. Radio Marti was on the air. It kicked things off with a news report about Castro's reprisals against the station, which included travel sanctions against the United States and suspension of the 1984 immigration treaty, which would have freed some 3,000 political prisoners from Cuban jails and allowed them to go to the States. It would have also required Cuba to take back almost 2,800 "boat people," including mental patients and criminals, who had made their way to the United States.[14] In addition, Castro threatened to jam American radio stations and demanded that Radio Marti cease operations.

Radio Marti was designed to supplant the government-controlled Cuban media with information and cultural programming from American hard-liners in the Reagan Administration. The latter wanted Radio Marti to be patterned after the so-called surrogate stations, Radio Free Europe and Radio Liberty. Indeed, the Reagan administration wanted Radio Marti to tell Cubans "about their government's domestic mismanagement and its promotion of subversion and international terrorism." Liberals in Congress were concerned that fanatical Cuban exiles would seize control of Radio Marti and insisted that the facility be placed under the supervision of the Voice of America, in turn supervised by Wick's USIA to keep it on track. The Reagan White House agreed to this in order to obtain an initial $10 million annual budget from Congress.

At first, many listeners inside Cuba criticized Radio Marti's non-news programs for being out of step with the times, even those on the lackluster Communist island. One prime-time program featured a comedian who had been dead for several years. A ten-year-old soap opera produced in Miami featured a heroine named Esmeralda. "It sounds as if the programs were taped twenty-five years ago," complained one listener.[15] Said the *New York Times:* "Radio

Marti's 50s sound has Cubans tuning out. . . . [It is] old-fashioned and out of step with modern Cuban society."[16] Even musty old Radio Moscow suggested that Radio Marti make an attempt to "modernize" its foreign political broadcasts. And Castro himself, after his initial bluster, did not bother to jam Radio Marti's signals, suggesting that the program might even stimulate healthy competition. "No enemy is going to criticize us better than we criticize ourselves," he said defiantly. "We know better than our enemies what our problems are."

After Radio Marti's shaky start, it began to pressure the Castro government into being more open and aggressive in reporting problems inside Cuba. One broadcast suggested that Cuban soldiers involved in Angola's civil war were returning home infected by the AIDS virus. It featured interviews with exiled Cuban doctors and others who pointed out that over the previous ten years more than 400,000 Cuban troops had been stationed in Africa, "where AIDS has reached almost epidemic proportions." Later, Radio Marti obtained a secret tape of a meeting held in the Havana home of Ricardo Bofill, head of Cuba's human rights department, during which human rights violations were raised and denounced. It was aired on a 90-minute special, "Cuba without Censorship." Programs such as this would help Radio Marti's audience grow.[17] And as Radio Marti improved, it was perceived as providing an alternative source of information to the Cuban government line. It developed a list of important journalists and other opinion leaders around the world, to whom it mailed a quarterly update report of political information on Cuba and its problems. The Cuban media was conspicuously silent about the Chernobyl nuclear disaster in the Soviet Union. Radio Marti carried the news, and in addition reported construction by the Soviets of a nuclear power plant in Cuba. Marti also reported on the failing Cuban sugar production and the killing of more than a dozen young people whose pleasure boat was sunk by Cuban military planes as it sailed toward Florida. Radio Marti provided tide and weather reports for the 90-mile area between the Communist island and the American mainland, and reported successful crossings, including those undertaken with inner tubes. "Marti encouraged us to try," said one of four men rescued by a fishing boat near the U.S. shore after five days at sea.[18]

As a result, the Cuban government's bureaucracy sought

to revitalize its own media. Cuba's Radio Rebelde expanded to a 24-hour format, increasing the number of news reports and adding sixteen new programs, several of which were designed to appeal to young people. A new school of journalism was opened at the University of Havana with a mission to improve the quality of the state-run press, which was being encouraged to become more critical and investigative. A Cuban Politburo directive noted that "the failure of the press to expose the shortcomings in the [Cuban] system allows the U.S.-based Radio Marti and the Voice of America to introduce their poisonous propaganda."[19] For the first time since Castro came to power in 1959, Cuban radio stations were permitted to play Frank Sinatra records. Cuban television also went to full-color transmissions, imported more soap operas from abroad, and premiered sixty movies. During the next five years, announced the government, it planned to invest twice as much money in its media as had been spent on it since the beginning of the revolution.[20] The government radio had a sympathetic listenership. While the concept of Radio Marti was to be a "local" service for Cuba, it was still being run by defectors living the good life in Miami. The nearly 11 million Cubans who remained on the squalid island resented being reminded of how miserable they were by Cubans who had left them behind to suffer.

Meantime, as the titular leader of 700,000 Cuban exiles in Florida, Jorge Mas continued to strengthen his political clout in Washington. He was appointed by Ronald Reagan to the congressional delegation observing El Salvador's presidential elections. He played a key role in lining up Democratic support on Capitol Hill for the Reagan Administration's military aid program for anti-government contra rebels in Nicaragua. The Cuban-American Foundation helped persuade Congress to repeal its ban on aid to anti-Communist Angolan rebels, who then had received $30 million in U.S. aid to fight Cuban troops in the African nation. Jorge Mas believed Castro would be weakened by a defeat of the Cuban-supported government in Angola. He received a hero's welcome from rebel leaders and thousands of their followers, all jammed into a soccer stadium in the West African nation and chanting, "Chairman Mas, Chairman Mas, President Mas, President Mas."

He would lash out at anyone who appeared soft on Castro. The Cuban Museum of Arts and Culture in Miami held an auction that included some works by Cuban artists who had not, in

Jorge Mas's view, been denounced by Castro with enough gusto. The director of the museum, Ramon Cernuda, countered that artists were selected by virtue of their talent and not their political views. Jorge Mas saw this as subversive behavior and publicly threatened to use his Washington connections to have Cernuda "investigated." Customs officials raided Cernuda's home and office and seized some two hundred paintings whose importation they claimed had violated the trade embargo against Cuba. A U.S. district judge ruled that the government had violated Cernuda's First Amendment rights of free speech, and ordered the paintings returned. The museum still lost $150,000 in state financing in addition to being picketed and bombed.[21]

Jorge Mas was not the only Cuban-American gaining influence within the Reagan Administration. There were more than twenty in key positions, a record number for any White House. Otto Juan Reich, one of the most visible, had arrived on a ferryboat from Havana with only $5 in his pocket.[22] Twenty-one years later he was an influential State Department official and a shaper of America's Central American policy. José Sorzano had worked in a Washington fast-food restaurant when he arrived from Cuba; two decades later, he was deputy U.S. ambassador to the United Nations. Another immigrant, José Manuel Casanova, was executive director of the Inter-American Development Bank and an adviser to the White House on Cuban exile problems. Such powerful Reagan appointees shared a fierce determination to rid Cuba of Fidel Castro.[23] One way to speed this process, so went the thinking, was by unleashing the awesome power of television. This was Jorge Mas's next project.

In 1986, James McKinney was chief of the Mass Media Bureau of the Federal Communications Commission, the division handling radio, television, satellite, and all forms of mass communications for the powerful regulatory agency. FCC chairman Mark Fowler telephoned McKinney to discuss the possibility of broadcasting television shows into Cuba. Fowler had earlier been asked about the idea by none other than Charles Z. Wick, who had also recommended Fowler for the FCC job, a plum appointment. Fowler and McKinney came to the conclusion that there would be serious problems getting a TV signal into Cuba. "A low-level television signal coming in from more than a hundred miles away would be weak and easy to jam," McKinney told Fowler. "In the cities especially, where most of the viewers are, you can put a little transmitter on a telephone pole at a main intersection downtown and wipe out a signal for six or eight blocks of apartment buildings. You can wipe out Havana that way from ever seeing the television programs."24 The CIA agreed with McKinney that TV Marti would be a complete waste of money.

Unlike AM radio signals, which bend with the curvature of the earth, TV signals travel in straight lines. Because Havana is 140 miles from the U.S. mainland, and below the horizon from even the southernmost tip, a TV signal from a standard-height TV transmitter aimed in the direction of Cuba could not reach it. The signal would need to be beamed from a sufficient height for a direct "line of sight" to gaze over the earth's curvature down into Havana. Moreover, a channel on which to telecast that would not interfere with existing Cuban TV stations had to be located so as not to violate international treaties to which the United States was a signatory. There was also the specter of retaliation by Castro, who could interfere with American radio stations by transmitting disruptive signals northward from Cuba. But Jorge Mas wanted it, and the Reagan White House wanted to keep him happy. The White House felt that a $20 million annual price tag for TV Marti would be a drop in the bucket.

Radio Marti and several Miami Spanish-language stations boomed signals into Cuba, and other radio stations from the southern United States and the Caribbean were easily picked up in Havana and elsewhere on the island. Cuba wasn't exactly in isolation. Its tourist industry was growing, and thousands of students were being exchanged each year between Cuba and non-Communist countries. Gary Gonzalez, vice president of the Cuban Institute of Radio and Television, noted that 42 percent of the movies being shown on Cuban TV were from America, and that Cuban TV also ran American situation comedies and miniseries. "Viewers already see the nice homes and cars in the United States," said Gonzalez. "What are you going to tell us? That we don't have enough food? We know that. That we don't have enough shoes? We know that."25 In fact, Cuban television was pirating commercial American programs from satellites. Officials said they would be only too happy to receive CNN, ABC, CBS, or NBC, or all of them in fact. What they did not want was an openly hostile U.S. government program service invading their airspace uninvited.

Wick asked me to meet with McKinney and look closer at the feasibility of a TV Marti service. Although McKinney and I were mindful that Jorge Mas had strong allies in the White House and on the Hill, we felt that TV Marti was a dumb idea and a waste of a lot of money. We also knew that if the Cuban lobby wanted it badly enough there wasn't much we could do to stop it. Nonetheless, we arranged a meeting between Wick and Fowler at which we would voice our reservations. My assistant, William Bell, attended the meeting with me so that he could do a standard memo of conversation, which meant that follow-up actions could be tracked and implemented. Bell took out his note pad. "Don't take any notes," Wick warned him. The entire question of TV Marti was politically charged, and Wick wanted an unvarnished exchange of views. He also didn't want a paper trail.

McKinney began by saying that Marti would have to use a VHF or "very high-frequency" spectrum (which included channels 2 through 13 on standard TV sets utilized in Cuba), but that because the signal would be coming in from a distance of 140 miles, his view was that the signal would be weak and easy to jam. He added that jamming would be quite inexpensive to do. Little transmitters, which cost about $30 and broadcast video and audio noise on the same channel as TV Marti, would wipe it out. "We know that Castro has huge big-power transmitters capable of causing widespread interference to the AM band throughout the United States," McKinney added. "Working with the CIA and other agencies, we have taken measurements and know precisely what kind of transmitter power Castro has, and how much power he has had since 1960 in all of his transmitters. They are in the hundreds of thousands of watts, which is a lot of power for the AM band." McKinney made it clear that if TV Marti ever went on the air, Castro could retaliate by aiming his transmitters at U.S. radio stations and knock them off the air.

If TV Marti was a fait accompli, McKinney and I made an alternative suggestion: that the TV signal be beamed in from space by satellite. It would provide a perfect picture, we said, and it would be almost impossible to jam. The CIA could drop satellite receivers and distribute them to our friends in Cuba to spread around. Fowler carried the idea a step further. "Why don't we send commandos into Cuba and put in satellite stations?" He then proposed how to deal with Castro if he retaliated by jamming U.S. radio stations: "We could do pinpoint bombing of Castro's transmitters." McKinney suggested to me later that Fowler had "probably been watching too many spy movies."[26]

There was indeed no stopping the politically charged project. The question was not whether television programs would be beamed into Cuba, but how quickly. One of TV Marti's chief sponsors in the Senate, Lawton Chiles of Florida, got the ball rolling. He attached an obscure rider to a larger authorization bill that earmarked $100,000 for TV Marti engineering studies. The Senate gave TV Marti its start without most of its members knowing it. I was appointed to a USIA task force that would review studies from engineering consulting firms, studies that confirmed that few Cubans would ever actually see TV Marti. Regular Cuban television signals could blot out TV Marti's picture and sound.[27]

One engineering firm suggested that transmitting from a fleet of airplanes flying in figure-eight formation could provide saturation coverage. Because the planes would be turning in circles for hours on end, however, the transmitter would have to be on a "gyro-stabilized platform . . . while the aircraft maneuvered and changed its positions," so that the antenna would always be pointing toward Havana.[28] Another engineering study suggested using "a propeller-type older plane that flies slowly, such as an old Lockheed Constellation, commonly called P-2." The idea was that the P-2 could fly over international waters as close to the Cuban shore as possible. The cost for such a plane and its electronics? $30 million. The report said a backup plane would be required as well for "equipment failures, repair and maintenance." Another $30 million.[29]

Then there was the consultant who outlined the construction of a 2,000-foot antenna (as tall as a 200-story building) to get a line-of-sight signal to Havana. The problem was that it would require a foundation so massive and heavy that a suitable location on the narrow Florida Keys peninsula would be hard to find; the whole rig would likely sink into the Florida marshland. Such a structure might take up one square mile of real estate. We were also told that a 2,000-foot tower wasn't tall enough, since the TV signal would shoot over the horizon and weaken before reaching Havana. Still another option was to place a transmitter in a balloon tethered to a "pirate" ship, again in international waters, some 25 miles from the Cuban shore. "Transmission of broadcast signals from . . . pirate ships operating from international waters . . . has been successfully achieved for years," assured this study. A balloon could be raised off the ship to a height of about 3,000 feet. The catch, warned the consultant, was that a short-range ground-to-air missile "accidentally" fired from Cuba could destroy the whole operation."[30] Moreover, two fully outfitted ships would cost $20 million each, not counting the cost of the crew, operation, and maintenance. "The difficulties of supplying and rotating full-time crews could be significant," the engineering report concluded.[31] Maybe it wasn't such a good idea. Finally came the plan for a balloon on a leash, or tether, moored from a fixed land-based location on the Florida Keys and capable of flying at 10,000 feet, or even higher.[32] The cost of a tethered balloon would run about $23 million, but only one would be needed, since it could be operational less than three hours a day and then pulled down for maintenance. An Air Force base at Cudjoe Key, near Key West, offered a location to which the balloon could be moored and dangled aloft. A full-time staff of at least nine persons would be required to operate the system.

Large inflated barge balloons or airships, sometimes called "aerostats," had been around since the turn of the century, and the technology really hadn't changed much. Aerostats are filled with inert, lighter-than-air helium gas, then released to hover high over one spot. Before World War II, they were used by the logging industry to lift big timbers out of backwoods that were otherwise inaccessible. During World War II, the military used them to hunt German submarines and as aircraft early warning devices. In the 1970s, the Air Force started experimenting with aerostats to lift surveillance radar platforms designed to keep watch on coastal defense areas and to look out for drug runners crossing U.S. borders. The aerostat itself looks like a huge, inflated toy airplane, with fuselage, wings, and a tail. Facing into the wind, its aerodynamic shape helps keep it steady.

The aerostat seemed like the most reasonable option, but there was still no getting around the fact that Castro's jammers could easily block the transmission simply by putting its own television signal on the same channel and overriding it. "An aerostat tethered at the Florida Keys would result in marginal coverage of Havana and could not readily adapt to overcome jamming," cautioned the author of one of the engineering studies done by A. D. Ring & Associates.[33] Sources inside Cuba told us that the majority of the TV sets and receiving antennas there were manufactured in the Soviet Union and not as sensitive as U.S. equipment. This meant they would not be very good at picking up TV signals from distant transmitters, and because Havana's television stations were located east of the city, home receiving antennas would be pointed away from the already weaker signal coming in from Key West. "If outdoor antennas were oriented toward Key West," said the A. D. Ring consultants, "it would be obvious from the street" that viewers were trying to pull in American television signals. "This would not be a prudent thing to do in a police state."[34] Other consultants' reports warned that stormy weather over southern Florida would keep the aerostat from flying at least one-third of the time. There was a danger the balloon might break from its moorings, or at least not be steady enough to beam the signal into Havana. It would not be able to fly during thunderstorms, when lighting could disrupt the signal or even destroy the aerostat and the millions of dollars' worth of TV equipment inside. Wick wrote to Senator Hollings—one of TV Marti's most fervent supporters—and warned him that TV Marti would be dark most of the time, but Hollings continued to push things ahead.

Next a channel had to be selected, one that would not interfere with existing stations in either Miami or Havana. As a signatory to the International Telecommunications Union (ITU), the United States was pledged not to interfere with the domestic broadcasting frequencies of other countries. A UN agency with over 165 member nations, the ITU coordinates the international use of broadcast frequencies registered to different countries. There is a difference between using international radio shortwave frequencies set aside to reach foreign audiences and broadcasting over the domestic television channels of other countries. "Extending international broadcasting to TV represents a new bold policy which could severely damage the U.S. image, respect, and influence at all future [ITU] international meetings," warned the Federal Communications Commission." It could be argued that if TV Marti deliberately causes interference to Cuban TV, it is a form of jamming. . . . Our political position with respect to Soviet jamming would probably suffer."

Jorge Mas was undeterred. The USIA Advisory Board for Cuba Broadcasting, which he chaired, hired the Washington law firm of Pierson, Ball & Dowd to investigate the regulatory issues and render an opinion. Pierson concluded that so long as TV Marti's signal originated from the United States and not from international waters, it would not violate the ITU agreement. The State Department also found a loophole: if a Cuban channel was not on the air at the time, TV Marti could use it. Cuban TV channels were in use during daytime and evening hours, so TV Marti might remain within the bounds of international law if it went on in the middle of the night. Jorge Mas had also concluded that TV Marti's "comparative susceptibility to Cuban jamming is low," and that an American television service would be popular because "most Cuban television programs are monotonous and boring." He cited opinion research involving recent Cuban émigrés who said there were too many long-winded political speeches on Cuban TV. He also pointed out that more than 90 percent of Cuban households had television sets.

Budget projections on what it would cost to get Marti on the air made their way to Capitol Hill. Although feasibility studies showed that TV Marti's yearly cost could easily exceed $100 million, lawmakers were fearful of voting against it. Its supporters were turning the issue into a referendum: "a vote against TV Marti would be a vote for Castro." Senator Lowell Weicker (D-CT) had been an opponent of TV Marti and had even visited with Castro in Cuba. Jorge Mas's Free Cuba political action committee zeroed in on Weicker and contributed to the campaign of his opponent, Joseph Lieberman, according to Federal Election Commission records. Weicker lost his seat in 1988. Congressman Dante Fascell (D-FL), chairman of the House Foreign Affairs Committee, was one of TV Marti's leading proponents in Congress. He received $33,387 from anti-Castro lobbyists over a five-year period. "If only one person in Cuba sees TV Marti, then it's worth its money," said Fascell. Congressman Bill Nelson (D-FL), who received political action committee donations from the Cuban lobby, said he interviewed defectors from the Communist island who told him that TV Marti would "open up the eyes" of Cubans.

On July 26, 1988, the Senate approved $7.5 million to start up TV Marti, which would cover the cost of a 90-day test run. The proposal was buried in a mixed-bag appropriations bill without prior hearings or authorizing legislation. TV Marti was blowing through Congress "on a very fast track," complained Representative George W. Crockett, Jr. (D-MI). "The House as a whole has been totally left out of the process.[35] Senator Claiborne Pell (D-RI), chairman of the Senate Foreign Relations Committee, charged that "the entire authorization process is being bypassed." Not surprisingly, the House Committee on Foreign Affairs gave its blessing to the proposal. Committee and subcommittee members received some $120,000 in campaign donations from the Free Cuba political action committee, which donated a total of $182,000 to both political parties in 1988.[36]

James McKinney, who by this point had left the FCC to work on the White House staff as deputy assistant to the president, saw the TV Marti appropriations request before it went to the president for signature. He wrote a memo to White House chief of staff Howard Baker, requesting that the White House not sign off on the bill. "Don't do it," implored McKinney. "It's a bad bill." Baker telephoned McKinney to set things straight. "You don't understand, Jim," Baker said. "This bill will be signed. Doesn't matter what anybody says. Doesn't matter how. This bill will be signed." And signed it was.[37]

Although the fate of TV Marti was now a foregone conclusion, a government interagency task force still had to go through the motions of endorsing it. Chaired by the Voice of America, which would oversee TV Marti, task force members included the departments of State, Defense, and Commerce, which were to assess the results of the 90-day test and make a recommendation to the White House whether the project should go forward. By this point, the White House was occupied by President Bush, who had already pledged his support of Jorge Mas's Cuban-American National Foundation. "I promise you today that I will help lead this administration's support of TV Marti," he had said in Miami.

The test run was to have begun in November, but was postponed from month to month due to various technical glitches. Construction of the transmitter was behind schedule. Winds gusting at 20 knots or more buffeted Cudjoe Key, grounding the balloon. Pressure tests had to be made to see if an old aerostat, lent by the Air Force, could make it all the way up to 10,000 feet. A seam ripped apart while the old canvas balloon was being pumped up with helium, and it exploded, its shredded canvas skin fluttering in the warm Florida breeze. The USIA asked the Air Force to lend it another balloon. On March 19, more than four months later than planned, the borrowed aerostat flew from Cudjoe Key, but only to a height of 50 feet. It underwent daily pressure tests, each day at a higher elevation until it reached 10,000 feet, the altitude level for transmission into Cuba.

The TV electronic war with Cuba began in the early morning hours of March 27, 1990, with TV Marti's long-awaited test transmission of a video signal aimed at Havana. The "test pattern" of TV Marti's logo was received only briefly in Havana before his jammers zeroed in on the signal, which fizzled and disappeared before Janet Jackson's MTV rock video could begin. The White House hailed the first test as a success, although it proved beyond question that TV Marti's signal could be easily and effectively jammed. "The programming aspects of it, technically and in terms of content, were successful," insisted White House press secretary Marlin Fitzwater.[38] Of course, all that viewers could see in Havana was TV Marti's logo and then a lot of squiggly lines. "We regret that Cuba has refused to permit the free flow of information and ideas," said State Department spokesperson Margaret Tutweiler. For his part, Castro claimed that he was merely trying to keep the sex, drugs, and violence of American television from infecting Cuban youth. "What can Yankee television teach our children?" he asked.[39]

The second night of the test, TV Marti signed onto Channel 13 at 3:45 A.M. Fuzzy pictures of baseball players appeared on the screen and were promptly replaced by wavy, horizontal jamming lines. More programs were run but were blotted out. TV Marti signed off the air at 6:45 A.M. Within a few minutes, Cuban TV signed on with the news and aerobics exercises. "The voice of freedom will not be stilled," said a defiant President George Bush.[40] "We want to send a daily picture of democracy," said Senator Bob Graham (D-FL).[41] At her morning briefing, Margaret Tutweiler was asked how TV Marti could be termed successful if it couldn't be seen. She agreed it couldn't but said testing would continue.[42] After all, Jorge Mas wanted it that way, and he was calling the shots.

Castro began to gloat that his $30 microwave dishes attached to trees and telephone polls could jam TV Marti's signal. Castro's jamming transmitters were just a few blocks from the receivers. Deciding to grandstand, he revved up his air force and sent helicopters and planes aloft with jamming devices cranked up. This would show how determined Cuba was to thwart the American imperialists. Cuban military officers were trotted out to do TV interviews. Sleek, Soviet-built MI-17 helicopters were seen sweeping across Havana, their jamming antennas poised for the kill, accompanied by Cuban army helicopters to protect jamming antennas from attack.[43] "This is an electronic war," said Cuban Lt. Colonel Manuel Rey Soberson. "The United States is attacking us, and we're just responding."[44] Castro further flexed his muscles by jamming Radio Marti's broadcasts, beginning on April 17, 1990, for the first time since it went on the air five years earlier. A three-hour speech by Castro knocked stations off the air in Florida, Alabama, North Carolina, Tennessee—where it was heard on country music stations in Nashville—and Texas. Radio station WHO in Des Moines, Iowa, where Reagan began his career as a play-by-play sportscaster, was bombarded with salsa music from Cuba. Castro displayed his sense of humor. Viewers of WCIX-TV in Miami were surprised to see Havana's Channel 6 on the air, which was playing the movie *Endless Love* along with clips from the Bay of Pigs invasion.

Castro's electronic interference got so bad that one Florida station owner had to take out a second mortgage on his home because of the loss of his station's advertising revenue. Capable of generating more than a million watts of power, Castro's transmitters were twenty times more powerful than stations in this country, which are limited by law to a maximum of 50,000 watts. The chief of staff of Cuba's armed forces threatened to use jamming transmitters to disrupt U.S. communications and defense installations. American intelligence agencies photographed Soviet-made SA-2 missiles being deployed around one of Cuba's jamming transmitters. Such missiles were said to be capable of carrying nuclear weapons and of hitting aircraft flying at 50,000 feet.

Despite this show of military force, the Castro government was lightening up a bit, beginning to play, and play expertly, the role of the small beleaguered country bullied by the Yankee imperialists. Things were starting to turn into a media circus. The Cuban government, which had provided few visas to U.S. newsmen, suddenly granted forty-six. Tours were organized to show off the array of jamming devices, and interviews with top Cuban officials were arranged for visiting journalists. President Bush, meantime, defended TV Marti in an address to the annual convention of the National Association of Broadcasters in Atlanta: "I do understand the concerns some of you have about [TV Marti]," said Bush. "But I also under-

stand that you represent the very principle TV Marti exists to serve—
the free flow of ideas."

To many observers the Reagan/Bush/Jorge Mas adven-
ture had badly missed the mark and was providing Castro with an
opportunity to strengthen his position while other Communist dicta-
tors in Eastern Europe and Central America were losing theirs. The
United States spent more than $20 million each year on a TV service
that couldn't be seen because of jamming that cost Castro only
$5,000. It was all an expensive, pointless exercise. According to one
foreign diplomat, "You turn it on, Castro jams it . . . and he puts another notch in his musket."[45]

Night after night during the test period TV Marti continued to be effectively jammed, and time was slipping by. President
Bush had to decide by June 27, 1989, the end of the 90-day test period, whether TV Marti should be turned on permanently or
scrapped. To boost its sagging image, TV Marti released the results of
an audience opinion poll taken during the first two weeks of the test
operation. Interviews with 543 émigrés, mainly tourists and older
people arriving in Miami to visit relatives, purportedly proved that
jamming was effective only in Havana and not in outlying areas of
the city, where it was claimed that 28 percent of TV households were
reached "occasionally." But an internal memorandum by Dr. Kristin
Juffer, Radio Marti's director of audience research, suggested that the
survey was critically flawed. Juffer claimed that the findings did not
"yield reliable and valid results." The survey relied on "hearsay information" and screened out large segments of the population, she
said. Other critics faulted the survey for polling predominantly older
persons in the sample. (Castro didn't allow young people to visit relatives in Miami for fear they would defect.) *Miami Herald* editor Carlos Verdasia said even Havanans who stayed up to watch TV Marti
couldn't find it. "TV Marti is totally blocked, totally nonexistent,"
he said. "I have family in Cuba and they stay up to the wee hours of
the night to watch TV Marti. They have never seen even the logo."[46]

Throughout the 90-day test period, a clandestine USIA
surveillance team crisscrossed Havana and the countryside in the
middle of the night, cutting a swath 10 miles wide and 60 miles
long. They gazed intently at their portable TV screens, hoping to
catch a glimpse of TV Marti. According to the team, TV Marti was
being watched without disruption by fewer than one percent of the

population, far less than the 28 percent the Marti-commissioned study had maintained. Flight logs on the aerostat at Cudjoe Key showed that during the test period, TV Marti was off the air 30 percent of the time: 26 percent because of bad weather and 4 percent because of technical problems.

Congress was beginning to voice doubts. Representative John D. Dingell (D-MI), chairman of the House Energy and Commerce Committee, questioned the legality of TV Marti, and asked for the government's General Accounting Office to investigate a possible conflict of interest between the station and Jorge Mas's Cuban-American National Foundation's links to the White House. Until this time, there had been no debate in either the Senate or House over TV Marti. On June 20, 1990, at the end of the 90-day technical test, a debate was held for the first time in the House. Representative Bill Alexander (D-AR) introduced an amendment that would have severely cut TV Marti's future funding. "TV Marti doesn't work," said Alexander on the House floor. "It gobbles up money which we can use in more effective ways here at home. . . . Let us pull the plug on this boondoggle." His amendment was narrowly defeated following an impassioned plea by Representative Dante Fascell (D-FL), who claimed that TV Marti was "partially" working, and with time would improve. The House voted to fund TV Marti for a full $16 million for the remainder of the year. Two months later, on August 28, 1990, President Bush approved final permanent funding for TV Marti.

But even though its programs were not being seen in Havana, the content of TV Marti's broadcasts raised some eyebrows. Under the supervision of the Voice of America, TV Marti's programs were to fall under the VOA's charter mission to present issues fairly and objectively. Yet in one news segment, a psychiatrist characterized Castro's behavior as cowardly and neurotic. Private-sector consultants who reviewed Marti's programs thought such segments inappropriate for a news broadcast purporting to be objective. Another report speculated that a Cuban who committed suicide in Angola did so because he was ordered to return home. On a news program later that same day, a former Cuban state security police officer was interviewed about his defection to the United States. The reporter asked the defector if Castro ought to be shot. Again, the consultants thought this type of comment was inappropriate. Marti's news program reported on an upcoming anti-Castro rally in New York, but

failed to mention that a pro-Castro demonstration was also scheduled. The anti-Castro rally was later given 20 minutes of live coverage, the pro-Castro demonstration only 2 minutes.

Expecting TV Marti to be objective was unrealistic. The
whole point of spending $20 million a year was to help rid Cuba of
Castro. The facility was being run by Cuban exiles dedicated to the
overthrow of the Cuban dictator. The president's Advisory Committee for Cuba Broadcasting was chaired by a man who was openly
seeking to take Castro's place as president, and whose foundation
was dedicated to bring this off as quickly as possible. It was foolish
to pretend that TV Marti was an objective purveyor of information.
Those in charge hated Castro, and they would select and report the
news accordingly.

Objective or wildly skewed, TV Marti was not being
watched. Even die-hard supporters in Congress who were on Jorge
Mas's political action committee payroll admitted privately that TV
Marti was a bust. "I can understand why people are pissed at Castro
for screwing up their country," said one congressman who insisted
on anonymity. "But you're not hurting him with 'Lassie' and 'Star
Trek' reruns at four o'clock in the morning." The dilemma was that
pulling the plug now would give Castro a major propaganda victory.
"The United States was in a catch-22," recalled former National Security Council adviser Richard V. Allen. "We had a nonexistent TV
station which was costing us over $30 million a year, but it was more
important to keep it on than to take it off and declare defeat. I
wouldn't touch it. The only reason there is a TV Marti is because
Jorge Mas twisted every political arm he could reach."[47] There
wasn't much doubt about where Congress or the president stood. It
was much safer to stay on the good side of Jorge Mas and the powerful Cuban exile community.

TV Marti would not die. Each year, as Congress held
aloft a stake to drive through TV Marti's heart, Jorge Mas would
come to its rescue. Syndicated columnist Georgie Ann Geyer called
Jorge Mas's pursuit of Radio and TV Marti a blatant effort to advance his "ambitions to be president of a post-Castro Cuba." The
Bush Administration certainly had no intention of running afoul of
the Cuban exile community, and later on neither would the Clinton
Administration. But even Jorge Mas couldn't get Fat Albert to work.
Flying at 10,000 feet in the air, the gigantic aerostat (some 270,000

cubic feet in mass and 185 feet long) could tug pretty hard on the tether that anchored it to the ground. A strong January wind in 1991 simply put too much strain on the tether, which snapped. The thousand-pound ground cable and the entire TV Marti payload—balloon, transmitter, and all the electronics—sailed toward the Everglades, eventually nose-diving into a mangrove swamp. The balloon and the sensitive electronic equipment it carried were mashed. Instead of leasing another aerostat from the Air Force, Bruce Gelb, Charlie Wick's successor as director of the USIA, thought it would be a good idea to buy one, at a cost of about $1 million. During House budget hearings, Congressman Bill Alexander (D-AR) asked Gelb if it was true the USIA wanted a million dollars for another balloon to bounce signals from Cudjoe Key to Havana. "I went down to Cudjoe Key," replied Gelb, earnestly. "I saw the installation, got my head up inside and looked at that equipment. It is really a remarkable technological achievement. And, interestingly, it works like gangbusters in terms of getting the signal out." Gelb also admitted under questioning that "jamming has been very effective."[48]

↔ **14** ↔

"I'm Not a Pantywaist!"

BRUCE GELB WAS A FOURTEEN-YEAR-OLD STUDENT AT PHILLIPS ACAD-
emy in Andover, Massachusetts, and was being hazed by an older
classmate, who had ordered him to move a huge couch across a
room. The scrawny Gelb was straining to do his best, but he couldn't
budge the heavy and cumbersome piece of furniture. Tears of frustration and rage in his eyes, he told the bully he couldn't lift it. The
bully promptly put a hammerlock on Gelb's head.

"Leave the kid alone," boomed an upper classman who
happened to be walking by. The bully let Gelb go. The knight in shining armor was young George Bush. In fifty years he would become
president of the United States, and Gelb would serve him as director
of the U.S. Information Agency. "You don't forget people who helped
you," Gelb said, after he had raised millions for Bush's presidential
campaign.[1]

There were many at the USIA who wondered if the Andover bully might have squeezed Gelb's head too hard. They thought
it might account for the bizarre behavior of the man who succeeded
Charlie Wick. Wick had come to the USIA as the man who had produced the film *Snow White and the Three Stooges,* but when he left

eight years later he was a kind of folk hero, far and away the most successful chief in the Agency's fifty-year history. Wick was a hard act to follow for a man whose background was directorship of a company that had produced Monster vitamins, Ban deodorant, and No-Doz. Gelb had been vice chairman of the pharmaceutical giant Bristol-Meyers, which his family owned and ran.

Tall and trim, Gelb at sixty-three looked like Central Casting's idea of a million-dollar-a-year *Fortune* 500 chief executive. But he was new to government and Washington politics and rattled the bureaucracy early on by informing Gorbachev that the Soviet leader could learn a lot from "the vipers and bloodsuckers in American business. That's what makes America tick."[2] Gelb offered to arrange a meeting between Gorbachev and chicken magnate Frank Perdue, so that Gorbachev could see for himself. Gelb also caused a stir when he proposed a tax on credit card purchases at a time when President Bush was telling people to read his lips about no new taxes. Gelb made his credit card proposal to two Democratic senators, who gleefully ran out of the room and leaked the story to the press to embarrass Bush. Gelb was astonished by the criticism he got for his tax proposal. "That's what happens when a creative mind is looking for new sources of funds,"[3] he replied.

In his first year as USIA director Gelb spent 20 percent of his time globe-trotting. While in South Africa on government business he met with the local Bristol-Meyers staff. In Rwanda he climbed the mountain featured in the movie *Gorillas in the Mist*. On a visit to Peru, he and eight bodyguards traveled to cocaine producing jungles, where the former drug company chief couldn't resist testing a new herbicide.[4]

But it was during the Persian Gulf War that Gelb's character really came through. A cable arrived from one of Gelb's former prep school classmates, who was in Saudi Arabia on business. "Bruce," it read, "for those Americans who are over here, I think it would be a good idea if the VOA started broadcasting lessons about how to deal with the heat, like 'stay inside, cover yourself and drink lots of fruit juices.' The VOA should broadcast it as well in Arabic for the local population." Gelb thought this was a wonderful idea, and a lot of people at the VOA spent a lot of time trying to convince him that it would be silly to broadcast lessons from the Americans back to Kuwait on how to deal with desert heat. Letters, faxes, and cables went back and forth between Washington and the Middle East. VOA officials held their breath, hoping it would go away. But it didn't, and several how-to stories about heat stroke prevention were carried on the VOA.

In the meantime, the VOA was being roundly criticized in some quarters for being too soft on Iraqi president Sadaam Hussein. "By not saying every fifteen seconds that Sadaam was a blood-sucking viper whose mother copulates with camels in the desert, we were somehow taking Sadaam's side," said former VOA chief of staff Michael Schoenfeld. "Some American ambassadors in the Middle East, who had not heard our broadcasts but who heard from a friend of a friend, were told we were pushing the other side."[5] When Sadaam made a comment, the VOA would cover it. Egypt's President Hosni Mubarak couldn't understand why the VOA was giving airtime to the other side and telephoned Bush to complain.[6]

The issue established the atmosphere for coverage of the Gulf War. Critics of the VOA seized the opportunity to discredit the radio service and began leaking stories to the press involving classified cables from disgruntled U.S. ambassadors in the Middle East. A story surfaced that the head of the VOA's Arabic-language service, although an American citizen, was an Iraqi by birth, and this was taken as prima facie evidence that the VOA was being subverted. Independent reviews of the VOA's Arabic programming were later conducted by the Hudson Institute and the Institute for Strategic and International Studies, both of which concluded that the VOA's Gulf War coverage had been scrupulously fair.

Gelb became paranoid about leaks to the press. "He didn't talk to his deputy for six months because he didn't trust him," said one USIA official. There was a bathroom between their offices, and Gelb suspected the deputy sat on the toilet listening to his conversations. Gelb returned to work one morning to notice that his office was in disarray, with papers scattered over his desk. He was convinced someone had come in over the weekend to bug his office, and told USIA's security chief Brian Dowling to call in the FBI. Four agents showed up and tore out an office wall to look for eavesdropping devices. Nothing was found. They returned a few hours later and tore out another wall.[7] No recording devices were found. The agents did discover a "quirk" in Gelb's speaker phone, through which conversations from his office could be transmitted to some adjoining rooms. "Aha!" said Gelb. "I told you so."

A few weeks later Gelb came to work and saw something else suspicious. He summoned three top aides to his office, and motioned them over to a loveseat near the couch. Gelb pointed to a stain on the loveseat's cushion. "What's that?" he asked. The three shrugged. Finally one of them volunteered, "It's a spot." "Somebody's been fucking on my couch!" Gelb exclaimed. The three stared at one another.

Gelb insisted that Brian Dowling investigate. "What's that?" Gelb asked Dowling, nodding to the spot on the loveseat. "I don't know, Mr. Gelb," replied Dowling. "Somebody's been fucking on my couch, Brian," Gelb fumed. "And I know who it is." He didn't elaborate, and no one asked him to. The piece of furniture in question was a tiny two-seater. "But they would have to be midgets or contortionists to fit into this thing," Dowling replied. "I want this cushion taken to the FBI lab for analysis," announced Gelb.

Dowling was not about to call the FBI. Instead, he took the cushion around the corner to a dry cleaner and asked the owner to run it through tests. The next day Dowling came back to the cleaning store. The stain on the cushion was identified as hot chocolate. The news of Gelb's stain spread throughout the USIA's offices and then overseas to the American embassies. Diplomats in Burkina Faso, Ougadugu, and Muscat convulsed with laughter.

In mid-September 1990, before the Gulf War, Gelb toured countries in the Desert Storm conflict area and became very interested in figuring out a way to send a stronger VOA radio signal into Iraq. Tariq A. Almoayed, minister of information from neighboring Bahrain, offered to provide the VOA with a site and temporary radio transmitter from his country, as a contribution to the cause. Gelb accepted the offer, but didn't clear it with the White House first. Almoayed said he would refuse to take compensation for the transmitter and so Gelb, in his desire to please Almoayed, invited the minister's daughter, a student at American University, to come live with him and his wife, Luisa, and to use the family car.

As it turned out, Almoayed had no intention of making a transmitter in Bahrain available to the United States. He was only interested in public relations value for himself by hobnobbing with top American government officials. Almoayed began to report delays in getting necessary equipment for the transmitter and then requested $1 million in used American radio equipment to help put the facility on the air. Almoayed also asked the United States to build roads in Bahrain while it worked on the transmitter. The Bahrainis were conducting an elaborate shakedown. Gelb stayed in the game, and even made a trip to Bahrain to express U.S. solidarity and friendship. Gelb requested assistance from the secretary of defense to ship equipment from the VOA facility in Belize. The Pentagon agreed and airlifted the supplies and personnel needed to build the broadcast facility, which finally went on the air well after the Persian Gulf War with Iraq had ended. The transmitter signal was weak, "a mere whisper in the wind," according to a U.S. engineer who conducted tests at the facility.

Gelb was struggling to find his niche, the equivalent of what Charlie Wick had found with Worldnet. He concocted elaborate plans for a mammoth American pavilion at the Seville World's Fair in 1992, celebrating the 500th anniversary of the discovery of America by Columbus. Because of poor planning, costs skyrocketed and the project went $10 million over budget. The corporate funding that had been counted on never arrived, so Gelb frantically began to look for money within the Agency to pay for the project. He planned to carve $2.9 million from the Voice of America's budget. The VOA's politically astute director, Richard Carlson, thought of a way to throw Gelb off track. Carlson announced he would eliminate six language services and their fifty-seven long-time employees. "This will cripple our efforts at a time of unprecedented change and opportunity," admitted Carlson, playing to sympathetic VOA employees and Congress. Carlson had taken what is called the "Washington Monument approach"—he fought back by cutting some sacred landmarks: the VOA's language services. Ethnic groups flooded Congress with letters of protest. At an employee meeting in the VOA auditorium, Carlson said, "This is the most painful thing I have ever had to do." He then proceeded to read the names of every one of the 57 persons who were to be fired, as well as the numbers of years each had served with the VOA. Most of the employees (several of whom had been with the VOA for more than thirty years) were foreign nationals who would be sent back to their country of origin. While Carlson did this,

VOA employees wiped tears from their eyes, in full view of members of the press who had been invited to attend.

It was a public relations masterpiece. Howls of protest went up among the media and from influential congressmen and senators on the Hill. Senator Hollings informed Gelb that VOA language services were not to be cut and that the USIA would have to look elsewhere to find the money to fund the Seville World's Fair. "Be advised that Seville has no priority with me," Hollings told Gelb. "Our highest priority has to be getting the Agency's basic funding stabilized and not worrying about fairs."[8] Gelb backed down, and plans for the American Pavilion at the Seville Fair were scaled down. Gelb then summoned Carlson to his office to tell him he was fired. "You can't fire me," replied Carlson. "I work for the president." Both Gelb and Carlson were summoned to the White House, where they were convinced to work out their differences.

The truth was, the White House was fed up with Gelb. They stopped sending him information on foreign policy decisions because they didn't trust him. He was kept out of the loop while preparations were being made to invade Panama. When word of the invasion was announced on television, the USIA's operations center frantically tried to reach Gelb in Washington by telephone to give him the news. They got an answering machine. So they rushed over to his residence and banged on his door. No one answered. Gelb, it turned out, was asleep. A sleeping pill kept the U.S. government's top information chief from being aware of the military action until he got to his office the next morning.[9]

Despite what he'd told the White House, Gelb was not finished with Carlson, who had become one of his obsessions. Gelb was engineering what would be called, in the vernacular of the business world, a "hostile takeover" of the VOA. Without informing Carlson, he announced a major reorganization of the VOA, whose personnel and budget departments were to be consolidated into the parent USIA. This came on the heels of several earlier and awkward Gelb attempts to interfere with VOA news content. Gelb had tried and failed to prevent the VOA from carrying an interview with a Chinese dissident who had been released from jail, so as not to upset the Beijing regime.[10] VOA employees, concerned that Gelb's real motive was to impose ideological censorship on them, circulated a petition bearing hundreds of signatures that demanded the VOA have complete autonomy from the USIA. Nothing like this had ever happened before at the USIA. Newspapers across the country carried stories with headlines like "VOA Employees Rebel." The press started asking the White House to tell them what was going on.

Gelb decided to call a public meeting and explain to all VOA employees why administrative consolidation was a good idea. Carlson was on vacation in the Caribbean when he received a telephone call from Gelb. "We're going to have this public meeting to air our differences," Gelb told him. "Bruce, this is nutty," replied Carlson. "First of all, we're not going to work out our differences by referendum. Next, this will escalate out of control. The press is going to be there. It's going to embarrass you, it will embarrass me, and it will embarrass the President." Gelb replied tartly, "This is not a matter for discussion. You will be there or I will have grounds to fire you for insubordination."

There has sometimes been a strained relationship between the VOA, struggling for news independence, and the USIA, with its policy ties to the State Department and the White House. But the strain was never worse than it was at that time. Anyone "from across the street" at the USIA headquarters was considered hostile. Many of the ethnic groups represented within the VOA's language services—some fifty in all—saw no shades of gray: you were either with them or against them, and if the latter, you were the enemy.

Nearly a thousand people jammed into the shabby, New Deal–era VOA auditorium, with its high ceilings and WPA murals and long, ceiling-to-floor dingy white drapes. On the wooden stage was a single podium and three wooden chairs, which were for Gelb's aides: management director Henry Hockeimer, foreign service counselor Michael Pistor, and USIA deputy director Eugene Kopp. Hockeimer, a Reagan holdover, had become a chief aide to Gelb and the architect of Gelb's clumsy VOA power grab. It was a face-off, with Gelb's henchmen sitting on an empty stage facing a thousand very angry, very hostile people from seventy countries muttering curses under their breath in Farsi, Dari, Arabic, Pashto, Romanian, Bulgarian, and several dozen other languages. What might have been a typical if unfortunate bureaucratic squabble had become a public relations disaster for the White House, with two presidential appointees at open war against each other. "Yes, Dick and I disagree on some issues," Gelb began. "But I am not myself a pantywaist." The comment was met with astonishment, then with derisive laughter. "This is your meeting, Bruce," Carlson declared. "I have no intention of resigning." His comment was met with thunderous applause and cheers. A State Department official who was there described the public meeting as probably the single biggest management blunder in Washington history.

Several days later, Gelb was relieved of his job and appointed ambassador to Belgium. The White House also found a place for Carlson—as ambassador to the Seychelles Islands in the East Indian Ocean. To defuse things, the White House had separated the two combatants by putting them halfway around the world from each other. VOA staffers set about their business, sporting "I am not a pantywaist" buttons.

Gelb was replaced as USIA director by Henry Catto, formerly American ambassador to Great Britain. Catto, who had married into the Hobby family, one of Houston's oldest and wealthiest, spent a lot of time jetting between his wife's homes in San Antonio, Virginia, and Aspen, where she was building condos with a former ski instructor.[11] Catto hadn't won too many friends in Great Britain when he described the Royal Family as "boring." At the USIA he kept a low profile and avoided controversy. All he wanted was to get back overseas as an ambassador and as soon as possible. Nothing of consequence occurred at the USIA on Henry Catto's watch. Like the Royal Family, it was boring. Until Bill Clinton arrived from Arkansas.

↔ 15 ↔

Adventures in the Nanny Trade

PUBLIC DIPLOMACY MAY HAVE BEEN WASHINGTON'S GROWTH INDUS-try during the 1980s,[1] but Bill Clinton helped to make the nanny trade one of the growth industries of the 1990s. Record numbers of pretty, blue-eyed, blond nannies from Western Europe invaded the United States each year because Clinton wanted to fill Justice Department and Supreme Court vacancies with individuals who, he later learned, had violated the law. The minute Clinton's team hit the White House they purged the travel office to make way for friends of the president and fired elderly telephone switchboard operators who had been at the White House since the Truman Administration. However, no one dared lay a hand on the government's child care employment agency, which was doing a land-office business supplying full-time, tax-exempt babysitters to influential Americans.

  Zoe Baird, general counsel at Aetna Life & Casualty, had been Clinton's original nominee for attorney general, but her name was withdrawn when she revealed she had not paid Social Security taxes on wages for a Peruvian couple she hired as household help. Judge Stephen Bryer, who was under consideration to replace Justice Byron White on the Supreme Court, had a similar problem, and that was why Ruth Ginsburg got the nod. Bryer got a second chance, of course. Judge Kimba Wood also had hired an illegal alien, which put her out of the running as the nation's top law enforcement officer. Clinton's choice to head the Social Security Administration, Shirley S. Chater, also failed to pay Social Security taxes for part-time babysitters over a six-year period. All of this caused a stampede to the doorstep of the travel agency that supplies documented, legal, tax-free au pair babysitters and housekeepers to ambitious Americans.

And who, you might ask, runs this employment agency? The Immigration and Naturalization Service of the Justice Department? The Labor Department? Wrong. Congress insisted that the United States Information Agency run the overseas nanny trade. Why the USIA? Because as part of its mandate, the USIA handles cultural, educational, and international visitor exchanges, and apparently Congress thought washing dishes and changing diapers fit these categories. According to former USIA associate director Ronald Trowbridge, whose department administered the program, "Thousands of people, and I'm talking about high rollers, were flouting immigration laws by getting child care this way." One of the reasons it's run by the Agency is that a lot of senators and congressmen have au pairs and want to maintain the program.

The Mutual Educational and Cultural Exchange Act of 1961 established so-called J-Visas, enabling non-immigrant "bona fide" students to study in America, to participate in cultural and educational activities, and to "increase mutual understanding" between countries. This included teachers, medical students, research scholars, airplane pilots, and au pairs. Issued a J-Visa, an immigrant does not require certification from the Labor Department to work full-time. And while au pair girls (and they usually are girls) are permitted to receive wages for babysitting and housecleaning, their employers, or "host family," need not pay Social Security taxes or fill out IRS W-2 employment forms (which is what Zoe Baird and Stephen Bryer failed to do with their non-J-Visa au pairs). Immigration lawyer Thomas J. Fadoul, Jr., believes au pairs should be on working visas. "You ought to call it what it is," he said. "It's just another employment situation, and it's wrongful that no taxes are paid on au pair wages."[2]

Some 30,000 au pairs are employed in American homes annually. They must be between the ages of 18 and 26 and can stay for 12 months. This is how the system works. There are eight "sponsor" agencies certified by the USIA, and they have affiliate offices throughout Europe. Au pair candidates are first screened, then the agency tries to match up the candidate with the right family. The sponsor agency is paid $3,750 by the host family, which also pays the nanny $115 a week plus room and board. Nannies are supposed to work no more than 45 hours per week, but frequently work much more. The Labor Department says a 40-hour week constitutes full-time employment. There are tax breaks for au pair hosts, who may legally qualify for child care tax deductions of up to $960 per year. If a host family member has an employer who has set up a Dependent Care Spending Account (DSCA), through which au pairs can be paid, there are additional benefits. One of the sponsor agencies, E.F. Au Pair, has a brochure that reads: "DCSAs provide important tax advantages because the money you designate to be deposited into a DCSA is not included in your taxable income. So, you pay less federal income tax . . . less state and local income tax."

The largest of the eight tax-exempt, licensed au pair agencies is the American Institute for Foreign Study Scholarship Foundation (AIFS) and its subsidiary, Au Pair in America. AIFS was founded in 1986 by a former Procter & Gamble ad man who sold the USIA on the idea of starting a pilot au pair program. An AIFS representative admitted that the name of the organization was misleading. "The au pair isn't required to go to the school," admitted a spokesman. The au pair's responsibilities include: "Looking after, feeding, bathing and playing with the children . . . Driving children to and from school, appointments, outings or errands if required by family. . . . Preparing meals for the children, looking after their belongings, making the children's beds, doing their laundry and straightening out their rooms." To appeal to working parents, sponsor newspaper and magazine ads often state that the nanny (not the au pair) can be left in "sole charge" of children. Ads also claim that nannies are "qualified," implying they possess recognized child care credentials, which is rarely the case. Nowhere is studying mentioned. The USIA's general counsel's office feels the au pair program exceeds the agency's mandate. It concedes, "An educational component is entirely optional. It is not the function of the USIA to monitor whether the au pair attends classes, and the agency has no specified method of doing so."

After she returned home, one au pair summed up her educational experience in the United States in a letter to her sponsoring agency. "I learned special things about Americans," said Marie Pechilga of France. "For example, they eat with their arm under the table, cut sometimes with the right hand and sometimes with the left, they eat potatoes with the skin." A young mother in the program said her au pairs went out partying at night after taking care of the kids all day. "They have a list of discos before they get here," she said. What the USIA doesn't realize, says Uta Christianson of the Inter-Exchange agency, "is the value of experiential education."[3] Senator Christopher J. Dodd describes the au pair program as one of the most successful cultural exchange programs in the country. "The current au pair programs have proven their ability as enriching cross cultural experiences for American families and young Europeans alike," said Senator Dodd, in whose state, Connecticut, the largest au pair–sanctioned agency, Au Pair in America, is located.[4]

About 20 percent of the match-ups don't work out, usually because the au pair feels overworked. Anne Dotson, a coordinator for Au Pair Homestay, says, "One problem that comes up again and again is the family with two careers. The au pairs come here expecting a warm, fuzzy family experience. What they find is a situation where you have two attorneys, and they're never home by ten, and the au pair has responsibility for some very needy children."[5] In West Hartford, Connecticut, John Monahan's family was matched with a young au pair whose fiancé was studying at the University of Massachusetts, a two-hour drive from their home. "It was obvious that her primary reason for being in this country was not a crosscultural exchange," complained Monahan to the sponsoring agency, which he believed had been aware of the situation and advised the au pair not to mention it in her introductory letter or her visa application. He also claimed that the au pair had stolen money from him and from others for whom she had previously worked.[6] In another instance, a New York couple filed a $100 million civil lawsuit against a Swiss au pair and the agency that hired her, E. F. Au Pair, in the arson death of their three-month-old daughter. Flammable liquid was poured over the child. The lawsuit claimed the au pair's references had been forged, and that the E. F. Au Pair agency had not properly screened her or verified her references.[7] A nineteen-year-old Dutch au pair was charged with shaking to death an infant in her care near

Washington. Another au pair was deported because of child abuse. One family heard from neighbors that their two-year-old child, supposedly being watched by an au pair, was seen wandering down the street alone.[8]

Another reason the nannies arrive via the USIA is because influential sponsoring groups want it that way. They reap millions by keeping the program housed in an agency that doesn't want it and therefore monitors it loosely. Because they and thousands of their constituents use it, congressmen hide the program, with bipartisan support, in the USIA, where it is virtually invisible. Because of the Smith-Mundt Act, restricting agency programs to audiences overseas, the American public knows little about what goes on in the mammoth international public relations organization that is the USIA. Congress, which decides which USIA programs are funded, feels it has a stealth weapon in the USIA. Were the Labor Department to get involved in the au pair program, it would instantly confront opposition from the AFL-CIO labor unions, which would see it, quite correctly, as a threat to their workers. The J. Visas also restrict the au pairs to Europe. Moving the program to another visa category and expanding it to other parts of the world would mean moving the au pair trade to the Immigration and Naturalization Service in the Justice Department. Regulators would scrutinize and probably kill the whole boondoggle.

The au pair program was designated as a two-year experimental project, after which it was to be evaluated for continuation. In 1988, near the end of the trial period, a government-wide task force was appointed and issued its findings. Speaking for the group, the late USIA general counsel Normand Poirier informed Congress that "a household domestic work program does not appear to be included within any of the terms of the [congressional] legislation," and that it did not belong in the USIA. He also contended that au pairs are admitted to the United States without regard to their impact on the domestic work force. "Other foreign nationals coming to the United States to work as live-in domestics," said Poirier, "must first have certification from the Department of Labor that sufficient qualified U.S. workers are not available for the job and that wages and working conditions attached to the job offer will not adversely affect similarly employed U.S. workers."[9] The thing that really set off Congress was Poirier's order to trim back the au pair's work week from

45 to 30 hours. At that point, "All hell broke loose," said Poirier.[10] The au pair agencies were unwilling to make any changes in the work week and boasted they had enough clout in Congress to make the USIA back down.

Congressman Dante Fascell (D-FL) claimed the program wasn't broken and didn't need to be fixed: "It has been operated as a cultural exchange program . . . and has become one of the most successful cultural exchange programs in the country." Fascell said limiting the number of au pair work hours "would discourage virtually every American family with two working parents from participating as a host family." In one month alone, Poirier's staff logged a record number of 52 phone calls and 41 letters from members of Congress protesting the proposed changes.[11] "Poirier felt there was a real prospect of other projects blossoming into work programs and proliferating," said former USIA general counsel Alberto J. Mora. Congress also set up the Q-Visa, known as the "Disney visa," because it enabled thousands of Europeans to get work at the Disney theme parks. Disney had urged Congress to set up this special category when it appeared that some changes might be made in the J-Visas.

Congress extended the J-Visa program for another two years in 1988, and in 1990 it mandated that the USIA continue administering the au pairs without change "until such au pair programs are authorized and implemented by another agency of the United States government."[12] What is behind keeping the au pairs in the USIA is purely European snob appeal. Having an attractive, blue-eyed, blond teenager from the Alps caring for your kids is like having a Mercedes-Benz parked in your driveway. It makes a statement to neighbors and business associates. It is said that the biggest crimes in Washington are the legal ones, and nobody skirts the laws better than the people who write them. Discrimination on the basis of race or religion or ethnic background may be illegal, but the U.S. government, which writes and enforces those regulations, prefers its au pairs to be blue-eyed blondes from thirteen Western European countries. The United States itself isn't an equal opportunity employer. Lairold M. Street, a staff attorney with the U.S. Equal Employment Opportunity Commission, believes it is deeply discriminatory to limit the program to Europe. "I wonder about the moral and international human rights implications of our country excluding people of color from such 'educational' and/or work opportunities in the United States which appear to be only available to Europeans," wrote Street. "If we are going to have a government-sponsored program, then it should be free of discrimination and open to all races and nationalities."[13]

Yet there is E. F. Au Pair of Cambridge, Massachusetts, advertising that its program offers "a legal alternative to traditional American child care." Prospective clients are told that "a well-educated, English European [will be] living in your home as a family member." Au Pair in America advertises that it uses "carefully selected" young people from Western Europe. In au pair ads, everything is white: the au pairs, the kids, the furniture, the pets, and the stuffed animals. According to a congressional source who refused to be identified, "If the program were opened up to other parts of the world its whole complexion would be different. You want someone who is bright and curious about the world, to get higher quality child care. It's a big business and the whole market would change." The key word is *complexion*. While casting doubt on the morality of the government's au pair programs, the Equal Employment Opportunity Commission says they are not within its jurisdiction. It gets involved only when "employers" discriminate. It doesn't do "exchange programs."

Domestic nanny agencies, which employ many blacks and Hispanics, say au pairs have had a devastating effect on their business. They are at a disadvantage because foreign au pairs are paid $115 per week by host families who do not have to pay Social Security and unemployment taxes. American live-in nannies, whose taxes must be paid, can cost up to $25,000 per year. The cost of an au pair, including round-trip air fare and all other expenses, averages $10,000 per year. Congress, which seems to ignore that in French *au pair* means "in equality," has forced the USIA to be the lily-white Mary Poppins of domestic child care.

By the mid-1990s, the au pair program was growing rapidly, particularly where government workers who go through periodic background checks need technically legal child care. "This Zoe Baird thing contributed enormously to our growth," said Celia Gaston, executive director of Eurapair, an agency in California. "Especially in the Washington area. The growth trend there has been spectacular."[14] The Internal Revenue Service reported that the number of 1993 tax returns for domestic help rose for the first time in twenty-five years. Some taxpayers reported back liabilities for as much as $25,000.[15]

USIA general counsel Alberto Mora was rightly concerned that if the USIA didn't toe the line on the au pair program, Congress would use it as an excuse to pile on other abuses. "Other work-based programs," said Mora, "would be attached to the agency, and with every step the agency would be getting into programs further away from its primary function of educational and cultural exchange and getting close to becoming an organization involving the U.S. labor market, because of well-organized, well-funded groups."[16] For example, one au pair organization wanted to start Eldercare, a program to place au pairs in the homes of elderly people, thereby providing non-nursing companionship and care. Although perfectly legitimate, this is not the kind of cultural exchange program that the USIA should be conducting.

Against its will, however, the USIA has been saddled with other projects, such as the summer work, travel, and camp counselor programs. There is no obvious educational component in these programs, either, which mostly involve young people going into the labor market and flipping hamburgers, becoming lifeguards, or clerking in stores. Two European automobile mechanics came to the States on a USIA program and performed the same type of work here. A chef from Hong Kong with twenty years' experience worked as a cook in a Washington Chinese restaurant under the USIA program. "I had people tell me with a straight face that the Chinese chef with twenty years' experience would be getting an educational and cultural experience by cooking for Americans," said Alberto Mora.[17] Three other participants worked in florist shops planting, pruning, spraying, and shipping flowers and plants.[18]

There are 1,200 sponsors in the USIA exchange programs, and they are reaping big profits. Under the J-Visa program alone, about 175,000 participants come here each year for "educational and cultural" purposes.[19] Many of the programs have turned into big business, such as flight training programs, whose participants fork over $20,000. There are a growing number of flight schools that are increasingly focusing their attention away from American students and looking abroad, because there is greater opportunity for profit and growth. It costs a flight student much less to get a pilot's license in the United States than it would overseas. Consequently, these programs market their services overseas. The controversial part of the training program is not the original instruction, but the eighteen-month period of so-called classical training required by regulation after a pilot earns a license. The trainees are cut loose in the American labor market to look for jobs, with no supervision at all from the sponsoring agencies. Foreigners therefore compete with American pilots for a limited number of jobs. Apart from assuring that the training promised is actually being delivered, the USIA is also responsible for trying to monitor the financial stability of these programs. In a two-year period, two of thirty sanctioned schools went bankrupt and a third was suspended by the USIA for violations of regulations.

Then there is the "Future Farmers of America" program, where a significant number of young foreigners are placed in jobs, usually without training, and where no instructional syllabus is provided.

And, of course, thousands of exchange students who come to the United States with temporary visas don't return home, despite a congressional requirement that after completing their U.S. stay, certain participants must go back to their native country for at least two years. The system has lots of loopholes. The agencies can get waivers of the foreign resident requirement if they can show that such waivers are in the national interest. Participants can also get waivers if they can prove that returning home will create hardships for themselves or their families, or if they would be subject to persecution in their home country. "It's always a hardship case," said former USIA General Counsel Thomas Harvey, "and it usually works, so they stay here."[20] The notion that someone comes to the United States to learn, and then goes home to share the benefits of that learning with his or her own countrymen, is too often a myth.

Finally, we shouldn't forget Congress's very own pork barrel fund, neatly hidden in the USIA's $225 million cultural and educational exchange budget. Over a six-year period, $3.34 million was spent on the international travel club for former members of Congress, the Institute for Representative Government.[21] It was terminated in 1995.

The president has the authority to conduct the government's foreign exchange activities, but neither Reagan, Bush, nor Clinton wanted to put an end to the au pair travesty by executive order. Attention had been focused on Bill Clinton's USIA director, Dr. Joseph Duffey, a man with impeccable educational credentials. Duffey's wife, Anne Wexler, had lobbied Congress on behalf of the biggest USIA-approved nanny agency to keep the au pair work week at 45 hours. She ceased this activity before Duffey became USIA director. Ms. Wexler, a former official of the Carter Administration, had every right to make her own way in the business world. But in Washington, perceptions are critical. Duffey indeed did not stipulate that the au pair 45-hour work week be trimmed, which the USIA has long lobbied for, so as to provide young Europeans the time to go to school in America. He also dropped a proposed nine-hour work limit on au pair workdays and changed his mind about raising the au pair's weekly stipend from $100 to $150 per week. He yielded to the whining of the "nonprofit" au pair agencies and settled on a $115 per week stipend, the first raise for au pairs since 1985. New guidelines now require that au pairs must go through criminal record checks, and that au pairs taking care of children under two must be at least twenty-one years of age and have documented child care experience.

Congress has played fast and loose on immigration matters. It has coerced a little-known agency of government to implement a brazenly disguised, self-serving work program, feebly packaged as an educational and cultural program. Congress wasn't about to introduce legislation that would remove their cloak of invisibility at the USIA. And Joe Duffey and Bill Clinton weren't about to rock the nanny's boat, either.

↔ 16 ↔

Caught in the Smith-Mundt Act

AMES, IOWA, IS A UNIVERSITY TOWN WITH A SOPHISTICATED POP-
ulation. As editor and co-owner of the *Ames Daily Tribune,* the
town's most important newspaper, Michael G. Gartner thought it
would be educational for his readers to see occasional reprints of
Voice of America editorials so that they could keep abreast of government policies on some important world issues and learn how the
VOA was presenting these policies to listeners abroad. He telephoned the VOA in Washington to request that editorials be mailed
or faxed to him. The VOA refused; the Smith-Mundt Act of 1948
prohibited the domestic dissemination of USIA program materials.[1]
But, said a VOA representative, Gartner was welcome to come to
Washington to examine the editorials—though he would not be permitted to photocopy them or take verbatim notes. Gartner had no
desire to make the trip from Iowa and felt the editorials could be easily faxed or mailed to him. Nor did he feel that the restrictions on
copying and note-taking made any sense. Indeed, he believed they in-
fringed on his First Amendment rights to receive and disseminate information. Therefore, with money that he had set aside to buy his
wife a new car, Gartner filed suit against the USIA in 1989.

James M. Weitzman, a Washington communications lawyer, recalled that years earlier, when he was in high school in Milwaukee, he had written a letter to the VOA directed to the famous jazz announcer Willis Conover requesting information about a record Conover had played. "Several weeks later I got back a two-page letter that looked like a bill from a lawyer who doesn't want you to know what he's doing on a day-to-day basis," said Weitzman. "They gave me all the reasons why they couldn't supply me with the name of the song. It came in a government-franked envelope, and I said to myself, how ridiculous. For the same postage and less effort they could have just scribbled down the name of the song."[2]

The Smith-Mundt Act was designed for another era, when the memory of Nazi propaganda was fresh. When the VOA first signed on, on February 24, 1942, the announcer promised that the listener would hear the truth, the good news as well as the bad. Three decades later, in the 1970s, as head of a government panel, former CBS president Frank Stanton conducted a wide-ranging study of this country's overseas information programs and advocated lifting the ban on domestic dissemination. If the VOA tells nothing but the truth, he reasoned, shouldn't everyone be able to hear it? The answer from Congress was still no.

Today, as we speed headlong along the information superhighway toward the twenty-first century, we are bombarded with information that fifty years ago would never have been accessible. Technology has rendered pointless any of Congress's efforts to muffle government broadcasts. USIA satellites cover the United States, making government TV programs easily available, and anyone with a modem can download transcripts of VOA news reports from the Internet worldwide computer network.

Because they have vast news and information resources of their own, the major American radio and television networks traditionally have not shown much interest in getting access to USIA programs. The hundreds of new cable operations springing up, however, are eager to receive and retransmit free government programs, sight unseen. Despite all the accessibility the new technology makes possible, or perhaps because of it, Congress remains concerned that relaxing Smith-Mundt opens the door for anyone occupying the White House to use VOA and other USIA media products to advance his own political agenda. Said the late Senator Edward Zorinsky, a member of the Foreign Relations Committee, as he introduced an amendment to reinforce the ban on domestic dissemination, Smith-Mundt "distinguishes us, as a free society, from the Soviet Union, where domestic propaganda is a principal government activity. . . . The American taxpayer certainly does not need or want his tax dollars used to support U.S. government propaganda directed at him or her." According to Jon Beard of the USIA's congressional relations staff, the obstacle is Republican disenchantment with Clinton Administration policies: "It's one thing if the editorials are intended to be available for foreign audiences. But if they are readily available and are in fact distributed as well to folks in North Carolina, you can bet your bottom dollar we're going to have problems with Senator Helms and others."[3]

The government does promote itself with taxpayers' money, from the White House and congressional press and communications offices on down. "Government press releases, speeches, briefings, tours of military facilities, publications are all propaganda of sorts," Michael Gartner maintains. "Propaganda is just information to support a viewpoint, and the beauty of a democracy is that it enables you to hear or read every viewpoint and then make up your own mind on an issue."[4] To those who fear that American citizens would be brainwashed by USIA material, Gartner offered some advice: "Bring them up press releases from other government agencies and then bring them up VOA material and ask them which they think is the straighter."[5] In *Gartner v. United States Information Agency,* Judge Donald O'Brien held that "the First Amendment proscribes the government from passing laws abridging the right to free speech; the First Amendment does not prescribe a duty upon the government to assure easy access to information for members of the press." The judge added, however, that even though it was the law, "it would be easy to conclude that USIA's position is inappropriate or even stupid."[6] Later, Michael Gartner became president of NBC News, and again he was rebuffed by the USIA. "I wanted to read what the VOA was saying about some international crisis or another, and I called down to Washington and asked again if they would send me material, and they declined," he recalled. "So I asked our London bureau chief to call Washington and ask for the same thing. . . . The VOA gladly faxed them the material. London then faxed it to me. I got what I wanted. It just cost the government a few dollars more, and it struck me as exceedingly silly."[7]

Although Gartner lost his case against the USIA, Judge O'Brien made it clear that the press could print anything it got its hands on. "There is no case or controversy as to plaintiffs' ability to publish verbatim transcripts already in their hands," wrote Judge O'Brien. Accordingly, the USIA's general counsel's office wrote the following internal memo to the agency staff: "Agency officials may rightfully continue to refuse to disseminate USIA materials domestically. They should take care, however, not to imply that the public may not disseminate USIA materials domestically." Although anyone examining documents was still prohibited from taking verbatim notes, no one would inspect their notes. However, laptop computers and photocopying were still not permitted. In November 1990, shortly after Judge O'Brien's decision, Congress somewhat relaxed the regulations, permitting USIA material to be released in America twelve years after it was used.

An immediate beneficiary of this new policy was James Weitzman, who for years had tried to educate some of his broadcasting clients, especially multiple–radio station owners, about the business opportunities presented by a multicultural audience. He conceived of the idea after realizing how many persons of foreign origin crossed his path each day. How, he wondered, do they all stay in touch with their roots, with their countries of origin? He took his own advice and bought a small gospel radio station, WUST, in Washington, changed its format, and called it New World Radio. Then he began to seek out foreign-language programs. Weitzman researched the *Gartner* case and decided that his station could broadcast VOA language programs—provided he could find a way to get access to them. When he telephoned the VOA for instructions on how to receive the more than forty foreign-language programs fed overseas via satellite, "They were very polite, but they wouldn't offer any help. To find out really how to do it took a little bit more intrigue than being a Watergate burglar." Someone finally gave him a number to call at the VOA. Weitzman telephoned and, as instructed, refrained from telling the person who he was or why he was calling. "He supplied information, but then he said, 'You didn't talk to me,' and he hung up the phone."[8]

A satellite dish appeared on New World Radio's roof, and

without fanfare the station went on the air. "We started broadcasting in Cambodian, Korean, Chinese, Amharic, Vietnamese, Filipino, and other languages, and the phones went crazy," said Weitzman. "We didn't understand what they were saying, but one thing was clear. Some people were crying tears of joy. These were people who were suddenly making a connection. It's their link to their origins and it's their handshake to America."[9]

Several years ago, C-SPAN decided to use its satellite subcarriers to transmit audio signals, thereby providing an additional service to subscribers who watched congressional proceedings. It signed up the BBC World Service and arranged to carry other English-language broadcasts from Korea, Japan, France, and Israel, among others, as well as Radio Beijing and Radio Havana. After the *Gartner* decision, according to general counsel Bruce D. Collins, C-SPAN decided it was safe to pick up the VOA as well. "It was their interpretation of the statute after the famous *Gartner* decision," said Collins, "that while we could do whatever we wanted with the information if we could get it, they weren't going to lift a finger to help us." To get a high-quality feed, C-SPAN sought permission to put in a hard-line wire connection between the VOA studio and its own, a distance of about six blocks. The answer was no. C-SPAN engineers then expended considerable amounts of energy and cash and rigged up a special "black box" that would receive a clear satellite signal. Because of C-SPAN ingenuity, VOA English-language programs are now available to some six million cable households. "C-SPAN long ago stopped thinking of itself as a television network," said Collins. "It thinks of itself, as do most information providers these days in the digital world, as an information network. And as information moves from analog to digital it's all going to be much easier to distribute." He is confident that any government attempt to control the free flow of information will fail.[10]

In January 1994, VOA took a bold step forward by placing transcripts of its news and English-language broadcasts on the Internet computer service. The initiative was approved by USIA lawyers even though this meant that Internet users in the United States could also access the VOA. During its first few months of operation, an average of 4,000 to 7,000 files were downloaded each day by Internet users. "If you know how to do it, you can pull it in here," said Carol Epstein, USIA assistant general counsel. "But we're not telling you to do that. . . . There is a legitimate overseas distribution purpose in this, and there is some spillover because technology has overtaken this law [Smith-Mundt]." Epstein noted that the Smith-Mundt Act never carried with it any enforcement authority.[11] Former USIA attorney John Lindburg points out, however, that while the Smith-Mundt Act carries no penalties and is really a law without teeth, the USIA doesn't want to push its luck. If the Agency went too far, "some senator or congressman up on Capitol Hill is going to slap their wrist for it. . . . [By] cutting their funds or passing even more restrictive legislation."[12]

The Internet gateway isn't the only way in. Anyone with a backyard satellite dish can pick up signals from Worldnet, whose swath of satellite coverage blankets the United States and the world with its 24-hour, multilingual broadcasts. We have come a long way from the days when USIA films were dispatched by dogsled. Some critics, like Richard W. McBride, a former majority staff consultant to the House Foreign Affairs Committee, are worried that a weakened Smith-Mundt bill will mean abuse. "The people put at the top of the USIA are political appointees who see the value of domestic publicity to promote the White House point of view and themselves," said McBride. "There would be the temptation to divert resources from the overseas mission."[13] For now, there is still a thin veil of censorship. You still can't bring in your own copier when you review USIA documents.

↔ **17** ↔

Public Diplomacy Goes Private

Perhaps the most powerful factor determining bureaucratic behavior is the instinct of organizational self-preservation. Like other forms of life, bureaucracies tend to pursue survival before all other goals. . . . Bureaucratic entities are, as a result, notoriously difficult to kill off, even after their original reason for being has disappeared.[1]

The Russians knew better than most what a bureaucracy was all about. "To introduce a television or radio program is a cultural event," remarked veteran Radio Moscow reporter Boris Kalyagin. "But to take it off the air is a political decision."[2]

Kalyagin has turned out to be quite right. The recent debate in Congress over the future of America's cold war broadcasting instruments—the Voice of America, Radio Free Europe, and Radio Liberty—involved past conquests and bureaucratic self-preservation. In 1995, seven years after the collapse of the Berlin Wall, the U.S. radios together broadcast more than 70 language services (15 of which were redundant) from 160 transmitters, mostly trained on former Communist Eastern Europe and the old Soviet Union. Nary a word about new technologies available to promote U.S. public diplomacy objectives abroad was uttered in the congressional debate.

Since the end of the cold war, mighty bureaucracies have been fighting to stay alive by being creative. The Soviet "evil empire" may have vanished, but emerging in its place, says the FBI, is the first mafia-controlled nuclear state. FBI chief Louis J. Freeh warns that the rapid growth of the Russian mafia is such that it might soon get its hands on material to make nuclear bombs. A grim-faced Freeh told Congress that the FBI had information about serious "nuclear thefts," and that Russian crime links with the United States were being established. He toured nine former Communist nations in early July 1994 and announced that an FBI office would be opened in Moscow because of "a mounting threat to the safety and well-being" of America.[3] Leaders of other nations in Eastern and Central Europe pleaded with Freeh to open FBI offices in their countries. By suggesting this, Freeh was invading the turf of the beleaguered Central Intelligence Agency, America's overseas cloak-and-dagger operation, as well as the Arms Control and Disarmament Agency, established to prevent nuclear proliferation. This meant a triplication of effort. For its part, the CIA has been getting into domestic terrorism prevention, the FBI's turf. New fiefdoms are being established. Bereft of its old Communist enemy, the National Security Agency has expanded its domain from global communications surveillance to establishing a standard to crack domestic computer codes. The Internal Revenue Service was testing the system, to the dismay of the business community.[4]

Watching its budget shrink, the Pentagon saw an area of opportunity in this new information age by invading what had been the purview of the USIA for almost fifty years. The Air Force was preparing to use broadcast satellites to beam propaganda to world trouble spots to undermine hostile governments. (Plans also included using satellite technology to jam troublesome local television signals that the Pentagon didn't want audiences abroad to see.) The Pentagon planned to transmit television programs from airplanes outfitted with equipment tested during the Persian Gulf War. It began by beaming propaganda to Haiti, to which the Voice of America was already broadcasting, in an attempt to encourage the population to oust the nation's military dictatorship.

Not about to be left behind, the USIA looked for ways to build a domestic constituency. The Agency began hosting meetings with U.S. business leaders and local politicians to help them find new joint ventures abroad. Traditionally, this was the turf of the Commerce Department. The USIA knew that to pique the interest of President Clinton and Congress, it had to rally domestic support. It was clear to USIA insiders that Clinton could not have cared less about public diplomacy efforts, which he shunted off to third-echelon White House and State Department aides. During Reagan's administration, ambassadors and their public affairs officers were encouraged to "think television," to get America's story out. "At one time, we would have leaped at the opportunity to have talked to a small, cultural organization at a tire factory around the corner," said Philip Brown, former public affairs officer at the American Embassy in Moscow. "We now had to be very brutal and say, 'Your organization isn't important enough.'"[5] Ambassadors overseas learned to work with their personal computers, hooked up to their political advisors and public affairs officer. (There has been scant desire among career diplomats abroad to spread the word of assistant secretary of state Peter Tarnoff, who remarked that the world should not look to America for leadership.)

When the Iron Curtain collapsed, permitting the free flow of information, shortwave radio died. Local radio stations were now providing their own services. Hardest hit were surrogate stations such as Radio Free Europe and Radio Liberty, which had provided the local and regional information services that gave them their largest audiences. In February 1993, the Clinton administration's budget had called for Radio Free Europe and Radio Liberty to be phased out by 1996 at a savings of some $210 million per year. By June 1993, however, after a ferocious bipartisan lobbying campaign promoting the surrogate stations, Clinton wavered. On behalf of his former Russian enemies, Lech Walesa made "save the radios" pleas directly to Clinton, while Boris Yeltsin and Mikhail Gorbachev lent their testimonials as part of an ad campaign on TV and in U.S. national publications, featuring *babushkas* recalling the impact Western information had on their lives during the cold war. In the end, perhaps predictably, Clinton announced RFE/RL would be preserved—along with all other nonmilitary U.S. international broadcasting operations—under an independent board, which would also address issues involving the duplication of language services, and technical and administrative services. Clinton even went a step further, by supporting a whole new broadcasting bureaucracy called Radio Free Asia, at a start-up cost of at least $60 million. Under the plan, as Radio Free Europe and Radio Liberty were preparing to wind down in Eastern Europe and Russia, they were to direct their efforts toward Asia, where they had no experience. At least $30 million per year would be spent for a new Asian shortwave service that would parallel the VOA broadcasts already directed to that part of the world.

All of this, inconceivably, came at a time when FM stereo stations, video- and audiocassettes, and, of course, television were all competing for audiences. For every international shortwave broadcaster, radio listenership was rapidly declining. "The growth of regional powerhouse radio stations in the 1970s and 1980s and in particular of high-fidelity FM are killing shortwave in many parts of the world," read the USIA's own research report. "Just as few of us turn on our TVs to watch commercials, relatively few people tune in to a foreign station on shortwave or hear the news of the sponsoring government. They tolerate them, that's all."[6] The VOA's largest audience was in China, to which it beamed 21 hours of programming each day (10 hours in Mandarin, 1 hour in Cantonese, 2 hours in Tibetan, and 8 hours in English.) But although the VOA was the most popular foreign radio service in China, fewer than one percent of those who had shortwave radios listened to the VOA at least once a week. VOA research analyst Dr. Kim Andrew Elliott told me he had noticed that the 1995 Radio Shack catalogue offered five shortwave radio receivers, down from nine the year before. The decline in shortwave listening will be rapid, he said, when direct broadcast satellite receivers rival shortwave radio sets in price in a few years. When the Soviet Union jammed the VOA during the cold war, 13 percent of the population listened to the radio service. In the mid-1990s, when VOA shortwave programs entered Russia unencumbered, the number of listeners had dropped to 5 percent. Gone were the propaganda broadcasts of Albania's Radio Tirana and Czechoslovakia's Radio Prague. By 1994 Radio Moscow had cut the number of its language broadcasts in half, and its weekly hours of programming from a high of over 2,000 in the 1980s to 1,300 in 1994. Its strident propaganda had been replaced by news broadcasts, which had to compete with nongovernmental, independent stations. In 1995—to work around the decline in shortwave listening—getting "placed" on local radio stations abroad was the American buzzword, with programs being plucked from satellites and played live via AM or FM frequencies to local audiences. But as local stations in developing democracies matured and added more of their own programs relating to local audiences, such outlets soon began to disappear.

USIA executives, protective of their shortwave radio fiefdoms, reluctantly admit that the dominance of television is not limited to the developed world. Agency surveys for several years have shown that television viewing surpasses radio listening even in poor Third World countries. In Karachi, Hanoi, Bulgaria, Algiers, and in remote provinces of China such as Nanning, practically every household has a TV.[7] The new Star TV satellite, in which media baron Rupert Murdoch bought controlling interest in July 1993, is seen by an estimated 30 million people in 38 nations in its coverage swath from Asia to the Middle East.[8] Millions in China are already watching CNN, MTV, BBC-TV, and other international program providers on their own satellite dishes. Tunisia, Turkey, Morocco, and Egypt had started daily TV satellite programming reaching an estimated 5 million Arab speakers in Europe, North Africa, and the Middle East.[9] But the United States was still pouring its money into shortwave radios in its 1996 budget, at a funding ratio of 17 to 1 over television.

In these difficult, competitive, confusing times, several international broadcasting organizations are thriving. The BBC's World Service Television is leaving the U.S. government Worldnet, as well as America's Public Broadcasting Service, in the dust. Its self-funded, satellite-delivered international commercial operation, launched November 1991, costs the British taxpayer nothing. Other privatized systems are also flourishing by being attentive to commercial marketplace forces and having shaken loose from their own government "mush-mouth brigade," as columnist William Safire has labeled obstructive State Department bureaucrats.[10] Through a holding company, the French government owns popular and profitable commercial broadcast properties, including TV and Radio Monte Carlo, which promote French interests. The French, generally acknowledged as the world's most aggressive government broadcast service, live by the credo: "Speak French, think French, buy French." France's Radio Monte Carlo is the dominant Western station throughout the Middle East, dwarfing the VOA's audience, which is smaller than in the period preceding the 1991 Gulf War.[11]

There is a lesson here, one we must learn. The new Congress should shrink government by letting go of its international broadcasting services. My belief is that these services should be privatized. Worldnet and the radio services should be combined with the Public Broadcasting Service, National Public Radio, and American Public Radio (which should also be privatized). Free of government funding and control, public broadcasters can more readily adapt to the changing international media marketplace and make their way as private entrepreneurs. Gone would be congressional mandates for expensive and unnecessary language services, including Kurdish and Tibetan, that exist only because of their domestic constituency on the Hill. Neither could an expensive, redundant shortwave service be decreed for Asia. The Voice of America has instant international name recognition, and America's public broadcasters have the programming. And with new digital TV satellites that deliver crystal clear signals and a wide range of channels, the future is promising for a commercial international TV and radio service. Satellite TV revenues in the Pacific Rim are expected to triple by the year 2002, according to London-based CIT Research.[12] Richard Carlson, who is currently president and CEO of the Corporation for Public Broadcasting, the funding arm of PBS, finds it "ironic indeed that while we can now reach through satellites billions of people directly, the images and the voices and the ideas and the perceptions of America that those people receive are so unrepresentative of what this country is really like." A U.S. international TV system would provide quality programming from America. For example, he said, "The Bold and the Beautiful" and "Baywatch," two of the most popular American TV programs abroad, are not noticeably realistic or perceptive in their portrayal of American life. Carlson points out that there are about 350 local PBS stations and "tens of thousands of hours of very good programming sitting on the shelves in these stations . . . [including] the very best children's and educational television programs that have ever been produced."[13] Foreign correspondents assigned to Washington and New York are on limited budgets and simply cannot cover the great diversity of America that would be of great interest overseas. A worldwide public television satellite network, resources of National Public Radio, the VOA, and RFE/RL consolidated—it would be an unbeatable combination.

I would also recommend putting the brakes immediately on the VOA, which continues its multi-billion-dollar program to put still more shortwave radio transmitting facilities overseas, construction that will extend into the year 2003. An additional $1 billion for capital construction abroad is in the VOA's plan, half of which is for modernization projects not yet begun.[14] What began as a five-year modernization plan back in 1983 has turned into a twenty-year modernization plan. It is a colossal misallocation of resources. "Shortwave will continue to be the backbone of the [VOA's] signal delivery for many years to come," read a recent VOA engineers' report. The new buzz term is "surge broadcasting," which means to "increase the capacity to increase the number and duration of shortwave signals during crises."[15] To further justify the 140 new engineers, many of whom came aboard well after the Berlin Wall had tumbled, the VOA has established additional technical offices. One, named ACT (Advance Communications Technology), has "tiger teams" working on new projects. The latest attempt to justify exorbitant expenditures involves using redundant shortwave stations. They are needed, says the VOA, in order to provide clearer signals, sending them to the same audience from different directions. "The vagaries of shortwave radio signal propagation demand three simultaneous signals from different relay stations to ensure reliable level of service at all times under all circumstances," the engineers' report continued.[16]

Ten years after the start of the VOA's $1.3 billion cold war modernization program began, and five years after the collapse of the Berlin Wall and the Communist empire, the VOA's shortwave facility in Morocco finally and unbelievably went on the air. The waterlogged tract of land that the VOA had leased was drained and packed with landfill, and the shortwave station was partially operational. It had all cost $215 million. Then the wet earth beneath the massive concrete foundations began to settle and foundations under the seventy-story-high transmitters started to crack (by 1996 the problem was expected to be rectified). Government managers had vastly overestimated their ability to handle such a large and complex technical project. Terry Balazs, a VOA engineering manager, lamented, "There were so many parts that had to come together sequentially, and things just didn't mesh."

In 1995, the following classified ad ran several times in *Broadcasting & Cable* magazine:

> SURPLUS PROPERTY SALES, U.S. Information Agency, disposal of the Voice of America's medium wave radio station broadcasting facilities and personal property located in Punta Gorda, Belize, Central America. All responsible sources may submit an offer which will be considered.

↔ Epilogue ↔

Charles Z. Wick returned to Hollywood, where he deals in investments for Rupert Murdoch from an office on the lot of the Twentieth-Century Fox film studio, not far from Melrose Place.

Valentin Falin moved to Germany, where he opened a small art gallery near Munich.

Alexandr Yakovlev, always the survivor, was appointed by Boris Yeltsin to be head of the Russian public television network.

Michael Gartner, back in Iowa as editor of the *Ames Daily Tribune,* now broadcasts editorials over the Voice of America, which he once sued.

Alvin Snyder is a freelance journalist and communications consultant in Washington.

Weather permitting, Fat Albert still bobs high over Cudjoe Key, Florida, beaming to Cuba TV Marti's programs, which no one on the island can see.

NOTES

PREFACE

1. The dinner was held on November 17, 1988, in the Hall of Flags at the headquarters of the Organization of American States.
2. British Independent Committee of Enquiry into the BBC's Overseas Information Service, April 1954.
3. Zbigniew Brzezinski, *The Grand Failure: The Birth and Death of Communism in the Twentieth Century* (New York: Charles Scribner's Sons, 1989), p. 254.

CHAPTER 1: LETTING WICK BE WICK

1. Remarks at a dinner honoring Charles Z. Wick, director of the USIA, 17 November 1988.
2. Eric Konigsberg, "Empires of the Sons; and the Friends, and the Mistresses . . . ," *Washington Monthly*, June 1992, p. 12.
3. Author's interview with Peter Galbraith, former staff aide, Senate Foreign Relations Committee, 24 July 1992.
4. Cheryl Arvidson, "Charles Z. Wick: A Profile," Cox News Service, 27 May 1984.
5. Jack Anderson and Dale Van Atta, "Loaded for Bear at USIA," *Washington Post*, 3 November 1989.
6. David Corn and Norley Jefferson, "Capitalism Triumphs over USIA," *Nation*, 10 October 1988, p. 299.
7. Author's interview with Terrence A. Catherman, who accompanied Wick on the European trip, 13 August 1992.

8. Arvidson, "Charles Z. Wick."
9. Charles Z. Wick, dictated daily notes, 4 October 1983.
10. USIA, memorandum of conversation, 14 October 1984.
11. Author's interview with Leonard Garment, 15 February 1995.
12. James H. Andrews, "Legal Combat in the U.S. Capital," *Christian Science Monitor,* 26 November 1991, p. 15.
13. Bumiller, "Wick Whirlwind."
14. Arvidson, "Charles Z. Wick."
15. Author's interview with Charles Z. Wick, 30 May 1995.
16. Garry Clifford, "Couples," *People* magazine, 26 January 1981, pp. 85–88.
17. Clifford, "Couples," p. 6.
18. John LeBoutillier, *New York Times,* "Reaching the Soviet People," 12 April 1981.
19. David Gergen to Ed Meese, Jim Baker, and Mike Deaver, memorandum, 21 December 1982.
20. Bumiller, "Wick Whirlwind."
21. Author's interview with former Wick aide Robert Earle, September 1994.
22. Ibid.
23. Bumiller, "Wick Whirlwind."
24. Minutes of the meeting held at the USIA's Foreign Press Center, 6 January 1982.
25. U.S. Advisory Commission on Public Diplomacy, annual report, 1982. In accordance with the requirements of Section 8, Reorganization Plan no. 2 of Public Law 96-60, the U.S. Advisory Commission on Public Diplomacy submits its annual report on the USIA, and activities of the U.S. government involving public diplomacy, to the Congress and to the president.
26. Hans N. Tuch, *Communicating with the World: U.S. Public Diplomacy Overseas* (New York: St. Martin's Press, New York), p. 49.
27. Author's interview with Catherman.

CHAPTER 2: TOWARD A PUBLIC DIPLOMACY

1. House Appropriations Committee, discussion of policy toward showing certain films abroad, Department of State, appropriations hearings for 1948, 21 March 1947, pp. 447–78.
2. Ibid.
3. William Benton, assistant secretary of state, memorandum to the secretary of state, 18 March 1946.
4. Colmer Committee on Postwar Economic Development, 20 December 1946.

5. Department of State press release, 18 September 1950. The group called on President Truman 12:30 P.M. that day, and later met with Commerce Secretary Charles Sawyer at 3:30 P.M.

6. USIA, study conducted in Western Europe (England, West Germany, France, and Italy), 1962.

7. Milton Lehman, "We Must Sell America Abroad," *Saturday Evening Post,* 15 November 1947, pp. 147–48.

8. Teresa Priory, "People of Europe Being Offered a New Picture of Life in the U.S.," *New York Herald Tribune,* 28 December 1947, pp. 1, 8.

9. Paul Leicester Ford, ed., *The Writings of Thomas Jefferson* (New York: G. P. Putnam & Sons, 1898).

10. Author's interview with Kim Andrew Elliott, Voice of America researcher, 19 June 1995.

11. From a videotape entitled "Finally, the Main Points Again," produced and written by Jonathan Marks for a VOA conference, "International Broadcasting in the 1990s and Beyond," Washington, D.C., November 3–6, 1992.

12. Holly Cowan Shulman, *The Voice of America: Propaganda and Democracy, 1941–1945* (Madison: University of Wisconsin Press, 1990), p. 100.

13. U.S. Advisory Commission on Public Diplomacy, report, 1977, p. 10.

14. Congressional Quarterly Information Service, *Congress and the Nation: 1945–1964,* (Washington, D.C.: Government Printing Office, 1965), p. 210.

15. "USIA Advisory Commission on Public Diplomacy," report, 1972, p. 12.

16. Author's telephone interview with Abbott Washburn, 10 July 1995.

17. The Mutual Educational and Cultural Exchange Act of 1961 authorized the academic exchanges of American and foreign graduate students and teachers, and grants to emerging foreign leaders.

18. Radio Free Europe began broadcasting in July 1950 following the Berlin blockade and the Soviet invasion of Czechoslovakia. Radio Liberation began broadcasts to the Soviet Union in March 1953, changing its name to Radio Liberty in 1963. CIA funding of RFE/RL was revealed in 1971, and the Board for International Broadcasting (BIB) was established as an oversight agency in October 1973, with funding from Congress. In 1976, RFE/RL, Inc., an independent federal agency, was created with the merger of the two radio services, under the BIB.

19. *Variety,* 20 April 1955.

20. John F. Kennedy, memorandum for the director of the USIA, 25 January 1963.

21. House Subcommittee on International Organizations and Movements of the Committee on Foreign Affairs, *Ideological Operations and Foreign Policy: Winning the Cold War: The U.S. Ideological Offensive,* Report No. 2, 27 April 1964.

22. Ibid.
23. Legislative Reference Service, Library of Congress, *The U.S. Ideological Effort: Government Agencies and Programs,* study prepared for the House Subcommittee on International Organizations and Movements of the Committee on Foreign Affairs, 3 January 1964.
24. Ibid.
25. Thomas A. Johnson, "Call at Cape Town by Ship Opposed," *New York Times,* 2 February 1967, p. 12.
26. Benjamin Welles, "Navy Stands Firm on Capetown Visit," *New York Times,* 3 February 1967, p. 10.
27. "Diver and 100 Go Ashore," Reuters, 5 July 1987.
28. "Carrier Leaves Cape Town for U.S.," *New York Times,* 7 February 1967, p. 7.
29. House Subcommittee on International Organizations and Movements of the Committee on Foreign Affairs, *The Future of United States Public Diplomacy,* Report No. 6, *Winning the Cold War: The U.S. Ideological Offensive,* 2 November 1968.
30. Ibid.
31. Joseph Gelmis, "It's Not Hollywood's War," *New York Newsday,* 20 November 1971.
32. Joseph McBride, "Drums along the Mekong," *Sight and Sound,* Autumn 1972.
33. Gelmis, "It's Not Hollywood's War."
34. The U.S. Advisory Commission on Public Diplomacy, 1972 report, p. 21.
35. From a historical record of USIA television, compiled by Jack DeViney, 1993.
36. Author's telephone interview with Victor Sheymov, 21 October 1993.
37. Victor Sheymov, *Tower of Secrets* (Annapolis: Naval Institute Press, 1993), p. 132.
38. Author's interview with Victor Sheymov, 19 October 1993.
39. Historical record of USIA television, Jack DeViney.
40. The Trendex report covered U.S. audience reaction to the week-long television series, broadcast January 23–30, 1977.
41. Jonathan Eyal, "Recent Developments in the Jamming of Western Radio Stations Broadcasting to the USSR and Eastern Europe," *Radio Liberty Research* (a monthly publication of Radio Liberty), 7 November 1986.
42. Ibid.
43. Julia Wishnevsky, "Western Radio Stations and Soviet Law," *Radio Liberty Research,* 16 January 1985.
44. Ibid.
45. Senate Select Committee to Study Governmental Operations with Respect to Intelligence Activities, hearings, October 1975, *Mail Opening,* Volume 4.

46. Wishnevsky, "Western Radio Stations and Soviet Law."
47. Ibid.
48. *Kontinent,* no. 12, 1977, p. 271. Cited in Wishnevsky, "Western Radio Stations and Soviet Law."
49. Tass, 25 August 1982.
50. Novosti in English, 24 August 1982.
51. Serge Voronitsyn, *Sovetskaya Rossiya,* as reported in *Radio Liberty Research,* 5 July 1982.
52. Ibid.
53. *Vodnyi transport,* 23 January 1982, as reported in *Radio Liberty Research,* 5 July 1982.

CHAPTER 3. CRANKING UP THE VOLUME

1. Kenneth L. Adelman, "Speaking of America: Public Diplomacy in Our Time," *Foreign Affairs,* Spring 1981.
2. House Foreign Affairs Committee, House Report No. 97-480, 2 April 1982.
3. Author's interview with Dr. Carnes Lord, Army War College, Fort McNair, Washington, D.C., 11 August 1992.
4. National Security Decision Document (NSDD) number 45 (July 15, 1982) directed that the "VOA . . . will undertake a major, long-term program of modernization and expansion," and that "acquisition of new transmitting sites and facilities should be a priority matter on the political agenda of bilateral relations with appropriate countries." NSDD 77 (January 14, 1983) reinforced the administration's commitments to VOA modernization, and requested details of how it would be implemented. NSDD 130 (March 8, 1984) restated the priority of VOA modernization.
5. The NSC directed the Voice of America to expand coverage into the Near East, Far East, Africa, and the Caribbean Basin; defeat jamming of the VOA broadcasts by the Soviet Union; and increase weekly program hours from 960 to 1,148.
6. Author's interview with Lord.
7. Author's interview with Kenneth L. Peel, Washington, D.C., 17 July 1992.
8. MIT Research Program on Communications Policy, "A Study of Future Directions for the Voice of America in the Changing World of International Broadcasting," 25 April 1983, p. 20.
9. General Accounting Office, "The Voice of America Should Address Existing Problems to Ensure High Performance," GAO/ID-82-37, 29 July 1982.

10. "Tuning Up the Voice," editorial, *Los Angeles Times,* 2 January 1985, p. 4.
11. James Reston, "The Other Star Wars," *New York Times,* 20 March 1985, p. A27.
12. Tim Matthews, "Broadcasting to the World," *Broadcast Sound,* March/April 1984.
13. The author was on hand at the conference. Supplementary information from *USIA World,* July/August 1983, and from author interviews with USIA staffers Philip Rogers, David Cohen, and Hugh Foster, January 1995.
14. Minutes of a session of the Soviet Politburo, 31 May 1983, as translated by Lena Milman in the *Bulletin of the Cold War International History Project of the Woodrow Wilson International Center for Scholars,* Washington, D.C., Fall 1994, pp. 77–80.
15. Ibid.

CHAPTER 4: THE FIVE-MINUTE TAPE GAP

1. The International Civil Aviation Organization (based in Montreal) issued its findings on the shooting down of the Korean airliner on 31 August 1993.
2. "Retrospective on the End of the Cold War," a symposium held at the Woodrow Wilson School of International Studies, Princeton University, February 1993.
3. George P. Shultz, *Turmoil and Triumph: My Years as Secretary of State* (New York: Charles Scribner's Sons, 1993), p. 361.
4. Author's interview with Gregory J. Newell, 1 June 1993.
5. Seymour Hersh, *The Target Is Destroyed* (New York: Random House, 1986), p. 112.
6. 1983 Politburo session on KE-007 (*Rossiyskiye Vesti*), Moscow, 25 August 1992, as reported in the CIA's Federal Broadcast Information Service, 27 August 1992.
7. Shultz, *Turmoil and Triumph,* pp. 363–64.
8. William Chapman, *Washington Post,* 3 September 1983.
9. Associated Press, English translation of Russian-language statement, *Washington Post,* 3 September 1983.
10. Woodrow Wilson School of International Studies, "Retrospective on the End of the Cold War," symposium held in February 1993.
11. Christopher Andrew and Oleg Gordievsky, *KGB: The Inside Story* (New York: HarperCollins, 1990), p. 499.
12. *International Civil Aviation Organization,* final report on KE-007, 6 August 1993, p. 9.
13. "From Lies to Remedies," *New York Times* editorial, 7 September 1983, p. A22.

14. David Shribman, *New York Times,* "U.S. Experts Say Soviet Didn't See Jet Was Civilian," 7 October 1983, p. 1.
15. Murray Sayle, "Closing the File on Flight 007," *New Yorker,* 13 December 1993, p. 101.
16. "How U.S. Would Act in Airspace Invasion," *New York Times,* 2 September 1983.

CHAPTER 5: CASTING WIDE THE WORLDNET

1. James Reston, *New York Times,* 17 September 1983.
2. Author's interview with Larry Speakes, Washington, D.C., 25 August 1992.
3. Data from Paul Kagan Associates' newsletter, *Cable TV Franchising,* 1982.
4. Charles Z. Wick and George S. Vest, U.S. representative to the EEC, memorandum of conversation at the U.S. Embassy, Brussels, Belgium, 13 February 1982.
5. Charles Z. Wick, dictated daily notes, 23 September 1982.
6. USIA Office of Research, "Western European Public Support for NATO Widespread," report, 15 May 1981.
7. From a major policy speech by Ronald Reagan to the British Parliament, 8 June 1982.
8. OECS members were Antigua, Barbuda, Dominica, Grenada, Montserrat, St. Lucia, St. Kitts–Nevis, St. Vincent, and the Grenadines.
9. Fay S. Joyce, *New York Times,* 27 October 1983, p. 1A.
10. A detailed account of the U.S. action in Grenada can be found in George P. Shultz, *Turmoil and Triumph: My Years as Secretary of State* (New York: Charles Scribner's Sons, 1993), pp. 323–45.
11. Steven A. Holmes, "Less Strategic Now, Grenada Is to Lose American Embassy," *New York Times,* 2 May 1994, pp. 1, A6.
12. Penny Pagano, "TV Goes Global on Worldnet," *Los Angeles Times,* 2 March 1985, part V, p. 2.
13. USIA translation of "Jewel in the Crown," *Poznan Daily Gazeta,* 12 April 1987.
14. "News over the Atlantic," *Wall Street Journal* editorial, 27 December 1983.
15. Michael Davie, "Uncle Sam Gets Message Across on Celestial TV," (London) *Observer,* 7 July 1985, p. 44.
16. Rod Townley, "This Is One Show That's Driving the Russians Crazy," *TV Guide,* 22 December 1984.
17. Charles Z. Wick, conversation with public affairs officer Jim Magee in New Delhi, India, daily notes, 31 October 1983.
18. Richard Levy, deputy director, USIA Television and Film Service, weekly activity report memorandum, 5 April 1984.

19. Paul Mongo, *Variety*, 7 November 1984, p. 1.
20. Author's interview with Alexander Shalnev, *Izvestia* U.S. correspondent, National Press Building, Washington, D.C., 5 October 1992.
21. The going rate per satellite dish location in Europe was approximately $3,500 per hour.
22. Wick arranged a "turnkey" contract for delivery of 520 hours per year of Worldnet programming in Europe and the Middle East via an unlimited number of satellite dishes for $1.6 million—a savings of roughly 90 percent over the standard commercial rates.
23. Lynn Rosellini, "Reagan Aides Show Capital Luxury Style," *New York Times*, 16 August 1981.
24. John M. Goshko, "USIA Develops Space-Age Propaganda Role," *Washington Post*, 31 March 1986, p. 1.
25. Russian archives, Moscow, June 1993.
26. An exception was made for the use of two high-powered "Ekran" satellites that transmitted to small dishes in remote Siberia, whose 20 million residents would otherwise have been without a TV signal. Television was considered an important link to home for those in remote areas; it kept them from getting homesick and wishing to get back to the big city.
27. *Argumenty i Fakty*, no. 42, 1986.
28. USIA, "The Rapid Expansion in Soviet Satellite TV Broadcasting," research report prepared by George Jacobs and Associates, Inc., consulting engineers, February 1985.
29. Ibid.

CHAPTER 6: BRILLIANT PEBBLES, ETHNIC GUNS, AND BABY PARTS

1. Nancy Whelan, "A Flair for Disinformation," *Government Executive*, February 1987, p. 14.
2. Author's telephone interviews with Todd Leventhal and Herbert Romerstein, and USIA memoranda of conversations relating to disinformation discussions with the Soviets.
3. U.S. Information Agency Report, "Soviet Active Measures in the 'Post–Cold War Era' 1988–1991," a report prepared at the request of the U.S. House of Representatives Committee on Appropriations, June 1992, p. 120.
4. Author's interviews, Leventhal and Romerstein; USIA memos.
5. Ibid.
6. Central Committee of the Communist Party of the Soviet Union, "On the Hostile Speeches of the President of the U.S.A.," 25 September 1985; "Revelations from the Russian Archives," exhibit in Madison Gallery, Library of Congress, Washington, D.C., June 1992.

7. "Soviet Active Measures," pp. 6–7.
8. Ibid.
9. William Preston, Jr., and Ellen Ray, "Disinformation and Mass Deception: Democracy as a Cover Story," *Freedom at Risk: Secrecy, Censorship, and Repression in the 1980s,* edited by Richard O. Curry (Philadelphia: Temple University Press, 1988), p. 212.
10. Cdr. Merle Macbain, USN Retired, "Russia's Propaganda Machine," *Retired Officer,* April 1981.
11. "The Barbery Wars," Robert Wallace, *Smithsonian Magazine,* January 1975.
12. Fitzhugh Green, *American Propaganda Abroad from Benjamin Franklin to Ronald Reagan* (New York: Hippocrene Books, 1988), p. 7.
13. Senate Select Committee to Study Governmental Operations with Respect to Intelligence Activities, 4 and 5 December 1975.
14. Statement of Karl F. Inderfurth, professional staff member of the Senate Select Committee to Study Governmental Operations with Respect to Intelligence Activities, 4 December 1975.
15. Comment by Senator Frank Church, chairman, Senate Select Committee on Intelligence, 4 December 1975.
16. Walter Pincus, "European Press Said Target of '78 CIA Program," *Washington Post,* 23 October 1984, p. 1A.
17. David Whitman, "The Press and the Neutron Bomb," Harvard University study, October 1984.
18. Laurien Alexandre, *The Voice of America: From Détente to the Reagan Doctrine* (Norwood, N.J.: Ablex Publishing, 1988), p. 112.
19. Angelo M. Codevilla, Ph.D., senior research fellow at the Hoover Institute of War, Revolution and Peace, Stanford University, in *Political Warfare and Psychological Operations, Rethinking the U.S. Approach,* edited by Carnes Lord and Frank R. Barnett (Washington, D.C.: National Defense University Press in cooperation with National Strategy Information Center, 1989), p. 83.
20. Author's telephone interview with Bruce Koch, 2 May 1995.
21. In March 1985, the CIA reported in its de-classified research paper, "Reshaping the News: Moscow's Media Presence in Developing Countries," that the Soviets had Tass or Novosti bureaus in 67 developing countries, 24 more than in 1970. Africa was the fastest growing region, going from 16 bureaus in 1970 to 31 in 1985. Five new bureaus were added during this period in Latin America. Eight Soviet news organizations had 15 correspondents in Afghanistan.
22. Department of State, "Active Measures: A Report on the Substance and Process of Anti-U.S. Disinformation and Propaganda Campaigns," August 1986.
23. Vera Tolz, "The Changing Character of Soviet Media Coverage of American Life," *Radio Liberty Research,* 1 July 1985.

24. USIA, research on media programs for Latin America, 22 March 1985.
25. *Komsomol'skaya Pravda,* 6 July 1984.
26. Radio Moscow, 15 May 1985.
27. Tolz, "Changing Character of Soviet Media Coverage."
28. Ibid.
29. The USIA was not to be outdone by the Soviets. In 1985, under its American Participants Program (AMPARTS) about 850 private-sector speakers were sent abroad to lecture on democracy-building themes, such as electoral reforms and foreign policies and defense. Additionally, some 50 U.S. performing arts groups traveled overseas under U.S. auspices. The President's International Youth Exchange was extended to 34 countries for young people 15 to 25 years of age. Additionally, the Fulbright Program, America's flagship educational exchange program, permitted the exchange of almost 2,000 American and West European students, teachers, lecturers, and researchers.
30. Testimony by CIA director William Colby before the Senate Select Committee to Study Government Operations with Respect to Intelligence Activities, 16 September 1975.
31. Tass, 28 June 1994.
32. Department of State, "Active Measures."
33. Ibid.
34. *Le Monde,* special Olympics supplement, 20–21 October 1985.
35. Narrative, *Hello, Los Angeles,* half-hour documentary film produced by Meyer Odze for USIA, 1983.
36. *Algerie Actualite,* 13–19 March 1985.
37. The congressional staff in the investigation of USIA's Worldnet operations in London, Paris, and Brussels included Richard McBride, Susan Andross, and Kenneth Peel from the House International Operations subcommittee; Thomas Harvey of the USIA; and Bruce Gregory of the USIA Advisory Committee on Public Diplomacy. The itinerary ran January 12–18, 1986.
38. Philip Taubman, "Through a Soviet Lens: Gomorrah on the Hudson," *New York Times,* 7 April 1986.
39. John F. Kordek, USIA director for Europe, to Charles Z. Wick, memorandum, 9 April 1986.
40. Taubman, "Through a Soviet Lens."
41. Department of State, "Soviet Influence Activities: A Report on Active Measures and Propaganda, 1986–87," August 1987.
42. Ibid.
43. Ibid.
44. Russian archival collection, Madison Gallery, Library of Congress.
45. David A. Spetrino, "AIDS Disinformation," Central Intelligence Agency report, Winter 1988.

46. Author's interview with Todd Leventhal, 13 October 1993.

47. Such allegations appeared in the Soviet press on 12 February 1989 in an article in *Novosti Military Bulletin*, "Virus under a Nuclear Cloud," by N. Suglobov. The article, which distorted a British magazine's story on the subject, began, "The discharge of radioactive elements into the atmosphere during nuclear weapons tests is one of the main causes for the appearance of the AIDS virus and the rapid spread of the epidemic of this dangerous disease in the United States and Africa."

48. Author's interview with Leventhal.

49. Ibid.

50. Memorandum of conversation from U.S.-USSR Information Talks: Government-to-Government Panel, first session, 26 September 1988, at Novosti Foreign Press Center, Moscow.

51. In 1988 Falin became head of the International Department of the Central Committee of the Communist party of the Soviet Union. Falin would report to Alexandr Yakovlev, a Gorbachev confidant.

52. Memorandum of conversation between Falin and Wick from 5 June 1987 meeting, contained in cable from American Embassy in Moscow to USIA in Washington, D.C.

53. Ibid.

54. Bill Keller, "American Outraged by Soviet Article," *New York Times*, 6 June 1987, p. 5.

55. Cable from the American Embassy in Moscow to USIA headquarters in Washington, 5 June 1987.

56. Todd Leventhal, "The Baby Parts Myth: The Anatomy of a Rumor," USIA paper, June 1994.

57. Letter released by Assistant Secretary for Health James Mason and Surgeon General C. Everett Koop, 6 June 1989.

58. Ibid.

59. Ibid.

60. Author's interview with Sherwood Demitz, 4 November 1992.

61. "Baby Parts" received media usage in, among other places, Austria, Denmark, West Germany, Finland, Greece, Ireland, the Netherlands, Norway, Portugal, Sweden, Switzerland, and Great Britain.

62. Jack Shick, "Reshaping the News: Moscow's Media Presence in Developing Countries," CIA Office of Central Reference, March 1985.

63. Ronald Reagan, speech from the White House Oval Office, 23 March 1983.

64. Mikhail Gorbachev and Georges Marchais, leader of the French Communist party, joint communiqué, September 1985.

65. William Burr, "Soviet Cold War Military Strategy: Using Reclassified History," Woodrow Wilson International Center for Scholars, *Cold War International History Project Bulletin*, Fall 1994, p. 30.

66. Ibid., p. 12.
67. Sergei Rogov, "Is a New Model of Soviet-American Relations Possible?" USSR's Institute on the United States and Canada, 1989 monograph.
68. ACDA publication 122, August 1986.
69. Eduard Shevardnadze in the Soviet weekly *New Times,* issue 40, 1991.
70. Robert McFarlane, "Consider What Star Wars Accomplished," op-ed, *New York Times,* 24 August 1993, p. A15.
71. George P. Shultz, *Turmoil and Triumph: My Years as Secretary of State,* (New York: Charles Scribner's Sons, 1993), p. 250.
72. Ibid., p. 492.
73. General Accounting Office, report no. 94-219, July 1994.
74. Tass, 4 November 1987.
75. McFarlane, "Consider What Star Wars Accomplished."
76. Mikhail Gorbachev, *Perestroika: New Thinking for Our Country and the World* (New York: Harper & Row, 1987), pp. 140–41.
77. General Vladimar Lobov, (USSR) *Military Historical Journal,* November 1991.
78. *Moscow News,* issue 44, November 1991.
79. Mikhail Gorbachev, speech, Moscow, 15 November 1989.

CHAPTER 7: ANTENNA TOWERS AND ASPARAGUS STALKS

1. Amity Shlaes, "Berlin: Developing the Diepgen Factor," *Wall Street Journal,* 22 January 1986.
2. *Economist,* 3 March 1990, p. 43.
3. Stephen Kinzer, "Cold War Institution Fades from Airwaves in Berlin," *New York Times,* 4 January 1994.
4. Ibid.
5. USIA, "Extent of Western Influence on the East German Population," study conducted July through September 1957. An attempt was made to determine the most popular media in the German East Communist Zone. RIAS Radio was mentioned by 67 percent of the respondents as having been heard, SFB by 60 percent, while the Voice of America was mentioned by 51 percent. Only 14 percent said they would like to go to the U.S. library/cultural center in Berlin, the Amerika Haus.
6. Author's interview with Patrick E. Nieburg, Arlington, Va., 22 April 1994.
7. Shlaes, "Berlin: Developing the Diepgen Factor."
8. Stan Burnett to Charles Wick, memorandum, 7 November 1986.
9. From a feasibility study by VideoConsult of Hamburg, West Germany, completed in August 1984.

10. Patrick E. Nieburg to Hans N. Tuch, U.S. Embassy, Bonn, letter, 6 June 1984.
11. Warren Christopher to Paul Bartlett, letter, 26 March 1979.
12. State Department, "Study of the Bartlett Proposal for the Establishment of an American Radio and Television Station in West Berlin," March 1979.
13. Hans Tuch to Charles Wick, letter, 30 August 1984.
14. Ibid.
15. In his memorandum to USIA director Charles Z. Wick of 31 January 1986, Thomas E. Harvey advised that neither the West German nor the U.S. government "through a private citizen was entitled to operate radio facilities in Germany under the terms of any German-American agreement."
16. USIA memorandum of record covering meeting with Ernst Cramer, 23 May 1984.
17. Meeting with Ambassador Richard Burt, 21 March 1986, at USIA headquarters, Washington, D.C.
18. USIA memorandum of record covering meeting held on April 2, 1985, between Charles Wick and other USIA officials, and Mayor Eberhard Diepgen of Berlin.
19. The study, commissioned by the state-run television networks ARD and ZDF and the Bertelsmann Foundation, was based on interviews with 4,011 West Germans aged 12 to 30. The study was published in Hamburg, February 1986.
20. U.S. Mission in Berlin to USIA headquarters in Washington, cable, March 1986.
21. At the request of RIAS Radio intendant Peter Schiwy, Professor Klaus Schoenbach, of Hannover, West Germany, conducted a viewer potential survey for RIAS-TV. The survey was conducted from January 9 through February 4, 1986.
22. U.S. Mission in Berlin to USIA in Washington, cable, January 1986.
23. Telecast on German Channel Two's (ZDF) "Kennzeichen D," a political news magazine program, 12 February 1986.
24. From article commemorating the fortieth anniversary of RIAS Radio, *Bildzeitung,* 1 February 1986.
25. Memorandum of meeting between Wick and Diepgen in Washington, D.C., 21 February 1986.
26. Reuter and UPI news services, 8 July 1987.
27. The nightly news debuted on RIAS-TV in August 1988, and the morning news in October 1988.

CHAPTER 8: THAT'S ENTERTAINMENT!

1. Jackson Diehl, "VCRs on Fast Forward in Eastern Europe," *Washington Post*, 17 April 1988, p. A26.
2. William Burger with Joyce Barnathan, "Moscow's Video Generation," *Newsweek*, 18 August 1986, p. 16.
3. Ibid.
4. The original test locations were: Ankara, Turkey; Bridgetown, Barbados; Gabarone, Botswana; Caracas, Venezuela; Kuala Lumpur, Malaysia; Manila, the Philippines; Lagos, Nigeria; Islamabad, Pakistan; Riyadh, Saudi Arabia; and Bonn, West Germany.
5. Robert L. M. Nevitt to Alvin Snyder, memorandum, 17 July 1983.
6. USIA Research, 22 March 1985.
7. Leo Jaffe, remarks at "A Tribute to Leo Jaffe," sponsored by the USIA and Jaffe's many friends, at the Beverly Hills Hotel, Beverly Hills, Calif., 17 October 1986.
8. Mo Rothman to Leo Jaffe, letter, 31 October 1983.
9. Al Snyder to Charles Z. Wick, memorandum, 16 May 1986.
10. United States Advisory Commission on Public Diplomacy, "Annual Report," 1986.
11. *USIA World*, November 1987.
12. USIA cable from Sofia to Washington, 1 May 1987.
13. USIA, "Video Library Program: Status Report," 21 July 1987.
14. Author's interview with Jackson Diehl, *Washington Post* newsroom, Washington, D.C., 25 October 1993.
15. Ibid.
16. Celestine Bohlen, "Moscow Joins the Video Revolution," *Washington Post*, 12 January 1986.
17. Victor Yasman, "Satellite Television in the USSR: Toward a New Dimension," *Radio Liberty Research*, 29 June 1987.
18. Diehl, "VCRs on Fast Forward in Eastern Europe."
19. Jackson Diehl, "Dissident Poles Exploit VCR Boom," *Washington Post*, 12 March 1986, p. A24.
20. Neil Hickey, "The Message for Poland's Rulers: Beware of Fresh Ideas —Your Control is Slipping," *TV Guide*, 29 August 1987.
21. Yasman, "Satellite Television in the USSR."
22. Bohdan Nahaylo, "*Sovetskaya Rossiya* Pans Soviet Film Attacking Radio Liberty," *Radio Liberty Research*, 24 May 1985.
23. Ibid.
24. Michael Parks, "Soviets Free the Dreaded Photocopier," *Los Angeles Times*, 5 October 1989, p. 8.
25. Vladimir Voinovich, "The Electronic Enemy of the People," *Radio Liberty Research*, 10 January 1986.
26. Ibid.

27. *Literaturnaya Gazeta,* 14 March 1985.

28. A commentary by Vladimir Voinovich, "The Electronic Enemy of the People," broadcast on Radio Liberty's Russian Service, April 1985.

29. Ibid.

CHAPTER 9: THE FAUSTIAN BARGAIN

1. USIA, "Status of Information Issues in CSCE Countries," 15 March 1989.

2. John Mueller, "New, Improved Opiates for the Masses," *Wall Street Journal,* 23 May 1989, p. A18.

3. *Sovetskaya Rossiya,* 22 March 1987.

4. USIA memorandum covering staff meeting with Charles Z. Wick, 14 January 1986.

5. Simon Baker, "Watching the West," *Cable & Satellite Europe,* February 1987, p. 17.

6. John F. Kordek to Charles Wick, memorandum, 10 April 1987.

7. Ibid.

8. USIA translation of article in *Poznan Daily Gazeta Poznanska,* 28 March 1987.

9. Kordek to Wick, memorandum, 14 April 1987.

10. Baker, "Watching the West," p. 17.

11. "Television without Frontiers," Reuter, 12 May 1989.

12. Baker, "Watching the West," p. 15.

13. Simon Baker, "The People's Dish Factory," *Cable & Satellite Europe,* February 1987, p. 20.

14. Cable and Satellite Communications Europe [CSCE] Information Forum Survey Data, 15 March 1989, p. 62.

15. Notes taken at meeting of Central Committee Ideological/International Secretaries, Warsaw, Poland, January 1987.

16. Viktor Yasman, "Satellite Television in the USSR: Toward a New Dimension," *Radio Liberty Research,* 29 June 1987.

17. Ibid.

18. Douglas Hamilton, "Caviar and Marlboros Mark New Style for Gorbachev Speech," Reuter, dateline Bonn, West Germany, 18 August 1986.

19. Ibid.

20. *La Nazione* (Florence, Italy), 24 August 1986.

21. Yasman, "Satellite Television in the USSR."

22. Statistics from the TV Bureau of Advertising, New York, a private organization.

23. BBC, *World Broadcasting Information,* no. 34, 23 August 1984, p. 2A.

24. "Ostankino-87," *Izvestia,* 27 January 1987.

25. Christopher Walker, dispatch from Moscow, (London) *Times*, 3 March 1987.

26. David Remnick, *Lenin's Tomb: The Last Days of the Soviet Empire* (New York: Vintage Books, 1994), pp. 146–47.

27. *Sovetskaya kul'tura*, 13 September 1986, p. 3.

28. Viktor Yasman, "Telebridges with the West: Vaccination against Ideological Contamination," *Radio Liberty Research*, 8 April 1987.

29. Ibid., p. 2.

30. Letter to *Izvestia*, 14 March 1987, p. 7, with copies to the KGB and Gosteleradio, as reported by Yasman, "Telebridges with the West."

31. Soviet commentator Aleksandr Bovin, as reported by Yasman, "Telebridges with the West."

32. *Electronic Week*, "Soviet TV Playing in U.S.: From News to 1 Million Ruble Movie," reprint of *Detroit News* article, 19 November 1984.

33. Neil Hickey, "Good Morning, USSR!" *TV Guide*, 3 September 1988.

CHAPTER 10: CLEARING THE VOICE

1. Article 19 of the United Nations Declaration of Human Rights guarantees the right to "seek, receive, and impart information and ideas through any media and regardless of frontiers."

2. From a book by V. N. Yaroshenko, "Black Waves," quoted in *Argumenty i Fakty*, 1 April 1986, p. 7.

3. Article 19, UN resolution.

4. State Department, "Issue Paper on Jamming," 28 August 1986.

5. The USSR began jamming the VOA, BBC, and Deutsche Welle on August 20, 1980, following Soviet invasion of Afghanistan.

6. Stanton H. Burnett to Charles Z. Wick, memorandum, 19 September 1986.

7. "Truth Is in the Air," *Economist*, 6 June 1987, p. 20.

8. Robert G. Kaiser, *Why Gorbachev Happened* (New York: Simon and Schuster, 1991), p. 106.

9. Comments from Wick/Yakovlev meeting are from author's notes and from minutes by the USIA's Rick Ruth, country affairs officer for Europe.

10. "State Department Says 'Nyet' to NBC," *Broadcasting*, 8 September 1986, p. 105.

11. Nils H. Wessell, "Soviet Comment on U.S. Turn-Down of TV Debates," USIA memorandum, 10 September 1986.

12. William Safire, "You've Got a Deal," *New York Times*, 10 November 1986.

13. *Pravda*, 22 October 1986.

14. Woodrow Wilson International Center for Scholars, "Meeting of Polit-

buro of CPSU 22 October 1986," *Cold War International History Project Bulletin,* Fall 1994, pp. 84–85. A translation of "Top Secret" notes taken from Russian archives.

15. Ibid.
16. USIA, "Soviet Vulnerability and World Public Opinion," Office of Research memorandum, 11 December 1986.
17. Rick Ruth, "Glasnost and USIA Policy," USIA report, 6 April 1987.
18. Charles Z. Wick, speech, at Loyola Marymount University, Los Angeles, Calif., 2 May 1987.
19. Charles Z. Wick, report to the Council on Foreign Relations, New York City, 18 May 1988.
20. State Department cable to U.S. Embassy, Moscow, on U.S.-Soviet bilateral talks, August 25–26, 1987.
21. Author's interview with Todd Leventhal, 13 October 1993.
22. First meeting of U.S.-Soviet bilateral information talks, Soviet Embassy, Washington, D.C., 15 November 1988.
23. USIA memorandum of conversation, U.S.-Soviet information talks, government-to-government panel, Washington, D.C., 21 April 1988.
24. USIA meeting, Soviet Embassy in Washington, D.C., 15 November 1988.
25. Ibid.
26. USIA, confidential memorandum on information talks, 16 November 1988.
27. Alexandr Yakovlev, "Say and Hear the Truth," *New Times* (Soviet periodical), no. 41.88, October 1988, p. 13.
28. Leonard Zeidenberg, "USIA: All the World's an Audience," *Broadcasting,* 22 April 1985, p. 112.
29. "Letter From Washington," *National Review,* 28 June 1985, p. 14.
30. Charles Z. Wick, remarks at ceremony naming him Public Relations Professional of the Year at the PR News Silver Anniversary Awards Banquet, New York City, 19 May 1988.
31. U.S.-Soviet information talks, Washington, D.C., 20 April 1988.

CHAPTER 11: VOA FOLLIES

1. ABC, "World News Tonight," 15 June 1993.
2. Jacob Weisberg, "Citizen Djin," *New Republic,* 15 June 1992, p. 12. Also, Carolyn Weaver, "When the Voice of America Ignores its Charter," *Columbia Journalism Review,* November–December 1988.
3. ABC, "World News Tonight."
4. Ibid.
5. Michael Wright, ed., "The World at Arms," *Reader's Digest Illustrated*

History of World War II (London: Reader's Digest Association Limited, 1989).

6. Author's interview with Michael Schoenfeld, Washington, D.C., 10 April 1994.
7. Judith Haverman, "Prayer Area at VOA: A Corner of Controversy," *Washington Post,* 17 November 1987, p. A25.
8. Charles Stuart Kennedy's interview with Richard Carlson on behalf of the Association for Diplomatic Studies, Foreign Affairs Oral History Program, Georgetown University, Georgetown, Va., 2 March 1993.
9. Ibid.
10. Mary G. F. Bitterman (Carter appointee) 3/80–1/81; M. William Haratunian (acting) 1/81–8/81; James B. Conkling 8/81–3/82; John Hughes 3/82–8/82; Terry Catherman 8/82–12/82; Kenneth Y. Tomlinson 12/82–9/84; Gene Pell 9/84–10/85; Morton S. Smith (acting) 10/85–3/86; Richard W. Carlson 3/86 (acting)–9/86; Carlson served as director until 9/91.
11. Author's telephone interview with William Sheehan, 9 November 1993.
12. The VOA's relay station in Sri Lanka was planned to reach Soviet Central Asia, East Asia, Africa, and South and West Asia.
13. From Morocco the VOA planned to transmit its programs to Eastern Europe, the Soviet Union, Africa, and the Middle East.
14. Author's telephone interview with Maurice Rafensperger, 15 May 1995.
15. The Thailand station was planned for transmissions to the south and central Soviet Union, south and southeastern Asia, northern and eastern China, eastern India, and Burma.
16. USIA, Office of Inspector General, "Survey of VOA Modernization Program," 3 July 1986.
17. Author's interview with John Butcher, Washington, D.C., 10 August 1992.
18. USIA, "Survey of VOA Modernization Program."
19. Ibid.
20. Letter from Lola Secora to author, 1 February 1993.
21. Author's interview with Barry Malko, Washington, D.C., 7 July 1992.
22. USIA memorandum of meeting between Wick, Hockeimer, and VOA engineering managers, 16 April 1986.
23. Dr. Peter Berthold, bird migration scientist, letter to President Bill Clinton, 1 January 1993.
24. Ibid.
25. Board for International Broadcasting, "Talking Points on U.S. Relay Station in Israel," memorandum approved by the State Department and other interested government departments and agencies, 23 July 1990.
26. Dr. Bruno Bruderer, "Bird Migration in the Arava and the 'Voice of

America' Station," report submitted to USIA and other interested parties, 29 July 1991.

27. Ibid.
28. Morton Smith to Charles Z. Wick, memorandum, 13 November 1985.
29. USIA, Office of Inspector General, "Review of Selected VOA Modernization Issues," 27 July 1990.
30. Ibid.
31. Ibid.
32. USIA, Office of Inspector General, "Report on the Status of the Quesada Relay Station," 26 August 1987.
33. Ibid.
34. Charles Z. Wick, testimony before the House Committee on Foreign Affairs, Subcommittee on International Operations, 3 March 1987.
35. USIA, "Review of Selected VOA Modernization Issues."
36. USIA, Office of Inspector General, "Review of Allegations Concerning Selected VOA Broadcast Renovation Projects," March 1988. See also Jack Anderson and Joseph Spear, "VOA's Mismanaged Modernization," *Washington Post,* 21 October 1986, p. D12.
37. General Accounting Office, report on VOA management, July 1992.

CHAPTER 12: THE MUJAHIDEEN GO TO SCHOOL

1. Katherine Hinds, "From Freedom Fighter to the Fifth Form: The Long Journey of Masood Farivar '90," *Lawrentian* (alumni publication of the Lawrenceville School), Winter 1990.
2. Ibid.
3. David Barboza and Narendra Nandoe, "The Afghan War at Boston University," *Daily Free Press* (independent student newspaper at Boston University), 5 November 1986.
4. Library of Congress Congressional Research Service report, 1986.
5. Mary Linehan, "Eye on Afghanistan: New Ways to Help the World See," *Social Issues & Health Review,* January 1987.
6. John Kohler, "Afghan Media Project," report to USIA, 6 October 1985.
7. Ibid.
8. Edward Giradet, "Reporting Afghanistan's Brutal War," *Christian Science Monitor,* 24 December 1987.
9. Author's telephone interview with Gene Mater, Washington, D.C., 28 November 1993.
10. Letter from ten faculty members of Boston University's College of Communications to University Provost Jon Westling, November 1985. Also referenced in "Banned in Boston?" *Wall Street Journal,* 22 August 1986.

11. *Wall Street Journal*, 22 August 1986.
12. USIA, Islamabad to Washington headquarters, cable, 7 June 1989.
13. David Barboza and Narendra Nandoe, "Afghan Media Project Graduates 35 Students," *Daily Free Press* (Boston University), 23 March 1987, p. 1.
14. Marjorie Howard, "Hub Journalist Teaches Afghan Rebels," *Boston Herald*, 5 April 1987, p. 8.
15. Chris Nation, "Proposal for an Exhibition of AMRC Photography and Preliminary Budget Projection," March 1986.
16. William A. Rugh, USIA, to Charles Z. Wick, memorandum, 23 March 1990.
17. William A. Eames to USIA director, USIA-TV, memorandum, 17 March 1989.
18. In a report by the Afghan Media Resource Center, television reports and features were being broadcast in over 90 countries on six continents through Visnews and Eurovision/Asiavision—who sent AMRC video reports via satellite throughout the world. Stories appeared regularly on ITN and Thames TV in Great Britain, Swedish Television, Norwegian Television, FR 3 in France, and Pakistan Television.
19. The Reuter story, filed from Islamabad, Pakistan, 15 February 1989, said in part:

> The Afghan government has reinforced with Scud missiles its defense of the country's second city, Jalalabad, a rebel mujahideen news organization said Wednesday.
> The Afghan Media Resource Center said its correspondents inside Afghanistan did not know how many of the ground-to-ground missiles had been delivered to a special Afghan army unit trained to use them.
> They were quoted as saying 150 officers had been sent on a nine-month course in the Soviet Union to learn how to use the missiles and were now established in Jalalabad in charge of a new unit, the 95th Army Brigade.
> The news organization, based in the northwest Pakistan city of Peshawar, said its correspondents reported that the Afghan government had also shored up its defense of Jalalabad with a new unit to keep open the road to Kabul.
> The news organization said the second new force defending Jalalabad was the 60th Division and was stationed eight miles outside the city and had established new posts along the road to Kabul and was patrolling it with tanks and armored personnel carriers.
> It did not say how many men were in the division.

20. "Use of New Soviet Weapons," *Afghan Realities Fortnightly Bulletin,* no. 43, 16 October 1985, p. 13.
21. "Vehicles for AMRC," Branch Public Affairs Officer Richard Hoagland in Peshawar, Pakistan, to Country Public Affairs Officer William Lenderking in Islamabad, Pakistan, memorandum, 11 July 1989.
22. Frank Jossi, "Shop Talk at Thirty: The Afghan Media Resource Center," *Editor and Publisher,* 10 February 1990.
23. Richard Hoagland to William Lenderking, "Future of Afghan Women's Media Project," memorandum, 11 July 1989.
24. John Dixon to USIA, Washington, D.C., memorandum, 27 September 1989.
25. Ibid.
26. Hoagland to Lenderking, "Future of Afghan Women's Media Project."
27. John Dixon to USIA Assistant General Counsel Richard Swan, "American Sales for AMRC," memorandum, 27 March 1989.
28. Ibid. In 1988, the government of Canada contributed $83,000 to the Afghan Media Training Center. Private German contributions totaled $50,000 and Swedish private donations, $20,000. The government of Saudi Arabia contributed $250,000 for fiscal year 1989. A complete color film processing and printing lab was built with the help of a grant from the Swedish Relief Committee, and the Germans supplied video and film equipment.
29. USIA, Islamabad, Pakistan, to USIA, Washington, cable, 7 June 1989.
30. Ibid.
31. U.S. Embassy, Peshawar, to USIA, Washington, confidential cable, 14 March 1991.
32. Author's interview with Richard Hoagland, 5 January 1993.
33. Richard Hoagland to William Lenderking, "Prince Sadruddin at AMRC," cable, 7 January 1989.
34. Ibid.

CHAPTER 13: THE CAUDILLO OF MIAMI

1. "Cuban Television Station Measurements," FCC, Field Operations Bureau project report, 6 August 1989.
2. Larry Rohter, "A Rising Cuban-American Leader: Statesman to Some. Bully to Others," *New York Times,* 29 October 1992, p. A18.
3. Lee Hockstader and William Booth, "The Feud among Cuban Exiles, As Seen from D.C.," *Miami Herald,* 15 March 1992, p. 4C.
4. Celia W. Dugger, "Leader's Zeal Powers Exile Lobby," *Miami Herald,* 10 April 1988, p. 1.
5. Peter Slevin, "Jorge Mas Canosa: The Road to Havana," *Miami Herald,* 19 October 1992; Rohter, "A Rising Cuban-American Leader."

6. Donna Gehrke, "Mas Slugged Me, Brother Testifies," *Miami Herald,* 25 October 1990, p. 1B.
7. Ibid.
8. Author's interview with David Rivera, Miami, 13 November 1992.
9. Ibid.
10. Author's interview with Richard V. Allen, 11 March 1993.
11. Dugger, "Leader's Zeal Powers Exile Lobby."
12. Author's interview with Thomas Dine, 12 August 1993.
13. Slevin, "Jorge Mas Canosa."
14. Cuba signed a new immigration pact with the United States in December 1987. Radio Marti supporters saw this as realization by Castro that the radio facility was there to stay.
15. Edward Cody, "Marti Wafts Time Warp to Listeners in Havana," *Washington Post,* 3 June 1985.
16. Joseph B. Treaster, "Radio Marti's 50's Sound Had Cubans Tuning Out," *New York Times,* 4 June 1985.
17. Pat Norman, "The Radio Marti Program: A Special Mandate," *USIA World,* June 1988.
18. Terry E. Johnson, David Newall, and Ben Barber, "Adrift: Cuba's Raft People," *Newsweek,* 21 July 1986, p. 21.
19. Antonio Guernica, abstract, "Radio Marti's Effects on Cuba," Research and Policy Department, Radio Marti, 1984.
20. Ibid.
21. Ann Louise Bardach, "Our Man in Miami," *New Republic,* 3 October 1994.
22. Alfonso Chardy, "Reagan Aides Include Many Who Fled Fidel Castro," *Miami Herald,* 5 August 1984, p. 12A.
23. Ibid.
24. Author's interview with James McKinney, Washington, D.C., 14 July 1992.
25. Mimi Whitefield, "Don't Send TV Marti, Cubans on Island Say," *Miami Herald,* 26 March 1990, pp. 1A, 4A.
26. Author's interview with James McKinney.
27. A. D. Ring & Associates, P.C., "TV Marti: A Study of Technical Feasibility," March 11, 1988, pp. 2, 3.
28. Hammett & Edison, Inc., consulting engineers, San Francisco, "TV Marti Feasibility Study," section 8, option B, 1 April 1988.
29. Cohen and Dippell, P.C., feasibility study on TV Marti, February 1988.
30. Jules Cohen & Associates, P.C., consulting electronics engineers, commenting on various options proposed for TV Marti, 29 November 1988.
31. Ibid.
32. Jules Cohen & Associates, 31 March 1988.
33. A. D. Ring & Associates, "A Study of Technical Feasibility," p. 10.

34. Ibid.
35. Brian Barger, "TV Marti Slipped through Congress: House Chairman," *Multi-Channel News,* 26 September 1988, p. 52.
36. Stephen S. Rosenfeld, "Electronic Bay of Pigs," *Washington Post,* 18 May 1990, p. A19.
37. Author's interview with James McKinney.
38. David Lauter, "U.S. Begins Beaming TV Marti Signal to Cuba," *Los Angeles Times,* 28 March 1990, pp. F5, F7.
39. Reuter, "Cuba Jams TV Marti to Keep Out 'Sex, Drugs,'" *Washington Times,* 29 March 1990.
40. Mimi Whitefield, "Cuba Displays Its Ability to Jam TV Marti," *Miami Herald,* 3 April 1990.
41. Barry Klein, "Infiltrating Cuba over the Airwaves," *Electronic Media,* 21 August 1989.
42. Mimi Whitefield, "Cuba Again Zaps TV Marti's Signals to Block Reception," *Miami Herald,* 29 March 1990, p. 21A.
43. Howard W. French, "Cubans Parade Hardware to Jam TV Marti," *New York Times,* 4 April 1990, p. A12.
44. James M. Dorsey, "Cuba Tries Diplomacy to Ward Off TV Marti," *Washington Times,* 3 March 1990.
45. Don A. Schanche, "Cuba Calls for American TV Deal," *Los Angeles Times,* 31 March 1990, p. A8.
46. Author's interview with Carlos Verdasia, Miami, Florida, 11 November 1992.
47. Author's interview with Richard V. Allen, Washington, D.C., 15 February 1993.
48. House Appropriations Subcommittee, hearing, 20 March 1991.

CHAPTER 14: "I'M NOT A PANTYWAIST!"

1. Judith Havemann, "At USIA, The Beef Is over the Chief," *Washington Post,* 8 June 1990, p. B3.
2. Peter Pringle, "That's What Makes America Tick," *Independent* (London), 13 June 1990.
3. Havemann, "Beef Is over the Chief," p. B3.
4. Ibid.
5. Author's interview with Michael Schoenfeld, Washington, D.C., 10 April 1994.
6. Robert S. Greenberger, "Angry Critics Say US Arabic Language Service Was Not the Voice of America during Gulf War," *Wall Street Journal,* 13 June 1991, p. A18.
7. John Elvin, "Rip It Up," *Washington Times,* 22 January 1991, p. A6.
8. Senator Ernest F. Hollings (D-SC), chairman, Senate Appropriations

Subcommittee on Commerce, Justice, State, the Judiciary and Related Agencies, to Bruce Gelb, letter, 20 February 1990.

9. George Archibald, "USIA Chief Makes Waves, Enemies with Brash Acts," *Washington Times,* 7 January 1991, p. A4.

10. Ibid.

11. Claire Poole, "End of an Empire," *Forbes,* 8 June 1992, p. 21.

CHAPTER 15: ADVENTURES IN THE NANNY TRADE

1. Kenneth L. Adelman, "Speaking of America: Public Diplomacy in Our Time," *Foreign Affairs,* Spring 1981.

2. Author's telephone interview with Thomas J. Fadoul, Jr., 14 April 1993.

3. Author's telephone interview with Uta Christianson, 28 July 1993.

4. Senators Dodd, Pell, Moynihan, Helms, and Trible, joint letter to Wick, 1 February 1988.

5. Natalie Wexler, "Babysitter in a Strange Land," *Washington Post Magazine,* 22 May 1994, p. 26.

6. John P. Monahan to Child Care Placement Service, Inc., Brookline, Massachusetts, letter, 12 September 1989.

7. Associated Press, "Swiss Au Pair Sued in Death of Infant," *New York Times,* 3 December 1993, p. B5.

8. Wexler, "Babysitter in a Strange Land," p. 28.

9. Normand Poirier to Senator John C. Danforth, letter, 13 April 1988.

10. Peter Cary, "Should the USIA Be Importing Nannies?", *U.S. News and World Report,* 21 March 1988, p. 23.

11. Ibid.

12. Public Law 101-454, Section 8, congressional legislation requiring that the USIA oversee the J-Visa program indefinitely, 24 October 1990.

13. Lairold M. Street to the author, letter, 28 June 1983.

14. Alan McConagha, "Inside Politics," *Washington Times,* 22 April 1994, p. A7.

15. Paulette Thomas, "Going Straight on Nanny Tax Isn't an Easy Job," *Wall Street Journal,* 5 July 1994, p. B1.

16. Author's interview with Alberto Mora, 9 July 1993.

17. Ibid.

18. General Accounting Office, "Inappropriate Uses of Educational and Cultural Exchange Visas," GAO/NSIAD-90-61, February 1990.

19. General Accounting Office, "U.S. Information Agency: Waiver of Exchange Visitor Foreign Residence Requirement," GAO/NSIAD-90-212FS, July 1990.

20. Author's interview with Thomas Harvey, Washington, D.C., 12 January 1995.

21. A total of $3.341 million was provided for the program between 1988 and 1993. An estimated $600,000 was estimated for 1994.

CHAPTER 16: CAUGHT IN THE SMITH-MUNDT ACT

1. Section 501 of the United States Information and Educational Exchange Act of 1948, known as the Smith-Mundt Act, as amended, states in part:

   The Director [of USIA] is authorized . . . to provide for the preparation . . . and dissemination abroad, of information about the United States, its people, and its policies, through press, publication, radio, motion pictures, and other information media, and through information centers and instructors abroad. Any such information . . . shall not be disseminated within the United States, its territories, or possessions, but, on request, shall be available in the English language at the agency, at all reasonable times following its release as information abroad, for examination only by representatives of the United States press associations, newspapers, magazines, radio systems, and stations, and by research students and scholars, and on request shall be made available for examination only to members of Congress.

2. Alvin A. Snyder, "U.S. Foreign Affairs in the New Information Age: Charting a Course for the 21st Century," Annenberg Washington Program in Communications Policy Studies of Northwestern University, Washington, D.C., May 1994.
3. Ibid.
4. Michael Gartner, "Making America's Voice A Little More Audible," *Wall Street Journal,* 2 November 1989, p. A19.
5. Ibid.
6. Decision by U.S. District Court of the Southern District of Iowa, Central Division, *Gartner v. United States Information Agency,* 12 October 1989.
7. Ibid.
8. Ibid.
9. Ibid.
10. Ibid.
11. Author's telephone interview with Carol Epstein, 22 May 1995.
12. Author's telephone interview with John Lindburg, 15 April 1994.
13. Author's personal meeting with Richard W. McBride, Washington, D.C., 27 October 1993.

CHAPTER 17: PUBLIC DIPLOMACY GOES PRIVATE

1. Carnes Lord, *The Presidency and the Management of National Security* (New York: Free Press, 1988), p. 17.
2. Author's interview with Boris Kalyagin, Foreign Press Center, Washington, D.C., 4 September 1992.
3. R. Jeffrey Smith, "Freeh Warns of a New Russian Threat," *Washington Post,* 26 May 1994, pp. 1, 40.
4. John Markoff, "U.S. Code Agency Is Jostling for Civilian Turf," *New York Times,* 24 January 1994, p. D1.
5. Author's interview with Philip Brown, Washington, D.C., 1 September 1992.
6. Sherwood H. Demitz, with Elizabeth R. Fox and David G. Gibson, "International Broadcasting Faces the Challenge of the New Media," USIA Office of Research, July 1991.
7. David Gibson, "Foreign Radio Listening and Other Media Use in Nanning, China," USIA Office of Research, February 1990.
8. William J. Cook, Susan V. Lawrence, and Emily MacFarquhar, "The Great Asian TV Sweepstakes," *U.S. News and World Report,* 28 March 1994, p. 68.
9. *Communications Daily,* 10 February 1993, p. 9.
10. William Safire, "Needed: A China Policy," *New York Times,* 14 September 1992, p. A19.
11. David G. Gibson, "Radio Monte Carlo Dominant Western Station in Urban Audience Survey of Five Arab Countries," USIA Office of Research and Media Reaction, Audience Analysis Report, 27 December 1994.
12. *Broadcasting Abroad,* April 1993, p. 44.
13. Stated at a colloquium of the Annenberg Washington Program, "U.S. Foreign Affairs in the New Information Age," 2 February 1994.
14. General Accounting Office, "Station Modernization Projects Need to Be Justified," GAO/NSIAD-94-69, January 1994. Also see GAO report, "Addressing the Deficit," GAO/OCG-95-2, March 1995, pp. 91–94.
15. USIA Bureau of Broadcasting, "1992 Engineering Planning Committee Final Report," p. 11.
16. Ibid.

Appendix A

The following individuals agreed to be interviewed during the writing of this book. My thanks go to them all.

Richard V. Allen, Lyndon (Mort) Allin, Gerald A. Andersen, Terry Balazs, Leonard Baldyga, William J. A. Barnes, David Bartlett, Ralph Baruch, Jon M. Beard, William Bell, Ray Benson, Gerald A. Berman, Gerhard Besserer, Ernesto F. Betancourt, James Billington, Merton Bland, Kenneth Boles, Rolando Bonachea, Douglas Boyd, Philip Brenner, Clarence J. Brown, Philip C. Brown, Joseph B. Bruns, Stanton H. Burnett, John A. Butcher, Gerald L. Campbell, Graham Cannon, Richard W. Carlson, Frank Carlucci, Terrence Catherman, Robert L. Chatten, Eric Chenoweth, David Christian, Juan Clark, David A. Cohen, Sig Cohen, Bruce D. Collins, Eliot Corday, Robert Coonrod, Geoffrey Cowan, Jonathan Crane, Chris Current, Haji Daud, Sherwood H. Demitz, John H. DeViney, Jackson Diehl, Thomas Dine, Wilson Dizard, Leonid Dobrokhotov, Joseph D. Duffey, Nancy Dyke, William Eames, Robert Lee Earle, Kim Andrew Elliott, Fred Engle, Carol B. Epstein, Dante B. Fascell, Edwin J. Feulner, Jr., Mike Finley, Mike Fisher, Sherrie M. Fletcher, Roger Guy Folly, Hugh C. Foster, William A. Franco, Gregory B. Franklin, Neal and Jane Freeman, Barry Fulton, Jack Gaines, Peter Galbraith, Michael Garcia, Leonard Garment, Michael G. Gartner, William Gavin, Saul S. Gefter, Carl Gershman, William Gertz, David Gibson, Kimberly Godwin, Josie Graziadio, Bruce Gregory, Gregory Guroff, Rosemary Hackett, Edward Hanna, Lee Hanna, Thomas E. Harvey, Ashley L. Hawken, Harry Heintzen, David I. Hitchcock, Richard Hoagland, Henry Hockeimer, Sheldon Hoffman, Charles Horner, John Hughes, Roy Hutchins, Janet Irwin, Carey Isacco, Leo Jaffe, Linda S. Jamison, Frank Johnson, Tuleda P. Johnson, Charles Lichenstein, Frank Johnson, Kristin A. Juffer, Boris A. Kalyagin, John Katzka, John Kelly, Penn Kemble, Peter Kendall, Chris Kern, Roger Kirk, Jeane Kirkpatrick, Barbara Klein, Bruce Koch, John F. Kordek, Thomas C. Korologos, Michael Kristula, Theodore J. Kuligowski, Louis P. Lantner, Walter LaFleur, Kelly Lehman, Harvey I. Leifert, Robert S. Leiken, David Leiter, John Lenczowski, William Lenderking, Todd Leventhal, Richard Levy, Stanford Levy, Robyn Lieberman, John A. Lindburg, Richard Lobo, Steve Longo, Carnes Lord, Barbara Lukas, H. Joachim Maitre, Barry Malko, Martin Manning, Gary Marco, Gary Marrie, William Marsh, Kimberly Marteau, Gene P. Mater, Donald E. Mathes, Richard McBride, Joseph McCusker, Bryan McGuirk, Brian McKeon, James C. McKinney, Maury J. Mechanic, H. Donald Messer, Michael S.

Messinger, Daniel A. Mica, Linda Miller, Steve Monblatt, Alberto Mora, Tom Mullins, Neil Munro, Stephen Murphy, Antonio Navarro, Gregory Newell, John Nichols, Pat Nieburg, Lorie J. Nierenberg, Eugenio Nigro, Joseph D. O'Connell, Charles R. O'Regan, Kent Obee, Donna Oglesby, Wayne Olson, John Osthaus, Lawrence L. Ott, Jr., Irene Payne, Kenneth L. Peel, Richard Perle, Alison C. Pickeral, Mark Pomar, Maurice Rafensperger, Thomas Ramsey, Walter Raymond, Jr., Otto Reich, William H. Read, Manolo Reyes, Jack Reynolds, Vincent J. Ricardel, Ken Richards, Tim Rieser, Charles Rini, David Rivera, Walter Roberts, Philip Rogers, Herbert Romerstein, Robert Rostron, Jack Rubley, McKinney H. Russell, Rick Ruth, Ken Sale, Maria San Miguel, Bruce Sasser, Peter Schiwy, Robert Schmidt, Michael D. Schneider, Michael J. Schoenfeld, Stanley Schrager, David Seal, Stephen Shaffer, Alexandr A. Shalnev, Paul A. Shapiro, Janet Shannon, William Sheehan, Charles E. Shutt, Patricia Siemien, Stanley Silverman, John Silverman, Morton Smith, Jane Spain, Larry Speakes, Nancy Stetson, Rudolph Stewart, Thomas A. P. Stillitano, Jr., Marvin Stone, Ronald Trowbridge, Tony A. Trujillo, Hans N. Tuch, Carlos Verdasia, Bill Wagner, Rogene M. Waite, Abbott Washburn, David Webster, James M. Weitzman, Louise G. Wheeler, Timothy White, Douglas Wilson, Charles Z. Wick, David M. Wilson, Leonid A. Zolotarevsky, Barry Zorthian, Stanley Zuckerman

Appendix B

VOA Charter

The long-range interests of the United States are served by communicating directly with the people of the world by radio. To be effective, the Voice of America (The Broadcasting Service of the United States Information Agency) must win the attention and respect of listeners. These principles will therefore govern Voice of America (VOA) broadcasts:

> "(1) VOA will serve as a consistently reliable and authoritative source of news. VOA news will be accurate, objective, and comprehensive.

> "(2) VOA will represent America, not any single segment of American society, and will therefore present a balanced and comprehensive projection of significant American thought and institutions.

> "(3) VOA will present the policies of the United States clearly and effectively, and will also present responsible discussion and opinion on these policies."

Public Law 94-350
Gerald R. Ford,
President of the United States
Signed July 12, 1976

Sponsored by: Charles M. Percy (R.) Illinois
Bella S. Abzug (D.) New York

Appendix C

Title V—Disseminating Information about the United States Abroad

General Authorization

Section 501 of the U.S. Information and Educational Exchange Act of 1948 ("Smith-Mundt Act"), P.L. 80-42.

(a)   The Secretary is authorized, when he finds it appropriate, to provide for the preparation, and dissemination abroad, of information about the United States, its people, and its policies, through press, publications, radio, motion pictures, and other information media, and through information centers and instructors abroad. Subject to subsection (b) of this section, any such information (other than "Problems of Communism" and "English Teaching Forum" which may be sold by the Government Printing Office) shall not be disseminated within the United States, its territories, or possessions, but, on request, shall be available in the English Language at the Department of State, at all reasonable times following its release as information abroad, for examination only by representatives of the United States press associations, newspapers, magazines, radio systems, and stations, and by research students and scholars, and, on request, shall be made available for examination only to Members of Congress.

(b)   (1) The Director of the United States Information Agency shall make available to the Archivist of the United States, for domestic distribution, motion pictures, films, videotapes, and other material prepared for dissemination abroad 12 years after the initial dissemination of the material abroad, or, in the case of such material not disseminated abroad, 12 years after the preparation of the material.

(2) The Director of the United States Information Agency shall be reimbursed for any attendant expenses. Any reimbursement to the Director pursuant to this subsection shall be credited to the applicable appropriation of the United States Information Agency.

(3) The Archivist shall be the official custodian of the material and shall issue necessary regulation to ensure that persons seeking its release in the United States have secured and paid for necessary United States rights and licenses and that all costs associated with the provision of the material by the Archivist shall be paid by the persons seeking its release. The Archivist may charge fees to recover such costs, in accordance with section 2116(c) of Title 44. Such fees shall be paid into, administered, and expended as part of the National Archives Trust Fund.

Appendix D

Note: The KAL-007 videotape shown at the UN—and later published as a transcript in the *New York Times*—lacked the following portions of exchanges between the Sakhalin Island–based airbase ground control tower (GCT), the "deputat" (Sokol Airbase command post fighter commander), pilot 163, and pilot 805 (Osipovich), who shot the airliner down. The portions amount to approximately five minutes and show that Soviet ground control believed the intruder to be a U.S. military aircraft, that Osipovich could not identify the plane, that the weather conditions were overcast rather than clear, and that Osipovich attempted to warn the intruder by flashing his lights and firing warning shots.

GMT

17:48 GCT to deputat: "The cloud cover is spreading."

18:04 Deputat to pilot 805: "The target is military. As soon as it has violated state borders, destroy it. Arm your weapons."

18:10 Deputat to pilot 805: "Can you determine the [target's] type?" (Note: pilot 805's answer, "Unclear," was on our tape, but the question was not.)

18:13 Deputat to pilot 805: "Interrogate the target."

18:17 Pilot 163 to deputat: "Ask if the enemy's air navigation light is on or not."

18:17 Deputat to pilot 805: "The target has violated the state border. Destroy the target."

18:18 Deputat to pilot 805: "Flash your lights."

18:18 Deputat to pilot 805: "Flash your lights briefly."

18:18 Deputat to pilot 805: "Force it to land at our airbase."

18:18 Deputat to pilot 805: "[Fire] a warning burst from cannons."

18:18 Deputat to pilot 805: "Give a burst from the cannons."

INDEX